THE CAESARS
Might and Madness

BOOKS BY IVAR LISSNER

IVAR LISSNER

THE CAESARS
Might and Madness

Translated from the German

By J. MAXWELL BROWNJOHN, M.A. (Oxon.)

G. P. PUTNAM'S SONS NEW YORK

MANUFACTURED IN THE UNITED STATES OF AMERICA

VAN REES PRESS • NEW YORK

I SHOULD LIKE TO EXPRESS MY SINCERE THANKS TO
*Dr. Siegfried Lauffer, Professor of Ancient History
at Munich University, for scrutinizing the individual
chapters of this book and offering so many valuable
suggestions.*

CONTENTS

CONTENTS

CONTENTS

CONTENTS

THE CAESARS
Might and Madness

PROUD AND MIGHTY ROMAN WORLD

The history which I have assembled with such accuracy and regard for truth is not unfamiliar or unverified, nor merely borrowed from other sources, but still fresh in the minds of my readers.
—Herodian, *History of the Empire*, i, 1.

I have therefore decided to deal briefly with Augustus' death and then with the reign of Tiberius and his successors, without either hatred or liking— sine ira et studio.
—Tacitus, *Annals*, i, 1.

I HAVE always been fascinated by the knowledge that Julius Caesar's eyes were dark and lively, and that he brushed his hair forward and almost always wore a chaplet of laurel leaves or gold because he was embarrassed by his baldness.

Cleopatra was a proud young woman. She was no beauty, but her fine bearing and conversational gifts made her an attractive and likable companion.

The emperor Tiberius used to stroll through his gardens on the island of Capri in moody silence, a humorless, obstinate old man with a pathological anxiety neurosis and a marked streak of cruelty in his nature. A modern psychologist might have seen great significance in his being left-handed. With one finger he could bore through a crisp apple, and Suetonius tells us that with a single fillip he could break a boy's head. On the rare occasions when he joined in a conversation, he would accompany his remarks with a series of affected gestures. It is probable that Tiberius, with his large eyes, nervous mannerisms and penchant for murder, was not actually insane but had been driven to the border line of insanity by inner loneliness and misery. Such at least the traditional account of him implies.

Emperor Claudius was an extraordinarily casual and absent-minded person—so vague and forgetful, in fact, that after his wife Messalina had been done away with on his orders he asked his courtiers why the empress had not come to table.

As for Nero, he not only wrote good poetry, but wrote it with his own hand. This we have on the authority of an eyewitness who actually saw the original manuscripts covered with the emperor's corrections.

13

We owe our knowledge of all these vivid details to Roman and Greek historians. But truths become blurred by the passage of time, and the facts have been so distorted or suppressed by poets and romanticists of every period that the colorful personalities of imperial Rome have often become no more than a row of bloodless caricatures. In this book I have tried to reconstruct a picture of them based on ancient sources. I hope I have brought them to life.

On the other hand, I have made use of the best of modern research. Our knowledge has been greatly enhanced by the work of scholars in the great cultural centers of the world. Yet some scholars have been too quick to challenge the authenticity of old and once-respected sources. Until the middle of the nineteenth century the character sketches handed down to us by the great classical biographers and historians were taken on trust. It is only now, in a century which has made up for its lack of creative ability by becoming hypercritical, that people deprecate the magnificent psychological portraits painted for us by Tacitus, Suetonius and Plutarch. This book thus in general presents the traditional ancient literary portrait of the individuals treated. Contradictory facts have in many cases been discovered by recent scholars, yet the traditional portrait created here is that which the educated Roman of about 400 A.D. believed and which most educated men believed completely until the last century. Certainly this tradition, which formed the thoughts of so many great men, is of the utmost importance to us today.

Past and present are firmly interwoven—quite how firmly we are not always aware. We often forget that we are bearing a burden thousands of years old and that future generations will groan beneath the weight of our wars, our nuclear bombs, our novels and plays, our scientific discoveries, our ingenuity and stupidity. We have a regrettable tendency to judge everything that is old by the standards of our own day. We are blind to the lessons of history because we refuse to learn that there is nothing new under the sun, and no one generation is any more entitled to claim that it has arrived in the world at a "turning point" in history than any other.

Most people today are afraid of opening a Greek or Roman book. They have a deep-rooted and almost superstitious dread of anything they cannot understand at first glance. Modern so-called literature skirts cautiously around ancient sources like a skier negotiating a crevasse, with the result that our historical novels often continue to repeat the same old errors. Each adds something new to our store of misconceptions until the personalities of the past either become pale shadows of what they really were or are inflated far beyond their true importance. In the end we reach the stage where Claudius, pictured by Roman historians as a near-imbecile puppet of his wives and freedmen, is discovered by modern psychologists to have been a complex and, "in essence," good character.

Our information about Julius Caesar's dark and lively eyes comes from Suetonius, a distinguished scholar who was born about 70 A.D. and died about 140 A.D. He was an aristocrat who practiced law and subsequently became Hadrian's private secretary. Thus he had access to the state archives. He must have studied a vast amount of material during his researches: imperial speeches, letters, senatorial minutes, collections of anecdotes, biographies, and historical works by others. Reading his *Lives of the Caesars* is rather like steering a small boat through an immense sea of knowledge. His character studies are shrewd, his style clear, and his descriptions of the Roman emperors and their strange idiosyncrasies always invested with an extremely lifelike quality.

Many well-meaning schoolmasters succeed in turning history into something dry and boring, whereas others know how to capture their hearers' imagination. Their secret is simple: they follow the example which Tacitus set them so long ago and intersperse their subject with biographical material. From Tacitus to Ammian, the Roman historian's technique took on an increasingly biographical form. Roman biographers did not so much trace the development of a personality as describe its actual state or being, and by doing so they came—in my opinion—very near the mark. A man's personality is more easily determined from details of his family background and character than from a study of its development, since character is an immutable factor. In this way the biographers of the ancient world supplied us with an extraordinarily objective picture of their imperial masters. Again, classical historians and biographers did not always stick too closely to the chronological order of events, and only introduced political history as far as they considered necessary. This was not necessarily a symptom of weakness or partiality, as critical nineteenth-century historians liked to believe. Suetonius did distort some facts, it is true, but he never misrepresented the soul or the mental climate of anyone. He acknowledged the mad Nero's poetic talents, for instance, and mentioned that the tyrant Vespasian could never bring himself to pronounce a sentence of death, however well merited, without sighing and shedding tears. Details like these are of tremendous value and go a long way toward offsetting the omission of a few dates and figures.

Tacitus grew up under Nero, reached manhood under Domitian, and lived to enjoy the greater happiness and freedom which characterized the reigns of Nerva and Trajan, under whom he held important government posts. He had a sensitive nature and was very much aware of the evils of his own day. Because of this he matured early and withdrew completely into his private world of ideas, not becoming an historian until quite late in life by Roman standards, at the age of forty. He looked back with nostalgia to the good old days of individual liberty under the republic, days that he had never seen, but knew well from his studies, before Augustus came to power. It was true that the imperial regime was a guarantee of peace. But, however experienced a ruler the emperor might be, the absolute nature of his authority was apt to blur his moral sense and bound to turn his subjects into a crowd of sycophants. In Tacitus' opinion, everyone in Rome who tolerated the imperial regime was sacrificing his personal integrity, and the more distinguished the man in question, the bigger hypocrite he was.

Tacitus lived roughly between 55 and 120 A.D. This true-blue Roman is to my mind the greatest historian who ever lived. He was so talented a writer that it is all but impossible to pin down exactly where the magic of his technique lies. Yet even he has come under attack and been accused of taking liberties with factual accuracy and underestimating its importance. But all facts are fragmentary anyway, and the life of a man, like that of a nation, is a tapestry woven out of so many slender and infinitely varied threads that it would be unthinkable to dismiss the services of such a shrewd diagnostician of his times as Tacitus. His lively interpretation and expansion of the facts has nothing whatever to do with invention or fabrication.

Tacitus' style is a model of brevity and succinctness He writes concisely, summoning up his characters with a single stroke of the pen, and his taut, vigorous language instantly brings whatever he is describing into sharp focus. His pages are peopled with horrific characters, among them Tiberius, Sejanus, young Agrippina and Nero; and his dark forebodings about the Germans, whom he describes more fully and impressively than any other ancient writer, make enthralling reading. Yet the secret of his success was not artistry alone, for artistry was the hallmark of all the classical historians. There is an almost imperceptible deficiency in even the most precise historical writing of our own day, for wherever it ceases to be art and becomes pure science it somehow fails to arrive at the truth. It is left for Tacitus to show us how to keep the inner truth from being submerged by external truths.

Sallust was yet another extremely impartial historian with a vivid style. Far from being a "pathological case," as some have tried to make out, he felt far too deeply about his subject and took the ills of the Roman people far too much to heart to have written purely as a means of "suppressing his own vices."

In writing this book I have enlisted the aid—no less effective for being unseen, I hope—of masters of classical Latin like Cicero and Horace; Sallust; Suetonius, the diligent and inquisitive biographer of the Caesars; the brilliant historian Tacitus; Dio Cassius of Bithynia; Herodian of Alexandria; Lactantius, whose pages reveal signs of the upheavals to come; and Eusebius, who laid his last book on Emperor Constantine's tomb as a token of his undying loyalty. All these men have been close friends and collaborators of mine, and I have not resorted to translations of their works. The object of this book is to bring Caesars and their contemporaries, barbarians and Romans, Christians and pagans alike, back to life once more and, in an age overfond of distortion, to paint a picture of them as perhaps they really were, so that they stand before us again, if only for a little while, gay, grave or melancholy just as their fate, character or circumstances made them.

A vanished world?

Far from it.

We must never think of their world as a place which is dead and gone. The story of the ancient world is our own story. We are burdened not only with the evils but also with the blessings of Christian-Roman civilization. Everything we are and everything we own was passed on to us by or influenced by Rome: our religion, our concept of the state, our administrative and legal system, our church and code of chivalry, our standards of etiquette and fair play, our art and astronomy, mathematical and physical laws, our approach to sport, our ideas about love, marriage and upbringing, the names of our months, the choice of Sunday as our day of rest, and a hundred thousand other things which all have their place in our vast store of customs and go to make up Western civilization—of which we are part whether we like it or not.

Roman history is the history of a city and of what was originally a chiefly agricultural peasant race whose constructive energy produced the largest empire of the ancient world. The history of that empire represents one of man's best single lessons in the art of living, since its whole being and development can be traced in the finest detail from its earliest beginnings to its final downfall.

And since during the imperial era the destiny of the empire lay largely in the hands of a single man who represented the center of all political activity and, very often, of all religious observance, the story of the individual emperors gives us a clear key to the decline of Rome itself. Not only did the Romans move farther and farther into the world of the Asiatic steppe races with every eastward step they took, but their emperors also became on the whole increasingly oriental and alien in outlook.

Any process of enlargement, aggrandizement and expansion automatically leads toward disintegration. If the blessings of civilization are to remain at their best they can only be enjoyed by a small and cultured minority. Every concession to the taste of the masses, every simplification or blunting of spiritual values will inevitably result in a watering down of their original substance.

Civilization cannot be bought nor, equally, can it be prohibited. Freedom of thought goes on burning like a small flame during periods of oppression, and burns all the brighter under conditions of enforced secrecy. Like a difficult child, civilization has to be carefully reared, and few know the secret.

Cicero, Rome's finest stylist, politician and lawyer; Pompey, the dry and rather boring man who laid a whole new world at his countrymen's feet; Julius Caesar, the most versatile genius in the ancient world; Augustus, the great and, in his old age, lonely architect of governmental organization; Caligula, the emperor whose approach was greeted by whispers of "Here comes the Goat!"; Seneca, the immortal Roman philosopher whom Nero kissed and then forced to suicide; the good emperors Vespasian and Titus; Trajan, Rome's finest army officer; Hadrian and Gallienus, the Grecophiles; Marcus Aurelius, who spent lonely nights encamped on the frontiers of the barbarian world mentally wrestling for the freedom of his soul; Septimius Severus, the grim Phoenician; Elagabalus, who performed weird dances; Zenobia, the queen who rode like a boy, and her conqueror Aurelian; Diocletian, the administrative genius; and Constantine, first Christian emperor in the world—such they were, or such at least the ancient tradition says they were. In this book we shall be taking a closer look at them all and laying our fingers on the pulse of a great and vanished world.

It was a proud and mighty world, the Roman empire, a glittering and degenerate world wrapped in deceptive glamor. In these pages we shall meet the men who reigned over that world in such godlike splendor, meet them before its power fades altogether and its riches are scattered to the winds, meet them before we become so old and ignorant that we begin to tell ourselves it was all a colorful dream.

RIVALRY AND REVENGE

These events made it obvious even to the most simple-minded Roman that a change of tyranny, and not deliverance from it, was taking place. Marius was harsh and cruel from the very first, and accession to power only stimulated his natural inclinations. Sulla ... from his boyhood onwards a friend of gaiety and laughter ... only took to murder later in life, when he sated the city with executions beyond number. ...

—Plutarch, *Sulla*, 30 and 31.

FOR THIRTY YEARS, from 108 to 78 B.C., the affairs of the Roman people rested largely in the hands of two generals, Marius and Sulla, and, to their misfortune, the Roman people served more than once as mere pawns in the tale of the rivalry and revenge of this military pair.

Let us start with Marius, who precedes Sulla by almost a generation. Marius was born in the small village of Cereatae in the region of Arpinum in 156 B.C. Thirty-two years earlier, the inhabitants of this district had been given full Roman citizenship, and so Marius' position by virtue of his birth might be compared to that of a Puerto Rican, a full citizen, but from an outlying area with attendant social handicaps. When still a young man Marius made a name for himself as a brave intelligent soldier at Rome's siege of the Spanish city of Numantia. In 119 B.C., age thirty-seven, he became a tribune, but the real beginning of his political career came four years later when he was elected praetor and married a certain Julia, daughter of one of Rome's bluest-blooded families, which was again coming to the fore after a long period of obscurity. Some fifteen years after this wedding, a nephew of Julia's was born: history calls him Julius Caesar.

During this period Rome was becoming involved in military crises on two fronts. To the south trouble had started brewing in the year 116 B.C., when Rome arbitrated a partition of the African country, Numidia, between its two royal half brothers, Adherbal and Jugurtha. Jugurtha, the stronger of the two, paid little attention to Rome's decision and continued to attempt to gain control over the entire country by force. He brought matters to a head in 112 B.C. by permitting the murder of a corps of Italian residents who had helped Adherbal. (On the opposite front, meanwhile, Rome's strength was being drained by its first contact with the fierce barbarians from the north, the Cimbri and Teutons.)

It was to Africa that Marius was sent first. Affairs were not going well at all for the Romans. In 111 B.C., one Roman general had been forced to make an armistice with Jugurtha. In 110, a new general after accomplishing nothing himself in the battles he led, turned the army over to his brother who failed so completely that he had to surrender to Jugurtha. In 109 the consul Quintus Caecilius Metellus was put in charge of the African campaign, and he appointed Marius one of his deputy generals. Marius was now forty-seven, and this was his first big chance since the year of his praetorship and marriage half a decade before. For the next year Metellus gained some successes over Jugurtha, but could not bring about any decisive action. Marius now wangled permission from him to return to Rome, and by 107 had so belittled his commander and enhanced his own position that he was himself elected consul and appointed to command on the African front. He spent a year revitalizing the weary, by now undisciplined troops, and winning nondecisive skirmishes. Then in 106 he assigned his young paymaster, whom he considered more diplomatic than himself, to arrange the kidnaping of Jugurtha. This paymaster was none other than Lucius Cornelius Sulla, a member of an impoverished blue-blood family, who was now getting his start in Marius' army and had shown his courage in the recent campaign. Sulla succeeded in these negotiations, Jugurtha was taken, led through Rome, and finally executed like a common criminal in 105, thus ending for the Roman people a long, costly, and embarrassing war. Marius, the successful general who had replaced so many failures, was fifty-one, and Sulla, his paymaster with a flair for diplomacy, was thirty-three. Marius of course, as the commanding officer, received the triumph and the adulation of his people, but Sulla at the time had a signet designed for himself showing his part in capturing Jugurtha. This is said to have started the trouble between Marius and Sulla, and as Marius over the years came more and more to be associated with the popular party and Sulla with the aristocrats, the trusted paymaster became his bitter rival.

Meanwhile, in the year 113 B.C., just a year before Jugurtha precipitated the African crisis, a remarkable race of men almost unknown to the Romans approached the Alpine passes from the north. They were the Cimbri, most likely a Germanic people whose original home had been in the so-called Cimbrian Peninsula, near the present border between Denmark and Germany.

The Greek geographer Strabo records that some years earlier huge tidal waves had torn away whole stretches of the North Sea coasts, forcing the Cimbri to emigrate. They were joined by the Teutons, a related tribe who probably lived on the Baltic coast of northeast Germany. Together the two tribes pushed on toward the Danube, where they were temporarily held in check by the Balkan peoples whose resistance deflected the restless Cimbri to the west and south in search of a new home, with their women, children, and all their goods and chattels. They, their families and even their pet dogs all lived together beneath the leather roofs of their wagons.

The southerners were astonished at the appearance of these strange newcomers with their tall slim build, blond hair and pale blue eyes, their sturdy womenfolk, and their children with "old man's hair"—or so the flaxen heads of the northerners' offspring seemed to Italian eyes.

Having copied their Celtic enemies' up-to-date weapons of war, the Cimbri no longer contented themselves with sword, dagger and shield, but wore richly ornamented copper helmets and used the *materis*, an unusual type of throwing weapon. They also had cavalry and employed a battle formation in which men in the front rank were lashed together by their belts and thus forced to live or die together.

The German newcomers—if, as seems likely, they resembled the Germans described by Tactitus two centuries later—had some rough and ready ways. They ate their meat raw and their womenfolk frequently rallied alongside them in battle. Sometimes the date and place of a battle was arranged with the enemy in advance, and individual champions challenged each other to single combat before it began. Hostilities were preluded by the hurling of mutual insults and each side tried to intimidate the other by setting up a terrifying din, the men yelling their battle cries and the women and children drumming on the taut leather roofs of their wagons. The Cimbri considered that the only worthy way to die was "on the field of honor." When they were victorious, their white-robed priestesses used to sacrifice weapons, horses and prisoners to the gods of battle, foretelling the future from their slaughtered captives' blood.

Slowly, like a surging wave, the Germans' wagon camps rolled southward, taking rivers and mountains in their stride. When they did move fast it was only to strike like lightning and then withdraw before their enemies could assemble in strength. The first time a pitched battle was fought between Germans and Romans was in 113 B.C., not far from Noreia, in what is now northwestern Yugoslavia, and only a storm saved the Roman army from total annihilation.

Eight years later, while Marius was leading Jugurtha prisoner to Rome, the Romans suffered a terrible loss at Arausio (modern Orange) on the banks of the Rhone. Two Roman armies were defeated in the worst disaster since the massacre which Hannibal inflicted on the Romans at Cannae. However, instead of following up this victory by a decisive attempt against Italy itself, the Cimbri and Teutons spent three years raiding Spain and France, which interval Marius, who was immediately put in command of this critical front, used to great advantage to remake and strengthen the weakened Roman army. By 102 B.C. the Cimbri, Teutons, and several Helvetian tribes had joined forces and belatedly started a three-pronged offensive against Italy. Marius met the Teutons at Aquae Sextiae, about fifteen miles north of Marseille. There in the warm climate of southern France the Germans' battle formation failed them for the first time. Their human barricade crumbled and broke. Many of them were killed while others, the Teuton king Teutobod among them, were taken prisoner. The German women put up a desperate resistance in and around their wagons, spurred on by the knowledge that lifelong slavery awaited them if they were captured.

A year later the Cimbri, too, were defeated by the Romans under Marius near Vercellae in northern Italy. The date was July 30, 101 B.C. (by Roman reckoning, 653 years after the foundation of Rome), and the place the Raudian Fields, an extensive plain in which the Roman cavalry were able to make the most of their superiority. The Cimbri suffered total defeat, and were eliminated as a threat to Rome.

Marius' defeat of the German tribes earned him the title Savior of the Fatherland. He had now reached the height of his fame. He served as consul seven times in all, and inaugurated a complete reform of the Roman army the effects of which were so far-reaching that we must pause to examine them.

Before Marius, the army consisted of a citizen militia borrowed by the government for a single campaign at a time, receiving almost no pay, fighting because the defense of their country was involved. These were far from professional trained soldiers, but men anxious to get back to their crops, and ranked on a property basis into three groups on the idea that richer men could afford to arm themselves more heavily. They owed their loyalty to the republic as such, both in theory and in practice. Marius saw that in the grave crisis facing Rome this sort of army would not do, and so he started enlisting professional soldiers, not from the small landowners who had their crops to hurry back to, but from the idle proletarians, to whom steady work, even the hard steady work of fighting, with even the slight pay of the soldier, seemed to offer a new security. But in addition Marius held out to them the promise of land for themselves after sixteen or twenty years, and pensions. Here was the rub, for the land had to be obtained from somewhere, and this meant that the Senate had to approve giving out some conquered or unoccupied land to a general's veterans as they retired, or he would no longer have control of his men. If the Senate had always been faithful to these veterans, the army might in fact as well as in theory have remained bound to the republic first and foremost and to their general only as a magistrate of the republic. What happened however was the opposite, and it was this that made possible the rise to power of dictatorship of Marius, Sulla, Pompey, Caesar, and others.

Marius was now the leading figure in Rome, a man who had saved his country from disaster and whose name was universally respected. The aristocracy were forced to recognize him whether they liked it or not, and his allegedly humble origins made him popular with the lower classes. It only remained for the darling of the Roman people to show whether he was equal to the subtler demands of a Roman political career.

Alas, he was not. His manners were loud and uncouth as ever. Rome was rich and the Romans were a pampered race whose dress was as elegant as their conversation. Roman aristocrats had exquisite manners and lived luxuriously, as befitted the masters of a city which was the center of the known world. But Marius was hardly the type to feel at home among the refined and perfumed Roman politicians. He began to pay secret visits to Etruscan fortunetellers at night and followed their ludicrous advice as stubbornly as he disregarded the rules of polite society.

One day Marius appeared in the Senate house dressed in his triumphal robes. He was greeted with hoots of contemptuous laughter, and the news of his ignominious reception traveled through Rome like wildfire. By comparison with other members of the Senate, he was poor, although it has recently been proved that his father was considered well to do. What was worse, he lived modestly. Worse still, he loathed bribery and intrigue. Worst of all, perhaps, he kept a bad chef. But even that did not exhaust the list of blots on his social escutcheon. Being a peasant, he knew no language except Latin, which meant that if anyone spoke Greek in his presence he was reduced to embarrassed silence. In common with most upper-class Romans, he was bored to tears by Greek plays: the only difference was that he frankly admitted it. To immunize himself against the sarcastic gibes of society and the even more distasteful sympathy of his colleagues, he took to the bottle. Consul Marius became a notorious toper.

Marius' political ineptitude also led him to become embroiled in a series of intrigues which came to a head on December 10, 100 B.C. when fighting broke out in the great market place in Rome. The once-victorious general was no longer recognizable in the man who had been consul six times. He traveled to the East and on his return to Rome reopened his impressive mansion with the idea of giving banquets and parties for the capital's upper crust. No one accepted his invitations, however, and he was left to wander through the empty house alone, hoping and praying for an early end to the state of peace he feared and detested so greatly. But still no war broke out and peace reigned undisturbed.

Then in 91 B.C. the allied Italian cities began a campaign against Rome that threatened her very existence and the stability of the Mediterranean world. The Italians, who shared the burdens of Rome's wars, had long been demanding Roman citizenship, and the Roman Senate had been carrying on negotiations which a series of blundering incidents unfortunately broke off. Finally the Italian cities formed an independent government with its own senate and capital, took up arms against Rome, and thus started what is known as the Social War (*socii* is Latin for *allies*). Once again the Roman leaders played petty politics to their country's rue, for in an effort to snub the leader of the popular party, the country-boy Marius who had twice saved his Fatherland, they made him merely one of ten lieutenants under two inexperienced generals. In 90 B.C. one of these generals suffered losses in which he himself was killed, and Marius as highest-ranking officer took over the remnants of the troops. With his usual military genius, he turned the tables on his front and once again saved the day.

The next year the ungrateful Senate took his army away from him and gave it to another general who in turn lost his life. Meanwhile farther to the south, Sulla had taken over command and now won a series of victories that, coupled with Rome's at last granting citizenship to the Italians—their fair due in the first place—all but ended the Social War. Thus from 89 B.C. Roman history really became Italian history, and vast new strength was added to the nation. If only the unification had been managed well, this strength might have been sufficient to revive the dying republic. And if Marius had been given the command he so obviously deserved instead of being repeatedly snubbed, Rome might have been saved the two fantastic blood baths that followed.

For, as we have seen, a new star was rising at Rome in the person of Lucius Cornelius Sulla. In the year 88 B.C. Sulla became consul and was given command of an expedition against Mithradates, the king of Pontus in northern Asia Minor whose country formed part of what is now Turkey, and took its name from Pontus Euxinus, the Greek name for the Black Sea which bounded it in the north.

War had come at last, but the ever-ambitious Marius now suddenly found himself eclipsed by this newcomer. He resented it that, in spite of all his own past victories, command of the expedition against Mithradates had gone to Sulla. At this point a tribune named Sulpicius Rufus proposed some startling legislation, including among other items the transfer of the command against Mithradates to Marius. As a result riots broke out in the heart of Rome, and one of the consul's sons was killed while Sulla himself was said to have sought refuge in Marius' home. After a while he came out from Marius' house, canceled his opposition to Sulpicius' legislation and left the city. The law giving the command of the army to Marius was then quickly passed and messengers sent to the legions, informing them of this. Sulla however had arrived at his old army before these messengers and convinced his soldiers that many of them might lose their positions or benefits under Marius. Thus when the messengers from Rome came to announce the transfer of command to Marius, they were slain and Sulla marched on Rome itself at the head of his now-rebellious troops. For the first time in history a Roman army had rebelled against the government in Rome, and from that moment politics in the city became a farce, condemned to fade away whenever a successful general chose to defy the Senate.

Marius had no forces and could raise none on such short notice so he fled the city, and in a few hours Sulla was supreme. Sulla now set a dangerous and legally dubious precedent in declaring Marius an outlaw (i.e. his property was confiscated and anybody could legally kill him).

Marius fled and boarded a ship at Ostia bound for Africa. But the vessel was forced to land on the Italian coast once more by unfavorable winds and lack of supplies and the outlawed general wandered, footsore and hungry, through the countryside he had once saved. He was finally captured by Sulla's police in the coastal marshes at Minturnae, standing up to his waist in mud, and conveyed to a house to await execution. A foreign slave was detailed to carry out the sentence but the sight of the great conqueror's glowing eyes and the sound of his commanding voice evidently proved too much for him, for he ran off, crying loudly, "I cannot kill Marius." The officials at Minturnae were ashamed that a slave had shown more respect for the old general than his fellow citizens, and they accordingly released him and sent him to sea with a new ship and sufficient provisions.

At Rome, Sulla (who as one can imagine with the army at his feet had no difficulty in "persuading" any legislation he wanted) got the laws of Sulpicius, including the transfer of command to Marius, declared invalid—ironically, on the grounds that they had been carried by violence. Now begins the year 87 B.C. with two new consuls elected, Gnaeus Octavius and Lucius Cornelius Cinna. Sulla was not too pleased with the election of Cinna, as Cinna was known to have been a partisan of Marius, but to avoid the appearance of military despotism he contented himself with exacting an oath from Cinna to remain loyal to him while he went off at last against Mithradates. Sulla then left, only to have Cinna proceed to break his oath at once and propose anti-Sullan measures. Rioting broke out again in which Cinna was driven from the city by the other consul Octavius, who remained loyal to Sulla. Cinna proceeded to raise an army, and when Marius in Africa got tidings of Sulla's departure he came back, raising another army from among his veterans as he went. Cinna and Marius with their armies now jointly marched on and conquered Rome. Thereupon Marius, now completely brutalized, started a five-day reign of terror which Cinna finally ended. Marius and Cinna then appointed themselves consuls for the next year and of course declared Sulla an outlaw, but Marius died when only about two weeks in his seventh consulate on January 13, 86 B.C., a fine soldier but a deplorable politician.

Three years later Sulla returned from the East, to find his enemies had destroyed his house, confiscated his property, and almost murdered his family as well.

Sulla had scarcely set foot on Italian soil when civil war broke out. Whole legions went over to him, he captured Rome a second time and decided to settle accounts with his fellow countrymen. Mithradates was an expert in the art of wreaking revenge and Sulla had had ample opportunities of studying the king's brutal technique during his campaigns in the East. Thousands of innocent people were slaughtered at his command, public notices or "proscriptions" being posted daily in the Forum, listing the names of those who were to be executed the same day. Rivaling Ivan the Terrible, Sulla exterminated thousands of Italians who held out against him in the fortress of Praeneste near Rome. He auctioned off his victims' property and set their slaves free, loaded comedians, singers and whores with extravagant gifts, and invited the whole of Rome to an orgy of eating and drinking, throwing all the leftovers into the Tiber. Yet curiously enough, he also gave Rome quite a good new constitution and reorganized the legal system. He was, in effect, Rome's first Caesar, for by assuming the office of dictator for an unlimited term he paved the way for those who were to be Caesars in name.

Sulla pandered to the Romans' love of gory spectacles by forcing prisoners of war to fight organized battles in public. During one such entertainment a very elegant lady called Valeria happened to touch the hem of his toga, and he spent the rest of the show flirting with her while prisoners fought to the death in the arena below. Valeria became Sulla's fifth wife. He was fifty-eight at the time.

Inevitably there came a day when Sulla had had enough excitement for one lifetime. Dismissing his army, he set off for his country estate at Puteoli (modern Pozzuoli) where he settled down, apparently without considering the possibility of assassination, and spent most of his time in the company of actors and actresses—especially the latter. He also dabbled in poetry and wrote his memoirs. This happy state of affairs only lasted for a year, however, before he died.

The Romans decreed him a magnificent state funeral and his body was cremated in the presence of a vast crowd. Before his death he is said to have ordered the following inscription to be carved on his tomb: *I have always requited my friends with all that is good, and my enemies with all that is evil.*

No one could quarrel with the second part of that statement.

THE SWORD AND THE PURSE

Never before had any one, quite apart from defeating so terrible an enemy [Mithradates], subjugated so many large nations and at the same time pushed the frontiers of the Roman empire as far as the Euphrates.

—Appian on Pompey in *Roman History*, xii (War between the Romans and Mithradates), 116.

Pompey settled the pirates, who had hitherto been living in quite a different fashion, in towns. He also made an ally of Tigranes, whom he could have exhibited in his triumphal procession, declaring that he was more concerned with eternity than with a single day.

—Plutarch, *Comparison of Agesilaus with Pompey*, iii, 663.

OVER seven hundred thousand people lived in Rome in the year 106 B.C. The city, with its four- or five-storied apartment houses, was a maze of alleyways so narrow that a man could lean out of his window and shake hands with his neighbor opposite. The ill-ventilated houses were a breeding ground for every kind of disease, and, as in large cities everywhere up to the present day, the people who lived in the busy turmoil of Rome were often lonely. Filth was everywhere; the inhabitants lived crammed together, seven hundred thousand of them, in a city which was at that time much smaller than modern Rome. And yet, viewed from the roof of the temple on the Capitol, Rome's citadel, the great metropolis was a beautiful sight. The vista of murky, narrow streets was broken by a number of splendid marble buildings which soared above them. In the temples and temple courtyards stood the statues which Rome had purloined from the rest of the world, hundreds of works in bronze, magnificent sculptures in marble.

Among these sacred works of art wandered visiting Greeks, shaking their heads sadly as they renewed acquaintance with the gods which had been looted from them. Modern divers are now photographing sunken Roman ships which are veritable museums of classical Greek art.

There were vast warehouses in Rome heaped with salt, wheat, wine,

29

and writing paper from Egypt. Incidentally, if there was a drought in Egypt and the papyrus harvest was poor, the Romans had to write on wax.

During the rainy season people waded through the narrow Roman streets, and the drainage canals beneath the city walls became boiling torrents. Rome did have sewers, however, and no house was without its latrine. In aristocratic households and later in the imperial palace, these private thrones—precursors of the modern W.C.—were arranged in a semicircle to facilitate pleasant conversation. The aqueducts, those celebrated masterpieces of Roman engineering, brought over sixty million gallons of drinking and washing water into the interior of Rome each day, and public fountains and bathing places were located at every crossroads.

The Gauls introduced trousers into Italy, and the Germans brought furs. But for the most part the Romans dressed in a colored *tunica*, over which citizens of rank wore the white toga, with sandals or military boots which invariably left the toes bare. They were therefore obliged to wash their feet several times a day—an almost sacred ritual.

The city was pervaded by an indescribable bustle and din: there were the shouts of the retainers clearing a path for their aristocratic masters, who would only stroll along the narrow lanes if accompanied by a large entourage; there were the throngs of pedestrians, the rumbling carts and haulers' wagons, the litter bearers burdened with the swaying wooden frameworks which were a constant cause of traffic congestion, and the tradesmen loudly extolling the merits of their wares. Rome had markets dealing in fish, game, poultry, fruit, and delicacies from all over the world.

Outside Rome, some twelve miles away, lay the harbor of Ostia. The island situated at its mouth was later to be crowned by the celebrated Pharos, a lighthouse built on the orders of Emperor Claudius in the year 48 A.D. This gigantic freestone construction with four stories, of which three were square and the uppermost circular, was modeled on the lighthouse at Pharos, the island off Alexandria, built in about 280 B.C. by the architect Sostratus of Cnidus at a cost of some $1,000,000. This latter building survived until the fourteenth century when it was destroyed by an earthquake. It is interesting to note that another lighthouse, built by the emperor Caligula at Boulogne, France, was still to be seen in the seventeenth century. It even appears on old prints of the town. The Roman lighthouse at La Coruña in Spain, erected in

100 A.D., has been in continuous use right up to the present day. Forty-five lighthouse-keepers have served it since it was first built, each of them for an average term of forty years. Looked at in this way, the days of the Roman empire do not seem so very far off.

The year 106 B.C. saw the birth of two famous men: Cicero, Rome's greatest orator and lawyer, and Gnaeus Pompey, the scion of a plebeian family. Pompey's birthday fell on September 29 under the sign of Libra, the Scales, whose subjects are reputed to have an equal measure of fortune and misfortune in their lives.

Looking at Pompey's bust, one is compelled to agree with the German historian Theodor Mommsen when he declared him "a thoroughly ordinary person," rather the "efficient sergeant-major" type. Yet he became the most powerful man in the world for about twenty years.

A very competent soldier, though not an unduly talented strategist, he applied himself to every task with a remarkable degree of caution, only committing himself when he was sure of his ground. He was a fightingman, rather gauche and awkward, who combined disinterest, honesty and loyalty with a cool and unemotional nature. But his gaucherie was only confined to private life. In the field he was a skillful horseman and fighter. He was less of a peasant and less uncouth than the boorish Marius, yet he did have one thing in common with him: he was an unimaginative and irresolute politician. Marius makes a more sensual and emotional impact. Pompey was boring, dry, dignified and formal, a man of higher principles altogether.

Pompey enjoyed greater popularity in the country than in the city. In the outside world he behaved cordially towards all who had dealings with him and attempted to grant every request made of him. In Rome, however, he preferred to have as little as possible to do with the ordinary citizens, avoided the Forum as much as possible, and showed a reluctance to involve himself on other people's behalf, concentrating all his energies on his own plans. He could, when occasion demanded, rise to compelling heights of eloquence and seems to have been an attractive man, both in appearance and personality. He is said to have been handsome, even though our surviving sculptures of him are not exactly flattering. A courtesan called Flora still looked back with pleasure, even in her old age, on her association with him. Plutarch, the Greek historian, tells us that this somewhat promiscuous young lady claimed "never, when Pompey had enjoyed the delights of love with her, to have escaped the encounter unbitten." Her beauty, by the

31

way, won her so much fame that she was painted and her portrait hung in the temple of Castor and Pollux.

Pompey was the sword. We now come to the purse.

Even from a purely superficial point of view, Marcus Licinius Crassus was the very embodiment of wealth. About six years older than Pompey, Crassus was not particularly cultured or well-read and was a complete failure from a military point of view. On the other hand, his drive and initiative were unrivaled in his time. He was a great speculator, often buying up the goods which Pompey confiscated at dirt-cheap prices. He also undertook building projects as magnificent in architectural design as they were shrewdly planned financially. He was an astute banker, and anyone in Rome who needed money, senator and judge alike, called on Crassus. He was only too happy to arrange other people's legal affairs for them, bribing the courts and then taking a cut from his satisfied clients. If his name appeared in a will, it went without saying that it had been forged. Be that as it may, he lived unostentatiously, like any ordinary citizen.

Shortly before his death, Crassus' personal fortune was assessed at 170 million sesterces, making him the richest man in the Roman empire. A good judge of human nature, he never passed up an opportunity to expand his business connections and took care to greet every Roman citizen of note by name. He was a remarkably likable person, so much so that his constant preoccupation with other people's affairs often seemed almost like philanthropy. Whenever there was a chance of making money his keen commercial sense took him straight to the bottom of even the most protracted and wearisome business deals. He briefed himself thoroughly on every transaction in advance, no doubt partly because he was hard of hearing. Half Rome was in debt to him. He lent money ostensibly interest-free, but with the proviso that the eventual extent of repayment be fixed by himself. In that way the most influential men in the country became dependent on him. Like every wise financier since his time, he took no account of political parties, recognizing that political affiliations exercise a distracting influence upon men of his profession. He lent money to anyone who served his purposes and seemed credit-worthy.

Little by little, however, Crassus did develop political ambitions, borne along on the tide of his wealth, connections, and intrigues. Although he took care not to betray it, Crassus had always been jealous of Pompey. In his role as brilliant businessman and walking bank, he

This she-wolf, with her expression of strange disquiet, was already gazing into eternity in the year 500 B.C. At the time of Marius and Sulla she was standing on the Capitol in Rome. Cicero reports that she was struck by lightning and hurled from her pedestal in 65 B.C. (Traces of damage by lightning have actually been found on the bronze.) This work of art, now in the Capitoline Museum at Rome, was probably executed by an Italian craftsman who had been commissioned by the Etruscan rulers of the period. The twins—Romulus and Remus—are a much later Renaissance addition.

This furrowed Roman face, sculpted during the Republican era, demonstrates the harsh naturalism and realism of Roman sculpture—a far cry from the idealism of the Greeks (2nd century B.C.).

Lucius Cornelius Sulla (138-78 B.C.). This dictator was a statesman of the first rank.

Gaius Marius (156-86 B.C.), seven times Roman consul, was a brilliant general but a less able politician.

Pompey the Great (106-48 B.C.), a lifelong soldier who conquered three continents. He married five times. A remarkably shrewd, if cautious general, he was defeated by Julius Caesar.

Marcus Tullius Cicero (106-43 B.C.), politician, lawyer, orator, teacher of philosophy, and educator. His personality is intimately known to us, a great part of his private correspondence having survived.

The Mouth of Truth, an ancient marble disk which stands in the peristyle of the Church of Santa Maria in Cosmedin, Rome. The Romans used to place their right hand in the Mouth of Truth when swearing an oath. If they withdrew it unscathed, the oath was proved to have been made in good faith.

Gaius Julius Caesar (100-44 B.C.). "All scholars of any ability have pictured Caesar with the same essential traits, yet none has succeeded in reproducing them clearly. The secret lies in Caesar's perfection. Humanly and historically, Caesar stands at the point where the great antitheses of existence merge into one another" (Theodor Mommsen). This is a posthumous sculpture.

This Egyptian basalt sculpture of Julius Caesar, which clearly underlines the inspired side of his personality, reveals a mouth tense with repressed care and suffering and a lean, prematurely aged face.

The so-called Brutus at Rome does not portray Caesar's murderer but *Lucius Junius Brutus*, first consul of the Roman Republic in 510 B.C. By overthrowing the tyrant Tarquin he set an example to his descendant, Marcus Junius Brutus, who assassinated Caesar. The adjective *brutus* means "ponderous" or "stupid," and is the origin of our "brutal." (Bronze head, 12½ inches high.)

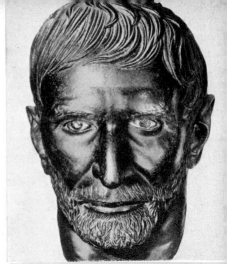

Mark Antony (83-30 B.C.), the brilliant man who was ruined by his infatuation for Cleopatra.

Octavia, sister of Octavian, married Mark Antony in 41 B.C. He was unfaithful to her with Cleopatra and divorced her in 32 B.C. "It was the Romans who knew Cleopatra who particularly pitied Antony, for they knew that Cleopatra was neither younger nor more beautiful than Octavia, the wife whom he had betrayed" (Plutarch).

Octavian was brought up by Julius Caesar and nominated as his heir. He defeated Mark Antony and, under the name Augustus, founded an imperial regime which was destined to last for five hundred years.

This head of *Cleopatra* in the British Museum probably gives us a good idea of the famous queen's appearance, for it bears a very strong resemblance to reliable portraits of her on coins.

Cleopatra probably knew this building, the celebrated Temple of Edfu, begun by Ptolemy III (Euergetes I) in 237 B.C. and completed by Cleopatra's father, Ptolemy XII (Neos Dionysos). It is better preserved than any other Egyptian temple.

outshone his far greater contemporary when both of them happened to be in Rome. But if Pompey was campaigning abroad his reputation and power greatly exceeded that of Crassus.

The year 82 B.C. found Pompey, then twenty-four, standing on the rubble of Carthage, watching with amusement as his troops scrabbled among the ruins in a feverish search for the lost treasures of the ancient Phoenician city. When it at last dawned on them that there was no gold to be found, he led them off to fight Domitius Ahenobarbus and won the north African campaign in forty days. Returning to Rome with his army, Pompey decided to enter the city in triumph, drawn by a team of elephants, but the city gate proved too narrow. However Sulla, the Roman dictator, greeted the twenty-six-year-old general with the title "the Great."

A few years later when Pompey was thirty, the Roman Senate made him proconsul and sent him to Spain against Sertorius, a former supporter of Marius who had set up an exile Roman government in Spain. Sertorius knew every hill and river, every nook and cranny of the Spanish countryside, and his remarkable skill in conducting guerrilla operations against Pompey won him the title, among his followers, of "the modern Hannibal." He was assassinated by a jealous subordinate in 72 B.C. while at a banquet, having held out against Rome for nine years. Pompey defeated his murderer, Perperna, and reconquered the province of Spain.

Meanwhile rebellion had broken out in Italy. The foreign slaves whom the Romans had captured in battle and trained to be professional fighters or gladiators rose in revolt under the leadership of a certain Spartacus. Spartacus had escaped from slavery in 73 B.C. and, collecting his companions in misfortune from the gladiatorial barracks, had occupied Vesuvius. He fought his way to the foot of the Alps, defeating various Roman armies as he went. Slaves flocked to join him in ever-increasing numbers. Leaving a trail of burned and looted towns in his wake, he seemed to be heading for the very gates of Rome with a large force.

Crassus, who had meanwhile become praetor, was now given supreme command of the operations against the slave uprising. His efforts to crush the rebellion which had terrorized Italy for three years were totally successful. He erected a grisly avenue of six thousand crosses, to each of which was nailed a captured slave. Crassus, Rome's greatest slave trader, knew how to deal with unruly slaves! We are told by Plutarch, incidentally, that he did not treat his own slaves badly.

Pompey was now thirty-five years old. His heart was set on the consulship but the Senate hesitated to permit him to run as he was not of legal age to do so. The result was an alliance between Pompey and Crassus, the sword and the purse. Military force backed by money is an irresistible combination, and the uneasy senators, many of them in debt to Crassus, found their hands forced. In 70 B.C. Pompey and Crassus were elected consuls of Rome. Crassus was always the jealous partner in this curious marriage of convenience, less popular and much less talented militarily than his fellow consul. When Pompey was given the task of clearing the Mediterranean of pirates—a task which he completed brilliantly within the space of forty days—Crassus, anxious to diminish Pompey's influence, joined forces with Julius Caesar.

But in the outside world Pompey gained military successes scarcely rivaled by any general before him. He chased Mithradates back behind the Caucasus. He conquered Syria and Palestine and defeated the king of Armenia. The distant Euphrates became the eastern border of the Roman empire. It must be mentioned, however, that Pompey's success was due largely to the Roman general Lucullus who in a ten-year campaign had so reduced Mithradates' forces that the defenses Pompey faced were no more than a façade. For his good services, the Senate refused Lucullus the forces he needed to complete the defeat of Mithradates and even acquiesced to Pompey's sending him home.

Pompey possessed to a marked degree the gift of knowing where to stop. He was an expert at biding his time and using it to best advantage. He founded colonies, continuously strengthened the ties between Rome and her provinces, built cities, and organized the whole of the East. He rarely marched off on wild-goose chases into distant regions which could never mean anything to Rome. (The exceptions were his campaigns in the Caucasus region which profoundly impressed his contemporaries.) Thus he was rarely in danger from strange and hostile nations in distant lands. He only became vulnerable at home, in Rome, at Roman hands, through Roman envy and Roman ambition. A great man, he carried his destiny within himself, in his own character and the character of his people.

ROME'S GREATEST ORATOR

But should my fate be determined once and for all by
my present misfortunes, then, my dear one, I have no
other wish than to see you once more and to die in
your arms.
—Cicero in a letter to his wife Terentia, 59 B.C.

POMPEY was absent from Rome for six long years, from 67 until 62 B.C. Throughout almost the whole of that period Rome was a seething cauldron of conspiracy and secret unrest. The hour of the Roman republic's slow decline had struck. The outlines of the bold plan for a complete political upheaval which Caesar hatched so cautiously, prepared so meticulously, and finally carried out with such audacity, now revealed themselves for the first time.

Rome was a republic, as it had been ever since the Romans overthrew their Etruscan rulers in 510 B.C. The republic survived for about 480 years, until 27 B.C., when the Principate of Octavian marked the technical beginning of the imperial era. These, at least, are the official dates, but actually Julius Caesar destroyed the republic almost two decades before its "official" death.

The period of the Roman republic's decline is one of the most interesting chapters in human history, not least because it embraces the lifetime of four great contemporaries: Pompey, Caesar, Cato and Cicero.

Rome was now like a ship struggling in the teeth of a gale. Power belonged to any man who could offer the people public festivals and do some judicious bribing during elections. Each tried to outbid the other in the splendor and attractions of his public entertainments. Roman society was morally bankrupt from top to bottom. Moneylenders flourished, great fortunes melted away, and property changed hands in a rapid and unmerited fashion. Two large proletariats took shape, one composed of slaves and the other of freemen. "Only the poor can understand the poor" became a popular catch phrase. And eventually it occurred to people that the penniless masses might be just as capable of constituting an independent political force as the oligarchy of the wealthy. Why shouldn't they play the tyrant for a change, they asked themselves, instead of submitting to tyranny? And, as always in such cases, this movement was aided and abetted by certain sections of the youthful aristocracy.

Many of them were in debt, and all those who had beggared themselves by laziness, extravagance or debauchery joined loudly in the cry for a nationwide moratorium on debts. To many people the idea of dividing the land among the poorer citizens seemed their last hope of salvation.

So, while great Pompey held the East in thrall and Rome was winning four Asiatic provinces, the republic was being internally undermined by clandestine schemes. Good men now had everything to fear, and bad men everything to hope for. The whole of Roman society, as well as the countryside for miles around, was honeycombed by a vast conspiracy. A cancerous disease, deadly, but as yet undeclared, was growing and germinating in secret: the now notorious Catilinarian conspiracy.

The Roman historian Sallust describes Lucius Catilina as having "great vigor both of mind and of body but an evil and degraded nature." Nonetheless he managed to gain the office of praetor and even became governor of the province of Africa. He came of a patrician family and his great grandfather was a tough soldier who had served with distinction in the campaigns against Hannibal, during which he sustained no less than twenty-seven wounds.

Catiline himself, however, was a pale-faced, shy man with a strong liking for the bottle. He had tarnished his name as a young man by joining Sulla's terrorists and indulging in bloodshed and brutality. He later fell in love with Aurelia Orestilla "in whom, apart from her personal appearance, no one ever found anything praiseworthy" (Sallust). Then, to clear his house for Rome's most unholy marriage, Catiline was believed even to have murdered his stepson, then a grown man.

The master conspirator was sly, an expert at hypocrisy and dissimulation, and eloquent as well. Every debauched and degenerate young man who had squandered his inheritance on loose living, depravity and gambling was his boon companion by nature. Libertines, adulterers, murderers, notorious perjurers, criminals who had already been convicted and other criminals still at large—all of them saw in revolution a chance of regaining their money and reputations.

Catiline was motivated partly by an innate lack of moderation, partly by thwarted ambition, partly by the audacity which springs from frequent failure and lack of money, and partly by resentment of the contempt with which society regarded him. He was a victim of his unsavory past. He also possessed—perhaps as a legacy from his great-grandfather—a certain amount of courage, a degree of military talent, the quick-witted gangster's knowledge of human nature, the fierce energy of a fanatical gambler, and a diabolical faculty for driving the immature or weak-minded to despair and then "helping" them by making them party to his darkest deeds.

Catiline had twice stood for the consulship, in the years 65 and 64, but had failed on each occasion. An attempt to assassinate the consuls of 65 B.C., intended to be the signal for a *coup d'état*, had come to nothing. Then in the year 64 B.C. he found himself opposed by Marcus Tullius Cicero, the leading orator of his day, the greatest in fact in the whole history of Rome. After this election defeat Catiline began a great conspiracy, setting the target date for autumn of the same year. The actual date of the uprising was to be October 28, 63 B.C., the anniversary of Sulla's victory.

The object of the revolution was to overthrow the existing government. It seems obvious that Catiline's chief motive was riches and plunder.

Cicero's bitter struggle against Catiline is one of the most gripping stories in human history, a contest between the fox and the snake which owes much of its fascination to the fact that we can follow its exact course in Cicero's correspondence and speeches. Cicero was Rome's most celebrated lawyer. In the year 63 he defeated Catiline for the consulship. By 62 B.C. he had not only frustrated Catiline's hopes of election again, but laid bare the conspiracy, forced Catiline to leave Rome, unmasked the machinations of Catiline's confederates and secured, with the aid of some magnificent oratory, the execution of five of them. Catiline himself was finally run to earth by his enemies and fell, together with three thousand followers, at the battle of Pistoria, north of Florence.

Rome had been saved from mortal danger. But the man who overthrew Catiline is worth a closer look, for it is upon his intellect and refinement of language that the foundations of European culture in good part rest.

Marcus Tullius Cicero's mother brought him into the world at Arpinum, Marius' home district, between Rome and Naples, on January 3, 106 B.C., "easily and without pain." He studied at Athens and on the island of Rhodes, the centers of contemporary learning, and lost his heart to each field of knowledge in turn. Whoever the teacher and whatever the subject, he was always an avid student but he cherished a secret passion for poetry.

Forty-eight of Cicero's speeches have been lost but fifty-eight survive. They hardly represent a core of justice, nor do they ever give the object of his indictments a chance. Yet this is only natural, for Cicero's speeches are those of an advocate or a politician, not an historian or a judge. Piling charge upon charge, accusation upon accusation, Cicero brought mountains of arguments to bear upon his opponents. Employing Attic wit and the subtlest of irony, fair means and foul, he recruited every ounce of available material into the service of his sublime command of words, an eloquence which left its mark on Latin for all time and made the language of Rome a classical medium of expression.

Apart from this, Cicero always took pains to be well informed about his opponents. A secret seldom stays a secret for long once a pretty woman hears of it, and in Catiline's case the source of the leak was a woman called Fulvia.

We shall now go back and take a closer look at just how Cicero thwarted Catiline's dangerous conspiracy.

Fulvia was an aristocratic Roman lady of promiscuous habits. Curius, an impudent, immoral and depraved individual who was one of Catiline's fellow conspirators, had long been madly in love with her, loading her with so many presents that he completely ruined himself. Then, since Fulvia's favors were only to be had for gold and tangible gifts, Curius—desperately infatuated—began to tell her of his great prospects and the wealth and prosperity which were shortly to be his. At first he only dropped vague hints but later, spurred on by desire, he became more explicit. At last, intoxicated by his dreams of the future, he threw caution to the winds. And because she was not altogether discreet, vague rumors of rebellion started to circulate in Rome. Fulvia was always in need of money and her knowledge was valuable and easily converted into cash. It was for money, therefore, that she eventually revealed Catiline's dangerous schemes to Cicero's intermediaries. Curius, too, was easily bought over, and a continuous stream of reliable information flowed in.

Few men who got caught up in the grindstones of a Ciceronian indictment could hope to escape unscathed. *"Quo usque tandem?"*— "How much longer?" The famous opening words of Cicero's third speech against Catiline still preserve their ominous ring today. "How much longer, Catiline, will you abuse our patience? How much longer will your wild behavior be the object of our scorn? When will you, in your unbridled effrontery, cease glorifying yourself?" Cicero's genius, both as a politician and a lawyer, is clearly recognizable in the unrivaled perfection of the Latin style which graced his speeches.

His letters reveal a volatile temperament which made him self-confident in time of success, irresolute and even unnerved when faced by disaster. Many of these letters are addressed to Atticus, who lived for twenty-three years—from 88 to 65 B.C.—in Athens where he had taken refuge from Sulla's agents. Atticus was an astute merchant, financier and publisher who owned land in Epirus and was a patron of the arts. He was a practical man, always ready to help people, and he was much wiser in the ways of the world than Cicero, who was a bit of a romantic. Atticus looked after Cicero's finances, published his writings, acted as his lifelong adviser, and provided a sort of placid reservoir into which all his brilliant protégé's miseries, fears, hopes, passions and joys could flow without restraint.

Cicero dictated many of his letters to his secretary and friend Tiro. It was his habit to walk up and down while doing so, and he spoke so fast that Tiro, himself a talented man, invented a shorthand which also enabled him to take down Cicero's speeches verbatim. Latin stenography later took its name from him and his system, "*notae Tironianae*," was still being used by the monks of medieval times. Tiro, incidentally, was originally a slave whom Cicero freed because of his unusual ability. He was also the author of a work on the usage and meaning of the Latin language.

Cicero was well aware that he would go down in human history as a man of very rare genius. He wrote to Atticus: "As soon as I have completed the history of my consulship I will send it to you, and you can expect yet another one in verse. For since I am to praise myself for once, it shall be done in every possible way. If the world has something great to show, let it applaud it and not criticize. But what I am writing is, in fact, not so much a panegyric as a plain statement of historical truth." It was a remarkably bold assertion but it came from his heart.

Cicero's letters (we have 931 of them) show a lively, attractive mind and a capacity for evolving an inexhaustible wealth of ideas about one and the same subject. They sparkle with intellect, wit, mockery, irony, charm. They bring us face to face with the worries and cares of a hard-working man, of a devoted father, and of a husband who found happiness with his passionate, jealous and energetic wife only when he had plumbed the depths of personal misery. Terentia brought him a dowry of 120,000 denarii on their marriage and was heir to another 90,000. "On this fortune he lived in a wise and decent manner, in the company of erudite Greeks and Romans who enjoyed his society," as Plutarch puts it. In addition, Cicero owned a fine estate at Arpinum, two farms at Naples and Pompeii, and a number of beautiful country houses—probably eighteen of them—in various parts of Italy.

Cicero wrote a whole library of rhetorical and philosophical works. There were books on orators and the art of rhetoric, on the ideal form of government, on law, on moral obligation, on the nature of the gods, on old age, on fate, on friendship, and many other subjects. The earth was popularly held to be a disk in those days, but Cicero describes it— like Plato before him—as a ball: "For human beings are created on condition that they inhabit this sphere which you see here in the midst of the universe, the sphere which people call the earth. . . . The constellations and stars, which are spherical and round, are animated by divine spirit. They complete their circuits and revolutions with marvelous speed. . . . But the measurements of the round stars exceeded the size of the earth. The earth itself seemed to me so small that I was overcome by a sense of shame at all our activity, which, when all is said and done, affects but one point upon the tiny earth."

On December 5th in the year 63 B.C. Cicero summoned the Roman Senate to confer on the fate of the captured Catilinarians. Junius Silanus, consul-designate for the following year, demanded the death penalty and all the ex-consuls present supported this proposal. Only Caesar, who had already been elected to the praetorship, rejected capital punishment in favor of life imprisonment, offering plausible and cogent reasons for his attitude of prudent clemency. Silanus and other friends of Cicero were getting ready to vote with Caesar when Marcus Porcius Cato came out so strongly in favor of executing the Catilinarians that he left everyone in a renewed state of indecision.

Cato, descendant of the Carthage-hater, was an odd individual. Mommsen called him "the Don Quixote of the aristocracy" and "a dreamer in the sphere of abstract morality," but this judgment is probably too harsh. Cato was a Stoic, a stickler for what he believed to be the ancient Roman standards, and an extreme conservative, a slow-thinking but model citizen who wandered through the vice-ridden capital holding everything up to the mirror of virtue. He always went about on foot—like King Romulus, the legendary founder of Rome. Above all else, he yearned for the good old days and made no secret of the fact. But he was seldom taken seriously and only once did his honesty come in useful—in 58 B.C. when the wealthy island of Cyprus was about to become a Roman province and he was sent there to organize the administration, being the only man who could be trusted not to feather his own nest in the process.

After Cato had delivered his unyielding demand to the Senate to pronounce sentence of death upon the instigators of this liberal, if not anarchical, conspiracy, Cicero rose and launched into the last of his famous *Catilinarian Orations,* a veritable masterpiece of psychological persuasion. While managing to give an appearance of complete impartiality, he succeeded, by constantly varying his tactics, in steering his listeners toward their intended destination. The Senate voted for the death penalty. Accompanied by a party of friends and citizens, Cicero personally removed the first conspirator, Lentulus Sura, from his place of detention by the Palatine Hill and conducted him through the streets of Rome to prison, where the executioners threw the luckless rebel into a cramped dungeon, the Tullianum, and throttled him with a cord. The remainder of the condemned men speedily met a similar fate, being executed the same night, December 5, 63 B.C.

Cicero felt that the day he saved the republic from the conspiracy was the greatest in his life. He was escorted home in a triumphal procession through the brightly illuminated streets while crowds shouted his name from every window and rooftop, hailing him as the preserver and savior of Rome.

But he was to pay a bitter price for his action. When, on the last day of the year, he was about to conclude his term as consul with the customary speech before the assembly, he was brusquely cut short by the tribune Metellus Nepos. A man who had ordered the execution of Roman citizens without a hearing, he said, should not be allowed a hearing himself. Cicero rose to the occasion magnificently, asserting that he had saved Rome and the republic from the brink of disaster. But although his speech was publicly acclaimed, his reprieve was temporary. He was later exiled from Rome for political reasons.

His wife Terentia seems to have had a decisive influence on his life on at least two occasions. Her half sister, Fabia, was one of the priestesses of Vesta who were obliged by their vocation to live a life of complete chastity. When the Vestal virgin was suspected of carrying on a secret affair with Catiline, Terentia saw in his removal a chance of nipping this scandal in the bud and urged her husband to take proceedings against him.

The same thing applied in Clodius' case. Terentia thought that his sister Clodia had her eye on Cicero and was planning to marry him, so she persuaded her husband to bring evidence against Clodius. This man became Cicero's worst enemy and eventually brought about his exile from Rome, putting the great orator's houses up for sale or burning them.

Cicero was deeply hurt by his banishment. He continuously reproached himself, writing touching letters full of love and appreciation to his wife Terentia. "Unhappy wife, anguished and weakened in body and soul! How can I live without you? If I had you at my side I should not think myself utterly lost." And later: "I read, not without bitter tears, how they had taken you from the temple of Vesta by force and led you before the tribunes in the public market place. My life, my only love!"

Sixteen months later Pompey recalled Cicero from exile and his letters suddenly strike a different note: "The love of my brother and my daughter compensates me for everything. As for my remaining worry, it is of a strange kind." His "remaining worry" was Terentia. At the age of fifty-nine he divorced her, having developed a sudden distrust of her scrupulousness in money matters. They had lived together for thirty-one years. Now he married Publilia, a young heiress whose trustee he was.

Then something frightful happened. His daughter Tullia died. Beside himself with grief at the loss of the daughter he had worshiped, Cicero threw Publilia, who had never been fond of the girl, out of his house. But he found life only a pale shadow of what it had been. "A daughter, and what a daughter! How devoted she was to her father! How clever! How gentle, virtuous and lovable in her whole being! *My* face, *my* way of speaking, *my* intellect!" Thus Cicero wrote to his brother Quintus. Nothing could console him for the death of "Tulliola," as he used to call her. Shutting himself up in Astura, he spent days and nights by himself in the lonely woods. Was there a life after death? Cicero had pondered the question before. And if there was such a world hereafter, could one be reunited there with someone dear? Cicero found no answer to that last and most vital problem of existence, death and eternity, although he eventually found some solace in work.

Two years later, however, he won the hatred of Mark Antony, whose violent measures he had strongly attacked in his *Philippic Orations*. He had survived Caesar, Pompey, and Cato. But how? It seemed to him that he had done nothing all his life except work, worry, and fret. "You urge me, as you do so often, to be ambitious and to work," he once wrote to his brother. "I want to make the most of my abilities. But when am I to *live?*" Well, it was all over now, and he no longer wanted to stroll through his lovely gardens, write poetry, or philosophize. Now it was his turn to die, and he looked death boldly in the eye, as befitted a great philosopher.

Plutarch does the old man an injustice by suggesting that he should not have hidden from his assassins, undoubtedly Antony's partisans, who were after all only anticipating Nature by a few years. Cicero did not hide. It was true that he got into his litter intending to make for the coast. It was true that he tried to escape from his enemies. But he was a philosopher, not a fool, and knew the value of human life.

When he saw that his pursuers were gaining on him he ordered his litter to be set down and deliberately leaned out. The best head Rome possessed fell beneath the assassin's sword on December 7, 43 B.C. Cicero may have guessed in those last moments that he was going to see his beloved Tulliola again.

And, that being so, he had nothing more to fear.

UNDER THE SIGN OF LIBRA

*My Cornelia, you have so far known only one aspect of
life: good fortune. And, because it has stayed with me for
longer than is usual, you have perhaps been deceived. But
since we are mortals we must also endure ill fortune.*
— Pompey to his fifth wife, according to
Plutarch, *Life of Pompey*, 75, 1.

LET US RETURN now to Pompey. In summer of the year 62 B.C., after
an absence of six years, he began his slow return to Italy from the
East. The victorious general's homeward progress was one long pageant
of splendor, and he did not land at Brundisium until the end of 62 B.C.
He had completed the edifice of Roman sovereignty in Asia and
temporarily secured it against all threats. He had conquered many
lands, destroyed ancient cities, founded new ones—among them Nicopolis, Megalopolis, Zela, Diopolis and Pompeiopolis—and deposed and
enthroned kings. There has seldom been a general with so much power
who made such sparing and prudent use of it. But Pompey's moderation was probably not, as Mommsen believed, due to a lack of self-
confidence and initiative. He was remarkably wise and circumspect, if
only as a general and strategist. He served Rome tirelessly for nearly
thirty years as a cavalryman and a soldier, and he was a cautious and
unhurried man who rarely struck quickly, kept a sharp and attentive
eye on his enemy's smallest move, and often operated with an almost
Asiatic patience.

For all that, aristocratic society in Rome favored General Lucullus.
It was he, they said, who was the real conqueror of the East, and
Pompey had only supplanted him in order to snatch the laurels of
victory from his grasp.

In contrast to the aristocracy, the common people of Rome were
loud and rapturous in their praises of Pompey. They raised him to the
status of a hero, and Pompey let them do it. But life is like a mountain
path: it rarely ends at the highest peak. Plutarch says, quite rightly,
that it would have been far better if Pompey had ended his life at this
point when his name ranked with that of Alexander the Great.

In 61 B.C. a great triumphal procession passed through the streets of

Rome. Pompey was hailed as the conqueror of three continents, Europe (Spain), Africa, and Asia. His arrival caused a furore. Through the streets came prisoners from distant lands and treasures of unimaginable splendor: five children and a sister of the great Mithradates; the Jewish king Aristobulus; Tigranes, son of the Armenian king, together with his wife and daughter; hostages from Albania, Iberia (the remote district south of the Caucasus) and northern Syria; Olthaces, commander of the Colchians; the rulers of the Cilicians; women from the royal harem of Scythia; Menander, commanding general of Mithradates' cavalry; massive chests containing huge fortunes in coin, and emblems of victory. The procession was preceded by placards listing the lands and peoples conquered by Pompey. Pompey had captured a thousand fortresses and over nine hundred large towns, and had defeated twenty-two kings. He delivered to the public exchequer minted money and gold and silver vessels worth twenty thousand talents. His own appearance as he passed through Rome in the midst of this gigantic triumphal march was modest and unassuming, but he is said to have been wearing an overgarment, over 260 years old even at that time, which formerly belonged to Alexander the Great and had been found among the treasures of Mithradates.

And the populace? They did what they always do on such occasions: they cheered.

It was September 28, 61 B.C., or 593 years after the founding of Rome. It also happened to be the eve of Pompey's forty-fifth birthday. Rome struck coins in his honor.

But who could keep his footing on such a pinnacle of success? Slowly the tragic process of decline and disillusion set in. For thirty years Pompey had been on active service. For thirty years he had been without a home. Now sleep deserted him and when he did doze off he was startled from his slumbers by troubled dreams of dying oriental kings, charging cavalry, burning cities. The Roman aristocracy laughed at him and gave him ridiculous nicknames. They could not stomach greatness. Their sense of humor and penchant for sarcasm would not allow them to.

As for Pompey, his one desire was for peace. He longed to settle down with his wife and lead a quiet family life. Then he made his great mistake. He disbanded his army, whereupon the Senate refused to confirm his administrative measures in Asia or grant his soldiers their promised small holdings in the colonies.

It was during this period that Pompey concluded a pact of friendship with Julius Caesar. Caesar, then a man of forty-two, was an influential politician and a brilliant orator, lawyer and army officer from the patrician family of the Julians, who numbered kings and gods among their ancestors but who had only recently emerged from almost three centuries of obscurity. To set the seal on this pact of friendship Pompey married Caesar's only daughter Julia, a girl of twenty-three.

Pompey was twice as old as Julia yet his marriage lasted only six years, for Julia died at the early age of twenty-nine. Their only child died too. The scales of fortune were tipping more and more to Libra-born Pompey's disadvantage. But we are still in the year 59 B.C. when Pompey, Caesar and Crassus formed the first triumvirate or three-man government. Pompey was the general, Caesar the politician, and Crassus the capitalist. Pompey's veterans at last got their promised plots of land, his Asian policy was approved, and he became master of the greater part of the Roman empire. Caesar received only the governorships of Illyria and Gaul, but these were to form his steppingstones to subsequent power.

While Caesar was subduing Gaul from 58 to 51 B.C., Crassus endeavored to conquer Parthia, but was captured and put to death.

After Julia's death a rift grew between Caesar and Pompey, and eventually, on Pompey's insistence, the Senate ordered Caesar to relinquish his Gallic provinces and disband his army. Caesar, however, crossed the Rubicon, a small river forming the frontier between Italy and Gaul. "The die is cast," he declared, and before long he was master of Rome and all Italy.

Pompey fled to the East, was defeated at Pharsalus in Thessaly, was pursued by Caesar, and finally sought refuge in Egypt. The Egyptian court had learned of the disaster at Pharsalus and was preparing to resist Pompey's landing when the Egyptian king's court chamberlain devised a better scheme. A general was dispatched to Pompey's ship with a message inviting him to visit the king of Egypt. The water being shallow, Pompey went on board the Egyptian barge to be ferried ashore. However, as he was stepping on to the beach he was stabbed from behind, in full view of his fifth wife and his son, who must have witnessed the murder from the deck of their own ship.

It was September 28, 48 B.C., the very date on which Pompey had, thirteen years earlier, been drawn through the streets of Rome in triumph. His life had indeed been ruled by Libra, the Scales. The man who had borne the title "Great" since he was twenty-five and had laid the world and treasures without equal at Rome's feet met his end on a sand dune on the Egyptian coast.

Not long afterward, thinking he was still on Pompey's track, Caesar arrived in Egypt. They brought him the severed head of his son-in-law and former friend.

It is said that, deeply moved, Caesar averted his eyes and wept.

THE VERSATILE GENIUS

[When the vessel he was on was in grave danger]
Caesar said: "Take courage! You have Caesar
and Caesar's destiny aboard!"
—Plutarch, *Caesar*, 38.

Not even in the provinces were married women
safe from him.
—Suetonius.

"BUT YOU HAVE no reason for putting such a young boy to death," fellow Romans told the dictator Sulla. Sulla replied that they were unintelligent if they failed to see "many Mariuses" in the boy. His name was Julius Caesar.

As a member of the blue-blooded Julian clan, Caesar belonged to Rome's top aristocracy and was a leading light in fashionable Roman society. He could declaim and recite, was on good terms with men of letters, wrote poetry, and enjoyed the favors which the pretty girls of Rome lavished upon him. He was frivolous but he had a good head on his shoulders. The gods alone knew how he managed to lead his sort of life and still keep physically fit, but he did, perhaps because he fished, rode and swam.

His father had died when Caesar was sixteen, but he was very fond of his mother Aurelia, a highly respected woman. Theodor Mommsen says that Caesar was a passionate man, since without passion there cannot be genius; for all that, his passions never got the better of him.

At the age of sixteen Caesar became engaged to Cossutia, the daughter of an extremely rich man. It was not long, however, before he broke off this bethrothal and married Cinna's daughter Cornelia.

Life was sweet, Rome was a wonderful place, and Caesar was young. But he had heard whispers of things Sulla had said about him and was conscious of the dictator's hatred. He therefore moved to the country and roamed about from place to place. One night he happened upon Sulla's soldiers, who were searching out fugitives. Caesar bribed them, fled to the coast, and sailed for Bithynia, under orders from the praetor of Asia, where he sought to raise a fleet from King Nicomedes. He was later accused of having surrendered himself to this king's alleged unnatural desires.

Soon afterward Caesar set sail once more, only to be captured by pirates. He laughed them to scorn when they demanded a ransom of only twenty talents, scoffing at them for not realizing who their prisoner was. Offering them fifty talents, he sent his companions off to various cities to raise the money and meanwhile lived among the pirates in high style. He harangued them into keeping quiet when he wanted to sleep, joked and gambled with them, read them poems, jeered at them, and threatened that he would some day hang them. The bandits found themselves behaving like his body guard. It was almost as though he were their leader.

The ransom money arrived and Caesar was set free. At once he manned several ships, sailed against the pirates, caught most of them, and got his ransom back as prize money. In Pergamum he made good his playful threats by having all the pirates crucified. Such at least is one of the ancient traditions that have come down to us.

After Sulla's abdication from power Caesar returned to Rome and demonstrated his brilliant command of language as a lawyer. In private life he was polite, affable and civil in his demeanor toward everyone, and quickly won the love and affection of the people. His banquets were the talk of all Rome. His prestige in the state grew until it finally was suspected that his aim was to destroy it.

The great orator Cicero compared Caesar's political ability with the smiling serenity of a calm sea. He found it suspicious and menacing. Looking behind Caesar's mask of friendliness and cordiality, he saw not only the man's aristocratic nature but he scented tyrannical aspirations as well. "And yet when I see," said Cicero, "how artistically arranged his hair always is, when I see how he scratches himself with a single finger, it almost seems as though so great a crime as the overthrow of the Roman constitution could never enter his head."

Before long Caesar was able to do things in Rome which few other men would have dared attempt. He gave Julia, his father's sister and the widow of Marius, a magnificent funeral oration in the Forum and displayed portraits of her dead and despised husband in public, and the people cheered.

When his own wife, Cornelia, died at an early age, he accorded her the same honor. The people were touched, and the favor of the masses did not desert him even when he married Pompeia, Sulla's granddaughter, later. He continued to court popularity with the voting public, and it was not long before his debts totaled thirteen hundred talents.

During a stay in Spain at this time, Caesar saw a statue of Alexander the Great and tears came to his eyes. His friends inquired the reason. "Wouldn't you say," asked Caesar, "that I had cause to be sad, seeing that at my age Alexander was ruler of the world, while I have never yet done anything great or glorious?"

On the death of Quintus Caecilius Metellus Pius, the Pontifex Maximus of Rome, Caesar ran for the office which gave its incumbent charge of the temples and supervision of ritual and religious observance. But there were two other candidates for the appointment and it was a hard fight. When Aurelia, Caesar's mother, weepingly accompanied her son to the door on the day of the election, he told her: "Today, dear mother, you will see your son either as Pontifex Maximus or as an exile." Caesar was elected. He was then thirty-seven.

Next Caesar aimed for the praetorship, one of the two highest Roman judicial offices. But carving out a career in Rome was not easy. Everyone wooed the populace as best he could. Caesar won the praetorship, but Cato proposed that the Senate should dole out grain to the people and, since Caesar could not hope to match the Senate's vast distributions, his stock inevitably fell. It was a rule in Rome that success went to the highest bidder.

There was yet another incident which lowered Caesar's prestige in some quarters, although it was taken as a good joke in others. One of Rome's leading gallants was an arrogant individual named Publius Clodius, a man who was not only of noble birth but wealthy too. Clodius was in love with Pompeia, Caesar's wife, and Pompeia was perhaps not altogether indifferent to him. However, her quarters were constantly under the eagle eye of Aurelia, Caesar's strait-laced and virtuous mother, who put insurmountable obstacles in the would-be lovers' way.

The Romans had a goddess called Bona Dea in whose honor they held an annual women's festival from which men were excluded. Clodius, who was beardless and girlishly handsome, dressed himself up as a female harpist and slipped into the Regia, Caesar's official residence as Pontifex Maximus. He wandered round the rambling building for quite a while, avoiding the more brightly illuminated rooms, until one of Pompeia's slaves recognized him by his masculine voice. Aurelia at once suspended the festivities, covered up the sacred shrines, and

threw Clodius out of the house. Early the next morning the whole of
Rome was buzzing with the scandal and Caesar decided to divorce
Pompeia. But when the case came before a special court of inquiry
instituted by the Senate for this occasion, Caesar treated Clodius with
remarkable nonchalance, declaring that he personally had no knowledge of the man's guilt. Replying to people who asked him why, in
that case, he had divorced his wife, he said: "Because I demand of my
wife that she be above suspicion."

Caesar was appointed governor of the province of Farther Spain.
His creditors, however, made such an uproar about his departure that
he appealed to Crassus who paid off his most pressing debts.

After a highly successful tour of duty in Spain, Caesar returned to
Rome and effected a reconciliation between Pompey and Crassus under
which it was agreed, privately and unofficially, that Caesar, Pompey
and Crassus would co-ordinate their policy from then on. The triumvirate had been born. Caesar gave Pompey the hand of his daughter
Julia and contracted a fourth marriage himself, this time to Calpurnia,
the daughter of Piso.

In the year 59 B.C. the Roman people's assembly and the Senate between them granted Caesar the governorship of Cisalpine Gaul,
Illyricum, and Transalpine Gaul, which, after his coming conquests,
comprised modern France, Belgium and Holland as well as Italy north
of the Po. He was given four legions, or about 24,000 men, and his
term of office was initially set at five years although he later got it
extended by another five.

It is certain that Caesar was deeply influenced by his study of the
campaigns of Alexander the Great and other notable generals. Equally
certain is the fact that he cherished great plans for conquest, even if he
prevented any advance information about them from reaching the
ears of an eternally mistrustful Senate. In his work *De Bello Gallico*
he justifies his policy to the Romans and is always at pains to show how
the successful completion of a "defensive operation" forced him to
undertake a fresh one.

Following his defeat of the Helvetii, Caesar came up against
Ariovistus, the German king of the Suebi, and after a difficult campaign, defeated him on the plains of Alsace in September of the year
58 B.C.

Caesar's next target was present-day Belgium, and he did in fact
manage to subdue the whole of northern Gaul.

But he went even farther afield. On two occasions, in 55 and 54 B.C., he crossed the Channel and landed in Britain, although he contented himself with exacting tribute from Cassivellaunus, king of certain of the British Celts "since among this wretched and poverty-stricken nation there was nothing worth while to take" (Plutarch). The Britons, incidentally, probably never paid the tribute Caesar imposed upon them.

Caesar never tried to conquer modern Germany, although he did make a show of force there by crossing the Rhine twice, in 55 and 53 B.C. Thus the Rhine formed the frontier between the Gauls and the Germans, between Roman sovereignty and the "barbarians."

This ability to call a halt when once his objective had been reached has been called the true secret of Caesar's genius. At the Thames, as at the Rhine, Caesar turned back before it was too late. He never failed, once he realized that his run of luck was at an end, to obey this inner voice.

Less than two years later Vercingetorix, a chieftain of the Celtic Arverni from central Gaul, rallied the central Gauls in a great uprising against Caesar and Roman domination. But Caesar finally blockaded Vercingetorix in Alesia and the Gaulish hero was forced to surrender. In 46 B.C. he was led through Rome in a triumphal procession and later was decapitated in the Carcer Mamertinus.

In all Caesar spent seven long years (58-51 B.C.) fighting in Gaul. The Greek historian Plutarch considers that as a strategist he surpassed all the Roman generals before him, Fabius, Scipio, Metellus, Sulla, Marius, the two Luculli or even the great Pompey. He points out that Caesar fought the most battles, and killed the greatest number of enemies. He took over eight hundred towns by storm and subjugated three hundred different tribes.

Caesar boldly met every danger halfway and never shirked any difficulty or hardship. He despised death and astounded everyone by the toughness of his constitution, for he was a lean man whose white skin made him look almost pale. What is little known is that he suffered from epilepsy, and Plutarch regarded his military service as a kind of therapy, forced marches, an extremely simple diet and continuous outdoor living keeping his body strong against attacks. He normally slept in a carriage or a litter. A secretary was in constant attendance on him, ready to take dictation even on the march, while behind him usually stood a solitary soldier armed with a sword.

Caesar used to travel so rapidly that the first time he went from Rome to Gaul it only took him a week to get to the Rhone. And during the Gallic campaigns he even dictated on horseback, employing two or more scribes for that purpose. In Caesar's view "written conversations" saved time, and he found short letters far less irksome than long conferences. We can see, therefore, that Caesar between the ages of forty-three and fifty was quite another person from the spoilt, versifying youth of twenty.

It was true that he still had his affairs and successes with women but he never allowed them to exert any influence on his decisions. Even so, he probably retained some of his youthful vanity, for he carefully concealed his baldness with an ever-present laurel wreath.

Caesar was possibly the most versatile genius ever born. He was a consummate politician, a general who always subordinated his military measures to the overriding considerations of his political aims, an author with an extraordinarily graphic style and great simplicity of expression, and a born ruler who knew how to captivate everyone from the common citizen and the tough non-commissioned officer to the noble ladies of Rome, from the princesses of Egypt and Mauretania to his two ill-assorted partners, the brave cavalry general and the crafty banker.

All the historians, authors and poets who have tried to capture something of his unique perfection have failed in one respect: none has never managed to catch the strange luster, the glow, the sheer positive radiance which endued all his deeds and actions and his personality itself.

THE SECRET OF SUCCESS

When, at supper on the day before, ... they were
discussing which death was best, Caesar cried in a
loud voice before anyone else could answer: "The
unexpected one!"

—Plutarch, *Caesar*, 63, 4 (737).

THE CONNECTION between genius and success is something which the little minds of this world will never understand. Like a radiant sun, Caesar walked the earth—so gray and dismal to millions of other men— as though pursued by luck. Yet it was not "luck" as such. Caesar forged his own luck and knew how to retain it.

We call him Caesar, but the name which became a title of supreme rulership all over the world was actually pronounced "kaisar" by the Romans.

Crassus had met his death fighting against the Parthians. Only one man now stood in Caesar's way: Pompey, his great rival and the general whose victories in Asia rivalled Caesar's own.

Rome was like a ship without a helmsman. Near anarchy reigned and power belonged to anyone who could entertain the people. The Senate was corrupt, the constitution on the point of collapse.

In Rome Pompey tried to prevent Caesar's re-election to the consulship in 48 B.C. On reaching the Rubicon, the river which separated Cisalpine Gaul from Italy, Caesar paused, lost in thought. Then, after lengthy deliberations as to whether he should attempt a bold coup against Rome, the Senate and Pompey, he decided to cross the Rubicon, the point of no return. Within sixty days he had won a bloodless victory and was master of all Italy.

Then came the chase culminating in the battle of Pharsalus on August 9, 48 B.C., in which Pompey was defeated once and for all and fled to Egypt where, as mentioned before, he was murdered.

Then Caesar landed at Alexandria and with godlike self-confidence began to reorganize the state of utter chaos which prevailed there. Egypt was being governed by the king's prime minister, the eunuch Pothinus. The king and queen were Ptolemy and his sister Cleopatra who, following the normal Egyptian custom, were married although at the time Ptolemy was only twelve years old while Cleopatra was nineteen. It was now three years after this marriage, and Cleopatra had been driven out of the country by Pothinus and was in Syria, scheming to regain her royal prerogatives by force of arms.

The wily regent Pothinus was far from overjoyed by Caesar's arrival, for the father of the fifteen-year-old king owed the triumvirs 17½ million drachmas and Caesar now demanded the repayment of 10 million for the upkeep of his troops. Pothinus advised him to quit Egypt and carry out his world-wide projects but Caesar replied that Egyptian advice was the last thing he would take. Instead of leaving the country, he secretly sent for the exiled Cleopatra.

Accompanied only by a Sicilian, Apollodorus, the princess entered a small boat and landed near the royal palace at twilight. In order to reach Caesar's presence undetected she hid herself in a mattress (not a carpet, by the way!) which Apollodorus tied up with cord and brought to Caesar.

We can well imagine how affected the hard, middle-aged soldier must have been at the sight of the girl. She may not have been beautiful, but she was certainly attractive. In Plutarch's own words: "Her society and charms made a great impression upon Caesar." Caesar reconciled Cleopatra with her brother, Cleopatra naturally having stipulated that she should take a share in the government from then on. There followed a ceremonial banquet designed to seal the reconciliation.

An attempt on Caesar's life planned by Pothinus and his general, Achillas, was now unmasked by Caesar's barber, a slave who, although he was the most timid man in the camp, was an expert spy and eavesdropper. Caesar posted guards all around the conspirators' rendezvous but although he got rid of Pothinus he failed to catch Achillas, who escaped and immediately took up arms against him. The Egyptians blocked all the canals and sources of water supply with the result that Caesar's troops nearly died of thirst. Then Achillas tried to make off with Caesar's fleet. Caesar set fire to the naval arsenal.

Caesar was himself exposed to great danger during this melee. The battle was raging near the island of Pharos and its celebrated lighthouse when he jumped off the mole into a small boat to go to the aid of his troops. Egyptian vessels came swooping down on him from all sides. He plunged into the sea to elude them and swam to safety through a hail of shots, holding some important documents above the water with one hand. The young king had meanwhile gone over to Achillas, but Caesar inflicted a decisive defeat on the Egyptians. The boy-king was probably drowned in the Nile.

Leaving Cleopatra behind as queen of Egypt, Caesar traveled to Syria while Cleopatra shortly afterwards gave birth to a son whom the Alexandrians, logically enough, called Caesarion, or "Little Caesar." Caesar's next step, in 47 B.C., was to defeat Mithradates' son Pharnaces at Zela, south of the Black Sea. His way of transmitting the news to Rome as speedily as possible was to write to his friend Amintius: "I came, saw, and conquered." Caesar's defeat of Pharnaces, incidentally, was the work of a single short hour.

The brilliance with which Caesar parried the blows of fate, his genius for improvisation, and his deliberate independence of what is commonly called luck are all demonstrated by his African campaign during the winter of 47–46 B.C. And this campaign is a perfect illustration of the way Caesar inevitably managed, despite a succession of mishaps and the most unfavorable prospects, to come home with total victory in his pocket.

Africa was the chief stronghold of republican opposition, for it was here that all the opponents of Caesar and tyranny in general were concentrated. They included the survivors of the army defeated at Pharsalus, and the garrisons of Dyrrhachium (Durazzo), Corcyra and the Peloponnesus. The senior general Quintus Metellus Scipio, Pompey's father-in-law, had also arrived there, as had the leader of the republican anti-Caesarian faction, Marcus Cato, the man who "would sooner have let the Republic fall in ruins for a proper cause than save it by irregular means" (Mommsen). There, too, were to be found Pompey's son, Sextus, as well as Labienus, an efficient officer who had earlier been Caesar's ablest subordinate in Gaul but had now gone over to his enemies' side. In all, this stubborn remnant of Pompey's former supporters had collected more than ten legions together. The chief backer of this menacing coalition was the African king Juba.

While Caesar was assembling forces in southern Italy in preparation for the African expedition, mutiny almost broke out. His legionaries, wearied by an endless succession of campaigns, were discontented, especially since the rewards and privileges they had been granted had not come up to their expectations. So they went marching off to Rome in wild and undisciplined bodies with the declared intention of telling Caesar himself how they felt.

But then the legionaries found themselves standing before Caesar, who came out to greet them suddenly and unannounced. His manner was calm as he demanded: "What do you want?"

The legionaries then informed him that they wanted their discharge, knowing that Caesar needed them more urgently than ever before for his African enterprise and could not afford to let them go.

Caesar's reply was as succinct as it was unexpected. "You are right, Quirites," he said. "Heavy fighting and wounds have tired you out. You may go."

"Quirites" ("fellow citizens") he called them, not "comrades"— as though they had ceased to be soldiers and were already civilians! "I do not need you any longer," he said. "I discharge you."

For a moment the soldiers stood there dumbly.

Then they begged to be allowed to remain with him.

Reading this, one cannot quite grasp why the mutinous legionaries let themselves be pacified so easily. But it was not just Caesar's words which did it. It was something which, after almost two thousand years, one finds hard to comprehend. Once again Caesar's extraordinary personality had enthralled his soldiers. Once again they stood there before him abashed, irresolute, like wax in his hands. Mommsen says: "History knows no greater psychological stroke of genius."

The actual expedition in Africa was a long series of mishaps with one single exception: the battle of Thapsus, the final struggle and the only decisive engagement, which Caesar, true to form, won. No sooner had he sailed for Africa on December 25, 47 B.C., than an equinoctial storm blew up and his fleet went astray among the storm-tossed waves. He landed at Hadrumetum (Sousse) with a mere three thousand men, most of them recruits. Stepping ashore, Caesar stumbled and fell, an occurrence which struck terror into his superstitious soldiers. But with great presence of mind he pretended that he had thrown himself to the ground on purpose. "I seize you, Africa!" he cried.

The remainder of Caesar's ships eventually hove in sight. Next he managed to extricate his legions from a surprise attack by Labienus, but only with heavy losses. In this kind of situation Caesar revealed an iron nerve and inexhaustible reserves of patience. Stage by stage, he gleaned for his side whatever advantages he could, always avoiding a decisive battle. He mobilized Gaetulian tribes of herdsmen against Juba, drew Mauretanian kings into an alliance, won over various towns and their citizens, and incited the native inhabitants of the African coast against the republicans. He seized the harbors of Ruspina

(Monastir) and Leptis Parva, conveniently situated in case of a possible evacuation, and there dug himself in. He thought of everything. When horse fodder ran out, he ordered his men to gather seaweed. When his troops showed that they were incapable of dealing with the enemy's war elephants, he had circus elephants brought over from Italy. He trained his younger soldiers in African-style guerrilla warfare and conducted daily maneuvers.

Then Caesar chose precisely the right moment to lure his adversaries into a fatal trap. On February 7, 46 B.C., Scipio was stationed with his army only a mile away on the narrowest point of the isthmus in front of Thapsus, the enemy-occupied naval fortress, with the open sea on one flank and a lagoon on the other. Caesar's veterans could hardly be restrained, and he himself galloped toward the enemy at their head—a man of fifty-four, let it be remembered, with a long history of successful campaigns behind him. His veterans wreaked terrible havoc in the enemy's ranks and Caesar won a total victory.

The enemy commander in chief, Quintus Metellus Scipio, committed suicide when his escaping fleet was trapped. As for King Juba, he had devised a dramatic end for himself. He intended to be burned on an immense pyre in Zama, his capital, along with his family, his treasures, and all his citizens. The people of Zama, however, were not overly keen on playing their part in this mad orgy of death and destruction and they shut the city gates on their king as he approached. So, after a sumptuous banquet, the savage monomaniac challenged Petreius to mortal combat. Petreius fell and Juba, who was wounded, had himself stabbed to death by a slave. Labienus and Pompey's sons escaped to Spain.

Cato's death at Utica marked the spiritual end of the civil war and the end of the conflict between the republican forces and Caesar. This indomitable man chose to die a martyr's death for the republican cause. Caesar would have been only too happy to pardon him, if only for the sake of gaining a reputation for magnanimity, but Cato felt that Caesar's mercy would close the gates of immortality to him forever. When he recommended to his son that he go to Caesar, his son asked: "Why do you not do the same?" "I was born in an era," answered Cato, "when one could act and speak freely. At my age I cannot accustom myself to servitude so quickly, but you are a child of the times and must make friends with the spirit of your century." Then the greatest republican of his day sat down to read Plato's dialogue, the *Phaedo*. At midnight he drove a dagger into his body and when they bound up his wound, tore out his own entrails. Thus even Caesar's genius foundered on the inflexibility of this reactionary Roman nobleman, Stoic and idealist. "He did not even grant me the glory of allowing him to live," grumbled Caesar.

Nevertheless the monarchy had been forged, and Caesar's triumphal march through Rome was the triumph of a man who had defended and enlarged the empire, not that of a victor in a civil war. One day of the festivities was set aside for Gaul, another for Egypt, another for Pontus, and yet another for Africa. The triumphal procession included, apart from huge quantities of booty, prisoners such as Princess Arsinoë of Egypt, young Prince Juba of Numidia, and the famed Vercingetorix, former hero and leader of the Gauls. Then came Caesar himself and the wagons full of gold for his soldiers. Each legionary received a gratuity of 5,000 denarii, and each centurion 10,000.

To no one's surprise, Caesar was elected dictator, first for a term of ten years and then, as *dictator perpetuus*, for life.

A final murderous battle against Pompey's sons which took place near the town of Munda in Spain led Caesar into such personal danger that when it was over he declared that, although he had often fought for victory, this was the first time he had fought for his life. It was the last battle he ever fought.

The Romans had become used to Caesar's triumphs. The victor was now their absolute master and Rome stood at the mercy of his whims. However, it was hoped in the capital that one-man rule would at last bring relief from civil war and its attendant tribulations, and so the Romans willingly elected Caesar dictator for his lifetime. Yet the moment he was granted unlimited power for an unlimited term, Caesar became a tyrant and a dictator in the modern sense.

Then began the grotesque game of flattering a man who was ultimately bound, by the sheer plethora of the honors heaped upon him, to look ridiculous. An orgy of adulation and exaggerated hero worship, taking strange and often offensive forms, made Caesar a detested figure even in the eyes of the good-natured citizenry. And most extravagant of all in their panegyrics and eulogies were Caesar's enemies.

Caesar re-erected Pompey's statue. But when several of his friends advised him to provide himself with a body guard, he replied: "It is better to die once than always to be expecting death." Distributions of grain, entertainments, grants of colonial land to veterans, all these things

Caesar tossed at the people like so many pieces of bait. At the same time he forged great plans. He wanted to outdo his existing military successes. He wanted to march against the Parthians. He wanted to push into the Caucasus, skirt the Black Sea, and force his way into Scythia. Then he proposed to return to Italy by a long and circuitous route through Germany and Gaul, conquering every country on the way, until he reached the oceans which marked "the frontiers of the world."

What was there left, he asked himself, for a man with so much power? What worth-while enterprise still lay open to someone who was master of the world? He devised a plan to cut a canal through the isthmus of Corinth. He decided to dam the Tiber and divert it into the sea near Terracina. A vast project involving thousands of people hovered before his eyes—the draining of the Pontine marshes. He intended to construct moles on the coast, eliminate the dangerous reefs and shoals in the port of Ostia, and install harbors and anchorages. He summoned the greatest philosophers and mathematicians of the day and ordered them to devise a new time-system. He introduced the whole Roman empire to the solar year and the Julian calendar which was adopted by the world at large and is still, as amended by Pope Gregory XIII in the year 1582, in force today.

But even all this was not enough for Caesar. Perhaps he wanted to become a king, the greatest king in the world. Or perhaps he was driven to his destiny against his will. At any event when the Senate tried to hail him as king and bestow on him even more exaggerated marks of honor, Caesar refused to rise from the rostra and declared that the offer should be withdrawn. That went down badly, both with the Senate and the people. Caesar went home, laid aside his toga, and told his friends that anyone who wanted to kill him was free to do so. Then he apologized. It was his illness, he said. A man with epilepsy easily became confused if he had to address the people in a standing position. Any shock or violent movement made him dizzy. Here one Cornelius Balbus cut short Caesar's apologies by telling him: "Do not forget that you are Caesar. Let yourself be revered as a superior being."

Caesar sat on a golden chair in his triumphal robes. He was proffered a laurel wreath and a diadem. When Caesar pushed the diadem away, the people clapped loudly. He was again offered the diadem. Again he refused it, and again the crowd clapped. Reluctantly perhaps, he rose and ordered the wreath to be carried to the Capitol.

However, Caesar's enemies secretly adorned his statues with diadems. Two tribunes of the people were detailed to remove them and the men who had hailed Caesar were thrown into prison on the dictator's own orders. The convicted men were accompanied to prison by a jubilant mob.

Marcus Brutus was an enemy of tyranny. Caesar had pardoned him after Pharsalus where he had fought for Pompey, and he enjoyed the dictator's particular confidence. He was praetor and Caesar was backing him as a candidate for the consulship. But Cassius, who instigated the plot against Caesar's life, knew that Brutus could be won over through ambition. It was of Cassius, incidentally, that Caesar once said: "I do not like Cassius' paleness." On another occasion when someone tried to cast suspicion on Antonius Dolabella, the dictator remarked: "I am not afraid of well-covered gentlemen, only lean and pale ones." The inference was plain.

The Greek geographer Strabo tells us that sinister portents were observed at this time. Fiery figures were seen, for instance, and when Caesar sacrificed he could find no heart inside the victim. A soothsayer warned Caesar particularly to beware of great danger on the fifteenth of March. But on the morning of that day Caesar greeted the soothsayer on the way to the assembly with the words: "Well, the fifteenth of March is here." Whereupon the soothsayer replied: "Here, yes, but not yet gone!"

When at supper the day before they were discussing which death was best, Caesar had called out loudly: "An unexpected one!" Then that night all the doors and windows of his bedroom sprang open and his wife Calpurnia sighed and talked in her sleep. When morning came Calpurnia begged Caesar to postpone the session in the Senate and not to venture out. Caesar was disturbed, for he had never noticed any superstitious tendencies in his wife before.

He had decided not to attend the sitting after all when one of his favorites took him by the hand and drew him outside, pouring scorn on all the soothsayers' predictions. An unknown slave came to beg a quick word with Caesar but failed to get there in time. He told Calpurnia that he had a message of the utmost importance to deliver to her husband. A certain Artemidorus even pushed a note into Caesar's hand which would have unmasked the whole conspiracy, but

Caesar merely handed it to an attendant. Artemidorus stepped close to Caesar and told him: "Read it, Caesar, quickly and without delay." Caesar took the letter back but was prevented from reading it by the pressure of the crowd.

The Senate was assembled in the magnificent hall which Pompey had built onto the theater and which also housed a statue of him. Gazing at Pompey's statue, Cassius mutely called upon the figure for support. Then Caesar entered the chamber and the senators rose respectfully to their feet.

As they did so, a man called Tullius Cimber handed Caesar a petition on behalf of his exiled brother and followed him to his chair, pleading with him as he went. But Caesar, taking his seat, flatly rejected the petition. Then Tullius took Caesar's toga in both hands and dragged it from his neck. The first to strike the doomed dictator was the tribune Casca who stabbed him in the neck with his dagger. Casca's blade did not penetrate deeply, however, and Caesar wrenched the weapon away from him, shouting: "Casca, you madman, what are you doing?"

At that, each of the conspirators drew a weapon, for they had agreed that each of them should participate in the murder. Hemmed in on every side, Caesar eluded the dagger blows aimed at his face and eyes, squirming under his murderers' hands like a cornered beast. Then Brutus dealt him a blow in the chest. Caesar had been writhing to and fro, screaming at the top of his voice, but when he saw the sword in Brutus' hand he offered no further resistance. He fell near the base of Pompey's statue, spattering it with his blood. It was almost as though Pompey were taking his own revenge on his erstwhile friend. Rome's greatest general and politician died with twenty-three wounds in his body. Such at least is the account passed on to us.

The powerful guardian angel which had always watched over Caesar during his lifetime followed him into death as the avenger of his murder. It tracked down his assassins wherever they went, on land or sea, and all of them met a violent end or took their own lives. Brutus defeated at Philippi by Octavian and Antony, fled to the top of a steep hill and there plunged a sword into his breast.

"It is better to die once than always to be expecting death," Caesar had said.

THE BEAR AND THE HONEY

*Her appearance and her words had such an effect that she
drew into her toils even the most unemotional man, the most
inveterate woman-hater.*
—Dio Cassius, xlii, 34.

*There was an irresistible charm in her closer acquaintance, and
her appearance, engaging conversation, fine manners and general
demeanor never failed to make a deep impression.*
—Plutarch, *Marcus Antonius*, 27.

SOON AFTER Caesar's death his murderers were forced to acknowledge
that, while they had killed the man, they had not killed his popularity.
Furthermore the soil which had produced the dictatorship of a Caesar
remained as fertile for Caesardom and monarchy as it ever was. The
daggers of a Cassius and a Brutus, the fervent speeches of a Cicero, the
hatred and opposition of a Cato—all these had done virtually nothing
to change the course of history.

It is unwise to assassinate a dictator: far wiser to let him destroy
himself.

It was not until seventeen years after Caesar's death that the age of
the mighty Caesars, the Roman emperors, the great monarchs, the
sometimes capricious and iniquitous rulers of the world, began. The
main candidates for power in the interim were Antony and Octavian.

Marcus Antonius had served under Caesar in Gaul and later became
consul in the shadow of Caesar's dictatorship. He was now the most
prominent man in Rome, having helped to prejudice Caesar's veterans
and the citizens in favor of Caesar's memory and against his assassins.

Octavius was just eighteen years old. Caesar had adopted him, made
him heir to his immense fortune, and appointed him executor of his
political testament. Now Octavius became Gaius Julius Caesar Octavianus. It took courage to be a Caesar's heir.

The triumvirate of Octavian, Mark Antony and Lepidus was formed.
Before long Mark Antony and Octavian were in action together
against Cassius and Brutus, and at the battle of Philippi (42 B.C.)
Caesar's murderers were defeated. Then Lepidus was relieved of all
active duties by his victorious colleagues. Mark Antony eventually

became ruler of the eastern part of the Roman empire while Octavian took over the West, reigning supreme over Spain, Italy, west Africa (i.e. not Egypt) and Gaul. Both men now were apparently extremely happy.

But there is always latent danger in any such partition of the world. The feud between Caesar and Pompey was still fresh in all minds. Pompey had married Caesar's daughter, yet even so the two great Romans became deadly enemies. Mark Antony and Octavian tried at times to get on together. But both men were ambitious and therein lay the seeds of the great conflict to come.

Mark Antony was a fine-looking man with broad shoulders, a strong nose, and manliness and decision in his every movement—altogether a Herculean figure. He was boastful and sarcastic, yet tough, courageous and daring in battle without ever being bereft of a good general's caution.

His soldiers loved him because he was fond of chatting with them, sat down at their tables, drank with them, and was exceedingly generous. He hated to skimp or save and had nothing but loathing for the parsimonious. He threw out anyone who came to him with complaints and flatly refused to listen to anyone else's worries.

Women, on the other hand, were his ruling passion. He spent his nights feasting and theater-going with comedians, jesters, ladies of easy virtue and, above all, with a former slave-girl, Cytheris, who enjoyed a most unsavory reputation and whom he had carried behind him in a litter from town to town when he went traveling. On reaching a grove of trees or a beautiful river he would set up marquees and serve banquets on golden plate. Sometimes he used to hitch his chariot to a team of lions, and he made a practice of billeting his favorite whores and musicians in the houses of respectable men and women. His third wife, Fulvia, had enough energy and exactly the sort of temperament needed to control such a difficult husband. But Antony was not often in Rome. In Asia he spent his time with flute-players, dancers, buffoons and evil riff-raff, and his bouts of debauchery were so open and unabashed that they became the gossip of Rome.

Antony was a frivolous and carefree character. He liked to laugh at others but was just as fond of being laughed at himself, thinking that his ostensible friends' witticisms were not meant in earnest. Naturally his court was soon invaded by an absurd rabble of flatterers who took advantage of his good-natured gullibility. But they took care to season their lies with a little frankness occasionally, so that Antony would think they were men who dared to speak openly and were not afraid to tell him the truth.

With his honey-fuddled bear's nature, Antony might have come through life quite successfully if fate had not marked him out for a piece of very bad luck. He fell in love with Cleopatra!

Antony was at Tarsus in Cilicia, near the southern coast of modern Turkey, making preparations for a campaign against the Parthians when he ordered Cleopatra to visit him so that he could interrogate her about the financial and military support which she had given Cassius, Caesar's murderer.

Cleopatra was no longer the immature girl of twenty-two who had once been brought to Caesar in a mattress. She remembered her effect upon him; she knew how he had fallen under her spell; and she hoped to have a far easier time with Antony. Now twenty-nine, she had reached her prime and was a woman of considerable intelligence. She amassed a large number of gifts for Antony, including money and jewelry, but she pinned her main hopes on her own fascination and charm.

As she lay beneath the purple sails of her royal yacht, propelled by silver oars which moved to the rhythm of harps and flutes, Cleopatra had arrayed herself like one of the contemporary pictures of Aphrodite. Pages cooled the air with fans and slave-girls of unusual beauty, dressed as Nereids and Graces, stood at the steering oars and ropes. Thousands of incense candles wafted their perfume to the banks of the river up which the fairy-tale ship had to pass on its journey inland. Throngs of spectators accompanied it all the way from the estuary to its destination.

Antony was sitting in judgment in the market place when he suddenly found himself deserted. All the inhabitants had run off to see the new "sensation" from Egypt. As soon as he learned of the ship's arrival he invited Cleopatra to dine, only to have Cleopatra reply that it would be better if Antony came to her.

Antony came.

He was dazzled by the splendor of the ship. Cleopatra had ordered the lighting of tens of thousands of torches arranged in circles and ornamental patterns.

On the following day she paid Antony a return visit, but the pomp and splendor which Antony had hastily thrown together was rather modest by comparison. Antony himself ridiculed its lack of taste and Cleopatra immediately realized, from Antony's crude jibes, that she was not dealing with a cultivated man like Caesar. Always adaptable, she played the role of a pert and unaffected girl.

It is interesting to set aside the labyrinth of biographies, novels, plays and romantically distorted portrayals of later times, and search for the truth about Cleopatra and her relationship with Antony in ancient sources alone. According to them, Cleopatra was neither abnormally beautiful nor did she seem, at first sight, particularly desirable. But on closer acquaintance—as Plutarch expressly remarks—she had an irresistible charm. Her winning conversational ways, her well-bred, elegant demeanor, her figure—all these things added to her attraction. In addition she had a pleasant speaking voice and had mastered a remarkable number of languages: Ethiopian, Hebrew, Arabic, Syrian, Median and Parthian among them—not to mention Latin and Egyptian. Plutarch emphasizes that of all the Ptolemaic kings who ruled Egypt before her not one had even taken the trouble to understand Egyptian.

Cleopatra was Macedonian by birth and her native tongue was Greek. The founder of her ruling house, the Ptolemaic dynasty, had been one of the seven body guards of Alexander the Great.

Since most of the Egyptian kings were the products of inter-family marriages, the Ptolemaic dynasty probably preserved its Macedonian characteristics intact. We must therefore picture Cleopatra as European, not as one of the dark-skinned Egyptian people.

Antony had summoned Cleopatra to Tarsus in order to reprimand her. Instead he let her bear him off to Alexandria, gave himself up to gambling and pleasure like an indolent youth, and lightheartedly allowed time, that most precious of all commodities, to pass him by. Day by day the two surrendered themselves to their desires and appetites, doing whatever came into their heads. Their chef once roasted eight wild boar one after the other because each dish had to be at its best whenever the lovers suddenly decided to dine and he could never, he remarked with a smile, guess the time in advance.

Cleopatra never left Antony's side, day or night. She traded jokes with him, devised one novel form of entertainment after the other, and knew when to flatter or scold him. She played dice with him and accompanied him on drinking bouts, hunting excursions, even military exercises.

At night Antony would stagger tipsily up to commoners' doors and windows and play practical jokes on them. Cleopatra used to stroll through the streets on his arm dressed as a slave-girl, clapping her hands in high glee whenever her unrecognized hero got himself a sound thrashing. The Alexandrians were delighted with their general and conqueror's entertaining habits, and used to boast that while Antony only showed the Romans his serious side, they were favored with the mask of comedy.

To impress Cleopatra Antony once made divers swim down and attach fish to his line, triumphantly pulling out two or three at once. The young queen countered by sending down her own divers to put a salted herring on her lover's hook. There were hoots of laughter when Antony thought he had made a good catch. "Leave fishing to us kings, O Emperor," Cleopatra mocked him. "*You* must catch cities and countries!"

GOSSIP AT ROME

The Romans who were particularly sorry for Antony were those who had actually seen Cleopatra, for they knew that she was no more beautiful and no younger than Octavia, the wife whom he had betrayed.

—Plutarch, *Marcus Antonius, 57.*

ANTONY, now back in Italy, in 40 B.C. married Octavian's thirty-year-old sister Octavia whose first husband, Gaius Marcellus, had died a short while before. Octavia had brains as well as beauty, and Octavian must have been very fond of her. Certainly he had every hope that her relationship with Antony would be a happy one, for the sake of Rome and the world.

But the man to whom Octavian gave his sister's hand was far from being an ideal marriage partner. He had tasted the opium of Cleopatra's charms and was to become an addict. He made no bones about his affair with her either, even in Rome, though certainly he was not at this time in love with her. His marriage to Octavia did in fact last for three very happy years. He took her to Greece with him and Octavia saw to it that the friendship between her brother and her husband remained intact.

But then in 37 B.C. Antony sent his wife back to Italy and summoned Cleopatra to meet him in Antioch. She came and soon Antony was hopelessly in love with her.

Some months after her first encounter with Antony, Cleopatra had given birth to twins and Antony now acknowledged them as his own children (calling the boy Alexander and the girl Cleopatra). And when he capped that by giving them the additional names Sun and Moon, gossip really ran riot in the city on the Tiber.

In March of 35 B.C. Octavia made one last desperate attempt to save her marriage with Antony and prevent a breach between him and her brother. She set off to see her husband in person but in Athens she received a message from him telling her to stay where she was.

Cleopatra had seen the red light. She realized that Octavia intended to have a showdown with her and, fearing Octavia's dignity and prestige as well as her beauty, she now acted as though she were mortally enamored of Antony. She started dieting. If Antony looked at her she would go into a sort of ecstasy. If he went out she gazed after him dejectedly with languishing eyes. Again she would make a pretense of crying, and then hastily wipe the tears away when he stole a glance at her as though she had not wanted him to notice.

Antony was contemplating a campaign against the Parthians but Cleopatra bound him to her with all the artifices of love. Weepingly she complained that Octavia was only clinging to him for the sake of her brother and the Romans. She herself, on the other hand, although queen of a great nation, stood in full view of the world as his lover. She could bear this fate just as long as he remained with her, but she would never survive a separation.

From then on, Antony was saddled with the additional burden of Cleopatra's strong will. Yet certainly this was compensated for to a certain degree by her wealth, and by the fact that her caution was after all prudent. Certainly the Parthian campaign was a great and unwarranted risk on Antony's part.

Back in Rome, Octavian ordered his sister to put an end to the scandal and move back into her own house but Octavia stayed on in Antony's home, not only looking after her own children but those of Fulvia as well. She stood up for Antony's friends and remained loyal and devoted to him, behavior for which Antony rewarded her ill.

On a silver stage at Alexandria he erected two thrones in 34 B.C., one for himself and the other for Cleopatra, and declared Cleopatra queen of Egypt and Cyprus, appointing Caesarion, the child of Cleopatra's union with Caesar, as coregent. To Alexander, his own son by Cleopatra, he gave Armenia, Media and Parthia—which were still to be conquered. His second son by Cleopatra, Ptolemy Philadelphus, he made king of Syria and Cilicia. To the boy's twin sister he gave Cyrenaica and Libya. Cleopatra herself had for two years appeared before the people dressed as the goddess Isis and was also called Aphrodite.

Rome was shocked. The populace knew that Antony was capable of conquering countries as well as giving them away, but they were enraged by his motives. Certainly they thought it disgraceful to lose bits of their empire merely to satisfy the romantic whims of an aging and infatuated general. Cleopatra became the talk of Rome once more.

Meanwhile Octavian spent a great deal of time complaining to the Senate. The Romans were now sorry not only for Octavia but also for

Antony. Cleopatra was no stranger to them. She had visited Rome during Caesar's lifetime and was there when he died, so they had seen her with their own eyes and knew that she had no more to recommend her than Octavia, either in age or looks. More and more charges were leveled at her. It was said that Mark Antony had given her the library of Pergamum with its 200,000 works; that he had knelt and stroked his mistress's feet in the presence of a crowd of people. In the end the Senate voted to declare war on Cleopatra and relieve Antony of his official authority. Octavian gave it as his opinion that drugs and love philters had robbed Antony of his sanity.

Hardly had war been declared than all the soothsayers, astrologers and augurs came forward to announce that they had seen portents which boded ill for Antony. Pisaurum (modern Pesaro, not far from Rimini), a town on the Adriatic founded by Antony, was destroyed by an earthquake. Sweat oozed from a statue of Antony at Alba and did not dry up even when wiped away. While Antony was at Patrae at the entrance to the Gulf of Corinth, lightning struck the temple of Hercules and burned it to the ground. At Athens the statue of Dionysus was caught up by a whirlwind and hurled into the theater. The same gale blew down the colossi of Eumenes and Attalos on which Antony's name was inscribed.

On September 2, 31 B.C., a naval battle was fought between the fleets of Antony and Octavian at Actium, off the coast of Epirus. During the engagement Antony saw Cleopatra's ships sailing away. Oblivious of all else, he left his forces in the lurch and went chasing off after his mistress. In that moment she cost him an empire.

When Cleopatra saw Antony's standard at the masthead, she let his ship catch up to hers. Antony came aboard and without giving Cleopatra a glance he went to the forepart of the ship and quietly sat down by himself, resting his head in his hands.

For three days he sat there alone in the bows. Only when the ship put in at Taenarum—Cape Matapan, at the southern tip of the Peloponnesus—did Cleopatra's ladies-in-waiting manage to effect a meeting between Antony and their mistress.

Sending Cleopatra on to Egypt in advance, Antony gave himself up to solitude. Nervous, miserable, and quite unlike his old heroic self, he roamed about in the company of two friends. He even tried to take his life but his friends foiled the attempt and brought him back to Alexandria.

Once there, he had to acknowledge that Cleopatra was made of sterner stuff than he. She was still full of daring and initiative. There was no canal across Suez in those days, so Cleopatra now proposed to haul her fleet across the desert sand to the Red Sea. From there she intended to sail off into the blue and find a new home in some distant land where Octavian and Rome could not follow, and where she could feel safe from enslavement.

But since the Arabs immediately burned the first ships to be hauled laboriously ashore, and since Antony proved to be mistaken in his belief that his land forces were still intact at Actium, Cleopatra abandoned her project and began reinforcing her frontier garrisons.

Antony built himself a house, surrounded by water, on one of the moles leading out to sea at Pharos. There, weary of disloyalty and jealousy, he meant to lead a lonely life like Timon, the Athenian misanthrope. However, Cleopatra fetched him back into her castle at Alexandria.

The two of them formed a new club, "the companions in death," which was joined by many friends who wanted to die with them. Meanwhile they spent their time making merry, drinking and enjoying themselves.

The stage was set for as shrewd a duel with death as the world had ever witnessed.

THE FINAL SACRIFICE

*I do not weep because I have lost you. I shall be joining you
soon enough. No, what hurts me is that such a great general as
I should be surpassed in courage by a woman.*
—Plutarch, *Marcus Antonius*, 76.

THE SUMMER OF 30 B.C. was a time of uneasiness and fear for both
Cleopatra and Antony. Danger shimmered in the sun-baked streets of
Alexandria; everywhere there was a sense of impending doom. Octa-
vian, the victor of Actium, was advancing on Egypt from Syria, and
Cleopatra and Antony could muster no significant forces against him.

It appears that Cleopatra may secretly have been corresponding
with Octavian during the weeks preceding the final disaster. It is also
probable that she received a guarantee from him that her life would
be spared if she managed to get rid of Antony. Octavian's envoy to
Cleopatra was an ex-slave named Thyrsus, and certainly he conducted
some negotiations with the queen, who was as convinced as ever of
her beauty and charm.

In his despair and loneliness, Antony became jealous. He had Thyrsus
watched, arrested and flogged. Then he sent him back to Octavian
with a letter telling him that, in spite of his predicament, Thyrsus'
conduct had offended him. "And if you are annoyed that I have
flogged your ambassador, there is always my freedman Hipparchus.
You can have *him* hung up by the arms and flogged, and then we shall
be quits." It must be explained that Hipparchus had been one of the
first men in Antony's entourage to go over to Octavian.

Weary, irritable and overwrought, Antony saw himself surrounded
by enemies. He mistrusted everyone and even began to regard Cleopatra with suspicion. For her part, she behaved most tenderly, plying
him with sweet words and flattery. She made no mention of her own
birthday but celebrated her lover's with extravagant splendor. Guests
who came to this "last supper" poor left the festivities as rich men.

But hour by hour Octavian's generals ate up the miles of desert which
lay between them and Alexandria. Hour by hour Octavian's shadow
loomed larger and more menacing.

Cleopatra had taken care to provide herself with a splendid mausoleum well in advance. Whether it was a pyramid or a monument of

some other kind we do not know. We only know that it was a building of extraordinary beauty and that it stood next to the temple of Isis.

Into it Cleopatra transported the most priceless of her royal treasures —gold, silver, emeralds, pearls, ebony, ivory, cinnamon and, last but not least, numerous torches and large quantities of pitch. On hearing this, the ever-wary Octavian began to fear that Cleopatra would burn her vast store of treasures before he could lay hands on it. Wishing to prevent her from committing this final act of desperation, he sent couriers to her with messages designed to raise her hopes. And at last he arrived outside the city with his army.

Here Antony led a desperate sortie, fighting so bravely that he put Octavian's cavalry to flight. But no sooner had he won this victory than he went back to the royal palace, kissed his beloved, and paraded before her in full armor. Then he sent an emissary to Octavian challenging him to single combat. Octavian replied: "There are many ways of dying open to you."

Antony realized that his opponent was right. He was going to die one way or another, and his only remaining choice was the manner of his death.

At supper he drank liberally and ate with gusto, remarking to his servants that none could tell whether they would be waiting on him tomorrow, or on a new master. They were troubled only by the thought that they themselves might be dead by the following day.

At dawn the next day Antony deployed his army on the hills before the city. From his vantage point on the high ground he watched his ships as they left the harbor to engage Octavian's fleet. But as soon as his ships were near enough to the enemy the crews raised their oars in salute. His whole fleet had gone over to Octavian and the combined force now moved in on Alexandria. At the same time Antony's cavalry deserted as well. He rushed back into the city, raving that he had been betrayed.

Cleopatra had already taken refuge in her tomb. But before entering her eerie vault, accompanied by two of her most loyal slave-women, Eiras and Charmion, she sent a message to Antony telling him that she had taken her life.

Antony was at his wit's end as he went to his room and put his armor on. "Ah, Cleopatra!" he said. "I do not weep because I have lost you. I shall be joining you soon enough. No, what hurts me is that such a great general as I should be surpassed in courage by a woman."

Antony then ordered his faithful slave Eros to kill him. But Eros drew his sword, raised his arm—and stabbed himself. He sank to the ground at Antony's feet.

"Worthy Eros!" cried Antony. "You were right. You could not do it. But you have shown me what I must do."

Stabbing himself in the stomach, he fell back onto a bed. Before long, however, the blood stopped flowing from his wound and he regained consciousness. Desperately he ordered the onlookers to give him the *coup de grâce,* screaming and tossing about in terror, but his friends ran from the room. Then Diomedes, Cleopatra's private secretary, rushed in with orders from his mistress to bring Antony to her tomb.

In his death throes, Antony told his attendants to carry him to the mausoleum. Cleopatra would not open the door but appeared at an upper window and let down some ropes. Antony was tied to them, and Eiras and Charmion pulled him up. As they did so Antony's wound started to bleed again, and he struggled in agony and stretched out his hands to Cleopatra. The two serving-women began to weaken but Cleopatra, her features racked with the effort, refused to abandon her hold on the ropes.

She laid Antony on her bed. She tore her clothes with grief. She lacerated her breasts with her nails and wiped the blood from her lover's body with her face, calling him her lord, her husband and emperor. Her own misfortunes were quite forgotten.

Weakly Antony asked for wine and told Cleopatra to save herself, always providing it could be done without dishonor. "Do not mourn me because of my unhappy end," he said. "Think rather of the many good things I enjoyed, of my great reputation and power: and remember that it is no disgrace for a Roman to be vanquished by a Roman." With that he died.

Meanwhile they had brought the bloodstained sword with which Antony had mortally wounded himself to Octavian, who went straight into his tent and wept for the man who had been his brother-in-law, his coregent, and his companion in so many battles and enterprises. He read Antony's letters to his friends to prove that whereas he, Octavian, had always sought friendship, Antony had answered in truculent and aggressive vein. Then he sent Proculeius off to see that Cleopatra was kept alive at all costs, thinking of her treasures and probably too, of his future triumphal march through Rome.

But Cleopatra declined to return with Proculeius. Opening a small shutter in her trap door, she demanded that the government of Egypt be handed over to her sons.

Next Octavian sent a general named Gallus to speak to Cleopatra. Again there was a conversation through the trap door. But this time while Gallus spun the interview out Proculeius climbed up a ladder and in through the upper window.

Catching sight of Proculeius at last, Cleopatra tried to stab herself with a dagger but he twisted the weapon out of her hand and searched her clothing for fear that she had some poison on her. Then a sentry was posted in the tomb and ordered to treat Cleopatra with every courtesy.

A few days later Octavian came to speak with the captive queen in person. He found her a mass of cuts, racked by a high fever, and almost starved to death. Yet on his entrance she jumped up from her couch, her hair tangled, her eyes swollen with weeping, her voice trembling and her face twisted with grief, and threw herself at his feet. Even now her old faith in her looks was not quite gone, and something of her old self-confidence lurked in her ravaged face. She at once began to justify herself, blaming her everlasting fear of Antony for all that had happened. And when Octavian demolished her arguments one by one, she resorted to pleading and tried to arouse his sympathy, behaving as though she wanted to cling to life with every fiber of her being. At last, in desperation, she gave Octavian an inventory of her treasures.

One of Cleopatra's stewards, who was present, accused her of having neglected to mention several items of value and, jumping up in a rage, she took the man by the hair and rained blows in his face. Octavian laughed and tried to soothe her. "Do you deny," she cried, "that it is insufferable for me to be reproached by my own slaves while you treat me honorably, even in my present circumstances?"

Octavian was now convinced that Cleopatra wanted to live, and he assured her that he would treat her magnanimously and that she would be allowed to go and live in Italy, surrounded by all that was dear to her. He left feeling certain that he had taken her in completely and hidden his real intention to lead the Egyptian queen in triumph through the streets of Rome. Cleopatra, however, knew or guessed this and the fear of such an indignity steeled her determination to disappoint Octavian.

She begged permission to take Antony a funeral offering and, going to his tomb, she threw herself on his coffin. "Antony," she cried, "I bring you this offering as a closely guarded prisoner. I must not injure this body of mine, enslaved and guarded as a symbol of triumph over you, with tears or blows. These are the last funeral offerings which Cleopatra will ever bring you. In life nothing could part us. In death we shall not, in all likelihood, lie beside each other."

She then decorated the coffin with garlands and ordered a bath to be prepared for her. After her bath she sat down to a sumptuous meal.

A little later a man arrived from the country carrying a small basket. When the sentries asked what it contained the fellow opened it and, removing some leaves on top, showed them that it was full of figs. The sentries marveled at the size and beauty of the fruit, and the man smilingly offered them a few. They allowed him to take the basket inside.

After her meal Cleopatra wrote on a tablet, sealed it, and sent it to Octavian. Then, ordering everyone to leave the room, she locked herself in with her two serving-women.

Octavian unsealed the writing tablet. In it he read Cleopatra's fervent request to be buried at Antony's side. Realizing what had happened, he hurriedly sent messengers to Cleopatra, but it was too late. They found her dead on a golden couch, dressed in her royal finery. One of her attendants, Eiras, was dying at her feet. The other, Charmion, swayed and stumbled, still trying to adjust the diadem encircling Cleopatra's brow.

Hidden beneath the leaves and figs had been an asp. She had removed a few leaves, seen the snake, and crying "There it is!" presented her bare arm to its fangs.

Some say that Cleopatra teased the asp with a golden needle until it struck at her arm and hung there. They also say that her arm bore the marks of two minute punctures. At all events, Octavian later had a picture carried in his triumphal procession which showed Cleopatra with an asp hanging from her arm.

On Octavian's orders, Cleopatra was buried in regal state at Antony's side.

Of course modern scholars these days have recreated quite a different story. The above however is a combination of the many and varied details passed down to us from different ancient sources. Perhaps the details are overly romanticized, but one of the great faults of modern science is its all but total disregard of legend, tradition and romance. So, modern man of science, I beg your indulgence in this tale to which the world has thrilled and wept for almost two thousand years.

"HAVE I ACTED OUT THE COMEDY WELL?"

*After the main meal he would withdraw to the couch in his
study. There he stayed until far into the night, until he had
completed the rest of the day's affairs. Then he went to bed,
but seldom slept longer than seven hours, and then not un-
interruptedly. He used to wake up three or four times. If he
could not get to sleep again ... he would summon a reader or
storyteller and thus induce himself to fall asleep once more. ...
He never lay awake in the dark without someone sitting by
his bed.*

—Suetonius, *Augustus*, 78.

WITHIN fourteen years Octavian had rid himself of all other con-
tenders, actual or potential, for supreme power: first Caesar's murderers, Brutus and Cassius, then Pompey's son, then Lepidus, and finally,
after the naval battle at Actium, Mark Antony and his mistress, the
Egyptian queen Cleopatra.

He continued to reign, a coolheaded and competent ruler, for another forty-five years. He ushered in a new era of world history which
not only outlasted his lifetime but survived for century after century
and has extended, in some form, despite tumbling thrones and abandoned scepters, into our own day. He became master of the world,
the first real Roman emperor. His Greek motto ran *speûde bradéōs*,
"make haste slowly," the watchword of any statesman with lasting
achievements to his credit. What is done well, Augustus used to say,
always happens soon enough.

He always held several government appointments at the same time.
He commanded the army in his capacity as Imperator. Much later,
in 12 B.C., he got himself elected Pontifex Maximus, the head of the
Roman state religion. But long before this, in 27 B.C., the Senate voted
him the honorific Augustus, the exact significance of which defies
description, but which may be taken as recognition its holder had
commended himself to gods as well as men. Sextilis, the month in which
Octavian conquered Egypt in 30 B.C., was rechristened Augustus in
his honor and has become our August. Many towns still bear his name
today, among them Augsburg, Aoasta, Autun, and Saragossa. Yet,

for all the authority he himself possessed, Augustus was wise enough to surround himself with the ablest men of his day. Agrippa fought his battles and Maecenas was his diplomat.

Augustus' entire career is an object lesson to us that a statesman can always achieve more than a soldier, and that a brilliant politician is worth more than all the generals put together. No victory delighted Augustus more than his treaty with the Parthian king, which guaranteed peace on the eastern frontier of the Roman empire and effected the return to Rome of all the legions' standards ever captured by the Parthians. The Ara Pacis Augustae (Altar of the Augustan Peace) at Rome is one of the most important works of art produced during the classical Augustan age.

Years later, when Publius Quintilius Varus, defeated by the Cheruscan prince Arminius in the famous battle of the Teutoburger Wald, threw himself on his sword, the then seventy-two-year-old emperor let his beard and hair grow long in mourning and lamented them bitterly. He even developed an aversion for his German bodyguards and dismissed them, loyal men though they were. They had suddenly become sinister in his eyes.

Some modern historians consider Augustus harder to understand than any other historical figure. Although he spent fifty-seven of his seventy-seven years in a fierce blaze of publicity, he kept his motives and secrets concealed behind a veil of silence.

For all that, Augustus is not really such a mysterious figure. In the year 40 B.C. he was still the cold, inexorable avenger and tyrant. One has only to think of Perugia and the massacre which he instigated there before the altar of Julius Caesar on the anniversary of his death, the Ides of March. "*Moriendum est*"—"Let there be death," he said. Yet from 30 B.C. to 14 A.D., a period of forty-four years, the same Augustus was the most just and intelligent ruler which Rome, so used to bloodshed, had ever known. Never perhaps did the Romans enjoy a time of greater peace and prosperity than when Augustus was their absolute ruler.

Considering the high aesthetic standards of the day, we can form some idea of Augustus' appearance from the fact that the Romans considered him a strikingly handsome man. He was "approaching blond" and not very tall, hence his fondness for wearing shoes with built-up heels. He had a pleasant voice and peculiarly radiant eyes of whose effect he was well aware. His eyes were unusually large too,

79

which was held by the people to be a sign of divinity. He is said to have had no difficulty in conquering womanly hearts and, although the reports may be exaggerations of his enemies, to have seduced the wives of friends and political opponents alike, countering any reproaches with the plea that he was sacrificing everything for Roman policy. Fortunately, these reports continue, his wife Livia was wise enough to put up with his philandering habits, even going to the lengths of providing him with young girls whenever the warm summer nights made him restive.

Livia was one of the shrewdest women in Rome and became, as the years went by, a sort of unofficial secretary of state. Yet her marriage to Octavian had caused great indignation because her first husband, Tiberius Nero, had "passed her on" to Octavian when she already had one child (the future Emperor Tiberius) and three days before she wed Octavian she gave birth to a second son.

It is understandable that historians find Augustus difficult to analyze, for his dual personality was apparent in everything he did. The man who was so fond of philandering behaved, in other respects, like any ordinary citizen. Indeed, his only wish was to be first citizen, which was why he liked to be known as *Princeps,* "the First." He wept on receiving the title Father of the Fatherland, and refused to be addressed as *Domine* or "Lord," even in the family circle. When offered the title Dictator, which Caesar had held, he declined in horror. He gave the state a "constitution" which was not supposed to be a monarchy but a form of improved republic. His house on the Palatine hill was deliberately unostentatious, even though all subsequent "palaces" in history take their name from that building. He insisted on a frugally run household, allowing himself only the plainest fare and a minimum of drink. He was also a collector and a patron of the arts and he built himself a villa on Capri where he collected interesting fossils, mammoth bones among them. He was a man of almost Spartan habits. But he believed in shaving himself daily, which was by no means the rule among the Roman males of his day.

When it came to civil engineering, Augustus built on a bolder and a grander scale than any Roman ruler before him. Nile canals in Egypt, aqueducts and bridges in southern France, the controlling of the river Tiber, the Temple of Apollo on the Palatine in Rome—all these projects were born in his mind and then transformed into marble and stone. Indeed, Rome ceased to be a city of brick and became a

Emperor Augustus was born in 63 B.C. and died in 14 A.D. at the age of seventy-seven. "His outward appearance was distinguished by remarkable beauty and always by extreme grace, though he scorned all aids to beauty," writes Suetonius. The month of August is named after him.

Livia Drusilla, wife of Octavian (Augustus), was one of the shrewdest women in Roman history. The Romans were outraged when she married Octavian at the age of twenty, for she was more or less passed on to him by her first husband, Tiberius Claudius Nero. Livia was beautiful, intelligent, and a first-class adviser to her husband, but she was also inordinately ambitious.

The Palatine was the most important of the Seven Hills of Rome. Dominating the Tiber, its summit was the site not only of the earliest Roman settlement but also of the houses of Sulla, Cicero (whose mansion cost $1 million), Crassus and Mark Antony. In Augustus' day the Palatine became an imperial residence, and it was subsequently built on by Tiberius, Nero, Domitian, Hadrian and Severus.

Agrippina, mother of Caligula and wife of Germanicus. She starved herself to death in 33 A.D., after she had been exiled and imprisoned by Tiberius.

Emperor Caligula. If not actually insane, he was certainly prone to crazy ideas and probably constituted a "border-line case." The historian Suetonius reports that: "Once, when the sacrificial beast stood ready at the altar, he appeared in the role of sacrificial slaughterer, swung the axe high in the air—and struck the assistant priest dead."

A silver denarius bearing the head of Tiberius. This was the sort of coin which Christ held in his hand when the Pharisees asked him whether it was right to pay tribute to Caesar. The reverse depicts Livia Augusta, the emperor's mother.

Tiberius built his citadel high up on the eastern tip of Capri. "No one can land there unobserved by the sentries," wrote Tacitus. This was the emperor's home for the last eleven years of his life.

Tiberius, the grim and sinister figure who died at the age of seventy-eight.

1

2

1. *Emperor Claudius* was born at Lyons in 10 B.C. and died in 54 A.D.—probably poisoned by Julia Agrippina.

2. *Antonia* (36 B.C.-37 A.D.) used to call her son Claudius "a monster of a man" whom Nature had begun but never completed. She was the daughter of Mark Antony and Octavia, Augustus' sister.

3. *Julia Agrippina* (15-19 A.D.). She married Claudius, who was her uncle, in the year 49, and is said to have participated in his murder in order to put her son Nero on the throne.

4. *Tessallina Valeria*, wife of Claudius. Notorious at Rome for her dissipated way of life, she was put to death in 41 A.D. at the command of Claudius, quite justly.

3

4

Augustus' house on the Palatine, bought by the Emperor from the heirs of the orator Hortensius and converted for his own and his wife Livia's use. Augustus' Palatium has given its name, in the form "palace," to all the princely homes in Europe since his day.

The *Via Appia* or Appian Way, leading from Rome through Campania, was named after Appius Claudius Caecus, who constructed it. It spanned the 100 miles between Rome and Capua and was the most famous arterial road in Italy. The Romans built massive tombs along its verges.

Poppaea Sabina became Nero's mistress and persuaded him to murder his mother Agrippina and his wife Octavia. Nero married her in 62 A.D. but kicked her to death three years later because she nagged him for coming home late.

Emperor Nero ruled Rome for fourteen years, from 54 to 68 A.D. At the age of fifteen he married Octavia, who was three years younger than himself, and at seventeen he came to the throne. Nero had genuine poetic ability.

city of marble as Augustus re-erected eighty-two temples and built a huge pantheon on the principle that one could never tell with gods and it was better to be sure! His other works included the Baths of Agrippa, the Temple of Neptune, the Theater of Marcellus, promenades, and a kind of triumphal avenue—all of it borrowed splendor, of course, because it was all a reflection of Greek art.

Augustus was fortunate enough to be a contemporary of great poets like Virgil, Horace, Propertius and Ovid. He spent happy hours discussing ancient Roman history with Livy of Padua, the great historian. And it was these men who really set Octavian Augustus on the pedestal of divinity and endowed him with his halo of immortality. Some of it stuck to him, as something always does, and no other Roman emperor was worshiped as a god after his death with such pious sincerity.

His health was not good, either, even though he did reach the age of seventy-seven. He had himself frequently rubbed with ointment, sweated over a fire, and took sulphur baths in the Albula springs between Rome and Tibur. He fished, threw dice, and played marbles with little slave-boys. He took great pleasure in the laughter of these youngsters and had them fetched from all parts of the world, especially Syria and Mauretania.

Once his personal physician Antonius Musa, a Greek, prescribed a cold-water treatment which cured him of a serious illness when everyone else had given him up for lost. Yet when Marcellus, his heir presumptive, tried the same treatment he dropped dead. Augustus believed in giving the people *panem et circenses*, "bread and circuses," and his public entertainments included animal baiting, gladiatorial shows, and a sham sea battle fought on an artificial lake by three thousand combatants.

In the course of centuries the Romans had become increasingly dissolute and self-indulgent, and childless marriages were common. Now Augustus disqualified all unmarried men worth over 100,000 sesterces from inheriting, unless they were relatives of the party making the will. And in his books and tracts he waged a bitter fight for morality, at a time when the Jewish people were witnessing the birth of the Messiah in Palestine.

With the growth of his power and responsibilities, the young and unscrupulous despot in Augustus gave way to the mature statesman. Then, with shocking suddenness, his youthful misdemeanors sprang to life again in his daughter Julia whose impudent and shameless behavior became such a public scandal in Rome that Augustus was eventually forced to punish her like a common criminal and send her out of the country to the island of Pandateria. Yet he had brought her up very strictly as a young girl, never allowing her to do anything which might cause public offense. Once when a young nobleman had called on her in Baiae to pay his respects, Augustus sent him a letter reproving him for his lack of tact.

Now that his daughter had been exiled, he saw to it that she was denied all the creature comforts. No wine was allowed to pass her lips and no man, not even a male slave, could visit her without first obtaining Augustus' permission. Even then a careful note was taken of the visitor's age, height, color of eyes, and possible scars or blemishes. Nobody was to be allowed to insinuate himself into Julia's presence, and she was never to escape surveillance again.

Augustus spent a lonely old age. It was his greatest misfortune that, having no sons of his own, the men whom he desired as his successors died before him, including Marcellus, Agrippa, and even his two grandsons Lucius and Gaius who were the comfort of his declining years.

The whole of Italy and the Roman empire had reached a golden age. But Augustus was old now, and very tired. At Nola, near Pompeii, he sent for Tiberius, Livia's son by her first marriage and one of the ablest generals and administrators in the Roman world, to name him heir apparent.

"Are the people already mourning outside?" he asked, shortly before his death. "Have I acted out the comedy well? If the spectacle of my life has pleased you, applaud!"

Augustus died in Livia's arms. During his lifetime he had built himself and his family a mausoleum on the Field of Mars, a magnificent circular building of great size which has survived the millennia until our own day. In it were placed his ashes and a record, compiled by himself, of all his achievements, engraved on two bronze plaques. The plaques have disappeared but a copy of this *index rerum gestarum*, the celebrated *Monumentum Ancyranum*, was discovered on a temple wall in Ankara fifteen hundred years after Augustus' death.

There were some of Augustus' friends who swore that, as the flames blazed up beneath the great man's pyre and the sparks flew hissing into the sky, they saw the emperor rise heavenwards.

THE SINISTER RECLUSE OF CAPRI

*I am very well aware that much of what I have related and shall
further relate may be found trivial and unimportant. Yet it is
probably not valueless to subject events which are at first sight
unimportant to closer scrutiny. For they are often the causes of
great upheavals.*

—Tacitus, *Annals,* iv, 32.

A GLOOMY and mistrustful man who found himself at odds with both
himself and the world, Emperor Tiberius cuts a tragic, sinister and
puzzling figure.

Certainly he is one of those great historical personalities whose
character has all but eluded the grasp of historical research. The reason
for this is that he was nearly always doomed to be the pawn of other
men whose machinations obscured his own character and destiny. Much
written about him by the Roman historians is unfavorable, yet there
is no denying that the empire was very ably administered all during
his reign.

When the Roman historian Tacitus produced his main work, the
Annals, about 115 A.D., he was writing only seventy-eight years after
Tiberius' death. And in the *Annals* Tacitus gives us a remarkable picture of the dangerous world of intrigue which surrounded the dramatic
figure of Tiberius. He pictures the emperor as of a cold and rigid
nature; a curious blend of mistrust, tenacity, hatred and fear of
humanity, moderation, intelligence and, sometimes even, the occasional
spark of genius.

The imperial era, which lasted for five hundred years, had got off to
a flying start with the first emperor, Augustus, and his forty years of
one-man rule. What successor, however strong and able, could hope
to maintain such greatness and impetus?

Who then was Augustus' successor, of whom the crumbling ruins
of villas and palaces on the island of Capri still stand as a mute reminder?

There is a passage in the Gospels (Matthew xxii: 17–22) which describes Jesus holding a coin in his hand. "Whose is this image and
superscription?" He asks. "Caesar's," comes the answer. "Render therefore unto Caesar the things which are Caesar's," He replies, "and unto
God the things that are God's." The coin in Jesus' hand was a denarius,

83

a silver coin worth about 11½ cents, and the head on the denarius was that of the Emperor Tiberius. When Christ was born the throne was occupied by Emperor Augustus, and Tiberius was about thirty-five years old. When Christ, having been condemned to death by the Roman procurator Pontius Pilatus, was nailed to the Cross—about 30 A.D.—Emperor Tiberius was seventy-two years old. "Crucify him!" shouted the Jews in Jerusalem. A little later the mobs in Rome were shouting, "Into the Tiber with Tiberius!"—"*Tiberium in Tiberim!*" Pun or not, it was uttered in grim earnest.

Tiberius' father was one Tiberius Claudius Nero, of an old and distinguished patrician family and one of Julius Caesar's officers. But it was his mother, Livia Drusilla, who really made him what he was by so captivating the great Octavian that he took her away from her husband, whether against her will or not is uncertain.

Livia was an exceedingly ambitious woman and kept a sharp eye on every aspect of her growing sons' careers. Tiberius spent half his life on active service in Spain, Armenia, Gaul, and Germany, where he fought at his brother Drusus' side. The soldiers soon got used to his strict ways and, even though their private name for him was not Tiberius but *Biberius*, "the drinker," they obeyed him. At the age of twenty-nine, his brother fell from his horse and later died of his injuries. Livia only had Tiberius left now, and since it was her secret wish that he should become emperor, she wasted no time in buttressing Tiberius' position. He and the emperor were not blood relations, it was true, but the emperor regarded Tiberius highly so Livia shrewdly devised a means of strengthening the ties between them, almost certainly with the emperor's help. Augustus' daughter Julia, whom we met in the preceding chapter, had been married to Agrippa, Augustus' best friend and one of the victors of Actium, but was now a widow with five children. On his mother's and the Emperor's insistence Tiberius married her.

This would not have been so bad, perhaps, if Tiberius had not already had a wife, Vipsania, with whom he was very much in love. What was more, Vipsania was Agrippa's daughter by an earlier marriage. Tiberius was thus being forced to marry his wife's stepmother. This was only the first bitter cup which Tiberius had to accept for political reasons, for Julia's depravity was the talk of the capital, and her loyalties—as the whole of Rome knew—were with no one but herself.

Once, later on, when Tiberius accidentally met Vipsania, he gazed at her with tears in his eyes. From that day forth they made sure that he never again set eyes on the woman he had really loved.

Augustus now adopted his stepson and son-in-law, appointed him coregent and copartner in the tribunitian power, and presented him to his armies as the successor to his throne. And after Agrippa's death he also entrusted him with the most difficult military assignments. When the subject peoples between the Danube and the Adriatic staged a concerted uprising, it was Tiberius who quelled it after three years of heavy fighting. When the Roman interests in Germany collapsed after the battle of the Teutoburger Wald, it was he who secured the Rhine frontier.

Yet now Augustus was not completely happy about his successor for he did not altogether trust him. Perhaps he did not want the splendor, fame and magnificence of his own reign to be overshadowed.

Julius Caesar had been fifty-six when he died. Tiberius was fifty-six when he came to the throne in 14 A.D. Until then he had stood in the shadow of a more than life-size Augustus. Now he was to rule under the influence and guidance of a woman, his mother Livia. This may have been logical enough since it was to her that he owed his throne, but it was unpleasant to submit to continuous restraint. He wavered uneasily between fear, suspicion and hatred.

Tiberius was evasive when the Senate asked him to assume power, making all sorts of allusions to the magnitude of the empire and his own inadequacies. Only a mind like that of the deified Augustus, he said, was equal to such an immense task. Augustus had allowed him to share in the problems of government, so he already knew from personal experience what a Herculean task the over-all administration of the empire was. The state had such a wealth of brilliant men that there was really no need to burden any one individual with everything. . . .

There was a fine, estimable ring to all Tiberius' arguments. One and all applauded the new man, but no one believed him. Yet that was always Tiberius' way: he had an innate fondness for indulging in obscure and ambiguous turns of phrase. Now, on the threshold of his reign, he was forced by a lack of constitutional precedent to exercise the utmost caution, and therefore expressed himself even more vaguely and obscurely than usual. He was unwilling even to accept the title Imperator, and he rose from his seat when the consuls entered the chamber.

The senators, on the other hand, redoubled their pleas, and implored

Tiberius to accept, embracing his knees with tears in their eyes and raising their arms to heaven and to the effigy of Augustus. Their adulatory and obsequious attitude also extended to Livia, who now bore the honorary title Augusta. They proposed that she should receive the additional honorific Mother of the Fatherland. Tiberius did not take kindly to this last. The marks of respect paid to a woman, he declared, must be kept within bounds. He also tried to limit to reasonable proportions the honors bestowed upon himself.

He was justly wary of his uncommonly astute, clever and calculating mother, afraid of her measureless ambition, afraid of the woman who had managed her marriage to Augustus with such subtle intuition and remarkable adaptability.

Tiberius at first showed himself a determined and experienced ruler. He attempted no further conquests in Germany, but contented himself with holding the Rhine frontier, removing his popular nephew Germanicus from command when it became obvious that Germanicus was running against the emperor's own policy of prudence. He maintained peace and order in the provinces, and his conduct of governmental affairs at Rome was characterized by intelligence and imagination.

Livia Augusta did not die until 29 A.D., having reached the ripe old age of eighty-four. Thereafter Tiberius consolidated his government. The degenerate Senate lost much of its power and the people were no longer permitted to elect their own officials, who were now chosen for them by the Senate acting on the emperor's recommendation. Thus Augustus' revolution was carried still further. Indicting senators for lèse-majesté became a necessary protective measure.

Tiberius brought this idea of trials for lèse-majesté to a new prominence, while all sorts of informers flourished. There was a steep flight of steps, known as the Gemoniae, leading down from the Aventine Hill to the Tiber. In earlier times the custom of dragging people down them on the end of a hook and throwing them into the Tiber had been reserved for common criminals. Now, more than ever before, the public prosecutors found their hands full since fees were paid not only to themselves but also to the witnesses in a successful prosecution. Accusations, depositions and impeachments began to pile up. A large force of secret informers came into being, its ramifications even extending into private households where, as always, domestic slaves provided the most lucrative source of information. They could think up treasonable remarks of every description and put them into their masters' mouths, or at least make their life a hell with blackmail. Children, too, informed on their own parents.

Tiberius silently allowed this persecution, punishment and execution from behind the façade of a penal code, often trying to give the impression that it was his dearest wish to reduce the many well-merited sentences he had to pronounce. The fact that he was probably a practiced hypocrite seems to have escaped many of our modern historians. Tacitus, whose *Annals* gave us a pregnant description of the conditions prevailing at the time, has been regarded with unwavering skepticism by historians from the nineteenth century onward and has been accused of distorting and misrepresenting the figure of Tiberius. Ever since Mommsen, research into Roman history has been pervaded by a feeling of "we know better," and it is now thought fair to dismiss the accounts of Suetonius, Dio Cassius and Tacitus as too exaggerated. Fervent attempts are made to be "fair" to emperors like Tiberius, Caligula and Claudius. Only in very recent times and after thoroughgoing research has the factual reliability of the ancient Roman and Greek historians been acknowledged and an attempt been made (as with Erich Köstermann and H. Drexler in the case of Tiberius) to put the classical sources back into their true perspective.

Tiberius grew more and more suspicious as time went by. He discovered hidden allusions to himself in the most harmless remarks and dinner-table jokes, so that whenever he entered a room conversation dried up. He had simply forgotten how to get on with people. There was only one man in all his dreary life whom he trusted completely, and unfortunately he was a criminal, though not a conventional one. He was one of those artful, cunning, self-effacing, mealy-mouthed, ever smiling, almost Shakespearian villains whom we find exaggerated on the stage and hardly ever recognize in real life.

Lucius Aelius Sejanus was born at Vulsinii. Like Iago in Shakespeare's *Othello*, he was an officer, and his resemblance to that Shakespearian figure also extended to his character. When Sejanus became prefect, or commander, of Tiberius' bodyguard his power in Rome was virtually unlimited. Nothing could happen without his permission, and it was literally fatal for anyone to approach Tiberius without his knowledge. He was continually devising new ways to secure the emperor's favor, having long ago won that of his soldiers. The cohorts of the praetorian guard had formerly been housed in various parts of the city. They were now concentrated in one vast barracks where they were more easily controlled, and yet more conscious of their numerical strength. Sejanus visited this barracks frequently, often stopping to chat with individual officers and men. He even exercised the right of promotion on the emperor's behalf. Far from causing him any trouble, Tiberius commended him before Senate and people as his partner and collaborator, and gave permission for statues of him to be erected in theaters, public squares and military establishments. He trusted Sejanus.

And Sejanus?

He had but one aim: to make himself emperor of Rome. But the only way to achieve this aim was to get rid of all the potential heirs to the throne, a task rendered formidable by the number of children in the royal family. "It was," as Tacitus puts it, "an uncertain business, taking violent action against so many people at the same time. Their removal by stealth demanded time, and could only be accomplished at certain intervals." It was this secret course of action which Sejanus chose.

He decided to start with Drusus, Tiberius' son by his beloved wife Vipsania, for whom he cherished a particular loathing since Drusus had once struck him in the face during a quarrel.

Sejanus did not launch a frontal attack on Drusus. He went to work with subterfuge and slander, studiously keeping in the background. His first move was to approach Drusus' wife, also called Livia or Livilla, who had been plain as a child but had later developed into a great beauty. Sejanus wooed her so ardently that he finally succeeded in inducing her to commit adultery. Having attained his first objective, he went on to arouse her hopes of marriage, painting a glowing picture of himself upon the imperial throne with her, revered by the entire Roman Empire, at his side. Once he had kindled her imagination to this extent, he came out openly and urged her to murder her husband. And Livilla, grandniece of Augustus, daughter-in-law of Tiberius, actually agreed to this risky undertaking.

Livilla's friend and physician Eudemus, who often visited her on the pretext of giving her medical treatment, was initiated into the secret. To reassure his female accomplice Sejanus turned his wife Apicata, who had borne him three children, out of his house. All was now agreed between the conspirators and everything had been carefully planned. But the enormity of their intended crime perturbed Sejanus, Livia and Eudemus the physician, and they postponed it.

Drusus often complained about Sejanus, both to the Senate and his father. He pointed out that while he, the emperor's own son, was there, the emperor's chief adviser and right-hand man was a stranger. Before they knew it, he said, Sejanus would be coregent. Admittedly, the first steps to the throne were steep but, once they were past, friends and helpers would always be to hand.

Sejanus was worried now. There was no time to be lost. He had received accounts of what Drusus was saying about him in private from the unfaithful Livilla, and he realized he would have to get the murder over. He ordered a slow-acting poison which would bring on the symptoms of a normal illness to be prepared.

The poison was administered to Drusus by the eunuch Lygdus, and Drusus became seriously ill.

Tiberius continued to attend the Senate daily. Perhaps he wanted to exhibit his transcendence over family worries. In all events Drusus died, and Tiberius still continued to attend the Senate. And when the senators tried to offer their condolences he reminded them of their dignity. "I may be reproached for appearing before the Senate so recently bereaved," he declared, "but my devotion to the state has lent me strength and consolation." Was his grief genuine? We do not know.

As long as Drusus was alive Sejanus had not dared to do all he had in mind because he feared Drusus and knew how sharply he criticized him in his father's presence. But when he saw that Drusus' murder had passed off unnoticed and relatively unmourned, Sejanus began to think of ways of eliminating the remaining heirs to the throne. These were the sons of Germanicus, Tiberius' nephew, whose right of succession was indisputable. Since it was impracticable to kill off three people "just like that," Sejanus began to spread slanderous stories about them and simultaneously organized an insidious whispering campaign against their mother Agrippina. His intrigues were eminently successful.

Meanwhile, Livilla had become impatient and was demanding that Sejanus marry her as he had promised. So Sejanus obediently went to the emperor and asked for her hand in wedlock, only to have Tiberius refuse his request in a letter as polite as it was devious.

Sejanus then hit upon the idea of persuading the emperor to leave Rome on the hope that Tiberius would find the privacy of new surroundings so congenial that he would leave him, Sejanus, free to conduct affairs of state. He therefore began to outline to the emperor the advantages of peace and privacy.

Tiberius succumbed to the suggestion. He went to Capri and lived on that beautiful, peaceful island for eleven years, until his death. Only twice during this period did he travel to the mainland, and even then he did not enter Rome. People frightened him enough individually, let alone in the mass.

One of Tiberius' twelve houses on Capri stood on a clifftop high above the sea. This was probably the Villa Io, which took its name from Zeus' mistress. Somewhere nearby was the place from which condemned men reportedly were hurled into the sea on the emperor's orders, while fishermen stood by below to finish off any survivors with poles and oars.

The emperor apparently had no time either for the gods and their worship or for the dictates of conscience. He was completely wrapped up in astrology. Tiberius initiated only one man into the secrets of his horoscope. It was the duty of this man, an uneducated but well-muscled freedman, to escort all visiting astrologers who had met with the emperor's disapproval out of the house and hurl them off the cliff into the sea. Thus when Tiberius asked the astrologer Thrasyllus what his own horoscope portended that day, the stargazer blanched and started to shake with fright. He was threatened, he said fearfully, by terrible and almost mortal danger. Tiberius at once embraced the alarmed man and warmly congratulated him. From that day forth he treated him royally, regarding him as the *ne plus ultra* of clairvoyants, a walking Delphi and an oracle on two legs.

What else the emperor did on the island is not quite clear, but incredible rumors circulated. Tacitus tells us that "he was able to indulge his cruelty and lust with less distraction there than at Rome." But, although he wanted to withdraw himself and his "peculiar talents" from the Roman gaze, he never neglected affairs of state and maintained constant written communication with the capital.

Eight years after Drusus' murder, Sejanus received his just deserts. The emperor conducted such a thorough investigation into his crimes that in his zeal he mistakenly even had a friend of his from Rhodes stretched on the rack. Sejanus ultimately was led to his execution with a cloth over his head and a rope about his neck. His children were also handed over to the executioner, the sight of these innocent victims driving their mother, Sejanus' divorced wife Apicata, to such despair that she committed suicide. Eudemus the physician and Lygdus the eunuch became quite talkative on the rack. . . .

Six years later Tiberius died, still in Capri. He was seventy-eight years old. Mentally deranged and afflicted with hallucinations, he tried, to the very last, to conceal his deterioration behind a mask of artificial gaiety. On March 16, 37 A.D. his breathing appeared to have stopped. "Tiberius is dead," the imperial couriers announced. His successor, Gaius Caesar Caligula, started to accept congratulations on his accession to power.

Then it was suddenly announced that Tiberius had regained consciousness, that he had recovered from his coma and was asking for food. Caligula was rigid with fury. Having just seen his dearest wish fulfilled, he would now have to go on waiting for the death of a man who simply refused to die.

He ordered heavy rugs to be thrown over Tiberius, and the old man died of suffocation.

"HERE COMES THE GOAT!"

On one occasion he summoned three ex-consuls to his palace
at midnight, and told the men, who were half dead with terror
and feared the worst, to take their places on a stage. Appearing
suddenly, amid a tremendous din of flutes and foot-tapping,
dressed in a long cloak and a tunic which reached his ankles, he
performed a dance, and then disappeared again.

—Suetonius, *Caligula*, 54.

GAIUS CAESAR, also known as Caligula, was only twenty-four years old when he became Emperor. His mother was the Agrippina who had been exiled by Tiberius and his father was the long-dead and once very popular general Germanicus who had been Tiberius' nephew and thus a member of the imperial family itself. Caligula's family had suffered greatly from the murderous treatment of Sejanus and Tiberius, and he perhaps owed his survival to the fact that he had seemed too young and insignificant to merit killing. Apart from him, three of his sisters were still alive.

After his mother's arrest, Caligula had first been cared for by his grandmother Antonia and had later, at the age of nineteen, gone to the old emperor's court at Capri. Here he was forced, whether he liked it or not, to learn the art of dissimulation. Tiberius tried to draw him out by telling him things which might make him betray resentment, but Caligula never gave cause for suspicion. He appeared to remember nothing of his family's fate and acted as though Tiberius had never harmed a hair of their heads. So obsequious was his behavior that someone later said of him, very neatly, that there had never been a better slave or a worse master.

The young man's easygoing façade probably concealed, even at this stage, a leaning toward sadism, extravagance and self-indulgence, for it is recorded that he used to watch the torturing and execution of condemned men with avid interest. Dressed in wigs and flowing robes he visited disreputable taverns and brothels, behavior of which Emperor Tiberius was not unaware. Indeed, he once said, "Gaius has survived to the detriment of myself and everyone else." Fools and knaves were all that remained of the great line of Emperor Augustus. However, there flowed in Caligula's veins not only the blood of his great-grandfather Augustus but also that of Antony, so that in this young and easily corrupted offspring of an old and venerable tree both the victor and vanquished of Actium lived on. We shall see how Antony's blood declared itself in him, with its weakness for mawkish Oriental romanticism and incest.

The vicious and untrue rumor circulated that Caligula had poisoned Tiberius, that he had removed the emperor's ring while the old man was still breathing, and that when Tiberius refused to die straightaway he had throttled him with his bare hands.

It was a slow procession which moved along the ancient Via Appia from Misenum to Rome. Tiberius' body was carried by common soldiers, and at the head of the cortege came Caligula, cheered by crowds of hurriedly assembled onlookers. From altars erected on each side of the road clouds of incense and the smoke of thank offerings rose to the sky. Then Caligula left the main body and hastened on in advance to Rome where the royal proclamation was greeted with senatorial enthusiasm and roars of approval from the crowds outside. As usual, the Romans let themselves be carried away far too easily. Without any inkling of what they were in for, they solemnly swore by all the gods to die for Gaius Caesar. He was universally called Gaius Caesar, by the way, Caligula being only a nickname which he would not tolerate, even in private. It came from his youth when his mother Agrippina had put him into military uniform and heavy top boots or *caligae*, and the Rhine legionaries had adopted the diminutive of this word, *caligula*, as their pet name for him.

Caligula decreed Tiberius a modest funeral and delivered a funeral oration in which he said little about the dead man and a great deal about his own father Germanicus and his great-grandfather Augustus. That done, he set off for the islands in the Gulf of Campania where his mother and his brothers had met a ghastly end. Bringing his relatives' remains back to Rome, he ceremoniously interred them in the Mausoleum of Augustus and then requested the Senate to bestow every conceivable honor on his three sisters, the only surviving members of his family. That still left a young cousin and coheir of his, Tiberius, to be "taken care of." Caligula, then twenty-five, adopted seventeen-year-old Tiberius Gemellus as his son, gave him the title Prince of the Youth, and about six months after his accession ordered him to carry out his own death sentence.

Caligula's next victims were Macro, the prefect of the praetorian guard, and his wife. As successor to the notorious Sejanus, Macro had helped Caligula to secure the throne, but the emperor now found him a nuisance, so he appointed him viceroy of Egypt and then, before the unfortunate couple had a chance to set sail, sent him and his wife an order to commit suicide.

However, Caligula took great pains to win over the masses. He distributed largesse and arranged spectacular entertainments, including chariot races and lion, bear and panther hunts on a huge scale, ordering eight hundred wild beasts brought to Rome. He organized poetic contests and competitions in Greek and Roman rhetoric. The poet who did worst had to lick his composition off the writing tablet and was birched or ducked in the river. But Caligula did promise to abolish prosecutions for *lèse-majesté*, to recall those who had been exiled, and to publish a regular statement of public finances. In that respect he made a promising beginning.

The fickle populace had become tired of Tiberius and his dismal reign. Caligula dangled before them the prospect of halcyon days to come. And in an attempt to emulate Augustus he imported obelisks from Egypt. He did not notice that, while the pillars once brought over by Augustus were adorned with interesting hieroglyphics, his own obelisks had been forged.

Shortly after his accession Caligula became ill. People waited for nights on end in the streets near his palace. All were deeply concerned for his recovery and some even vowed that they would sacrifice their lives if he were cured. Yet no sooner had the emperor recovered from his illness than he started to show his true colors. On January 1, 38 A.D., he had induced the Senate to swear, one by one, that they would lay down their lives not only for himself but also for his sisters. By January 1, 40 A.D., two of those sisters were already imprisoned on lonely islands.

The third, Drusilla, had died previously and the emperor was inconsolable over her loss. Although she was the wife of an ex-consul, Lucius Cassius Longinus, he had then abducted her and publicly treated her as though she were his own legal wife, even naming her his heir. When she died Caligula stormed about Italy demanding that all he met should share his grief. He decreed days, weeks, and even months of public mourning. He prohibited laughing, bathing, and taking meals in the company of parents, wife and children, on pain of death. He even arranged Drusilla's admittance to the Pantheon, the national temple of Rome where hitherto only Julius Caesar and Augustus, the twin founders of the imperial regime, had been represented as gods. Caligula now erected altars for the new deity and sponsored a nationwide "Drusilla craze." One young senator who wisely and solemnly asserted that he had seen Drusilla ascending into the sky when she was cremated was handsomely rewarded.

Caligula twice abducted the brides of Roman noblemen in the middle of their weddings, only to repudiate them later. But his real passion in life was a woman, Caesonia, who was as extravagant and dissolute as she was lacking in looks and youth. He often made her ride at his side, arrayed in military cloak, helmet and shield, for the benefit of his troops, and occasionally exhibited her naked to his friends. When Caesonia presented him with a daughter he officially declared her his consort and the mother of his child—whom he recognized as his own flesh and blood by its ungovernable behavior. Then he began to "rule."

He made the most highly respected senators trot along beside his chariot in their togas or wait behind his couch at table, dressed in linen aprons like slaves. Other senators were secretly murdered on his orders, and he had his quaestor flogged, commanding that his clothes be ripped off him and laid beneath the soldiers' feet beforehand to give them a better foothold when plying their whips. During gladiatorial games he ordered the huge awning over the arena to be drawn back. The audience sweltered, but no one was allowed to leave the theater. From time to time he had half-starved wild beasts brought into the arena to be fought not by gladiators but by decrepit old graybeards.

But Caligula did not stop there. He wanted to play at being a god. Closing the granaries, he declared a state of famine. He combed the prisons for prisoners to throw to the beasts. When he could not make up his mind which to choose he simply ordered all the prisoners "between the first bald head and the last" to be marched off. Some convicts he branded or personally condemned to fight wild animals. Others he locked up like beasts of prey in cages where they could only move on all fours. He underlined the inhumanity of his behavior with gruesome pranks. For instance, he sent his exiled sisters a message saying that he not only had islands for them "but swords, too." And when he signed death warrants he would murmur to himself, "I am settling my accounts." His favorite instruction to the executioner was: "Strike him so he feels he is dying."

"Let them hate me, as long as they fear me!"—*oderint dum metuant* —was Caligula's motto. When the popular favorite in a race was not his own, he called out, "Oh that the Roman people had but a single neck!" He moaned about the general state of prosperity in the country. Believing that people would soon forget his reign if it was not distinguished by some great disaster or defeat, he prayed for famines, plagues, fires and earthquakes. During one sumptuous feast he suddenly became convulsed with wild laughter, and when the two consuls reclining near him asked why, replied, "I am laughing at the thought that I could have both your throats slit on the spot." He never kissed his wife or mistress on the neck without gently remarking, "This lovely head will fall too, as soon as I give the order." He once played a most unpleasant practical joke on the officials responsible for organizing the customary festival of remembrance for the battle of Actium. As great-grandson of Augustus and Mark Antony, he made an announcement: If the celebrations took place it would be an insult to the vanquished Antony and the officials' heads would roll. But if the celebrations did not take place it would be an affront to Augustus' memory and the officials would still forfeit their heads.

But all this was not enough for Caligula. He was determined to be a god here on earth, not a god of marble—a golden statue of him already stood in the temple—but a living god. Accordingly he had himself decked out in the sort of robes in which Greek sculptors usually portrayed their gods. When his courtiers declared themselves thrilled at his appearance, he paraded before the people dressed as Hercules, Bacchus or Apollo, and presided over the courts in the garb of Jupiter. The Roman people set about enrolling their emperor among the gods during his lifetime and the Senate voted him a temple out of public funds.

Caligula's only failure was with the Jews who protested loudly when the Roman administration attempted to erect a statue of him in the Temple at Jerusalem. If the emperor had not died in the nick of time, war might well have broken out. There were also disturbances in Egypt when attempts were made to introduce emperor worship into the Jewish synagogues there. Led by Philo, a great Jewish philosopher, a delegation arrived in Rome to lodge a protest but was curtly dismissed by the emperor.

Caligula designed a new sort of bath, thought up absurd dishes and exotic drinks. His pleasure boats on Lake Nemi, near Rome, boasted unheard-of luxuries. When the lake was drained twenty years ago remains of them were found lying ransacked on the bottom. Caligula built moles where the sea was deepest, bored tunnels where the rock was hardest, turned plains into mountains and mountains into plains. Everything had to be done at top speed, and anyone who dawdled forfeited his head. After a year of this, Caligula had run through 2,700,000,000 sesterces, the sum total of the fortune reputedly left him by Tiberius. Desperate, he started levying ridiculous taxes and wherever possible got himself named as "heir" to the richest men in the land. Anyone who lived too long after making such a will received a gift of poisoned delicacies from his imperial beneficiary. The public exchequer was also replenished by reckless confiscation.

Anxious to gain a military reputation, Caligula crossed the Rhine but there was little to do and the emperor's commanders were hard put to it to collect any prisoners of war. Eventually Caligula's German bodyguards were sent across the Rhine and told to hide in the undergrowth until they were "captured." The emperor's next objective was "the conquest of Britain." Leading his troops to the Channel coast, he deployed them in battle order. Then, having forgotten to provide the necessary transport for the crossing, he ordered them to collect sea shells. Only a few ships were available, so Caligula took a short pleasure cruise and then ordered a general withdrawal, at the same time dispatching couriers to the Senate to describe his heroic part in this victory. The only concrete result of the expedition was a lighthouse, two hundred feet high, which Caligula built at Boulogne. It was not demolished until 1544.

Caligula arrived back in Rome on his birthday, August 31, 40 A.D. He now proposed to become a sort of supergod and settle in Egypt, making Alexandria the capital of the Roman empire. But first he wanted to give the Roman aristocracy a final taste of his mettle.

Caligula was a tall pale man with an abnormally plump body, a scrawny neck, and skinny legs. His eyes were deep-set and his brows receding, his forehead broad and threatening. He tried to enhance the natural ferociousness of his ugly features by making frightful grimaces and contorting his face in front of the mirror. Although he was bald, his body was very hirsute. "Here comes the Goat!" his subjects whispered; although whispers like that could prove fatal.

The emperor found it impossible to rest; three hours' sleep a night was all he could manage. He crawled under his bed and cowered there. He donned women's clothes and a golden beard. In his right hand he brandished a lightning fork, a trident, or a snake-entwined rod, all emblems of the gods. He also gave ballet performances in the palace at night with himself as soloist.

The half-mad emperor reigned for three years, ten months and eight days. His crazy regime would have lasted even longer if one of his army officers had not decided to assassinate him.

Caligula's orgy of inquisition, murder and oppressive taxation had been an anathema to the officer corps. The man who put a stop to it was Cassius Chaerea, tribune of one of the praetorian cohorts. He was an elderly soldier with an outstanding military career behind him and had never shrunk from danger in his life. Indeed the emperor had always singled him out for the most unpleasant assignments and was fond of baiting him in front of his brother officers—unwisely, as it turned out.

Chaerea organized a small conspiracy. On January 24, 41 A.D., he lay in wait for the emperor in the underground gallery of the theater. Caligula was just leaving when Chaerea dealt him a heavy blow in the neck with his sword. Another sword pierced the emperor's chest. "So let your destiny be fulfilled!" Chaerea is said to have cried while Caligula writhed on the ground in agony. "I am still alive!" he screamed. There were thirty wounds in his body by the time they had finished with him. His wife Caesonia was also killed by a centurion and his little daughter's brains were dashed out against a wall.

The news of Caligula's assassination was received with disbelief. "The Goat has thought up the rumor himself," people whispered. "He's spreading it to test our reactions!"

Yet another madman was living on after his death. . . .

Such are some of the traditions passed on to us for what they are worth about Gaius Caesar Augustus Germanicus.

THE "POOR BOOBY"

*Sickly from childhood onwards and living in a state of perpetual
fear which made him pretend to be more stupid than he really
was, reared for a long time beneath the eye of his grandmother
Livia, then of his mother Antonia, and of women generally, he
lacked that masculine disposition which distinguishes the free
man. The master of Rome and the provinces was himself a slave.*
—Dio Cassius, lx, 2.

AT THE CONFLUENCE of the Rhône and the Saône stands Lyon, the
French city famous for its silk. Once called Lugdunum, it was perhaps
the chief city of Gaul, where once Caesar fought. It was also used by
the great Roman general Drusus, Tiberius' younger brother, as an
operational base during his campaign against the Germans in which
he lost his life after falling from his horse.

It was in Lugdunum, on August 1, 10 B.C., that a son was born to
Drusus and his wife Antonia. The child was given the names Tiberius
Claudius Drusus. Half a century later, in the year 41 A.D., he was
destined, as a man of fifty, to become emperor of Rome.

The uncle of Emperor Caligula and the nephew of Emperor
Tiberius, as a youth he had to contend with persistent ill-health. He was
considered, probably with justification, to be a physical weakling.
He was also considered by some certainly with no justification, to be
stupid—in fact almost insane. His own mother, Antonia, called him
"a monster" and declared that Nature had "only begun, not completed"
him. His grandmother Livia Augusta also treated him with contempt
and seldom spoke to him. When Claudius' sister Livilla heard that her
brother would someday inherit the throne, she bemoaned the unhappy
fate of the Roman people.

Augustus was also worried about his young relative. In a letter
recommending that an adviser be appointed to guide him, he wrote:
"We shall always be sweating, if we deliberate about each separate
case and do not make up our minds in advance whether we think he
can hold public offices or not." He also took care that young Claudius
never sat in the imperial box at the circus, so that he was not seen by
the public. In his will he treated him like a stranger by putting him
among beneficiaries of the third class.

CLAUDIUS

When young Claudius went to Tiberius and asked to be given consular duties his uncle sent him forty gold pieces and told him to have a good time at the Saturnalia. That was all he thought him capable of.

Later Claudius' house burned down and the Senate proposed to build him a new one at public expense, but Tiberius annulled the decision, saying he would make good the damage out of his own pocket since Claudius was weak. There is also a story, which many modern historians however discount, that when Claudius was deputed to congratulate Caligula, his nephew, on the unmasking of a conspiracy, Caligula flew into such a rage because they had picked on his uncle, of all people, for the job that he had Claudius thrown into the river.

If Claudius was late for a meal the other diners let him wander around the royal table until he found a seat. When he fell asleep during meals, as he often did, they would amuse themselves by throwing olive stones and date kernels at his head. And if he snored at table they would put slippers on his hands, so that when he woke and rubbed his eyes he got a shock, to the huge enjoyment of everyone present.

Not having anything worth-while to do, Claudius spent his time quietly by himself in his villa in Campania. But he also drank, gambled and, according to the historian Suetonius, associated with some very unsavory characters.

Was Claudius really nothing more than an oaf? Well, he was tutored by the great historian Livy and associated with Greek scientists and scholars. He took an interest in philology and phonetics. He made an exhaustive study of history and was himself the author of some apparently extremely interesting historical works, none of which, unfortunately, has survived. On his accession he introduced three new letters into the Roman alphabet, creating a distinction between u and v which had not until then been customary. (The new letters never really caught on.) It is not difficult to understand why an oddity like Claudius, whom no one had entrusted with any duties or offices, who had been subjected to continuous repression and contempt, and who had been left at times in the tender charge of a tough and brutal riding master, was hardly destined to be the ideal emperor for Rome.

Claudius was already fifty years old when the strange workings of fate set him upon the throne. Before assassinating Caligula the conspirators had decided to remove anyone who might disturb the proceedings, and Claudius was left in a summerhouse. But when he heard that the emperor had been murdered he ran to a nearby balcony and hid himself behind some curtains until a passing soldier, noticing a pair of feet peeping from under the curtains, pulled Claudius out, threw himself at his feet, and hailed him as Imperator. Then he took him along to his unit, where the troops deposited him in a litter and bore him into their camp. Claudius was terrified and quite ignorant of what was happening, and passers-by who recognized him in his litter thought he was being taken off for execution. Mobs thronged the streets of Rome and loudly demanded a new emperor while the Senate met to discuss whether it would not be better to abolish the Principate altogether. But it was too late. The troops were clamoring to swear allegiance to Claudius, who at last acquiesced, promising each soldier 15,000 sesterces, or about $420 apiece. By doing so he set a precedent, and in future no Roman emperor could take up office without giving the guard a gratuity in cash. In fact in later years the size of that gratuity on more than one occasion determined the length of an emperor's reign.

Claudius celebrated his accesion by declaring a general amnesty. He had his grandmother Livia Augusta enrolled among the gods and insisted on according his family the honors due to them: "By Augustus!" was his favorite oath.

The people soon found to their surprise that Claudius had a peculiar hobby. He loved to play the judge. He conducted interrogations, passed sentences and presided over court sessions even during the height of the Roman summer. He was extraordinarily inconsistent, however. Sometimes he acted with prudence and deliberation. Once when a woman refused to recognize a young man as her son, the emperor extracted an admission from her by ordering her to marry him. Yet occasionally he became childish and behaved like a buffoon. Let one of two parties fail to appear in court and he always decided in favor of the party present.

Perhaps the most remarkable feature of the emperor's judicial career was the amount of insolence he tolerated in court. Certainly many lawyers took gross advantage of the emperor's extraordinarily patient attitude. When he got down from the seat of judgment they would loudly call him back, holding him fast by the toga or even by the leg. One Greek lawyer even shouted at him, "You are both an old man and a fool!" And a Roman who had been charged with criminal offenses against women, but on the evidence of prostitutes bribed by his enemies, called Claudius "simple-minded" and "inhuman" and hurled a stylus and some wax tablets in his face, cutting him quite badly.

The emperor's public prosecutors were lazy and negligent, and red tape flourished. People whom Claudius charged with celibacy and childlessness demonstrated that they were respectable married men with large families. A man who was accused of trying to commit suicide with a dagger calmly undressed and exhibited his unmarked body. The emperor imposed penalties out of the blue because this man or that had left Italy "without the emperor's knowledge," or "without leave." This was something quite new to the Romans, who had hitherto usually been able to travel anywhere they pleased.

But Claudius was not merely a stupid and inconsistent judge with sudden flashes of inspiration. He made genuine efforts to deal with public affairs and did achieve some positive results. In particular, he considerably improved the administration of justice in the provinces. He granted Roman citizenship to a large number of Gauls. (Part of his address to the Senate on that occasion has been found inscribed on a bronze plaque at Lyon, the city of his birth.) Indeed, one prominent scholar, Theodor Birt, thinks that Claudius' lasting achievements in the spheres of policy and administration set him on a far higher plane than Tiberius or Caligula. Some historians think Claudius owed much of these achievements to his freedman Narcissus, whom he appointed chief of the imperial secretariat. Narcissus was a man of sound judgment who carried out his administrative duties without worrying too much about the vagaries of his royal master. Whatever the reason, the fact remains that while the regime at the imperial court and in the city of Rome was indeed a despotism because of Claudius' dependence on his wives and the imperial freedmen, the general administration of the empire was never better or more imaginative than during his reign.

Claudius always applied himself conscientiously to the problem of Rome's food supplies. He guaranteed supplies of grain during the winter months, granted large concessions to the shipbuilding industry and dredged the harbor at Ostia, which had silted up, an unusual technical achievement which Julius Caesar had attempted without success. Diverting spring water from the mountains nearly forty miles away, he brought it across the Campagna and into Rome to the Palatine, which until then had only been provided with storage tanks. The

Aqua Claudia survives today as one of the most impressive feats of Roman engineering. Claudius also diverted the waters of the Fucine Lake into a canal which 30,000 people took eleven years to build. Before the last soil was removed and the lake allowed to drain away, he held a mock sea battle. Those who had been forced to take part in it raised the customary cry: *"Ave, Imperator, morituri te salutant!"* or "Hail, Emperor, they salute you, those who are about to die!"—"Or aren't, as the case may be," answered the emperor. At once the men took this flippant remark for a pardon and flatly refused to fight, whereupon Claudius jumped up and hobbled all around the lake, ranting and raving at them to proceed, which they eventually did. The battle was fought between a Sicilian squadron and a squadron from Rhodes, each consisting of twelve three-deckers. The signal for the attack was blown on a conch by a silver Triton which rose from the lake by mechanical means.

Claudius presented spectacular entertainments and barbaric animal-baiting displays. There was always "something on" in the Circus Maximus for the spoilt and sensation-loving people of Rome. It might be chariot racing or hunting wild animals from Africa or the famous Thessalian horsemen who drove wild bulls around the arena until they were completely worn out, then leapt onto their necks and brought them down by the horns. The emperor always played the jovial host, personally rewarding the victors with gold pieces and encouraging the spectators to enjoy themselves.

Claudius was remarkably energetic in his provincial and foreign policy although he conducted only one war. Setting sail from Ostia he landed at Marseille, marched to the Channel coast and, without bloodshed, subdued part of Britain within the space of a few days. Six months later he returned to Rome and staged a splendid triumphal march. But the campaign had been carefully prepared by Narcissus whom Claudius had sent ahead to persuade the legions to leave their comfortable quarters on the Rhine frontier and take part in the expedition, for which they showed not the least enthusiasm. Nonetheless the conquest of Britain was a major achievement, and the wonder is that it was not accomplished sooner.

The emperor's reign otherwise was a succession of good things and bad, although the good outweighed the bad. He forbade certain persons to go farther from Rome than the third milestone. He conferred honors on elderly people and dished out sets of triumphal regalia.

In the same edict he could publish important government decrees and recommend the population to take a certain cough cure. Many owners of old and ailing slaves used to put them off on the Island of Aesculapius, a small island in the Tiber inside the city limits of Rome. Claudius decreed that in the event of their recovery such slaves should receive their freedom, and that if a master killed a sick slave instead of abandoning him, the master was guilty of murder.

Claudius banished the Jews from Rome "because, egged on by one Chrestus, they constantly stir up unrest." The expulsion of the Jews from Rome occurred in the year 49 A.D., the crucifixion of Christ having taken place during Tiberius' reign.

Claudius pronounced and carried out sentences of death with a complete lack of compunction. But, being absent-minded, the emperor sometimes forgot that he had ordered such executions shortly after they had taken place. He would invite the dead men to his house and then wonder why they did not turn up.

Claudius was a prodigious eater. It is recorded that slaves had to tickle his throat with a feather as he lay on his back after a meal, snoring, to help him void his stomach. Since he slept little at night, he used to get most of his sleep at court in the daytime. And however loudly the barristers bellowed their speeches, however much they shouted, nothing roused the royal Lord Chief Justice from his oblivion.

Behind all too many of the emperor's activities, two sinister influences were at work: emancipated slaves and women. And dominant among the women was the notorious Messalina.

"WHY DOESN'T THE EMPRESS COME TO TABLE?"

*She was bored by her love affairs because
she never encountered any opposition.*
Tacitus, *Annals*, xi, 26.

THE EMPEROR CLAUDIUS was a tall man who looked his best when reclining on a couch, but there is also said to have been a certain dignity about his appearance when standing or seated. In motion, however, his gait was unsteady. At times he foamed at the mouth when angry and he stuttered; furthermore, his head had an habitual tremor which grew perceptibly worse in moments of agitation. Other than this he appeared in good health—except for a stomach ailment which often gave him pain!

Perhaps he had some sadistic impulses. Certainly he was always reluctant to forgo any opportunity of conducting a grueling interrogation in person, and he insisted on attending all executions. On one occasion he was so taken with the idea of witnessing an "old-fashioned" execution that, when the executioner did not turn up, he left the criminal tied to his stake all day and waited there until a substitute executioner could be fetched from the capital. At mass executions he used to lull his conscience by turning the statue of Augustus around so that his milder forebear could not see the bloodshed.

He took a special delight in fights between wild beasts and also in *meridiani*, or "midday" gladiators, who had to fight to the death in the midday heat without any defensive armor. For Augustus' humane rule that gladiators should no longer fight to the death had long ago been abolished. Whenever a combat was scheduled Claudius hurried to the arena early in the morning and remain glued to his seat even in the long intermissions during which the spectators went off to eat. When he could not find enough professional fighters he condemned stage carpenters, mechanics and other members of the circus staff to mortal combat in the arena. The slightest pretext was sufficient: all that was needed was for some scenery or scaffolding to collapse or some machinery not to function properly.

As is often the case with such men, Claudius' marked streak of cruelty was allied with extreme timidity and perpetual distrust. He refused to visit an invalid unless sickroom, bed and bedclothes had been carefully searched in advance. He never felt happy at table unless he was surrounded by armed bodyguards. Everyone who visited the emperor had to submit to a thorough search. Only after lengthy remonstrances about the indignity of such a measure did he waive it in the case of women, boys, and young girls. He often complained bitterly that there was nowhere where he could feel safe.

Claudius was twice engaged. He broke off his first engagement to Aemilia Lepida before their wedding, and Livia Medullina, his second fiancée, died of a severe illness on the wedding day itself. He then married twice, only to obtain a divorce shortly afterward on each occasion, in the first instance because of petty irritations and in the second because his wife was promiscuous and he suspected her of murder.

Then he married again, this time Valeria Messalina, the daughter of his cousin Messala Barbatus, a woman whose name has an infamous ring even today.

When Claudius became emperor Messalina, as she was known, was just fifteen. She was therefore thirty-three years younger than her imperial husband. She was slim and probably golden-haired, although Juvenal casts doubt on this by alleging that she wore a wig. One thing is certain: she had a passionate and volatile temperament.

Messalina presented Claudius with an heir—probably the only positive contribution she ever made to history. Its true significance can only be measured when we reflect that neither Caligula, Tiberius or Augustus had any direct heir. Claudius was delighted and named the boy Britannicus in memory of the conquest of Britain.

As the woman who had brought this child into the world, Messalina could do no wrong, and she certainly made the most of her opportunities. She had affairs with every conceivable—and inconceivable—sort of man: with gladiators, with dancers, with the handsomest and sometimes, if she had a fancy, with the ugliest men in Rome. In all these activities she took the fullest advantage of her position and revenged herself pitilessly on any man foolhardy enough to rebuff her. One murder more or less meant nothing to her. She made enough pin money for her amusements by doing a brisk traffic in patents of citizenship, official appointments and other concessions.

In the end, bored by the increasing ease of her conquests as the list of her amours lengthened, Messalina abandoned herself to a career of debauchery such as even Rome had never known before.

All this left Claudius quite cold, so Messalina set to work on a certain Gaius Silius, reputedly the handsomest man in Rome. She broke up his marriage and made him her lover. And while Silius realized what a dangerous game he was playing, he also knew that it would be equally dangerous to throw in his hand. Messalina showered him with gifts and he, privately hoping that everything would turn out for the best, decided to enjoy the situation while it lasted. But clandestine love affairs had lost all savor for Messalina and the only way she could titillate her jaded palate was to shock the whole of Rome. Thus she never left Silius' side, showed herself in public with him, and visited his home accompanied by a large retinue. Tacitus tells us: "There came a stage when the emperor's slaves, freedmen and whole court were located at her lover's house, as though the throne had already passed to him." If Claudius knew of his wife's adulterous goings-on with Silius, he at least acted as if he were blind to them, with the result that Messalina and Silius grew even bolder and more presumptuous. Finally it occurred to Silius that actual danger might prove a remedy for potential danger. Not wishing to wait for the aging emperor to die, he decided to marry Messalina and adopt Britannicus.

Messalina, now bigamously married, waited for Claudius to divorce her. But the emperor did not act. Perhaps the enormity of the situation made people afraid to tell him. Perhaps Tacitus' assertion that Claudius knew nothing of what had occurred is really true.

Narcissus, the emperor's private secretary, was no mere intriguer; he was a most competent civil servant, and Messalina's meddling in public affairs had always irritated him. So, while Claudius was staying at Ostia, he persuaded two of the emperor's mistresses to inform him of the affair. One of them, Calpurnia, fell at the emperor's feet, crying, "Messalina has married Silius!" and the other woman confirmed the news. At Calpurnia's suggestion, Claudius consulted Narcissus. "Don't you know that you are a divorcé?" Narcissus asked him. "The people, the Senate and the army all witnessed Messalina's wedding to Silius. If you do not act quickly, Silius will be master of all Rome."

It was autumn, and Messalina was throwing a mammoth party to celebrate the vintage festival. Women danced in animal skins like frenzied bacchanals, while Messalina, more brazen than ever, disported herself with a Silius crowned with ivy. At the height of the orgy a man named Valens, another of Messalina's lovers, climbed a tree. "There's a storm blowing up from Ostia!" he shouted down. He was right. Claudius was approaching from Ostia, and with him was a detachment of praetorians under the command of Narcissus. He was not coming in the role of a vengeful husband, however, but trembling for his own safety and repeatedly asking his friends if he was still emperor. Messalina quickly made up her mind to go and meet her husband. Everyone had suddenly deserted her, including Silius, who excused himself by saying that he had business to attend to in the Forum. So she set out along the highroad to Ostia in a humble dung cart. No one sympathized with her. All that people could remember were her vices.

The emperor sat in his carriage, brooding apathetically, his head trembling as usual. And when Messalina drew near he simply looked the other way.

Messalina then fled with her mother to the gardens of Lucullus, for the first time in her life at a loss. She thought of pleading for mercy but her mother advised her to forestall the executioner by taking her own life. The last vestiges of honor had died within her, however, and before she had time for further deliberation the assassins had arrived with orders from Narcissus to settle matters quickly. Taking a sword, Messalina pressed it fearfully against her breast, then her throat. But her nerve failed her and one of the executioner's assistants stabbed her to death.

Claudius received the news just as he was sitting down to dinner. They did not tell him whether Messalina had died by her own hand or another's, and he did not ask. He merely called for a goblet and indulged in his usual bout of drinking. Then suddenly he seemed to remember something. "Why doesn't the Empress come to table?" he demanded.

The fifty-eight-year-old emperor later announced to his troops: "Since I have been unlucky in my marriages, I shall remain a bachelor from now on. If I fail to remain one, you may kill me."

Hardly had he made this declaration when he began courting again. He developed a fresh interest in Paetina, whom he had once divorced. Then he wooed Lollia Paulina, formerly the wife of Emperor Caligula. But it was Julia Agrippina who finally won the day.

Agrippina, the daughter of Germanicus, Claudius' brother, was thirty-three years old, ambitious, ruthless and calculating. Now she took advantage of her close relationship to kindle her elderly uncle's passions with blandishments and caresses. Normally a union with Agrippina would have counted as incest, so Claudius saw to it that the Senate "compelled" him to marry her "for the good of the state." What was more, he had marriage between niece and uncle made legally permissible by general decree.

"Rome was as if transformed. From now on everything went according to Agrippina's wishes. She did not merely toy with the state like the frivolous Messalina. Hers was a rigid and utterly masculine regime." Thus Tacitus describes the atmosphere in the capital in his famous *Annals*. As the *éminence grise* behind the throne, Agrippina was the real ruler of Rome. Tacitus informs us that she was born in "the capital of Ubii" and that she arranged for a veteran's colony to be founded there. It was after her, not Claudius, that the place was named in 50 A.D., becoming Colonia Agrippinensis, now Cologne, Germany.

Claudius, thoughtless or absent-minded as ever, added to the scandal his latest marriage had already caused by publicly referring to Agrippina as his "little daughter" or his "foster child," and by remarking in his speeches that he had carried her in his arms from birth. For all its vices, Rome found it hard to swallow this form of legitimized incest.

Agrippina's aim was to secure the right of succession for her son by her first marriage, Domitius Ahenobarbus, by fair means or foul. She succeeded in arranging the betrothal of the twelve-year-old boy to Octavia, Claudius' daughter. Thus, by becoming stepson and son-in-law of the emperor, the youngster was now on an equal footing with the heir apparent, Claudius' own son Britannicus. At the same time, Britannicus was edged farther and farther out of the limelight as Nero was schooled for a great career and given the famous philosopher Seneca as his tutor. Eventually Claudius adopted Ahenobarbus and gave him the title of prince and a new name, Nero Claudius Caesar. Agrippina was now within reach of her objective. But she had to act quickly, knowing that many people at court saw through her plans, and that her numerous crimes might one day effect a change of heart in Claudius. Accordingly, she served him a dish of his favorite mushrooms—toadstools, of course. From the notorious poisoner Locusta, whose deadly wares found a ready market in the unscrupulous Roman society of her day, she had obtained a remarkable poison which induced first mental derangement and then death.

It is said that Claudius lost the power of speech after enjoying his mushrooms. He tossed and turned all night in frightful pain, and by next morning he was dead. According to another story he brought up the poisoned food but was immediately given another dose, either in gruel or an enema.

Agrippina put all the entrances to the palace under guard. To prevent the innocent Britannicus from finding out that his father had been murdered, she clasped the youngster tightly to her as though she were beside herself with grief and needed comfort. Or could it, even worse, have been an effort to lure and win him over sexually? Tacitus has accused her of this and worse with her own son; why not with a mere stepson as well?

On October 13, 54 A.D., the gates of the imperial palace were flung open and out stepped seventeen-year-old Nero, to be greeted by rousing cheers from the soldiery. In the side streets old women whispered that Claudius had been distinctly heard to mutter over and over again, during his last session in court, that he had reached the end of his earthly life. What was more, a comet had appeared and his father's tomb had been struck by lightning; and everyone knew that they were omens of death.

HE REALLY WAS A POET

*Writing tablets and books have come into my possession bearing
very familiar verses written in his own hand. One can see at first
glance that they are neither borrowed from another nor written
at another's dictation, but worked out exactly as when one is
thinking and creating: so many things were erased and struck
through and written above the lines.*

—Suetonius, *Nero*, 52.

AGRIPPINA was now thirty-nine years old. Her life had so far been
dedicated to a single end: the securing of imperial status for her son
Nero. Having murdered Claudius, she would gladly be the true ruler
of Rome. *"Optima mater"*—"best of mothers"—was how Nero, on the
evening of October 13, 54 A.D., addressed the woman who had murdered her husband the day before.

"Our emperor is no orator," the citizens told each other. "He is
the first master of Rome to have his speeches composed by others."
There were smirks all round, and some people laughed out loud.

But seventeen-year-old Nero was not discouraged. This was
Claudius' funeral and he, Claudius' adoptive son and the new emperor,
was delivering the funeral address. Nero's father, also named Ahenobarbus, had been a red-bearded man, as the name implied, and the first
traces of red down were just beginning to appear on Nero's own
cheeks.

In his oration Nero spoke of the long history of the imperial family,
enumerating its ancestors, the consulships and triumphs they had won.
He pointed out that during the reign of his adoptive father Rome had
sustained no losses anywhere in the empire.

Greatly moved, the senators at once offered Nero the title Father
of the Fatherland. The new emperor made a very favorable impression
by thanking them courteously and declining the honor, saying that
he was too young for it.

He went on to speak of his predecessor's prudence and sagacity. But
that was too much. Nobody could keep a straight face. Tittle-tattle,
gossip and scandalous stories went the rounds of Roman society faster
than they do in London, Paris or Washington today. Domestic slaves

passed on whatever they picked up. The whole of Rome had enjoyed a generous sample of Claudius' "sagacity" and "prudence." And to hear these words from the mouth of Nero, the son of Agrippina, whose poisoning of Claudius was even then being discussed in whispers behind closed doors. . . .

The speech had, of course, been composed by the philosopher Seneca, Nero's friend and adviser. All Rome knew that Nero was not capable of composing an oration—or delivering one, either, the people now noticed. They were to learn later that he preferred to sing.

The Romans had heard the finest orators that ever mounted a platform. Augustus had spoken magnificently, like a real emperor. Tiberius, although he deliberately indulged in ambiguities and *double-entendres*, was a reliable speaker who weighed his words with care. And Claudius' elegant style of public speaking had always been impressive.

But Nero! He was a strange youth to be entrusted with the destiny of an empire. He sculpted, painted, took singing lessons, had a secret penchant for racing, and even wrote poetry. With such a modest and gentle man as emperor—even if he couldn't make speeches—the Romans saw golden times ahead. But then the Romans always saw golden times ahead when, after all the trouble he had caused, an emperor was buried on the Field of Mars and a new emperor treated them to the customary farce of a funeral oration.

Nero was too good to be true. He declared that he was nobody's enemy, that he harbored no ill will against anyone, and that he was mounting the throne free from any desire for revenge. He intended, he said, to do away with favoritism, lobbying for appointments, and corruption. He was going to wage no wars, to clean up the courts, and give the Senate every freedom. And like his predecessor, he naturally invoked the name of Augustus, still the brightest star in Rome's already murky imperial past.

But before he could devote himself to carrying out his fine resolutions he had some family business to attend to. Britannicus, Emperor Claudius' own son who might avenge his father's murder, was still alive.

At the festival of Saturnalia Nero, surrounded by a circle of friends, ordered Britannicus to stand up and sing, convinced that the boy would make a fool of himself. But Britannicus was quite unembarrassed and sang of how he had been deprived of his inheritance and his father's throne.

That was probably the moment when Nero decided to do away

with his stepbrother. He went to Julius Pollio, tribune of one of the praetorian cohorts, who was holding the celebrated Locusta in prison. He brought pressure to bear on the tribune and threatened Locusta with execution if she did not speedily prepare him an efficient poison: something which would, as he put it, bring him some peace of mind! Locusta brewed him a particularly deadly concoction which she guaranteed would act like a sword thrust.

Roman historians have handed the scene down to us in all its details. Nero shared his dining room with the royal children, among them Britannicus. The children took their meals seated while the older people reclined on couches.

Since a servant tasted all the food and drink intended for Britannicus, a subterfuge was employed. Britannicus was handed a very hot drink which the servant had already tasted. When, as was intended, he refused the drink because it was too hot, some cold water was hastily poured into it. This water contained the poison which permeated his body so quickly that his voice and breathing failed at once.

The children who were sitting near Britannicus fled while the adults in the secret stared at Nero lolling comfortably on his couch, looking as if nothing out of the way had occurred. Quite calmly he said that it was probably just another of the epileptic seizures which had afflicted Britannicus since his early childhood.

As for Agrippina, she was numb with shock and bewilderment. Perhaps she guessed that her son would one day murder her with the same cool deliberation. And Octavia, who had been compelled to marry Nero, only three years older than herself, when she was only twelve, had long since learned to suppress grief, love or any other emotion. And so, after a short pause, the meal resumed its merry course. Britannicus, the last male descendant of the Claudian line, had mutely met his death under the very eyes of his sister, stepbrother and stepmother, four months after his father's murder and Nero's accession.

Nero rewarded Locusta for her help by forgiving her all her previous crimes, giving her some property, and sending her some pupils to be instructed in the deadly art of poison brewing.

The emperor celebrated the success of his murderous act by giving handsome presents to his closest friends. Then he took care of the people, distributing a vast sum of money, four hundred sesterces apiece, to the population of Rome and presenting noblemen and senators who owned no property with a year's income. Rome did not fare badly during the first year of Nero's reign. Through the influence of Seneca and Burrus, the efficient prefect of the guard, many improvements were made in the judicature and the administration. Agrippina, too, supervised her son as best she could and gave him appropriate advice. And when the Senate wanted to offer him their thanks he modestly replied: "If I have deserved them."

Nero began to recite poetry, at first only at home but later in the theater as well where his audiences went wild with delight. When a death warrant was put in front of him for signature he cried: "I wish I could not write." Emperor Trajan later described the first five years of Nero's reign as the happiest period in the imperial age of Rome. If he was right, it was due to Seneca's influence.

Humane, affable, courteous, talented: that was the new emperor. He showed great interest in the theater and organized a large variety of entertainments, including youth sports (the *Iuvenales*), circus games, theater performances and gladiatorial contests. There were races between chariots drawn by four camels, and a leading Roman knight is said to have ridden an elephant down a tightrope into the arena. A comedy called *The Fire*, during the course of which an actual building was burned down, met with a great success. Among the presents distributed to the people were birds of every variety, delicacies, coupons for grain, gold, silver, precious stones, pearls, articles of clothing, slaves, and breeding cattle. But Nero's exuberant desire to be "kind" did not stop there. He even gave away ships, real estate, and whole blocks of houses.

Nero forbade the contestants in gladiatorial battles to fight to the death. But then he suddenly ordered four hundred senators and six hundred (another historian says forty and sixty) knights into the arena to fight with swords. "Just an odd whim," people said in the emperor's defense.

Naval engagements were staged on artificial salt-water lakes in which sea monsters swam about, and there were pyrrhic dances with very risqué passages. To the great excitement of all present, an unknown Icarus made his first attempt at flight, only to plunge to the ground close to Nero's box and spatter the emperor with blood.

Nero awarded prizes for Latin rhetoric, poetic composition and lute-playing. He took the prizes for poetic composition and rhetoric himself but modestly declined the victor's wreath for lute-playing.

During court sessions he would have the case for each side put to him verbally and then announced his verdict the next day, in writing. He introduced Rome to a new style of architecture after the great fire. Porches had to be built in front of every house so that their flat tops could serve as fire-fighting platforms, fires being a constant source of annoyance and danger in the capital. Nero built these arcades at his own expense.

He also tried to limit the growing extravagance of wealthy Roman society. Public feasts were to consist of a fixed number of courses while inns were only allowed to sell cold snacks, not cooked meals.

It is while describing the young emperor and the early portion of his reign that the Roman historian Suetonius makes an abrupt but interesting remark. Among Nero's "praiseworthy" measures he includes the death penalty which the emperor imposed upon the Christians, who Suetonius calls "the Christiani, a sect which had given itself up to a new superstition harmful to the public interest." This is the first explicit reference to the Christians made by the non-Christian Suetonius.

Some of Nero's laws not only demonstrate a genuine desire to remedy abuses but also show how thoroughly he went into matters. He issued a number of very sensible decrees against forgery and the falsification of wills.

Nero had no taste for conquest, a fact which was only partly due to Seneca's wise influence. For Nero was no mere buffoon or charlatan but possessed genuinely outstanding artistic ability. At all events, the first five years of his reign were not marred by any of the acts of inconceivable folly which characterized its last nine years.

Despite his ridiculous love of ostentation, despite his quite grotesque vanity, and despite his pathological yearning for recognition as an artist and a genius, the emperor was almost always meticulous in observing the rules of a competition. Should he ever modify the rules in his favor, he at least tried to delude himself that he had not.

One more thing: later historians have denied Nero, whose morbid propensities make him seem an outcast of Hell itself, even a nominal claim to poetic ability. In reality, Nero appears to have been a fluent poet. Writing between thirty and fifty years after Nero's death, Suetonius mentioned that he had seen tablets and papyrus scrolls bearing familiar verses written in Nero's own hand. He had immediately recognized, by the corrections and deletions, that these verses could not have been copied or dictated but must have been written by a man with a mind of his own who was carefully thinking things out for himself. Nero is also said to have tried his hand at painting and sculpture with considerable success.

Here may lie one of the root causes of his pathological striving for approbation. Had he been utterly without talent his lust for recognition might not have reached such insane proportions. But since he was obviously activated by strong artistic impulses (a fact which historians frequently disguise from us), since he gradually lost the ability to distinguish between flattery and genuine appreciation, since as time went by, his impulses were no longer curbed by his intelligence, and since he was eventually deserted by all the prerequisites of artistic creation: a sense of proportion, self-discipline, modesty, reverence, self-criticism, and faith—all that was left of Nero was a caricature of an artist and a dictator, tottering in the throes of near insanity.

STAGE FRIGHT

IMMEDIATELY after his accession, Nero engaged as his court musician a man called Terpnus, one of those singers who accompanied themselves on the cithara, a lyrelike instrument which the performer held in his hand and played in a standing position. Our words "zither" and "guitar" are derived from the Latin *cithara*, which was, in turn, borrowed through the Greek from the Persian *sithtar*, an instrument with three strings.

Terpnus was the outstanding cithara virtuoso of his time, and every night Nero listened until dawn while Terpnus played and sang. The capricious emperor and the lyre-player with the splendid voice, late at night in the hushed palace: it was a scene reminiscent of Saul, making the young David sing for him.

Before long Nero began to study singing and lyre-playing himself. He conscientiously followed all his teacher's instructions, even lying on his back for hours with slabs of lead on his chest to strengthen his voice. He rid himself of any "waste matter" which might obstruct his singing by taking laxatives and emetics. Singers were at that time advised to avoid eating fruit, and Nero extended this ban to include any food which might prove detrimental to his voice. To spare his throat he instituted monthly fast days during which he would not even touch bread.

We have already learned that Nero was no orator. His voice did not carry and lacked resonance. But, like so many people who suffer from some physical disability, he made his weakest point the focus of his greatest aspirations. Nero wanted to sing, and sing in public. So he practiced diligently, lured on by the attractions of the stage. "Unheard melodies are never sweet," he said.

With its blasé fondness for ridicule and criticism, Rome was hardly the right venue for his first appearance. Nero's first public performance took place at Naples. All the town's important citizens were invited to the theater, the news of the emperor's appearance also attracting the curious inhabitants of neighboring towns.

An earthquake shook the theater, but Nero went right on singing. Everyone had left the building, however, before it collapsed. Seeing this as a mark of divine providence, Nero continued his series of recitals. He also went and dined with the actors, promising them that when he had downed a few drinks to oil his vocal chords he would give them something to make the rafters ring. And when some visitors from Alexandria were loud in their applause, he sent for more shiploads of them.

Unfortunately as time went by, no kind of applause was loud enough for the emperor. He had young Roman aristocrats trained in the art of applauding and selected five thousand hefty young commoners, whom he divided into groups. Each group was then coached in a certain type of applause. There was *imbrix*, or clapping with the hands cupped, which got its name from the hollow roof tile; *testa*, or clapping with the hands flat, named after the flat building brick; and *bombus*, a beelike hum of applause. Nero's *claqueurs* were distinguished by their fine clothes and elegant hair styles. They were obliged to remove their knight's rings lest they hinder their applause. Their leaders received a salary of 400,000 sesterces, or about $11,000.

At last Nero decided to sing publicly in Rome and arranged a concert there. (The word concert originally meant "competition.") It was a grand contest on the Greek pattern, with events which included music, singing, poetic composition, rhetoric, field sports, chariot racing and riding. Nero christened these games the Neronia and built special baths and a gymnasium for the competitors. The Neronia were to take place every five years.

Nero sat impatiently in the orchestra, the rows of seats reserved for senators, while the vast circle of spectators clamored to hear his heavenly voice. Drawing his lot from the urn like all the other lyre-players, he joined the queue and when his turn came mounted the rostrum. Officers of his bodyguard carried his lyre for him. Having made the usual introductory speech, he bade the ex-consul Rufus announce that he would sing *Niobe*. He sang for a very long time, roughly from midday until four o'clock in the afternoon. Then, to give himself ample opportunity for more singing in the future, he postponed the award of the victor's wreath and the rest of the events until the following year.

Nero now began to take part in tragedies, complete with costume and mask, first seeing to it that the masks of gods, heroes and heroines resembled his own features or those of his current mistresses. Then he turned to equestrian sports. At first he was content to play with model horses on a table, but he soon began to visit the Rome races in secret. In the end he announced quite openly that he was very keen to take part in races and augment the number of his prizes. He began by practicing in his garden in front of slaves, and eventually appeared in the Circus Maximus as a charioteer.

The whole world was now familiar with Nero's fondness for prizes. All the Greek cities which held musical contests sent him victor's laurels for lyre-playing. "Only the Greeks have a fine ear for music. They alone are worthy of my art," declared Nero, and set off for Greece.

He visited all the festivals, and if they had already taken place, they were held all over again. Nobody was allowed to leave a theater once Nero had started to sing, not even women in labor. Men who simply could not stand his singing any longer climbed out furtively over the walls. Others pretended to fall dead and were carried from the theater feet first. During the Neronia of 65 A.D. a number of people were crushed to death or succumbed to the heat and lack of air. Such, at least, were the tales told in Suetonius' time.

The imperial artiste was always extremely nervous before a performance. He spoke to the judges and warned them to exclude the factor of chance. That done, he observed the rules with a punctiliousness which amounted almost to anxiety, but was only too happy to declare himself the winner when he was offered the laurel wreath. His way of obliterating the memory of earlier victors in the competitions was to have their busts and statues thrown into the latrines.

During a race at Olympia in Greece, Nero was thrown out of his chariot. He was picked up and installed in it again but failed to complete the course. Needless to say, he was still awarded a prize. The Olympic Games, which had been held regularly for eight hundred years at four-year intervals, were postponed for two years until Nero could come to Greece. On his departure he rewarded the whole province of Achaia by exempting it from taxation, an occasion he marked by giving an address at Corinth, the verbatim text of which has fortunately survived in an inscription: "My magnanimity, noble Greeks, always leaves room for the highest hopes, it is true, but I am granting you a boon of which you would never have dreamed. You are to receive freedom such as you never knew even in your happiest times, since you were forever defeating one another. Other rulers have given cities their freedom. Only a Nero has given a whole province its freedom."

Admittedly, this speech reflected Nero's inordinate self-conceit, and moreover it was all play-acting. But it was a first-class and even sincere piece of play-acting, for the truth was that Nero admired and revered everything Greek. He loved the Greeks and was convinced that their good taste, their festivals, their theater, their arts and their artistic appreciation had never been rivaled by any other people in the world. The emperor thus set the seal on this doubtless quite genuine conviction by granting the Greeks their freedom, which secured him their lasting affection. Indeed, after his death the Greeks saw Nero in a transfigured light as their savior and benefactor, and considered him worthy of divine worship. During the trials and tribulations of their later history they looked for his return, unwilling to believe that their Grecophile emperor could really be dead. Thus Nero, who strove for immortality and eternal renown throughout his life, at least found posthumous fulfillment of his dream in Greece.

The emperor firmly believed in his mission as an artist, actor, poet and singer, and many of the modern researchers are beginning to regard Suetonius' evidence of his great ability in these fields as entirely credible. Certainly Suetonius and Tacitus both showed elsewhere in their writings that they were far from being admirers of this unique emperor in other respects, so a few favorable remarks on their part surely deserve to be taken at face value.

Nero re-entered Rome in Augustus' triumphal chariot, dressed in a purple robe and a Greek cloak embroidered with golden stars, the Olympic victor's wreath on his head and a second, the Pythian, in his hand. He even slept with his precious wreaths of victory arranged about his bed. To avoid "wasting" his voice, he ceased to communicate with his troops except in writing, and he was constantly accompanied by a voice trainer whose job it was to remind him to spare his lungs or carry a handkerchief before his mouth.

Gradually Nero took to slinking out of his palace in disguise after dusk had fallen. He frequented disreputable taverns, assaulted people as they walked home through the streets, and threw them into privies, or broke into shops and robbed them, later auctioning off the loot at his house. Once when he made an indecent assault on a senator's wife, he was nearly beaten to death. From that day onward he never sallied forth without an escort of soldiers following at a distance.

He spun out his meals from midday to midnight, now and then refreshing himself with warm baths or cold, according to the weather.

Prostitutes and dancing-girls from all over the city served him at table, and when he traveled down the Tiber to Ostia brothels were set up for him at intervals along the banks.

Agrippina, Nero's mother, kept a sharp watch on her son's activities and frequently reprimanded him. She tried to intervene on behalf of Octavia, his wife, whom he scarcely noticed. His current mistress was an emancipated slave named Acte. Against his mother's opposition, he spoke of ultimately marrying her, and since a man of noble birth could not contract a legal marriage with a former slave, bruited it about that Acte was of royal descent. Slave or not, she remained true to Nero until his death and was buried at his side.

Then, while still on intimate terms with Acte, Nero began to court Poppaea Sabina, a woman of great beauty and intelligence, sending her husband, who had abetted the affair from the outset, off to Lusitania (modern Portugal) as governor. But as Nero's attachment to his lovely and ambitious mistress grew deeper, and as Poppaea herself made greater efforts to take Octavia's place and force Nero to divorce her, the relationship between mother and son became more and more strained, until finally there was a breach. Agrippina and Poppaea loathed each other. Only one of them could dominate Nero, and one of them had to go.

Faced with the necessity to choose, Nero decided to murder his mother. Poisoning her was impossible since she kept her household under strict supervision and ate only at home. He therefore lured her aboard a ship and sank it. Agrippina succeeded in swimming ashore and at once informed her son that she was still alive, pretending that it was an accident. Now the emperor summoned his two councilors of state, Burrus and Seneca, who had always been an opponent of Agrippina. Together they advised that the murder be entrusted to Anicetus, a former slave who had at one time been Nero's tutor. Agrippina's house was surrounded, her servants cut down, and she herself killed. She died on March 20, 59 A.D., at the age of fifty-four. As she saw the sword poised above her, she is said to have cried, "Smite the body that brought Nero into the world!"

Nero had also tried to strangle his young wife Octavia several times. Failing, he eventually divorced her on Poppaea's insistence, declaring that she was barren. Then he ordered her to be executed for conjugal infidelity. Every witness called during the judicial inquiry protested Octavia's innocence, save one: Nero had arranged for his former tutor Anicetus to give evidence for the prosecution and declare that he had secretly seduced her. Just twenty years old, Octavia had her veins opened. And when the blood would not flow, her executioners asphyxiated her in a steam bath.

"THE IGNOMINY AND DISGRACE OF IT!"

Nothing was to be seen but fire after fire.... There was fright-
ful chaos everywhere. Everyone ran wildly to and fro. Children,
women, young men and old, all sent up such a monstrous babble
of shouts and screams that, what with the smoke and the clamor,
it was impossible to hear or see a thing.
—Dio Cassius, xxii, 16.

THERE was no point in having money, thought Nero, unless one spent it lavishly. Hence his admiration for Caligula, his uncle, who had so quickly squandered the immense fortune left him by Tiberius.

Nero spent enormous sums on building projects. The vestibule of the Golden House, his new imperial palace, was so vast that it easily accommodated a colossal statue of himself, some 120 feet high. The hall consisted of three pillared arcades, one of which stretched for a mile. It contained a lake surrounded by buildings intended to represent cities, grain fields, vineyards, pastures, woods inhabited by animals tame and wild. The dining rooms had fretted ceilings with sliding panels of ivory concealing tubes which sprinkled the guests with sweet-smelling water. There were also baths with salt and fresh water, a luxury hitherto unknown even in Rome.

Sixteenth-century Romans christened the huge rooms "grottoes," and the murals in them, so different from the usual ecclesiastical paintings of those days, became "grottesco," or "as in the grottoes." It is to Nero therefore that we originally owe our expression "grotesque."

Since Rome could not provide enough laborers to carry out all the emperor's building schemes, he imported prisoners from all over the empire and ordered that in future criminals should be sentenced to penal servitude wherever possible.

It was not long before the funds in the public treasury were exhausted. And since provision still had to be made for the army's pay and veterans' pensions, Nero resorted to petty larceny. The estates of persons who had neglected to mention the emperor in their wills automatically went to the public treasury. Most government appointments had to be bought for hard cash. In the end he even laid hands on the dedicatory offerings in the temples and melted down silver images of the gods.

There came a day when Poppaea, whom he had now married, was forced to suffer the fate which she had so heartily wished on Octavia. Nero killed her by kicking her in the stomach when she was pregnant.

The Emperor sent his second councillor of state, Burrus, some medicine for a sore throat. Burrus dropped dead. He compelled his tutor Seneca to take his own life, perhaps here for good reason for there is evidence Seneca was in on the conspiracy to kill Nero. But first he toyed with Seneca. The old tutor fearfully applied for leave of absence and offered the emperor his whole estate, but Nero assured him that his worries were groundless and that he, Nero, would rather die than do him any harm. As for Corbulo, Nero's ablest general, who had defended the entire eastern frontier of the Roman empire from the Caucasus to the Euphrates, we can readily understand why he incurred the emperor's jealousy and was obliged to commit suicide.

When a conspiracy against him was discovered some time after the great fire Nero's bloodthirsty tendencies reached insane proportions. The plotters appeared in court triply chained. Some of them confessed without more ado, but others proudly declared that the best service any man could render Nero was to kill him.

By now the emperor's homicidal mania knew no bounds and Romans were condemned to death on the slightest provocation. One man, Paetus Thrasea, was ordered to commit suicide "because he had an expression like a cross schoolmaster." People who failed to carry out their own death sentences were "taken care of" by Nero's doctors; which meant, in the emperor's vocabulary, that their veins were opened. It is even said that he took delight in giving people to a notorious Egyptian glutton who was used to eating anything, including raw meat, and letting him devour them alive. As Nero himself declared proudly, "No prince before me ever realized the extent of his power." Yet he was wrong here, for certainly Caligula had.

No one knows for certain how the great fire which all but destroyed Rome during Nero's reign actually began. Yet for centuries it was held that, displeased by the ancient buildings and narrow, winding streets of Rome, Nero ordered the city set ablaze. The fire raged for seven days and six nights, and two-thirds of Rome was burned to the ground while the inhabitants sought refuge in vaults, tombs and temples. Most of the city's places of interest were gutted, including numerous temples and large palaces. Nero is said to have watched the fire from the tower of the Palace of Maecenas on the Esquiline Hill and, overwhelmed by the beauty of the scene, sung his own composition, "The Fall of Troy," and remarked that at last he could really picture the burning of Troy. (However, many modern scholars say he was not in Rome but at Antium, thirty-five miles away, when the fire started.)

After the fire broad new streets were laid out and buildings were not allowed to exceed a certain height. Nero undertook to build arcades in front of apartment houses. The installation of water mains was supervised to prevent anyone drawing off more than he really needed, and it became compulsory to keep fire-fighting apparatus in the forecourt of every house. But, although the city's appearance was somewhat improved, the Romans grumbled that the narrow alleyways and tall houses had been cooler than the broad, unshaded streets whose heat they found intolerable. They also suspected that Nero's sympathetic offers of reconstruction were only designed to camouflage the enormity of his act of pyromania. The dreadful rumor that he himself had set fire to the city spread from house to house like a virulent disease. To silence this dangerous gossip Nero put the blame on the Christians.

In this connection, Tacitus, who was probably born in northern Italy in 55 A.D., has given us some of the earliest non-Christian evidence about Jesus. The authenticity of the passage in question (*Annals* xv, 44) is acknowledged by philologists all over the world with the exception of Hochart and Drews. Its great value lies not only in its explicitness but in the fact that it comes from a Roman who regarded the Christians as criminals. "This name [Christians] comes from Christus, whom the procurator Pontius Pilate condemned to death during the reign of Tiberius. But the abominable superstition, which had been suppressed for a while, soon became widespread once more, not only in Judaea, its place of origin, but also in Rome, where all things shocking and odious in the world find their center and become popular."

The historian goes on to relate that people who openly acknowledged themselves to be Christians were arrested. They were not explicitly accused of arson, it is true, but were charged with "hatred for the human race." Nero turned the persecution of the Christians into a festival. The faithful were sewn up in animal skins and torn to pieces by dogs, nailed to the cross, or set on fire and turned into human torches. Yet Tacitus gives us a subtle indication that, even at this stage, the Romans began to be stirred by sympathy for the Christians "although they were guilty and had merited the harshest penalties." But they were victims of one man's ferocity, victims of Nero, and no one really took any pleasure in their death except the emperor, who opened his own gardens to the public for the Christian-burning display.

It is interesting to picture this man who ruled so autocratically on the brink of madness. Nero was of medium height. His skin was covered with blemishes and Suetonius expressly states that he suffered from body odor. His auburn hair was dressed in ringlets like a woman's but his features were not unhandsome. He gazed out rather timidly, through very shortsighted gray-blue eyes, at a strange world which tolerated his every whim. He had a bull neck and a protuberant belly, and his heavy torso was supported by two extremely spindly legs. He was probably blessed with a very robust constitution, for in spite of his dissipations he was only ill three times during his fourteen years on the throne.

For fourteen years the world tolerated him. Then, on the eighth anniversary of his mother's murder, he received news of a rebellion in Gaul under the leadership of Julius Vindex. Nero greeted the information with peculiar impassivity, almost as though he had a premonition of his downfall and death and felt he could not avert it. However, when he learned that the whole of Spain had joined the revolt he fainted dead away, and on regaining consciousness he rent his clothes and beat his brow. His old nurse pointed out that other rulers had been in similar straits, but Nero replied, "Never! Never has there been a misfortune like mine. I am losing my throne during my lifetime!" and taking his two most precious crystal goblets he dashed them to the floor.

One Roman historian reports that the emperor now planned to poison the whole Senate, murder all his military commanders, and put Rome to the torch once more, turning wild animals loose on the population to hinder any attempt at fire fighting, although this is almost certainly mere legend.

Then he relapsed into moody apathy. He declared that if he lost his throne he would live by his art. He would betake himself to Alexandria, where people had some artistic appreciation, and were loyal besides. . . . But soon that plan, too, was discarded. Nero announced his intention of going out to meet the rebel army alone and regaining their loyalty with his heart-rending tears. Next day, he said, he would be chanting paeans of victory. He at once started to compose lyrics for these songs.

But his remaining armies deserted him. Nero tore the gloomy dispatches into little pieces. He ordered Locusta to brew him a poison but could not summon up the courage to take it. He now proposed to appear before the people dressed in mourning and beg their forgiveness for all he had done. The completed draft of a speech on these lines was discovered after his death.

One night, toward midnight, he suddenly started out of his sleep. His bodyguards had abandoned him. He called for his court officials but no one answered. The servants had even stolen his bed linen and his box of poison. The emperor looked around for Spiculus, a famous gladiator, to give him the *coup de grâce*. But there was absolutely no one there. "Have I neither a friend nor a foe, then?" he shouted, and rushed out of the palace intending to throw himself into the Tiber.

Then he changed his mind. His freedman Phaon offered him refuge at his house. Nero jumped onto his horse and galloped through the night, his face covered with a handkerchief. There was a peal of thunder, an earth tremor, and the sound of soldiers shouting. His horse shied at a putrefying corpse by the roadside and the handkerchief fell from his face. A praetorian guardsman recognized him but let him pass. Arriving at Phaon's house, Nero threw himself onto a bed, whimpering.

His friends advised him to avoid dishonorable treatment by taking his life. Nero then ordered them to dig a grave to his measurements so that his body might be accorded a decent burial without delay. While they did so he wept and cried out repeatedly, "See, what a great artist is dying!" On hearing that the Senate had decreed that he should be flogged to death with rods, he picked up two daggers, intending to kill himself—and put them down again. "The ignominy and disgrace of it all!" he exclaimed. "This won't do for Nero. No, it won't do at all." Then, seeing horsemen galloping up to take him prisoner, he stabbed himself in the throat with the help of one Epaphroditus. The cavalryman who had been detailed to kill Nero now pretended that he had come to rescue him. "What loyalty!" gasped the dying emperor. It was the last mistake he ever made.

It is interesting to note that although Nero became intensely unpopular, it was not because he murdered and poisoned his intimate relations but originally because after an insurrection in Britain under one Queen

Boadicea the legions suffered a disastrous and unaccustomed defeat and because there was an immensely destructive earthquake in southern Italy. The Romans, always superstitious, did not object to a debauched and evil emperor but they objected violently to an unlucky one.

Nero died at the age of thirty-two, on the sixth anniversary of his wife Octavia's murder. There was jubilation among the elite in Rome and throughout the empire. And yet there were many who decked his grave with flowers for a long time afterward. For Nero's memory remained extremely popular with the urban mob. Suetonius writes: "Twenty years later an unknown man appeared among the Parthians claiming that he was Nero. I was only a young man at the time. But Nero's name was still held in such esteem, even at that date, that the Parthians supported him vigorously and only handed him over [to the Romans] with the utmost reluctance." (*Nero*, 57.2)

That was how long he took to die, this man who kindled and re-kindled the imagination of far-off races; who offered people of many lands not serious policies but entertainment, sport, art, and theatricals; who conquered the world's inhabitants not with logic but with startling and sensational pleasures—and all without their recognizing the perilous madness which lay beneath his actor's mask.

THE FEAST OF TRIMALCHIO

"Here lies Gaius Pompeius Trimalchio Maecenatianus. He was upright, staunch, true. He started with nothing and left a fortune worth thirty million sesterces. He never followed any particular philosopher. Farewell, you that read this." That was how the self-made freedman Trimalchio pictured the inscription on his tomb while in his cups.

—Petronius, *Satyricon.*

AMONG Nero's many victims was Petronius, of whom Tacitus tells us in the *Annals* (xvi, 18). He was an unusual man who slept during the day and pursued his pleasures by night, achieving an unparalleled mastery of the arts of hedonism and idleness. He had a mordant wit and a strong sense of humor, but he also showed, as proconsul of Bithynia and subsequently as consul, that under certain circumstances he could be an energetic and skillful political administrator.

It was Petronius whom Nero appointed his *arbiter elegantiae*, a sort of judge in matters of taste. This won Petronius the surname Arbiter, for whatever Petronius Arbiter recommended Nero was certain to find acceptable. Petronius probably succeeded in lending the thoroughly debased standards of entertainment at court some fresh refinement and splendor. But since his manners, his connoisseur's knowledge of genuinely worth-while things and his self-assured good taste put him head and shoulders above all the other men in Nero's entourage, it was only natural that he soon made enemies. Tigellinus, one of Nero's favorites, became jealous of him and bribed a slave to make perjurious allegations against him which led to the arrest of the century's most elegant man at Cumae in 66 A.D.

To escape execution Petronius opened his veins. True to his lifelong pursuit of pleasure, he arranged for someone to read cheerful poems and light verse to him while he lay dying, applied tourniquets from time to time to prevent his life ebbing away too quickly and chatted with his friends. He completed a list of Nero's vices, sent it off to his lord and master as a final dig, and died at the dining table as if death had come naturally and not as a violent form of punishment.

If this Petronius and the author of the *Satyricon* are one and the same as is now fairly unanimously assumed, the dead man was one of the most impudent rascals in the history of literature. His work probably comprised twenty volumes. Although only fragments of the fifteenth and sixteenth books have survived, they are a veritable thesaurus of contemporary slang and shed light on the lowest stratum of Roman society, its manners, good and bad, its amusements and dissipations. The *Cena Trimalchionis (Feast of Trimalchio)* gives us a taste of how a self-made man entertained his guests in those days. There is almost nothing in the whole of classical literature, apart from the wall inscriptions at Pompeii, which gives us a more direct and vivid impression of the Roman *nouveau riche* and the Roman in reduced circumstances.

A bald-headed old man in slippers and a red tunic, Trimalchio is discovered playing handball with some curly-headed boys. The evening begins with a steam bath followed by a cold plunge. Trimalchio is anointed with perfumed waters and then dried—not with linen towels but with the softest wool—wrapped in scarlet rugs, and carried home in a litter. A musician playing a small flute accompanies him all the way. On the door of his mansion is a signboard bearing the legend: *Any slave who leaves the house without his master's permission will get a hundred lashes.*

Before the start of the meal Alexandrian slaves pour snow-cooled water over the guests' hands while other slaves give them a pedicure. They sing as they work, for, like all the servants, they are trained in choral or solo singing.

A Roman feast consisted of at least seven courses, including hors d'oeuvres, two entrees, two meat courses, and a sweet. At Trimalchio's a third meat course is added.

The first of the hors d'oeuvres is a donkey of Corinthian bronze carrying panniers, one filled with green and the other with black olives. The donkey also carries silver bowls with small plates brazed onto them containing roast dormice steeped in honey and sprinkled with poppy seeds. There are damsons and pomegranates too, and sausages smoking on a silver grill. Trimalchio, ensconced on a pile of small cushions, is carried in to the strains of music. Then comes the first entree, a wooden hen with outspread wings beneath which are peahen's eggs bedded in straw. But in the eggs—a little surprise for the guests—are plump beccaficos in peppered egg yolk.

The dishes are borne away by a chanting choir and jugs of vintage Falernian wine are served. Trimalchio claps his hands and a second entree is placed on an enormous centerpiece, a circular disk ornamented with the signs of the zodiac, and on it twelve bowls of food appropriate to the various signs. Then comes the first of the three meat courses: a gigantic wild boar. As it is carved, live thrushes fly out and flutter round the room, to be caught by birdcatchers equipped with poles smeared in lime. One privileged boy hands around grapes, singing poems composed by his master as he does. When a guest begins to tell a story about a rich man and a poor man who were enemies, Trimalchio interrupts him with the question: "What does 'poor' mean?"

At the bidding of a jester, a boy dances to music on the rungs of a ladder, jumps through burning hoops, and balances a jug in his teeth. The host declares that he gets more fun out of jugglers and trumpeters than anything in the world, and that nothing else matters. He adds that he has also provided some actors, but he would sooner let them play the fool. Meanwhile, the boy—a slave, like all entertainers—falls from the ladder, and Trimalchio groans as though injured and at once grants the youth his freedom lest anyone should say that a great man like Trimalchio was hurt by a mere slave.

When shortly afterwards a roast pig is brought in, the host finds that it has not been gutted. The chef is summoned. He confesses that he has forgotten to prepare the animal. "Clothes off!" orders Trimalchio. "He shall be thrashed on the spot." Then he countermands the order. "Gut the pig in front of us," he bids the chef. Donning his clothes again, the man takes his knife and makes several incisions in the pig's belly—and out pours a cascade of roast sausages and black puddings. This jape is loudly applauded by the other servants. A toast is drunk to the chef and he is crowned with a silver wreath. The third meat course consists of a stewed calf.

To emphasize Trimalchio's wealth, his secretary reads out a list of facts. In a single day, thirty boys and forty girls were born on his master's country estate at Cumae, ten million sesterces were paid into his account, a slave was crucified for having made fun of him, and fire broke out in Trimalchio's gardens at Pompeii.

Panels in the ceiling slide apart and a huge ring, hung with golden wreaths and flasks of scented ointment, presents for the guests, descends. They begin to crack smutty jokes. Fortunata, Trimalchio's wife, behaves rather badly and the womenfolk get tipsy. A slave, pouring out wine and water, gives an imitation of a nightingale.

"Something else!" bellows our bald-headed Croesus. "Something else, go on, something else!" Before long the slaves of Trimalchio, a former slave himself, are allowed to join in the drinking. Their master announces that anyone who doesn't want a drink will have it poured over his head. Two boys enter carrying large jars. They pretend to quarrel and start scuffling. As they do so, oysters and mussels fall out of the jars and are collected in a bowl by another boy, who hands them around. Novelties like this go down very well with the guests.

Trimalchio at length becomes maudlin, demands that his will be brought in and reads it aloud to the sound of his servants' lamentations. Then he describes what his tombstone will look like. "We know we must die one day," says Trimalchio. "Why shouldn't we enjoy life? As true as I have your welfare at heart, let's take a bath. It's like an oven in here."

Later in the feast, and by this time tipsy as a fiddler, Trimalchio shows the guests his funeral toga trimmed with purple. "I hope it will become me as a corpse as well as it became me in my lifetime," he says. "Try and imagine you have been invited to my funeral." To trumpeters who enter the room he adds, "Pretend I'm dead, and play something nice." One of the slave musicians blows his instrument so lustily that he rouses the neighborhood and, thinking that Trimalchio's house is on fire, night watchmen come rushing up with water buckets and axes and break the door down. "We seized this favorable opportunity," the narrator tells us, "and took to our heels as though we really were escaping from a fire."

Just as the narrator of the "ludicrous feast" poked fun at himself and his surroundings, just as he unleashed his amazing powers of observation on all that he despised, just as the newly emancipated slave boy, a nervous guest at Trimalchio's table and in his bath, was forced to celebrate with his fat and stupid host whether he liked it or not, so it was, probably, with Petronius at Nero's court. Setting the fashion with a smile, this brilliant Cervantes of the ancient world played the part of an elegant fool and accepted the crumbs from his stage-struck master's table for as long as fate permitted. But no one, either before or after him, ever captured the vices of a decadent metropolis and held them up as a mirror before the face of posterity with such covert amusement or resigned candor.

WHAT IS MAN?

*A weak and fragile body, naked, defenseless by nature, depend-
ent on the help of others, susceptible to all the iniquities of
fate, apprehensive about his food, overabundance or lack of
which both spell his destruction.*

—Seneca.

BEFORE dismissing the dark days of Nero, let us take a closer look
at Nero's contemporary, Seneca. It is a quirk of history that Seneca,
one of the greatest educators of Western culture, should have been
Nero's tutor. The Nero-Seneca combination proves that character is
always stronger than upbringing and that a teacher can only mold and
develop his pupil's natural inclinations, never fundamentally change
them.

Strangely enough, Seneca's arrival in the world at Cordoba in
southern Spain almost coincided with the Christian Saviour's birth at
Bethlehem. It was in the shadow of Christ's presence that Seneca wrote:
"Divinity is near you. It is at your side. It is within you. There dwells
in us a holy spirit, the observer and guardian of all that is good and evil
in us. He treats us as we have treated him. No one is a good man without
God." (Seneca, *Letters to Lucilius.*)

While Gallio, Seneca's brother, was governor of Greece, Saint
Paul arrived in Corinth to preach the Gospel and was so remarkably
successful that the Jewish community there tried to get his teachings
banned. In the year 52 A.D., Gallio decided the issue between the Jews
and Paul in the latter's favor. It is quite possible that Seneca heard of
these events via Gallio's letters, for he was on good terms with his
brother and dedicated several of his works to him. But, apart from
that, Seneca must have been aware that there were Christians in Rome,
The whole world knew how Nero had blamed them for the great fire.
Since Seneca's views were so closely related to the concepts of Christianity, an idea subsequently grew up that Seneca was a Christian and
had corresponded with Paul. Saint Jerome believed in the authenticity
of the letters which have survived, but today they are regarded as
forgeries.

Seneca also spent a long time in Egypt where his uncle was governor.
There, too, he must have heard something of the Christian point of

view, since a fierce controversy was raging between the Jewish and Christian communities in Egypt at the time.

Seneca's father was a Roman knight, an orator and the author of several works on history and rhetoric. It was not long before he brought his young son Lucius Annaeus to Rome and sent him to study under Sotion and Attalus the Stoic. Seneca himself said of his tutors: "Whenever I listened to Attalus inveighing against the vices, fallacies and errors of this life, I pitied humanity and saw Attalus reigning high above all other mortals. I am not ashamed to confess the deep love for Pythagoras which Sotion inspired in me." Seneca was, incidentally, a dramatic poet of considerable repute. His tragedies, among them the *Medea, Phaedra* and *Oedipus,* all left their mark on world literature.

Under Caligula, Seneca became quaestor—and gave such impressive judicial addresses that the young emperor became jealous of him. He even made plans to have him killed but was murdered before he could carry them out. In the year 41 A.D. Emperor Claudius banished Seneca to Corsica. Seneca owed his eight years on that rugged island to Messalina's hatred.

Seneca was not recalled to Rome until after Messalina's death. Agrippina, Claudius' second wife, then secured him a senior government post at Rome and appointed him her son Nero's tutor.

Seneca did his utmost to keep his pupil on the straight and narrow path with the inevitable result that young Nero often saw him as a mere kill-joy who wanted to clip the wings of his imagination. But when he came to the throne Nero found he needed advisers. In Seneca and Burrus we are confronted by the unusual picture of two men who shared a single position of authority yet remained friends. Together they held the reins of world power, Burrus the praetorian prefect and Seneca the shrewd but kindly orator. "The bloodletting would have continued . . ." writes Tacitus, "but Burrus and Seneca opposed it."

But when Burrus died (obviously one of Nero's victims) Seneca's position also began to deteriorate. *Mors Burri infregit Senecae potentiam,* we read in Tacitus (*Annals* xiv, 52).

In the end Nero's murderous and all-embracing grasp fastened itself upon his old tutor. As Seneca himself admitted: "Who was ever unaware of Nero's cruelty? Having murdered his mother and his brothers and sisters, what was there left for him to do but murder his teacher and tutor?"

When Seneca received his orders to die he was probably better prepared for death than any mortal before or since. In the whole course of human history, rich as it is in murder and injustice, only one other philosopher went to his death with such utter serenity, with the aura of immortality shining so brightly about him: Socrates. It is no mere accident that Socrates the Greek was the spiritual father of Seneca the Roman. One cannot describe Seneca. To appreciate what a truly full life means and how it is possible to lay down that life with complete peace of mind, one must hear him.

Long before Seneca guessed that the emperor would one day force him to commit suicide, he had recognized the brevity of human existence, the value of each passing day, and the danger of letting time slip by unheeded and unfulfilled. "I have looked on each day as my last," he wrote to Lucilius.

There is an alarming note in some of Seneca's admonitions, and his essay "On the Brevity of Life" should be compulsory reading for everyone every ten years. "You live as though you will live forever. It never occurs to you how poorly provided you are. You squander time as though you had it in plenty, although the very day you devote to someone or something may be your last. You fear everything like creatures that must die, yet hanker after everything as though you could live for ever. . . . Just as travelers are beguiled by a conversation or a book until they suddenly notice to their astonishment that they have arrived, so busy men never notice their uninterrupted and remarkably swift journey through life until they have reached their destination. . . . Time runs out inaudibly, intangibly, noiselessly, unrecognized and unfamiliar. Yet it is the most precious commodity and the only real treasure we possess. Your lifetime," Seneca says, "will make no sound. It will not remind you of its haste. Silently it will flow away. . . . There is no more difficult art than that of living. But you must learn how to live while you live."

How should we use our time? How should we make sure that it is not wasted? Seneca gives us a clear answer. "Man is a being endowed with reason. This advantage attains perfection when he fulfills what he was born for. What does reason demand of him? The simplest thing in the world: to live in accordance with his nature. . . . Be safe: constantly remind yourself what a fine thing it is, having perfected your life before you die, to live out the rest of your time quietly, the possessor of a happy life. . . We tear life into little pieces and dismember it. . . . I wish you possession of yourself, so that your soul, driven this way and that by restless thoughts, finds a firm foothold at last and stands secure, so that it finds favor with itself and, because it has recognized the true blessings in our possession, needs no increase of years." Seneca advises us to ask ourselves every evening what we have done better during the day than ever before, and in what respects we must make still more progress.

Seneca had clearly recognized that there is but one worth-while thing in a man's life, namely what he *is:* his own faculties, his own ability to think, his own character. What he *has*, on the other hand, is much less important. "Never consider him fortunate who is dependent upon externals. The man who takes pleasure in things that come from outside has built upon fragile foundations. Each joy that comes from there will return there. But that which springs from within oneself is steadfast and true, grows, and stays with us to the end. The other things which arouse such great admiration are only fruitful and pleasant when the possessor of them is also in possession of himself. . . . Mightier than the whole of destiny is the soul. . . . It is a mistake to model our lives on others' and to do something only because many others show us how. To belong to oneself is a blessing beyond price."

Seneca knew that the only happy person is one who can follow his natural bents. He also knew that that is just what one should and must do, and that only these inner predispositions have any value. He had, in general, an amazing insight into the secret of "the happy life." "I deny that wealth is a good thing. For if it were, it would make men good."

On the other hand, Seneca was not unaware that money is useful, provided its importance is not overestimated. "For the rest, I acknowledge that it is allowable to possess wealth, that it is useful and brings life many advantages. . . . Can there be any doubt that a wise man has a greater opportunity to develop what is within him in wealth than in poverty? . . . Stop forbidding philosophers to possess money, therefore. No one has yet condemned wisdom to poverty." And Seneca himself amassed tremendous wealth.

But man must not be the servant of what he owns: what he owns must serve him. "Among the wise, wealth remains subservient; among fools it gains the upper hand. The wise man makes no concession to wealth; but *you* become used to it and depend on it as though someone had promised you everlasting possession of it."

It is amazing what a modern ring there is to every word this spiritual giant wrote nineteen hundred years ago. He grasped at every aspect of life, laying its meaning bare until he reached the ultimate mysteries of the world to come. In this he was always indifferent to popular opinion. "Things are not so well with mankind that the majority always prefers what is best. A large proportion always supports what is worst. In voting, one and the same thing is approved or condemned: that is the outcome of every decision made on a majority basis." Anyone suffering from "managerial disease," lack of leisure or pressure of work, should take time off to read Seneca's essays "On Peace of Mind" and "On the Brevity of Life." "Busy men have no time to review the past, and, even when they do, the memory of regrettable things pains them. Thus they are averse to thinking back on time misspent, and dare not hold their mistakes up before the light. . . . Anyone who ambitiously craves for much, arrogantly despises much, obtains much by force, extorts much by trickery, avariciously acquires much and wastefully squanders much, must necessarily fear his memory. The reward of a man with a carefree and tranquil mind is an ability to review every part of his lifetime. The soul of the busy man cannot look back. His life has vanished into the abyss."

From "On Peace of Mind": "Thus each man eternally flees from himself. But what good is it, if he cannot escape himself? He is his own escort and most burdensome of companions. . . . Hence restless journeys are made and seacoasts traversed. Vacillation, ever hostile to the present, tries first the sea, then the land. . . . Many an old man well advanced in years can produce no evidence of his having lived long other than his tale of years. . . . But do not believe that someone has lived a long time because of his gray hairs and wrinkles. He has not lived a long time, only existed a long time. . . . Living happily and living naturally are two ways of saying the same thing. . . .

"We live naturally when we watch our physical proclivities and the requirements of our nature carefully but not fearfully, as if they were something fleeting and only bestowed on us temporarily. . . . Virtue is to be found everywhere, in the temple, in the forum, in the assembly, standing before the walls, covered in dust, fresh-faced, with calloused hands; but sensual pleasure is to be found hiding in corners and seeking darkness, in bathhouses, sweatrooms, and places feared by the police, feeble, enervated, sodden with wine and scented oils, pale, rouged, painted with cosmetics. But the true mind never changes, nor is it ever repugnant to itself, and, since it is the best, it never changes anything within itself. The greatest blessing is harmony with oneself. . . . Insight and discernment, health, freedom and beauty of the soul. Why speak you of pleasure? I see the happiness of man, not of the belly—which is more capacious in cattle and animals! . . . Therefore learn how to enjoy yourself, but know that true joy is a serious matter. . . .

"What a splendid thing a good conscience is!" Seneca exclaims. "Men spend the greater part of their life doing evil, a large part of their life doing nothing, and the whole of their life doing anything other than that which they really should. . . . All that part of our lifetime which lies behind us holds death in its hands. Place all your hours side by side: you will be less dependent on the morrow if you make the most of today. The more you postpone life, the faster it hurries by."

Not even Nero could alarm a man who had attained such heights of knowledge. Of course, Seneca did not heedlessly throw his life away. When he realized that people who bore him a grudge were blackening him in the emperor's eyes, he requested an audience. He thanked the emperor with the utmost courtesy for all the favors he had received, declaring that he had been blessed with too much good fortune and that humility and moderation would be the losers. Then he begged Nero for aid "because I can no longer sustain my wealth. Allow my resources to be merged with your own." He wanted to lay everything at his former pupil's feet and end his days in peace.

But Nero declined. "It is you that hold me back when, in my youthful inexperience, I stray from the path and stumble. It is you that direct my energies for the best and take such good care of me. If you give me back your property, talk of my covetousness and your fear of my cruelty will be on every tongue." So saying, Nero embraced Seneca and kissed him. Seneca expressed his thanks—"which," as Tacitus remarks, "is how conversations with a ruler usually end."

After this interview Seneca was rarely seen in Rome. In 65 A.D. destiny caught up with him. The emperor charged him with complicity in the Pisonian conspiracy, and eventually sent the tribune Silvanus to order him to commit suicide. With complete composure Seneca asked for permission to make his will, but was prevented from setting down his last wishes. Noticing that his friends were weeping, he asked, "Where is that self-command in the face of adversity for which we have been girding ourselves all these years?" Then he embraced his wife Paulina, who announced her intention of dying with him. (She slashed her veins, but was later saved.)

Seneca died slowly. He severed several arteries with a single stroke, but the blood oozed reluctantly from his ancient frame. Then he tore open the veins in his legs and at the back of his knees, trying to disguise his frightful agony. Even at that late stage he dictated a longish speech to his amanuensis. When death still refused to come, he asked his doctor Annaeus to give him a poison, only to have the poison, too, fail to act.

Finally Seneca climbed into a hot bath. He sprinkled his favorite slave with water, declaring that he was offering a libation to Jupiter the Deliverer. Then he had himself carried into the steamroom, where he eventually died of asphyxiation.

"No one takes care to live wisely. Everyone worries about living long. But anyone can live a wise life, while no one can rely on a long one. He has comprehended wisdom who dies as free from care as he was born."

THE OLD MISER

*It is acknowledged that Sulpicius Galba was the wealthi-
est private person ever to enter the house of the Caesars.*
—Plutarch, *Galba*, 3.

NERO'S death marked the end of Julius Caesar's immediate line, for
Nero had no heirs and his successor, Galba, was unrelated to him
either by birth or adoption. Not a drop of the first six emperors' blood
flowed in the veins of the seventh.

Galba was born on December 24, in either 3 or 5 B.C. He came of a
very aristocratic family and called himself "descendant of Quintus
Catulus Capitolinus," tracing his ancestry back to the god Jupiter
and to Pasiphaë, the wife of Minos. More important to his status than
these legendary forebears, however, was his distant relationship with
Livia, Augustus' wife.

It was uncertain, even during the lifetime of this emperor, what the
name "Galba" meant. *Galbanum* is the resinous gum of a Syrian plant.
Galbeum was a woolen sling containing medicaments. *Galba* was the
Gallic expression for fat, and *galbae* were insects that bred in oak
trees. Galba's grandfather was a historian who wrote a thorough and
careful history, and Galba's father, a small misshapen man, was a hard-
working but not unduly talented lawyer. When Livia Ocellina, a rich
and outstandingly beautiful woman, declared her intention of marrying
him, he showed her his physical deformities. She was quite undeterred.

The man who later became Emperor Galba was not, however, a son
of Livia Ocellina, who was his father's second wife, but of his first
wife, Mummia Achaica. When astrologers prophesied to Tiberius
that young Galba would come to the throne late in life, the gloomy
old misanthrope said, "He can stay alive, then: that doesn't pertain
to me."

As a young man, Galba lived like any rich and pampered nobleman,
summering on a fine estate at Tusculum, a sort of Roman suburb where
well-to-do families had their villas. (Ruins of this place were found
near Frascati, fifteen miles from Rome.) Young Galba insisted on
feudal deference from his inferiors, and his freedmen and slaves were
obliged to parade before him twice a day in accordance with an

ancient Roman custom only he observed. Slaves and freedmen alike had to wish him good morning and good night at the beginning and end of each day. He received instruction in the principal branches of contemporary education, and also studied jurisprudence. He married once, but after the death of his wife Lepida steadfastly remained single —not, it may be said, because he had been particularly devoted to Lepida but because his personal preference was for stalwart men. Agrippina, Nero's widowed mother, had at one time taken an interest in him, but he was astute or indifferent enough to avoid her.

Galba became praetor at an early age. The Floralia, the games in honor of the flower-goddess Flora, were held each year on April 28. Praetor Galba made circus history at one of these festivals by exhibiting rope-dancing elephants, to the delight of Rome. Governor of the province of Aquitania in southwest France, consul-legate of Upper Germany and successful commander in action against the Germans— those were the highlights of a career which culminated in Galba's accession to the throne as an old man of seventy-three.

As soon as the news of Caligula's murder was abroad, many people tried to talk Galba into letting himself be proclaimed emperor. He prudently refrained, thereby winning himself the undying affection of Claudius, Caligula's successor.

Galba's next appointment was the governorship of Africa where he fully maintained his reputation as a martinet. Acting on the principle that the only way to toughen soldiers, whether veterans or recruits, was to keep them permanently on active service, he rejected all applications for leave. When one of his soldiers sold a bushel of his grain ration for about $20, Galba ordered that he should receive no rations at all if food ran short. The man starved to death.

Naturally Galba finished his term in Africa loaded with honors and triumphal regalia.

Nero was now emperor and Galba became increasingly cautious, living for the most part in retirement. Whenever he went on a trip he was followed by a second carriage which contained a million sesterces in gold, roughly $28,000, designed to meet any eventuality from greasing palms to financing a quick getaway.

Eventually Galba was given the governorship of Hispania Tarraconensis, a province which included territory in the north and east of the Iberian Peninsula. It was there, while he was sacrificing to the gods in a temple, that a miracle occurred. The hair of the boy holding the censer suddenly turned snow-white, an event which was interpreted as a sign that an old man would succeed a young man as emperor—that is that Galba would succeed Nero. But it took some time to happen. Galba administered his Spanish province for eight years, once again an object of fear to the troops, for discipline became tighter wherever he went. The local inhabitants on the other hand were delighted, because former procurators had plundered the country to their hearts' content. Galba was energetic, strict—even cruel. He chopped off a fraudulent moneylender's hands and had them nailed to his counter. A guardian who had poisoned his ward was sentenced to crucifixion but claimed his right of appeal to the emperor since, being a Roman citizen, he could apply to Nero in person. Galba at once "commuted" his sentence by erecting a considerably higher cross and having it nicely whitewashed. Otherwise the penalty remained the same.

In the end, however, Galba became perturbed by his own severity and, rather than do anything to offend Emperor Nero, he became indifferent and adopted a policy of laissez-faire. "No one can be prosecuted for doing nothing," he told himself. But two things happened to change the mind of the man whose one desire was to be left in peace. First, Galba intercepted a letter in which he read that Nero had issued a general order to the procurators to kill him; and second, someone reminded him of an ancient prophecy which stated that "the master of the world" would come from Spain. Like Charles V and Philip II after him, Galba took this prediction to apply to himself. He declared a state of war, recruited fresh legions, and posted reliable sentries outside his sleeping quarters.

Galba was very nearly killed before he reached the highest rung of the ladder which he had climbed so painstakingly. While walking down a narrow lane to the baths, he heard a voice exclaim, "Are we going to miss this fine opportunity?" What fine opportunity? thought Galba and arrested two slaves who confessed on the rack that Nero had hired them to assassinate him.

Then the incredible news arrived from Rome. Nero was dead and Galba learned that he had been accorded the oath of allegiance. The name Caesar had by now become a title reserved for the possessor of supreme power. Galba assumed that title in 68 A.D.

The new emperor was preceded by a bad reputation. Seventy-three years old, Galba did just about everything he could to make himself unpopular. He was afflicted with gout, and being a sufferer himself it did not worry him if others suffered too. Whenever his crooked nose showed itself at an unusually elegant dinner, his head steward knew what to expect. Galba would carp at the value of food being served and quietly tot up what it was going to cost him. The new emperor of the profligate Romans was a miser.

The emperor's shoes pinched him in the truest sense, for his limbs were so racked with gout that even the lightest sandals made him wince. He could not hold a scroll, either, since it was agony for him to open and close his fingers. Three men followed him everywhere like shadows: Titus Vinius, Cornelius Laco, and the freedman Icelus. Vinius, who was said to have filched a silver bowl from Emperor Claudius' table when invited to dinner, was rapacity personified; Laco was the walking embodiment of idleness; and Icelus was vice incarnate. Bereft of all will power, the gouty old man "reigned" in the shadow of these three ne'er-do-wells. On occasions when his gout was particularly painful he became indescribably harsh and avaricious. At such times the merest breath of suspicion would suffice to send someone to the executioner without a hearing.

Enlisting the help of a committee of fifty prominent Romans, the old miser cut by 90 per cent all the bequests made by Nero. He also protected notorious criminals like the eunuch Halotus and the former praetorian prefect Tigellinus, who had both been henchmen of Nero, even though the people repeatedly demanded the death of Tigellinus on the grounds that he had been one of the chief offenders during Nero's regime.

Finally, there was Galba's behavior toward his troops which was fraught with danger. He treated them all, soldiers and officers alike, with lack of consideration, never hid his distrust of them, and constantly insulted them. The first unit to swear allegiance to him was the army in Upper Germany, but the unpleasant old man, by this time afflicted with a painful fleshy protuberance on his right side, imagined that the officers despised him. Calling a parade, therefore, he publicly adopted a young nobleman called Piso Frugi Licinianus. The young man did not have long to enjoy his stroke of luck. Five days later, on January 15, 69 A.D., he was to die with Galba.

Galba started to do strange things. Sorting through his magpie's hoard of treasures, he picked out a necklace of pearls and precious stones, intending to adorn his Fortuna, a little bronze statuette which he kept on his estate at Tusculum. He had found the bronze goddess lying forlornly on his doorstep. Now he wanted to give her the finest piece of jewelry he possessed.

But his avarice got the better of him. He only wanted to sacrifice *one* piece of jewelry, so he dedicated the necklace which had been earmarked for his Fortuna to Capitoline Venus instead. The very next night Fortuna appeared to him in his sleep, screaming with rage. Half dreaming, half delirious, he saw her bundling together all she had ever given him. The old man awoke groaning and at once decided to make an expiatory sacrifice. Frenziedly, with the icy fingers of dementia already clawing at the fluttering hem of his toga, Galba raced off to Tusculum. But there, instead of a burning flame on the sacrificial altar, he found only hot ashes, and instead of a youth in a white robe, a trembling old man in deep mourning. "Your murderers are not far away," a soothsayer warned him.

Not long after, Marcus Salvius Otho seized power, and Galba was advised to take refuge in the praetorian camp. But he was weary, searing pains shot through his limbs, and he decided to stay in his palace. He mustered some troops for his personal protection, then donned a linen corselet. "Ah!" he groaned. "This will not avail me against many swords."

Soon shouts of triumph were heard. Apparently the revolt had been crushed. Messages of congratulation came, and some people reaffirmed their loyalty to the emperor. Deciding that good news ought to be met halfway, Galba left the palace. As he did so a soldier shouted to him that he had slain Otho. "On whose orders?" snapped the emperor, characteristically reluctant to give a reward. How could he know that his foe's party had sent men to tell him Otho was defeated to draw him from his lair to his death?

Galba was passing the Lacus Curtius on his way to the Forum when horsemen galloped up, scattering the crowds. In a moment the gouty old monster was deserted by his whole escort. Galba bowed to the inevitable, although one version of the story says he first made an attempt to bribe his assassins. Baring his neck to the assassins, he uttered the traditional formula used by Romans when slaughtering an animal for sacrifice: "Forward, strike home, since so it must be!"

Nobody made a move to save him. The old man lay where he had been felled. A passing soldier cut off his head, intending to take it with him. Finding it difficult to grip because of Galba's lack of hair,

Servius Sulpicius Galba was proclaimed emperor by the Spanish legions in 68 A.D.

Otho (32-69 A.D.) was as vain as a peacock and always wore a wig. He was so extravagant as a young man that he said, with justification: "My last hope lies in becoming Emperor." His end: suicide.

Aulus Vitellius (15-69 A.D.) was a clumsy giant of a man with a limp. His face was puce with wine-drinking and his body bloated by debauchery. Even taking Galba and Otho into account, Vitellius was the prize failure of the year 69 A.D. (Ancient sculpture in the Capitoline Museum)

Emperor Flavius Vespasian occupied the throne for ten years. The destruction of Jerusalem (70 A.D.) falls within his reign, as does the building of the Roman Colosseum.

Emperor Titus ruled well under the most adverse conditions. His short reign (79-81 A.D.) was beset by a series of disasters which included the destruction of Pompeii and Herculaneum, the Plague, and a great fire at Rome.

Bloodthirsty gladiatorial contests and animal-baiting displays took place here. The huge amphitheatre at Rome was started by Emperor Vespasian and opened by his son Titus in 80 A.D. with Games lasting a hundred days. The Romans called this building the Flavian Theatre, after the two emperors' family name. In the Middle Ages it became known as the Colosseum, from the colossus or huge statue of Nero which had been set up near by. The seats could be sheltered from the sun by means of huge awnings, and spectators reached their places via sixteen stairways and eighty arcades.

Vesuvius seen from the Bay of Naples. Pompeii and Herculaneum were engulfed on August 23 and 24, 79 A.D. Many of the wine jars which were dug up at Pompeii bore the inscription *Vesuvius wine*. During the time of the emperors this wine was reckoned among the best in Italy, and fine grapes still grow on the slopes of Vesuvius today.

Below: the Forum of Pompeii and the Temple of Jupiter.

Nothing is finer than beauty and nothing more fleeting. "I bear it manfully, though it turns me into an old man before my time," wrote Emperor Domitian of his baldness. He reigned in a state of permanent distrust from 81 A.D. until 96 A.D., persecuting the Christians and shedding torrents of blood.

Domitia, wife of Domitian, lived in constant terror of her royal husband's vengeance. The emperor had abducted her from Aelius Lamia. She eventually joined the conspiracy which brought about his assassination.

◄

The amphitheatre at Pompeii, the oldest surviving amphitheatre in Italy, was built in 80 B.C. Sunk far below ground level, it had thirty-five tiers of seats accommodating 20,000 spectators. A huge awning could be suspended above the arena and the public as a protection against the sun. Ferocious battles to the death used to take place here. (Excavated in 1815)

The triclinium in which the Feast of Trimalchio took place may have looked like this richly painted dining room belonging to the brothers Aulus Vettius Restitutus and Aulus Vettius Conviva, *nouveau-riche* wine merchants from Pompeii in the days of Nero. Their house was buried in mud during the eruption of Vesuvius in ◄ August, 79 A.D.

Titus captured Jerusalem in 70 A.D. on the orders of his father, Emperor Vespasian. When Titus died in the year 81, the Senate honored him by erecting the Arch of Titus, the oldest surviving triumphal arch in Rome. A relief in the passage through the arch shows the removal of the seven-branched candelabrum from the Temple in Jerusalem.

The passages in the Roman amphitheatre at Arles are mute evidence of amazing creative energy and great wealth. The old town in Southern Gaul of *Arelas* is mentioned by Caesar. Situated on the Rhône and the main road to Spain, Arles became a very important commercial center during the 1st century A.D. and was later the residence of Emperor Constantine.

he put his thumb into the imperial mouth and, like that, carried it to Otho who threw the head to some camp boys who stuck it on a spear and paraded it about the camp with jeers.

Argivus, Galba's major-domo, later buried his master's head and trunk in the imperial gardens by the Aurelian highroad. Galba was seventy-three when he ascended to the purple, surely too old to have been a successful emperor. He was still seventy-three when he died, having reigned for only about eight months. Had he never become emperor, remarks Tacitus, everyone would have gone on believing that he might have made a good one. And yet in retrospect one must confess that after Nero's extravagances, Galba's parsimony was a crying necessity, while lack of discipline in the army called for stern measures. Galba's story once again proves that the best of intentions alone is not enough to achieve success.

BETTER AT DYING THAN RULING

Scarcely had the freedman departed when Otho stood the sword upright between his hands and threw himself upon it. He experienced only enough pain to make him utter a single groan, thus betraying what had happened to those standing outside.

—Plutarch, *Otho*, 17

ROME had by now fallen prey to most of the vices that inevitably come with an advanced civilization. Greed and perversion, adultery and pederasty, sadism, treachery and injustice all made their presence felt among the seven hills which ruled the world. Caligula, Claudius, Nero and Galba had prepared the morass into which the new emperor, Otho, was to wade still deeper. Between the years 30 and 69 A.D. Rome's moral barometer showed its lowest reading.

Doomed to the fate of all tyrants, the emperors everlastingly shivered in their shoes. Their nights were made hideous by the memory of bloodshed, poison and judicial murder. They could scent conspiracy everywhere. More and more spies had to be employed until it seemed every wall had ears. Terror reigned supreme. A downtrodden and humiliated band of toadies and sycophants danced a witches' dance about the infallible person of the emperor, who could trust no one.

In the time of Augustus it was still customary to obtain senior political appointments on merit, by showing courage and competence. By Claudius' day a half century later the best method of making headway was to unmask a plot against the emperor's life. That was precisely the course adopted by Lucius Otho, the Emperor Otho's father. It did not take much doing since the conspiracy, which had been organized by a Roman knight, was revealed to Otho by a slave. The fawning Senate at once erected a statue of Otho in the Palatium and Emperor Claudius elevated him to patrician rank. "I could not wish for a better man than Otho," declared Claudius, "even among my own children."

Lucius Otho, the emperor's father whom we have already mentioned, was a man who adapted himself skillfully to the poison- and intrigue-ridden age in which he was born. Tiberius had been fond of him, and it may have been his good fortune to bear a strong resemblance to that emperor. On April 28, 32 A.D., his wife Albia Terentia, a woman of aristocratic birth, bore him a son. The child was bowlegged, and this imperfection—common enough among babies—stayed with him throughout the thirty-six years of his life.

However, young Marcus Salvius Otho developed other imperfections which did not suit his pronounced and precocious vanity half as well. The unscrupulous, degenerate and lascivious youth roamed nightly through the narrow Roman streets, waylaying drunks and beating them up. There were large gangs of these aristocratic delinquents in Rome during this period, although one must add that the comic dramatist Plautus had described an equally vicious type of young Roman more than two hundred years earlier, and history shows that all ages produce their share of vicious young men.

Otho senior soon awoke to his son's peculiar inclinations and thrashed him soundly and often. Marcus Salvius accepted his beatings and waited for the old man to die.

Lucius Otho had scarcely breathed his last when his son started to pay court to a dissipated freedwoman whose only redeeming feature was the fact that she was on good terms with Emperor Nero. By affecting a passion for her, Marcus Salvius Otho insinuated himself not only into the emperor's clique but also his affections. Actually his success was not so surprising because young Otho and the singing emperor were fairly similar in character. Like the mistress of some vain and stupid tyrant, Otho could twist Nero round his little finger.

It goes without saying that Otho was party to Nero's most intimate secrets. It was he who inveigled Poppaea Sabina, Nero's mistress, into committing adultery and then contracted a mock marriage with her. Having done so, he was unwilling to surrender her to his impatient lord, master and employer, and Nero had to send Otho off to Lusitania as governor before he could have Poppaea Sabina to himself. His indignation at his friend for having committed "adultery" with his own wife caused great amusement in Rome.

Otho administered his province for ten years, and we learn with some surprise that he made a thoroughly good quaestor. He was in on Galba's coup against Nero from the start, though even at that stage he cherished secret ambitions of becoming emperor himself, encouraged in this hope by the astrologer Seleucus. Seleucus (called "Ptolemaeus" by Tacitus and Plutarch) had long ago told him that he would survive Nero. Now the astrologer suddenly turned up with another prediction: "In a short time you will be emperor."

Otho made systematic preparations for his accession to the throne. Whenever Galba came to dine with him he distributed largesse to the emperor's bodyguard. Indeed, he made such a lavish bid for popularity with the praetorian cohorts that he soon had every guardsman favorably comparing his own openhandedness with Galba's tightfisted habits. For a while Otho hoped that Galba would adopt him, but as soon as he saw that it was not to be, he started to plan a *coup d'état*. Working on the snowball system, he confided his schemes to five bodyguards and instructed each of them to enlist two more. A large sum was paid for each new man recruited. When he had enough men bought, friendly as ever Otho went to call on the emperor, taking his leave when word came that "the architects had arrived." That was the signal for the *putsch*. The soldiers who murdered Galba acted on Otho's personal instructions.

Otho was now emperor, although he had no way of knowing that his triumph was to last for only ninety-five days. One of his first measures was to honor Nero by re-erecting his statues—a remarkable thing to do such a short time after Nero's death. He even let the people address him as "Nero" and made a grant of fifty million sesterces toward the completion of Nero's Golden House.

One morning screams were heard issuing from Otho's bedchamber and he was discovered lying on the floor by his bed. It seems that his murdered predecessor's ghost had appeared and hurled him to the ground. Then Otho stumbled during a storm and was heard to mutter, over and over again, in Greek, "What concern have I with long flutes?" (Suetonius, *Otho*, 7.) His throne was tottering even before he had settled himself properly upon it.

News now arrived that the army in Germany had sworn allegiance to Vitellius. Otho ordered the Senate to inform Vitellius by messenger that he, Otho, had already been elected emperor. Undeterred, Vitellius marched on Italy. Otho's forces fought two successful battles at the foot of the Alps but were defeated in the third at Bedriacum, between Mantua and Cremona.

Otho had never been a hero. He hated civil war. When a soldier announced that his army had been defeated at Betriacum, nobody believed him until before Otho's very eyes, the man threw himself on his sword. Among those present was the father of Suetonius the

Roman historian. He later told how Otho had called out in despair: "I shall no longer subject brave and devoted men to danger."

Otho said farewell to his brother and several friends, burned his correspondence, distributed gifts, and held an audience for anyone who wished to speak to him. Then, having drunk some cold water, he put a dagger beneath his pillow and fell sound asleep.

Although the cold-blooded determination with which Otho committed suicide early next morning may seem surprising, it was quite in keeping with his character. One sword thrust in the left side was enough. He groaned aloud. Servants came rushing into his bedchamber. Otho put his hand over the wound, then showed it to them, covered it again, and died.

There he lay, bowlegged as ever. Only then was it discovered that Otho did not have a single hair on his head. He had deceived his entourage for years by wearing a well-fitting wig. It had also been his desire to have a soft, smooth skin, and it is recorded that he had depilated himself by rubbing his face daily with moist bread.

Otho's death was in such striking contrast to his life that several of his soldiers wept, kissed his hands and feet and, running on their swords, followed their emperor into death. Roman citizens who had cursed him during his lifetime started to praise him now that he was dead. "Duels of imperial loyalty" were fought at Rome, the losers joining the emperor in the next world as though by divine decree. It was a strange age of aberration and debased values, an age when humanity had nothing to cling to. The Gospel of Christ was on its way—it already had its martyrs—but it had not yet conquered Rome in the year 69 A.D.

THE IMPERIAL GLUTTON

IT IS extremely difficult to describe Lucius Vitellius, father of Vitellius the emperor, in a few words. On the one hand he was a toady and a bootlicker of the first order. On the other he was an extremely able soldier and administrator who, having held the governorship of Syria, later became the highest official in the Roman empire, deputizing for Emperor Claudius during his campaign against Britain. Despite this, he aroused a great deal of scorn and ridicule by his infatuation for a former slavewoman whom he waited on hand and foot and followed around like a pet dog. Once, declaring that he was hoarse and that it would soothe his sore throat, he publicly downed a draught of her saliva mixed with honey.

"Caligula is a god," he announced and with these words sounded the keynote for a vogue of Caligula-worship. The Romans were no novices at this sort of thing. They had seen it all—insanity, perversion, and men who were a blend of emperor, god and animal—yet even some of them were taken aback. There was little enough left to offer Caligula in the way of honors, but Lucius Vitellius could always be relied on for new ideas. He made Caligula his god and danced attendance on him, spinning like a top in the fervor of his devotion.

Caligula's successor Claudius laughed at him delightedly. He liked Lucius. And Lucius lay on his belly before Messalina and begged for one of her shoes. Messalina put out her right foot and Lucius pulled the shoe off. From then on he always carried it between his toga and his tunic. He liked people to be watching when he suddenly produced the shoe and kissed it passionately.

Then he had a stroke and died the next day. The father was gone. What would the son be like?

We are still in 69 A.D., the undistinguished "year of the four emperors." Three of them, Galba, Otho or Vitellius, reigned for no more than a matter of months each. All of them were failures. Yet of the three, Vitellius certainly won the booby prize.

His given name was Aulus, but he was always known by the extremely obscene nickname "Spintria." Aulus had spent his early years in Capri as one of the band of degenerate adolescents whom Tiberius collected about him in the seclusion of that island and christened "*spintriae*."

Having won Tiberius' affections with such success, Aulus Vitellius
ingratiated himself in turn with Caligula, as his chariot driver, with
Claudius, as his gambling companion, and with Nero, as his *vox populi*,
or "spokesman of the people." (Once, when Nero was leaving the
circus—reluctantly, because he was itching to take part in a lyre-
playing contest—Aulus Vitellius brought him back, assuring him that
the public were clamoring to hear him.)

With the backing of so many emperors, Vitellius could hardly fail to
get ahead in life. The stages of his political career covered a senior
priesthood, the proconsulship of Africa, and finally the Roman equiva-
lent of the Ministry of Public Works. He murdered his son by his
first wife, Petronia; then his second wife, Galeria Fundana, bore him
another son whose tongue was so badly malformed that he could
hardly speak.

In the year 68 A.D., something quite unexpected happened. Galba
sent Vitellius to Lower Germany, a strange thing to do, because
Vitellius could well prove dangerous in his new job. But Galba said,
and he was probably right, that the least dangerous men are those
whose main interests lie in the direction of eating and drinking. And
Vitellius was a glutton such as even Rome, the home of gluttony,
could seldom boast.

Vitellius was also bankrupt. He rented an attic for his wife, son and
daughter, so that he could let his house, but he lived at such a rate that
all he amassed was debts. And now that he had been posted to Germany
he needed money. So desperate was he that he even visited his mother
and took a pearl earring out of her ear. He was dogged by duns and
creditors wherever he went, plagued by people whom he had cheated,
whose taxes he had embezzled. Vitellius turned, at bay. His omnipresent tormentors, who worried him by day and even awoke him
at night, had to be stopped or silenced, either by counteraccusations or
blackmail.

Vitellius was not without a certain native cunning. He made a practice of warmly embracing his private soldiers. Whenever he met livery-
men and travelers on the road he would greet them cordially, asking
them how they were. In camp he played the paternal, generous, benevo-
lent general. He canceled punishments, dismissed charges, extended
leave, and distributed presents. It was late one evening when his soldiers
finally gave vent to their affection for him. They hauled him out of
his quarters in his house-clothes and proclaimed him emperor.

They had not chosen a very auspicious time. It was January 2, 69 A.D., and the second day of each month was regarded as unlucky. Bleary-eyed with sleep, Vitellius was carried through the streets of Colonia Agrippinensis, holding a sword which had once belonged to the Deified Julius Caesar.

As dawn broke, flames leapt into the sky. It was the second unlucky omen. . . . The General's dining room had caught fire. Fortunately he had the presence of mind to quickly dispel any superstitious presentiments by exclaiming, "The sky is shining for us!"

Vitellius adopted the surname Germanicus, defeated Emperor Otho's legions, ordered some executions, and sat back to enjoy his victory. When told how his cohorts were burning and looting, he merely laughed. Slaves were set free, and there were floggings galore as Vitellius used brute force on anyone he disliked.

Mountains of dead lay on the battlefield at Betriacum, where Otho's forces had been defeated. Vitellius' staff recoiled from the mounds of decomposing flesh. Not so the new emperor. "Ah!" he cried. "Slaughtered enemies smell good, don't they, but dead Romans smell even better!" He handed around some flagons of wine and took a drink with his officers and men.

Then came the entry into Rome. Trumpet calls heralded a new era of imperial madness as the emperor marched in at the head of his legions, arrayed in his general's cloak. Vitellius seems to have modeled himself on Nero, for he held a memorial service in his honor and led the applause when some of Nero's songs were performed afterward. He even tried to out-Nero Nero. Referring to Nero's Golden House, he said that it was beyond his comprehension how Nero could have lived so poorly. Such of Nero's courtiers as were still alive rubbed their hands gleefully and looked forward to a return of the good old days.

Unfortunately Vitellius did not have much time to spare for his official duties and left the administration of public and private affairs to his favorite, Asiaticus, an emancipated slave with whom he was on only too intimate terms. Once, growing tired of his master's whims, Asiaticus ran away to Puteoli and became a seller of posca, a drink made of sour wine or vinegar mixed with water. Vitellius caught up with him, clapped him in irons, then freed him again. But his favorite became fractious once more, so he sold him to an itinerant trainer of gladiators. However, when the time came for young Asiaticus to enter the arena, Vitellius impulsively withdrew him from the contest and set him free.

Breakfast, lunch, dinner and, after it, a drinking session: these were the important events in the emperor's daily life. Roman historians could only explain his huge and unnatural capacity for food by assuming that he emptied his stomach after each meal by tickling his throat with a feather. Constant practice had made him an expert at vomiting. Unfortunately he seldom had any money, so he made a habit of visiting several wealthy Romans every day. Anyone who was honored in this way and spent less than four hundred thousand gold pieces to entertain his imperial guest was likely to forfeit his head.

To celebrate the emperor's arrival in Rome, his brother gave a banquet at which two thousand rare fish and seven thousand fowl were said to have been served. But perhaps the high spot in the history of the royal cuisine occurred when Vitellius dedicated to the goddess Minerva an immense silver dish containing pike livers, pheasant brains, peacock brains, flamingo tongues, and lamprey milt, all blended with the rarest oils and sauces. Vitellius' appetite grew with eating. There were times, between meals, when there was nothing to eat at all. The emperor found this unendurable, especially at night when the chefs were asleep. He would blunder about the palace, ransacking the cellars and leaving a trail of broken jars and pots in his wake. But there was something else in the emperor's life which brought him anguish: the smell of baked meat and cakes which rose to his nostrils when he was sacrificing. He could never refrain from snatching tidbits from the altar or the sacred fire and wolfing them on the spot.

Vitellius' inordinate appetite was matched only by his infinite cruelty. He ordained all sorts of subtle punishments and was always inventing new ways of getting rid of people. But he was at his most implacable when revenging himself on his creditors. He had only to catch sight of someone who had lent him money in the past to order his arrest. Sometimes, to make revenge even sweeter, he would reprieve men who had just been condemned and then have them slain before his very eyes. As under several of the emperor's predecessors, it again became dangerous to be remembered in a will, since the emperor frequently ordered the garroting of heirs as well as testators.

Then there were the astrologers. Known as "Chaldeans" because Babylon was the home of astrology, they had painstakingly forecast the date of the emperor's death. Vitellius banished them from Rome and persecuted them, killing many of their number. He is even said to have starved his mother to death when she fell sick because a Chattian woman had prophesied that he would reign in safety if he outlived her.

Vitellius reigned for eight months "in a constant stupor," as the Roman historian Dio Cassius puts it. Then his legions began to defect and swear to allegiance to Vespasian. Vitellius became frightened, began to bribe anyone whom he could still hope to win over with vast sums of money and made promises which he could never have kept, even if he had won, to those who volunteered to fight for him. He dispatched a fleet against the enemy under the command of his brother, but his army was defeated at Cremona in northern Italy by Vespasian's legions. When he learned of this defeat, Vitellius abdicated and announced his intention of retiring into private life, but was immediately dissuaded by his flatterers.

But his position was now deteriorating rapidly, so he suggested that the Senate should send envoys to discuss peace terms. By this time, however, Vespasian was close at hand so Vitellius attempted to escape, accompanied only by a baker and a cook. But, frightened, he soon gave up the attempt and returned to the imperial palace in Rome, only to find it forlorn and deserted. Buckling a belt full of gold pieces about his massive body, the emperor shut himself up in the porter's lodge, leaving a dog tied up outside and barricading the door with beds and other articles of furniture. Before long Vespasian's advance guard arrived. The soldiers searched every room until, finally, they came upon the strange porter.

"Where is Vitellius?" they asked him. The trembling emperor tried to keep up the deception, but he was recognized. He begged and implored them for mercy, telling them that they could lock him up as long as they did not kill him. He reminded them that he had been emperor, and knew things which could save Vespasian's life. All to no avail. The soldiers tied his hands behind his back, put a noose round his neck and half naked, his clothes in ribbons, he stumbled through the streets while his captors manhandled and reviled him. They even pulled his head back by the hair and strapped a sword to his chest, point uppermost, so that he could not bow his head and hide his face.

A man with so many victims to his credit was not allowed to die quickly. He was tortured to death with countless small wounds, then dragged into the Tiber on a hook. His brother and son followed him.

154

VITELLIUS

The war was over but, as Tacitus remarks, peace had not yet broken out. Vitellius' supporters were tracked down, both in Rome and the provinces, and some were annihilated by the revolutionaries. Vitellius died at the age of fifty-five. The soothsayers' forecast had been accurate.

HIS WITTY MAJESTY

[Caenis] received vast sums from many sources, sometimes selling governorships, sometimes procuratorships, generalships and priesthoods, and in some instances even imperial decisions. ... And to Titus, who expressed his indignation at the tax placed upon public urinals—one of the new taxes that had been established—he said, as he picked up some gold pieces that had been realized from this source and showed them to him: "See, my son, if they have any smell."

—Dio Cassius, lxv, 14.

ROME had had three emperors within a year as three army commanders had made their way to the throne. It was now to have a fourth. But where Galba of the Spanish legions, Otho of the Rhine legions and Vitellius of the Palatine troops had all failed to hold the imperial throne once they had attained it, Vespasian from the eastern command had the firmest grip and kept the prize. The line of born or adopted Caesars had died with Nero, and Caesar ceased to be a family name of the Roman emperors and became a title—both secular and, increasingly, religious as emphasis on worship of the ruler, Divus Caesar, the Caesar god, increased.

If the Flavian clan who now succeeded had no distinguished ancestors, their country had no need to be ashamed of them. Titus Flavius Vespasianus was born in the small hamlet of Falacrina, above Reate (modern Rieti) in Sabine territory. He was the son of a customs supervisor and of an energetic woman from Nursia, Polla Vespasia, who wanted her son to do big things in life and make a great political career. It is interesting to note, incidentally, that the Flavian family was of Etruscan stock.

Titus Flavius was brought up by his grandmother Tertulla on her country estate, and later, as Emperor Vespasian, he was often drawn back to this scene of his youth, and never forgot his grandmother's ministrations. He always drank from Tertulla's small silver wine goblet on feast days, and took care to see that her villa was maintained in its original condition, like a museum.

Vespasian's wife, Flavia Domitilla, who was the former mistress of a Roman knight, bore him three children: Titus, Domitian, and a daughter. After her death, before 69 A.D. he took a freedwoman, Caenis, who had once been secretary to Antonia, the mother of Claudius, as his concubine and, the historians tell us, treated her "almost in the place of a just wife."

Caenis possessed the two finest attributes a secretary can have: a good memory and a sense of discretion. Not surprisingly, the emperor remained faithful to her until she died. It was not until after her death that he acquired the numerous other concubines who, we are told on good authority, used to lie beside him in a row during his siesta.

Under Claudius, Vespasian had won a great reputation in Germany and, more particularly, in Britain, where he had fought thirty engagements on Rome's behalf, captured more than twenty towns, and conquered Vectis, now the Isle of Wight. In the year 63 A.D. he became governor of Africa, where he ruled extremely badly—according to Tacitus—and extremely well—according to Suetonius. But Vespasian was as unsuccessful at ingratiating himself with Nero as he had been successful with Caligula. He obviously could not stand Nero's interminable arias, because he was forbidden further access to the imperial court for falling asleep during performances.

It was at about this time that the little country where Jesus Christ had been born made several sudden, repeated and mysterious appearances on the stage of Roman history. The Jewish Messianic belief had produced a dangerous ideology. The Roman historian Suetonius records that there was prevalent in the East at this time a firm belief that out of Judaea would come "mastery over the world."

For several years this idea that they and their national God were destined to rule over every other nation on earth had caused outbursts of hatred and physical violence among the Jews in Caesarea and elsewhere. Palestine had long been under Roman control. And while it had been prophesied to the Jews that their God would hold sway over all other nations, they were now thinking of worldly, not spiritual domination. They rebelled—against Rome, every Roman, and every friend of Rome.

It was to combat this threat that fifty-eight-year-old Vespasian was given command of the legions in Judaea in the year 67. Taking his son Titus with him as second-in-command, Vespasian occupied Galilee and Samaria and after a series of engagements reached the Sea of Galilee.

Mount Tabor fell, as did the fortress of Jotapata with Titus the first Roman to set foot on the walls during the final assault.

The defender of Jotapata was a priest, Joseph ben Mattathias, who, when the town fell, saved his life by calmly walking over to the Roman camp. Standing before General Vespasian in chains, he made a momentous prophecy: "You have put me in fetters now, but in a year's time, as emperor, you will set me free."

The priest and prophet Joseph ben Mattathias became known to posterity as Josephus and is responsible for much of our detailed information about this period. He settled in Rome, became a Roman citizen, and wrote, among other important works, a twenty-volume history of the Jews from the Creation to 66 A.D.

The year 69 A.D. saw the fulfillment of the great Jewish historian's prophecy. On July 1 Vespasian was proclaimed emperor by the legions at Alexandria, and on July 3 by the army in Judaea. And once again we meet a reminder of Christ. Vespasian's authority lacked divine confirmation. People expected a miracle from him. In Egypt, a blind man and a cripple implored the emperor to cure them. Vespasian would have nothing to do with such superstition and advised them to go to a doctor, but friends talked him into trying to heal the two men, and history relates that he did in fact succeed. "And many false prophets shall rise, and shall deceive many," Christ had said (Matthew xxiv: 11). The Romans heard rumors of this miracle and the emperor's stock rose rapidly.

Many good things are reported of Vespasian. He subjected the Roman army to strict discipline and made sure that his authority was legally ratified by the Senate and the people. A tantalizing portion of the verbatim text of this statute survives on a metal plaque discovered in Rome. To one youth who reeked of perfume he said, "I'd sooner you stank of garlic."

Rome, large parts of which still lay in ruins as a result of the great fire of Nero's reign, was rebuilt under Vespasian who personally shoveled away the first pile of rubble. Owners of real estate who left their land vacant could now be dispossessed by anyone who cared to build on it. Near the Forum, Vespasian erected the Temple of Peace, and in the middle of the city, by the site of Nero's Golden House, there arose the great Flavian amphitheater which later became known as the Colosseum. It does not owe its name to its size, by the way, but to the immense statue or colossus of Emperor Nero which stood close by.

To bring a morally degenerate Rome to its senses, the emperor prompted the Senate to enact a decree whereby any woman who had an affair with another person's slave became a slave herself. People were not used to having such a virtuous emperor at the helm of the Roman empire. This man of humble origins who had won the throne and apparently wanted to make a clean sweep of everything was something quite new—almost scandalous. Amazing rumors went the rounds. Vespasian had no scores to settle. He was not fond of bloodshed. He felt so safe that he did not even post sentries outside his palace. It was true that he presented animal-baiting displays in the amphitheaters, but he took no pleasure in contests between human beings. He sighed and shed tears if ever he had to sign a death warrant. He set no store by outward marks of respect, and was straightforward, unostentatious and kind. His Imperial Majesty even took his own boots off, which the court found almost incredible.

One could make jokes about the emperor and abuse him to his face without risking punishment. Demetrius the Cynic was most disrespectful to the emperor on one occasion and went unpunished. Vespasian merely called him "dog," that was all. The Cynic philosophers, incidentally, took their name from the Cynosarges College in Athens, where they taught. Since they recommended a return to Nature and despised civilization, they represented a "dog's philosophy," so to speak—*kuōn* being the Greek for "dog." "You're doing your best to get me to kill you, but I don't kill dogs for barking," Vespasian said.

Vespasian was always in particularly good form at table. He loved to crack jokes and tell stories. And if some of his jokes were indecent, many were extremely witty, too. On one occasion Mestrius Florus pointed out to him that the Latin word for carts should be pronounced *plaustra*, not *plostra*. From then on, the emperor made a point of addressing Florus as "Flaurus."

Vespasian often poked fun at himself, which brings us to the thrifty side of the great man's nature which was forced on him by the general poverty following Nero and the Civil War. He found, at the very beginning of his reign, that he needed four billion sesterces, or nearly $112,000,000, to save the nation from the bankruptcy to which his predecessors had reduced it. Vespasian accordingly raised the level of taxation, increased the provincial tributes, and swung very clever business deals. He bought up scarce commodities and when his operations made them even scarcer unloaded them at a large profit. Suetonius asserts that he also sold official appointments and pardons. The Alexandrians called him "salt-fish dealer." Once, with a comedian called Favor giving the customary imitations of his mannerisms and tricks of speech, "Vespasian" asked how much his funeral would cost. Ten million sesterces, came the reply. "Then give me a hundred thousand and throw me into the Tiber!" he shouted. He had undoubtedly inherited some of his business acumen from his father the customs supervisor.

Vespasian introduced a tax on urine, a valuable commodity at this time since it was used as a tanning agent. When his son Titus protested about it, Vespasian held a coin under his nose and asked him, "Does it smell?" Titus agreed that it did not. Hence, perhaps, the celebrated expression *non olet*, "It doesn't smell," meaning money is money no matter from where it comes. Vespasian could be very witty. Even on his deathbed, when he realized that his illness was fatal, he cracked: "Dear me! I think I am becoming a god."

Vespasian was of medium height, sturdily built, but certainly not handsome. Indeed his face always wore the expression of one who was a martyr to poor digestion. He used to get up very early each morning to read the incoming mail and official reports, receiving his friends even while dressing. Then he worked on, allowing himself only a break for a short walk, until it was time for his afternoon rest. After that he took a bath. He was particularly fond of taking cold baths, a habit which is said to have brought on intestinal trouble. Even when he was sixty-nine and extremely ill he still transacted affairs of state from his bed, received deputations, and supervised the courts and their decisions.

He did not want to die—not lying down, at least. And so in his last moments he exerted all his remaining strength in an effort to stand up. Then, with the words "An emperor ought to die on his feet," the tough and virile old man breathed his last in the arms of the courtiers who were supporting him. Honest bourgeois, Etruscan, and son of the Sabine soil, he had lived for sixty-nine years, seven months, and seven days.

THE ERUPTION OF VESUVIUS

Ashes were already falling on us....I looked back. A
dense vapor was coming up behind us, like a stream
poured out on the ground....The darkness returned ...
[and, with it] such an intense and heavy rain of ashes that
we often had to stand up and shake them off to avoid
being covered over and stifled by their weight.
—Pliny the Younger to Cornelius
Tacitus, Book vi, Letter 20.

TITUS became emperor at the age of forty and was dead two years later, in his prime. But, although he reigned for only two years, people continued to sing his praises for centuries. He was like a beacon shining in the darkness of the imperial era of Rome. He was, as Suetonius aptly remarks, "the love and darling of mankind."

Titus Flavius Vespasianus was brought up at Nero's court with Britannicus, whom Nero poisoned. Indeed it is said that he was re-clining next to Britannicus at the time of his death and that he drank some of the poison, making himself extremely ill. That was in the year 55, when he was sixteen.

We have already heard how Vespasian took his son to Judaea, how Titus helped subjugate the country, and how he was the first to climb the walls of Jotapata. In the year 70 with his father now emperor, Titus besieged Jerusalem. Three fortified strongholds had to be taken individually: the Lower City, the Upper City, and the Temple. The Jews fought with a fire and determination born of their absolute faith in God, but bastion after bastion fell and the Temple at last went up in flames. The priests hurled themselves onto their enemies' swords, killed one another, or sprang into the flames. As Dio Cassius remarks (lxvi, 6): "In perishing thus, beneath the ruins of their temple, they all saw not death but victory, salvation and happiness."

As Titus was leaving Judaea, the soldiers hailed him as Imperator and implored him to stay or take them with him. A suspicion some-how arose that Titus intended to sever connections with his father and set himself up as emperor of the East. However, he hurried to Rome as fast as he could and greeted Vespasian with the words: "Here

161

I am, Father, here I am!" Examples of such mutual trust and understanding between father and son are rare in the history of the Caesars.

Titus played an active part in public affairs. He issued edicts and even dictated letters in his father's name, and was regarded by him as colleague. And as commander of the praetorian guard he became known for his forceful methods, and soon earned a reputation for severity by killing off several men whom he suspected of being a threat to his father or himself.

The Romans were not too sanguine about the heir apparent and his pleasure-loving disposition. He spent night after night drinking with friends; he consorted with a bunch of disreputable young men; and, worst of all, there was his scandalous affair with Queen Berenice.

Berenice was a sister of the Jewish king Herod Marcus Julius Agrippa II, with whom she maintained an incestuous relationship, having previously been married to two men in quick succesion. We learn (Acts xxvi) that she heard Saint Paul speak in Caesarea. Having helped to put Vespasian, Titus' father, on the throne, she now became the son's mistress, married him in secret, and bound him to her with the remarkable beauty for which she was renowned the world over. But the Romans knew too much about this woman. They were worried about Titus and his way of life, apprehensive of him even before he became emperor.

Their fears were unfounded. The moment he became Caesar, Titus broke with the worthless cronies of his youth, chose distinguished men as his advisers, and banished Berenice from Rome.

Few other rulers in human history were better-intentioned, yet few had so little time allowed them or were subjected to such severe ordeals. In 79 A.D., just two months after Titus became emperor, Italy was rent by a great natural catastrophy: the terrible eruption of Vesuvius which engulfed the towns of Herculaneum, Pompeii and Stabiae and had been heralded, from 63 A.D. onward, by a series of devastating earthquakes.

The Roman historian Dio Cassius, who was born in 155 A.D., gives a description, based upon hearsay, of how the eruption began: how flames burst from Vesuvius and "beings of superhuman size appeared on the mountains and floated through the air," how the air became oppressive and sultry and the ground trembled, how the whole of Campania "undulated" and the mountaintops "skipped." "Day turned to night, and light to darkness." A firsthand and thus more valuable account of the eruption of Vesuvius on August 23 and 24 can be found in the famous letters of Pliny the Younger. Pliny, who was born at Como in 62 A.D. and was to become a wealthy orator, author and patron of the sciences, was seventeen when Vesuvius erupted. In the course of the eruption his mother's brother, Pliny the Elder, lost his life. Pliny the Elder, besides being an admiral, was an extremely erudite man. Indeed he fell prey to his scientific curiosity for, whereas most people fled from the danger zone, the admiral sailed off to Stabiae (modern Castello a Mare) in the Bay of Naples in order to get as close to the natural phenomenon as he could, and was undeterred even when the showers of stones and clouds of vapor became intolerable.

Present-day scholars know almost precisely how the inhabitants of Pompeii and Herculaneum met their end since the lava ashes which buried them hardened and took on the shape of their bodies in the very moment of death. The bodies then decayed away to nothing, leaving only hollow concavities. In 1865 the Italian archaeologist Giuseppe Fionelli hit upon the idea of filling these concavities with liquid plaster of Paris. As a result, human figures were recovered, still wearing on their faces the expressions which they had worn when they died on that dreadful day in 79 A.D. The catastrophe seemed to have taken its victims completely unaware. Their posture still denoted quite clearly that, even at the moment of their death, death itself was very far from their thoughts. Hence the plaster "reincarnations" of people sitting, sleeping, or making love. In one shop a customer was found with coins still lying on the counter before him.

What actually killed all these unsuspecting people? Was it the volcano's poisonous gases? Were the inhabitants suffocated by a rain of ashes? Was it the heat?

The historian Tacitus tried to elicit an exact account of his uncle's death from seventeen-year-old Pliny. In Pliny's letter of reply we possess a precise description by a contemporary of the way in which the inhabitants of the flat land below Vesuvius met their end. Pliny, who was close at hand with his mother in Misenum, wrote: "Then the flames and the sulphurous smell which preceded them put the others to flight. But he [his uncle] was only heartened by them. He rose to his feet, supported by two slaves, but suddenly sank down again. In my opinion, the dense smoke had obstructed his breathing and blocked his stomach. When day came once more his body was found quite untouched, without injury, and still dressed in the same clothes. His expression was that of a man asleep, not dead."

The overwhelming of Pompeii and Herculaneum was followed by "a frightful plague, the like of which had never been seen before." It was assumed that this epidemic had been spread by the rain of ashes from the eruption. Dio Casius reports that their volume was so enormous that they even reached Africa and Syria.

Emperor Titus at once set off for Campania where he set up a relief organization, gave financial assistance to the victims of the disaster, and used the resources of those who had died intestate as a result of the eruption to help the survivors.

But in the following year, while he was still absent from the capital, Rome was devastated by a fire which raged for three days and nights, gutting the Capitol, the Temple of Jupiter, the Pantheon of Agrippa, the Theater of Balbus, and the Octavian buildings together with their libraries. Although Titus' first reaction was one of near despair, he soon pulled himself together and began to lend a hand. He ordered his own houses to be stripped of their ornamentation and used it for the reconstruction of buildings and temples.

Since Nero's time and during the reigns of Galba, Otho and Vitellius, a flourishing community of informers had grown up in Rome. But now Titus made a regular practice of flogging all informers and slanderers in the Forum. Then he had them paraded in the arena of the amphitheater and either auctioned them off as slaves or deported them to the most unhealthy islands in the empire.

No one was ever executed on Titus' orders after he became Pontifex Maximus or with his consent. "I would rather die than kill others," he said. Once when two patricians were brought before him on a charge of conspiring to usurp the throne, Titus told them quietly, "The throne is a gift of Destiny." He sent a message to the mother of one of the men, who was already having visions of her son being nailed to the cross, reassuring her as to his safety. On the following day he assigned them two seats close to his own in the amphitheater. And when the gladiators' weapons were presented for his inspection he handed them to the throne-struck patricians, despite the fact that they had probably been plotting his death.

But then Titus had all the attributes calculated to arouse admiration and affection in others. Although he was not built on heroic lines and had a slight tendency toward corpulence, he was a first-class swordsman and horseman. He was also a good speaker, and quite a talented poet, could sing and play the lyre, and was such an expert at shorthand that he used to compete with his secretaries for fun. He was also very adept at imitating handwriting, and claimed that he would have made a successful forger.

Titus' first wife was Arrecina Tertulla. On her death, he married Marcia Furnilla, who bore him a daughter, Julia, and whom he later divorced. Julia became Domitian's mistress and was ultimately deified.

The emperor was completely incorruptible and never accepted gifts or favors from anyone, whether private citizen, city corporation or foreign king, even though the whole of the contemporary world would gladly have laid its treasures at his feet. At the same time he was extremely generous. He turned the dedication of the Colosseum, which had been begun by Vespasian and only now, in the year 80, was completed, into a great national festival lasting a hundred days. He had cranes do battle first with dwarfs (Homer's *Iliad*), and then with four elephants. Nine thousand beasts were baited to death, some of them by women animal tamers. Gladiators fought land and sea battles (during which the arena of the Colosseum was filled with water), and there were performances by trained horses, bulls and other animals. The Colosseum had audiences estimated at 45,000, but since there were many numbered entrances and tickets corresponding to them, the vast crowds could always find their seats with ease and file out smoothly after each performance. Emperor Titus may well have been the inventor of the lottery. He had the spectators showered with little wooden balls containing small coupons which could be exchanged for the various articles marked on them, including items of clothing, silver and gold vessels, horses, cattle, goats, sheep, and even slaves.

The baths hurriedly constructed by Titus above Nero's Golden House (the famous Baths of Titus, where the Laocoön group was found) were also completed at this time, and their opening celebrated in a befitting manner. The people accepted all these blessings with a mixture of amazement, bewilderment and delight.

No one who approached the emperor with a request or petition was ever prevented from stating his case or sent away without hope. When people warned him that he would never be able to fulfill all the promises he made, he answered, "No one who has spoken to Titus shall go away disappointed." On another occasion, when it occurred to him at supper that he had done nobody a favor all day long, he said, "My friends, I have lost a day." For he was a ruler who never lost an opportunity to endear himself to his subjects. It was almost as though he guessed that he was only to be granted two years on the throne. He never omitted to give the poor free access to the public baths and—a shrewd stroke of psychology—at times even chose to let them in when he was bathing there himself.

As we have already seen, fate was unkind to this worthy emperor during his reign, with its volcanic eruptions, earthquakes, plagues and conflagrations. But Titus had another and perhaps even greater worry. His brother Domitian spent his whole time conspiring against him, stirring up disaffection in the army, and creating bad blood generally. Yet Titus never let himself be nettled into punishing or exiling him, but often implored him in confidence to return his own brotherly affection.

When the great festivals of dedication were over, the emperor wept bitterly in the presence of the people as if aware that his end was near. In the summer of 81 A.D. he set off for Sabine territory, only to be struck down by fever the very first night. He continued his journey by litter, pulling the curtains apart to gaze up into the sky, saying plaintively, "I do not deserve to have my life taken from me. I have done nought to repent of—save one thing."

The historians Suetonius and Dio Cassius assert that nobody knew what he was referring to. Some people presumed that Titus was thinking of the illicit relationship which he was supposed to have had with Domitia, his brother's wife. Against this, there is Domitia's solemn oath that no such relationship existed. Suetonius argues very plausibly that Domitia would never have denied such a thing if it had been true, since she was only too happy to brag about her other vices. Dio Cassius offers another and equally plausible explanation. He thinks that the emperor may have considered it a crime not to have executed his brother Domitian, who was quite openly plotting against his life. This would fit in with the belief, prevalent at the time, that Domitian either caused or accelerated his brother's death. There were rumors of poison. Dio Cassius asserts that Domitian put his brother, still breathing and possibly not beyond hope of recovery, into a receptacle filled with snow. He said it was to reduce his temperature but in reality he wanted to hasten his death.

Titus died at the age of forty-two in the same country house, the old family seat in Sabine country, where his father had died before him. The whole nation mourned the dead emperor, and the Senate heaped him with panegyrics and honors. The Jews, on the other hand, asserted that Titus' untimely end was a punishment for having destroyed the Temple at Jerusalem.

As for Domitian, he galloped off to Rome without even waiting for his brother to die, burst into the praetorian camp, and had himself proclaimed emperor.

THE EMPEROR IS CATCHING FLIES

Domitian was impetuous and quick-tempered, but he was also
spiteful and cunning. . . . He never genuinely liked any human
being, a few women excepted, and if he did act as though he liked
someone it was sure to be because he had earmarked him as his
next victim.

—Dio Cassius, lxvii, 1.

"IS ANYONE with the emperor?"

The question was directed at Vibius Crispus by a visitor who desired to speak to Emperor Domitian urgently.

"Not even a fly," came the answer.

Bewildered, the stranger repeated his question.

"Not even a fly," Crispus reiterated. The words were not as silly as they seemed. Although it was supposed to be a close secret, the whole court knew that the emperor retired to his private quarters for hours each day to catch flies. Having caught them, he would impale them on a sharpened stylus.

After his wife Domitia had borne him a son, Domitian saluted her as Augusta, or Empress, but he divorced her at short notice when she fell in love with the actor Paris. This handsome Casanova, who was idolized by ladies of the highest rank, incurred Domitian's jealousy and was murdered in the street. However, the emperor soon invited his divorced wife to rejoin him. "I don't know how I feel about it," he said, "but it is the will of the people." This was a brazen lie, of course. Domitia was the daughter of a famous general and had previously been married to Aelius Lamia, a most unfortunate individual. First the emperor seduced his wife, and then had him executed. Domitia, it may be added, went in constant fear of her imperial husband's displeasure.

Domitian sought to outdo all the emperors before him. He organized spectacles of fantastic splendor, presenting sea battles, animal-baiting and gladiatorial contests in the Colosseum, and arranging large-scale battles and two- or four-horse chariot races in the Circus Maximus. Other novelties included gladiatorial contests by torchlight and, as in Nero's time, between female combatants.

Domitian presented a strange appearance. His face was always red, probably with rouge—perhaps, as Tacitus suggests, because he wanted to hide his blushes, or perhaps because he sought to give an impression of vigor and energy. The eyes which stared into the arena were large but weak. In later years Domitian grew paunchy and bald, and was deeply offended if anyone joked about his lack of hair. He even wrote a small treatise on the care of the hair and presented it to a friend with a bald head with the following dedication: "You see what a tall, handsome figure I have: yet my hair will go the same way as yours. I bear it bravely, though it makes me an old man before my time. Always reflect that there is nothing finer and nothing more fleeting than beauty."

Whenever the emperor sat in his imperial box he was accompanied by a scarlet-clad dwarf with an extraordinarily small and malformed head. He was often heard chatting to this dwarf, and it was whispered that the big man discussed things of the utmost importance with his minute companion.

Domitian issued several strange decrees. He forbade actors and dancers to appear on the stage and only allowed them to perform at private houses. He prohibited castration and reduced the price of such eunuchs as the slave dealers still had "in stock." Women of doubtful reputation were forbidden to ride in litters or benefit under wills. Inchastity among Vestal virgins he at first punished by a simple death penalty, but he later treated them "after the custom of our fore-fathers." This meant that (as in the case of the chief Vestal Cornelia) they were buried alive and their lovers flogged to death with sticks. Domitian instigated many such trials, though Pliny tells us that the priestesses' guilt may not have been established in any instance.

Apparently Domitian's cruel streak only declared itself gradually, at first he seemed to shun all bloodshed, and even proposed to forbid the slaughter of oxen. Later he became spiteful and an expert at shock tactics. Issuing cordial invitations to the people whom he had marked out for brutal punishment, he put on his brightest manner, commended them heartily, and then pronounced their death sentence.

Domitian slowly bled his subjects white. Property was confiscated on the slightest pretext and trials for *lèse-majesté* took place as they had under Tiberius, who served as Domitian's model in this respect. The emperor's palaces swallowed up enormous sums. Each roof tile had to be overlaid with gold leaf. We are told that a special tax was imposed on the Jews, who had formerly paid their taxes to Jerusalem but since the time of Titus had paid them to the emperor as a sort of protection money which secured them religious toleration.

The Christians probably had to pay such protection too, since they came under the category of those "who disguised their origins." Certainly ecclesiastical history relates that Domitian actively oppressed the Christians, and the third Bishop of Rome was a victim of this persecution. Suetonius recalls that in his youth he was present when a ninety-year-old man was forced to show the procurator and a large tribunal whether he was circumcised or not to see if he was evading taxes.

Domitian was quite as arrogant as ever Nero was. On recalling his wife he declared that she was being allowed to take her place on the "couch of the gods" once again. "Hail to our Lord and Lady!" cried the audience in the amphitheater, and Domitian's edicts were prefaced by the words: "Our Lord and God commands . . ." He was thus the first emperor to demand baldly that the Romans recognize him as a god during his lifetime, thus following the example of Nero and Caligula to its logical conclusion. Indeed, it became his official mode of address. Domitian also took great care to see that the statues erected in his honor on the Capitol were of solid gold or silver. Their poundage was carefully calculated, and woe betide everyone if they proved to be underweight. And the emperor put up so many triumphal arches decorated with four-horse chariots and triumphal insignia that the people went out at night and scribbled *Enough!* on one of them.

The campaigns and wars of conquest which Domitian waged in the Taunus region on the German frontier, in Britain, and on the lower Danube owed their success at least in part to the fact that he had a number of competent military commanders. But, like Nero, he was jealous of his generals' achievements, often recalling them when they were on the verge of an expedition of any scope, as it was said he did with Agricola, the doughty general who reached Scotland.

It seems incredible that Domitian's kind of regime could have lasted for fifteen long years. The great historian Rostovtzeff compares it with a return to the worst times under Tiberius, Caligula and Nero. Wherever the emperor went, he aroused fear, alarm and hatred. Certainly conspirators constantly went about their silent and sinister work, usually aided and abetted by his wife Domitia. And as usual, the Chaldeans or soothsayers foretold the emperor's assassination. Pliny tells us that Domitian imported some white, marblelike stones from Cappadocia which shone like a mirror when they were polished, and used them to line the walls of the rooms and passages where he spent most of his time. Ever apprehensive of the assassin's dagger, he never took his weary eyes from the mirror-stones for he was only happy if he could see what was going on behind him. When he was interrogating prisoners he now shut himself in alone with them, holding their chains tightly in his hand.

The astrologer Ascletarion had predicted that Domitian would be murdered. Domitian then asked him how he, the astrologer, would meet his end. Ascletarion replied that he would shortly be torn to pieces by dogs. The emperor had him executed and ordered him to be carefully cremated so that no dog could come near him. But a storm blew the pyre over, and Ascletarion's half-burned body was, in fact, torn to pieces by dogs. This convinced Domitian that his own end was near. Sleep deserted him, and at night he would jump out of bed, order torches to be brought in, and stare about him wildly.

On September 16, 96 A.D., the moon entered Aquarius from which it was not due to emerge until September 18. What was more, Mars and Saturn were also under that sign simultaneously, a conjunction which was a sure portent of disaster. The emperor had been told that he would die at the fifth hour, and somewhere about that time he asked how late it was. To reassure him, he was told that it was six o'clock. Greatly relieved, Domitian headed for his bath. Then his steward Parthenius announced that a messenger had arrived and was seeking an immediate audience. Apparently he had discovered a plot against the emperor's life. Ordering everyone to withdraw, Domitian closeted himself alone in his bedroom with the messenger, one Stephanus, who was steward to his Christian niece Domitilla and looked harmless enough. He was wearing a woolen bandage on his left arm because of an injury which he said he had received, but between the bandage and his arm he had concealed a dagger. He handed the emperor a written denunciation of the alleged conspiracy and the emperor began to read it. At that moment Stephanus stabbed him in the groin.

We are told that after the first thrust Domitian called for his servants and bade them pass him the dagger which lay beneath his pillow, but all they found was a bladeless hilt. Mad with rage and terror, the emperor hurled himself on Stephanus. Throwing him to the ground, he tried with bleeding fingers and his last reserves of strength to gouge his eyes out, but Stephanus was too strong for him.

Domitian had reigned for fifteen years. Dio Cassius writes that he was never genuinely fond of any fellow creature. He is said to have been a fine bowman, and used to shoot arrows between the outstretched fingers of young slaves without harming them. He could be witty, too. "I wish," he once said, "I were as handsome as Maecius thinks he is." And, another time: "The sad thing about emperors is that, if they discover a conspiracy, no one believes them unless they are murdered."

Domitian led a lonely existence immediately before his death, even going out walking only in removed areas. But he remained dissolute to the last. After his assassination, Senators smashed his busts with joyous abandon.

LEAVE THE CHRISTIANS ALONE

*I always try, as emperor, to behave toward private citizens as I
had formerly, as a private citizen, wished emperors to behave
to me.*

—Trajan, taken from Eutropius, viii, 5.

SOMETHING new happened in Rome in the year 96 A.D. An emperor
was freely elected from among the members of the Senate. Senator
Nerva was probably sixty-six years old but he was a good lawyer, and
restored some much-needed equilibrium to the state.

All the people whom Domitian had thrown into jail for *lèse-majesté*
were immediately released and exiles were allowed to return to Italy.
On the other hand, many slaves who had denounced their masters during Domitian's reign of terror were now sentenced to death. Nerva
also forbade the prosecution of people "because of their Jewish way
of life"—which perhaps included the Christians. While Domitian's
acts were abolished, Nerva confirmed his benefactions, and a "welfare
fund" was set up for the benefit of destitute Romans. Nerva raised
money to purchase small holdings for these paupers. And when his
court got into financial straits Dio suggests that he sold clothing, gold,
silver plate and valuable household furniture from the imperial palace,
as well as several royal mansions.

The new emperor enforced his economies on the rest of Rome too.
He abolished extravagant sacrifices and limited expenditure on luxuries
such as race meetings and public entertainments. Castration was prohibited, as was marriage between uncle and niece. In his personal life
he was not as successful as in his public one, for he was addicted to drinking and engaged in sexual activities with boys.

Yet it is not surprising that Nerva was soon able to say of himself:
"I have done nothing which would stand in the way of my abdicating
and returning to private life unscathed."

But the worthy man was wrong. His life, too, was threatened.
Minor conspiracies were brewing here and there. At first the emperor
disconcerted the plotters by calmly appearing in their midst unarmed.
But when he got the feeling that people were abusing his kindness,
that they even despised him, perhaps because he was too old, he

The shaded area indicates the extent of the Roman Empire between 117 A.D. (death
Trajan) and 211 A.D. (death of Septimius Severus). The size of the empire remained vir•

ally static until the death of Theodosius in 395, the only territories relinquished being
Dacia (following the Gothic invasions of 250–270), Mesopotamia, and southwest Germany.

adopted the Roman governor of Upper Germany as his son and proclaimed him Caesar and a sharer of the imperial authority. It was the best and most important decision Nerva made during his reign. The Roman historian Eutropius called it an act of "godlike prevision." The fact that, by adopting the man who held the Army's loyalty, Nerva assured himself of that same loyalty must also be considered as a factor in Nerva's action.

Some months later he died and his new son became emperor Marcus Ulpius Traianus. He was a Spanish provincial (which was yet another novelty for Rome), and came of a Roman colonial family from Italica near Seville on the Guadalquivir. Actually Nerva had relatives of his own whom he could have put on the throne, but Rome and the Roman empire were more important to him than his family, and Trajan seemed the man for the job.

Trajan was forty-eight years old when he became emperor by an adoption which had been based on his own merits. That too was a new departure, but it became recognized procedure for the next hundred years, thereby guaranteeing Rome a series of efficient rulers which began with Nerva and ended with Marcus Aurelius, and turning the second century A.D. into the happiest and best period in the history of imperial Rome.

And Trajan, the great man who wanted to be another Alexander but never fully attained his ideal, set out on his career.

He made the most of his time. He rebuilt the dilapidated circus on a larger and more magnificent scale, planned public buildings, highroads and harbors, built a causeway across the Pontine marshes lined with houses and interspersed by numerous bridges, installed forts and crossing places on the German Rhine. His creative energy left its mark deep in the heart of the Danube area. In Africa he reached the borders of the desert and founded the colony of Timgad, the African Pompeii which was discovered under its shroud of sand by archaeologists of our own day.

Trajan loved hunting. He also loved banqueting, but only in moderation, and could drink a great deal of wine without getting drunk. For informers, who were his special bugbear, he reserved a special punishment, which was to flog them, put them on board ship, and send them out into a storm. In other respects he was always sparing in his punishments. He treated the Senate with courtesy and walked through the streets of Rome alone and unescorted.

Endless subterranean corridors in the Catacombs of Domitilla. In 95 A.D. Emperor
Domitian indicted Flavius Clemens and Flavia Domitilla, the parents of his adoptive
sons and heirs, on a charge of "Christian tendencies." Clemens was executed, while
Domitilla and a niece of the same name were exiled. Both women, together with
many other victims of Domitian's reign of terror, were buried in the Catacombs
of Domitilla on the Via Ardeatina, Rome. Their skeletons repose in the walls to
right and left.

The Forum of Nerva at Rome was completed by Emperor Nerva but has recently been proved to have been the work of Domitian. Only two pillars and a portion of the splendid frieze survive. In the foreground is a woman seated at her spindle and some girls stretching yarn. In the background on the right, a young river-god confronted by three girls, and on the left, a girl standing before a seated goddess. One of Martial's epigrams informs us that the Forum of Nerva contained booksellers' shops.

This Roman general's sarcophagus was found in the Villa Ludovisi at Rome, and is known as the "Ludovisi Sarcophagus." The figure with the outstretched arm in the center is the general himself.

Emperor Trajan (reigned 98-117 A.D.) richly merited the name Optimus, "the best," which was later bestowed on him. He was one of the most important and powerful Roman rulers, and under him the Roman Empire reached its point of greatest expansion.

Plotina, wife of Trajan, was renowned for her modesty, dignity, loyalty and virtue. She helped Hadrian to become Trajan's successor.

An interesting scene from the 155 reliefs on Trajan's Column shows Dacian princes reaching for a bowl of poison in their eagerness to commit suicide rather than be brought to Rome in Trajan's triumphal procession.

Trajan's Column, 125 feet high, is a picture book in marble comprising 155 individual scenes. The burial urns of Trajan and his wife Plotina were interred in its base. The column contains a circular staircase and was surmounted, until the Middle Ages, by a statue of Trajan.

Sabina was rarely happy. Emperor Hadrian's wife was a grandchild of Trajan's sister. Hadrian married her in 100 A.D. to help him secure his predecessor's throne.

Handsome Antinoüs was drowned during a trip up the Nile with Hadrian. Hadrian marked the spot by founding the now ruined city of Antinoopolis. The emperor's passion for this young man is one of Roman history's greatest enigmas. It has never been established how Antinoüs was drowned, but the emperor never fully recovered from his grief and built the dead youth numerous temples.

Emperor Hadrian. Genius emerges miraculously from the darkness of human history. Hadrian was a wise man such as the world only sees at intervals of several hundred years, a prince of peace, order and integrity who was endowed with an extraordinarily wide range of talents. He reigned from 117 to 138 A.D.

Hadrian built this tomb for himself and his successors. The burial vault still survives, but nothing has been found of the various emperors' urns and sarcophagi. The building was begun in 130 A.D. and completed by Antoninus Pius in 139. It is now known as the Castle of Santa Angelo, after the archangel who appeared to Pope Gregory the Great during a pilgrimage in 590.

The ruins of Hadrian's Villa, together with the various buildings belonging to it, occupy an area of about 160 acres. The emperor probably took a personal hand in designing the original plans. Sixteen portrayals of Antinoüs, among them statues, busts and reliefs, have been found in the grounds of the villa.

Roman legionaries wore helmets of metal or leather, and war equipment included trumpets. Archaeologists have even unearthed carefully drawn-up military commissions like that on the left.

Hadrian's Wall in England (below, left and extreme right) is almost 70 miles long. This photograph shows one of the forts in the line of defense.

When Pliny the Younger, who was governor of Bithynia under Trajan, wrote to the emperor asking what he should do with the Christians in his province, Trajan wrote back: "They are not to be sought out." Trajan's accession thus ushered in an age of humanity and tolerance. However, one must mention in passing that individuals formally charged as Christians still had to stand trial.

On the north bank of the lower Danube in the Seven Mountains region of Wallachia in eastern Hungary lived the Dacians. All the monographs written in ancient times describing them have been lost, and much of the evidence about them depends on how one interprets the column of Trajan. However it is possible to recreate the events of Trajan's encounters with them to a considerable degree.

Trajan advanced on the Dacians and worsted them, whereupon Decebalus, their highly intelligent, proud and wily King, behaved as though he intended to negotiate for peace and was prepared to make any concession. Then he fought on until his sister fell into Roman hands. Once more the barbarian king seemed willing to submit and even apparently paid homage to Trajan, falling on his knees before him, and throwing his weapons away. Trajan made peace and returned to Italy.

It was not long before news came that King Decebalus and his Dacians had thrown all their agreements overboard. Once again Trajan took personal command of the Roman army, Dacian troops began to desert, and soon King Decebalus was suing for peace again. But simultaneously he recruited a fresh army, bullied a number of tribes into joining forces with him against the Romans, and sent assassins into Trajan's camp who unfortunately for his plans were captured and tortured into admitting their guilt.

Decebalus then tried another ruse. He invited Longinus, a brilliant Roman general who had caused him a great deal of trouble, to pay him a visit and as soon as he had set foot in the barbarian king's camp made him prisoner. Decebalus then offered to release him in return for all the Roman-occupied territory along the Danube. Trajan's reply was couched in such ambiguous terms that he left Decebalus in the dark, but Longinus was loyal to his emperor and, before the barbarian king could do any more blackmailing, he poisoned himself.

Trajan then built a stone bridge across the Danube to help keep the Dacians on the run. Dio Cassius of Bithynia, in his eighty-volume history of Rome written about 229 A.D., gives a glowing description

177

of Trajan's bridge at the Iron Gate. In fact the piers of this bridge still exist to this day. Trajan's other feats of engineering were impressive enough, he writes, but this surpassed them all. The man who actually constructed it was a Greek called Apollodorus of Damascus, one of the greatest engineers and architects in the ancient world.

Using the bridge, Trajan then began a systematic conquest of the Dacians. Decebalus lost first his headquarters and then his whole country, and eventually, when he was threatened with capture, took his own life. His head was brought back to Rome in triumph, and Dacia became a Roman province. An enormous monument commemorating the victory was built in the Dobrudja, the Tropaeum Traiani. It became a city whose ruins were discovered by Moltke in 1837. The spot beneath the bed of the Ister where Decebalus had buried his royal treasures was betrayed to the Romans, who dug them up. It was there by the Ister that the stubborn king had built his residence, a strong fortress, so Dio Cassius tells us, which is surprising when we consider that the Dacians were largely a nomadic people. Their blood was subsequently mingled freely with that of Roman colonists, with the result that the region which they once occupied, now Romania, has a basically Latin language.

Trajan decreed victory celebrations lasting 130 days, during which thousands of wild animals tore each other to pieces and thousands of Dacian prisoners of war went through their paces in the arena. These gory spectacles gave the Roman public their first opportunity of seeing the bravery of the men whom Trajan had defeated. The emperor also put up libraries, commissioned the architect Apollodorus to build the Forum Traiani, a new square between the Capitoline and the Quirinal hills, and erected the most splendid example of Roman sculpture any-where, world-famous Trajan's Column, an amazing history book in stone which depicts the exploits of Roman legions on the Drave, the Save and the Danube in a series of 155 pictures encircling a pillar.

We are shown the bridge under construction; ships sailing along the river heavily laden with supplies; legionaries on the march, on sentry duty, and in action; the emperor himself, on foot as usual, among his troops; Dacian women and children in flight; and repeated portrayals of Quintus Lusius, Trajan's senior general, once a Moroccan sheik but now the emperor's right-hand man.

Of all the honorific titles which the Senate bestowed on Trajan, the one that probably meant the most to him: *Optimus,* "the Best," was a title which matched his character. He owed the rest to his military successes.

Trajan's marriage to Plotina was childless. The empress must have been extremely beautiful, if her coin-portraits are anything to go by. She lived a very quiet life and was a great friend of Marciana, Trajan's sister. On taking up her abode at the imperial palace, she said, "May I leave this house as free from any guilt as I now enter it." It was a vow she never broke.

Trajan could not bear inactivity. He was the last great soldier to occupy the Roman throne, a man who was not only a brilliant statesman but a simple, straightforward and uncommonly powerful personality with the military genius of a Caesar burning within him. He made up his mind to invade Parthia, inspired by the fact that there were Greek cities there culturally related to Rome, magnificent cities like Ctesiphon and Seleucia, which were in the hands of the barbarian Parthians.

Trajan victoriously retraced Alexander the Great's footsteps into the East. He reached Babylon and the Euphrates and ambassadors from India came to his camp. He pushed on into Media and satraps and kings laid gifts at his feet while a trained horse fell on its knees before him. His troops marched, without striking a blow, along the roads of Mesopotamia, Assyria, Armenia. Never before and never again would the Roman empire extend over so great an area as it did under Trajan. But at Antioch the emperor was unexpectedly involved in a terrible earthquake which claimed thousands of victims. (We are in the period between 114 and 116 A.D.) He escaped through the window of a house just before it collapsed, and spent several days in an alfresco bivouac on the local racecourse. Then he resumed his campaign and at last reached the Persian Gulf. The Indian Ocean lay before him, and now he built a fleet with the intention of conquering India, the land of Alexander's dreams.

But behind the Roman conqueror rebellion reared its head and conquered nations defected. That was one respect in which Trajan was unlike Alexander: he could not hold cities, kings or rulers under the spell of his personality or turn them into his permanent vassals. He was not a man to make political marriages, as Alexander did so successfully, and he did not exercise the same effect on Orientals as his glamorous and fortunate Macedonian predecessor. "I should have liked to go to India, too, if I had been younger," he mused resignedly as he watched a ship sailing off to the East.

While the Senate back in Rome was announcing Trajan's victories to the public—with considerable difficulty, since people found it hard to remember all the battles and thread their way through the names of so many distant and unfamiliar countries—Trajan was marching into Arabia against the Atreni, one of the many nations which had rebelled against him. Their capital was neither large nor prosperous and was surrounded by arid and desolate country. The water was bad, there was no wood or grazing and it was dangerous to besiege the place, since it stood "under the protection of the sun-god." Trajan's cavalry was routed and Trajan himself narrowly escaped being wounded. A sandstorm and a plague of flies then compelled the emperor to abandon the siege. That is all we know. We have no idea where the town of Atra or Hatra stood, or what desert dune now covers it.

Trajan still had a thousand plans, but he was old and sick, having long been afflicted with dropsy. He wanted to get back to Italy quickly rather than die on foreign soil, so, leaving one of his generals, Publius Aelius Hadrianus, behind in Syria with the army, he traveled to Cilicia in Asia Minor. There his condition deteriorated.

Trajan was now smitten by a dreadful suspicion that someone was trying to poison him. Then he suffered a stroke which left him partially paralyzed, and able to breathe only with difficulty.

Although the emperor had had plenty of time to arrange it, he had neglected to provide himself clearly with a successor until the end. Trajan died quietly, having reigned for nineteen years, six months and fifteen days.

A STATESMAN ON THE THRONE

EMPEROR TRAJAN was dead. How the legions all over the Roman empire, from Britain to the Nile, from the Guadalquivir in Spain to the Euphrates and Tigris, would mourn when they heard the news. How the Dacians north of the Danube would sigh with relief. Would it mean their freedom? And the Parthians? Would it raise their hopes of peace?

Emperor Trajan was dead, but there was much whispering around his deathbed

His wife Plotina was a clever and accomplished woman who was always one jump ahead of events, both in her ideas and her policies. She and Hadrian, one of her husband's ablest generals, had always got on extremely well, and their Platonic friendship had lasted for twenty years. Hadrian was now forty-one. Plotina wanted to make him emperor, but although Trajan had entrusted him with the highest political appointments and bestowed favors on him which clearly showed that he had made his choice, he had never adopted him.

So the whispering went on around Trajan's deathbed. Attianus and Plotina were very worried. What were they to do? The news of the emperor's death had not escaped the room yet, but beyond the heavy curtains stood sentries, senators talking in low tones, and tribunes awaiting orders for the legions and their generals in Germany, Britain, Egypt, and Parthia.

Suddenly Plotina had an idea. The emperor was dead, but nobody outside knew it yet. He could be made to whisper. Perhaps it was Attianus who impersonated him so effectively. At any event, there issued from the bedchamber of the dead Imperator a weak voice announcing the adoption of Hadrian.

Only then were the curtains drawn back to reveal that the emperor was dead. At last the dispatch riders could gallop off, carrying the news to the four corners of the far-flung empire. Ultimately they reached Antioch, the capital of Syria, where Hadrian was governor.

Publius Aelius Hadrianus enjoyed an unrivaled reputation in the Roman empire. He was also distantly related to Trajan and became his grandnephew by marriage. His father came from the same interesting part of the world as Trajan's, the banks of the Baetis, now the Guadalquivir.

Having lost his father at an early age, Hadrian became the ward of the Emperor Trajan and of the Knight Acilius Attianus. He studied the Greek language at Rome with burning enthusiasm for even as a youth Greece enthralled him. He was fascinated by Greek art and greatly admired Greek sculptors, statesmen and philosophers, especially Plato. The Romans even nicknamed him Graeculus, "the little Greek."

Hadrian joined the army in Spain at the age of fifteen, but his great passion was hunting, and he pursued it madly until Trajan recalled him to Rome about 93 A.D. The normal stages in a Roman public career followed, including a tour of duty with the legions on the Danube, more hunting, wine drinking and debts. Then, like a flash of lightning in the European sky, came the news of Trajan's accession.

Now twenty-two, Hadrian set off on a breakneck journey to Cologne, managing to arrive ahead of his brother-in-law Servianus, who disliked him and was always trying to bring him into Trajan's bad graces. Hadrian congratulated the new emperor.

Actually, Trajan and Hadrian could never have become intimate friends for they were too dissimilar in character. Nevertheless, with Plotina's support, Hadrian found a way of getting close to the emperor. He married Sabina, the granddaughter of Trajan's sister. Trajan was not too pleased with this union but Plotina managed to reconcile him to it. And through it all the Platonic friendship between Plotina and young Hadrian grew increasingly close. Thus, when the messengers galloped up to Hadrian with the news of Trajan's death, he may well have guessed at once that his friend Plotina was behind his own adoption. He informed the Senate of his wish to be confirmed as emperor, but at the same time he declined to accept, either then or in the future, any of the customary marks of honor.

Peace the world over: that was the new emperor's prime consideration from the earliest days of his reign onward. It was an ideal to which he remained true until his death.

There is no doubt that Hadrian's reign was one of the most prosperous and fortunate in ancient history. He was a quite remarkable personality, and for sheer versatility, he towered above every Roman emperor since Augustus. He embodied, for perhaps the last time, all the finest qualities which the ancient world produced: humanity and chivalry, imperviousness to physical hardship, courtesy, an excellent mind, and an amazing diversity of natural gifts.

The new emperor at once abandoned his predecessor's hard-won territory east of the Euphrates and Tigris, recognizing that these areas were untenable with the forces at his disposal. Trajan's conquests in Parthia, Assyria and Mesopotamia were therefore lost to Rome. It was not by caprice however, for Hadrian was a political genius of the first order. Knowing that unrest on such far-distant frontiers would overtax the resources of the Roman empire, he set himself a target: the Roman empire must become defensively strong, must remain entrenched in that position of strength and keep the peace.

It was an unpopular policy, and there were immediate murmurs from Rome's generals. Ambitious officers are never fond of seeing their careers frustrated by everlasting peace.

But Hadrian won the people's backing by the simple expedient of writing off all the sums of money owed by private citizens to the Roman exchequer. There was a tremendous outburst of rejoicing as thousands upon thousands of promissory notes went up in flames in the Forum.

Hadrian then began to put the public finances in order, probing every last detail with remarkable business acumen. He instituted welfare services and granted economic aid to the towns in Campania. He also built up a bond of intimacy between himself and the members of the Senate which rendered fruitful co-operation possible from the very start. He attended senatorial sessions punctually and in person. He safeguarded the Senate's reputation by ensuring that unsuitable candidates were not elected. He visited his friends when they were ill. He entertained a good deal but his banquets were largely devoted to the discussion of affairs of state. He secured the services of numerous shrewd and efficient men.

Hadrian achieved all this without a large outlay. He disliked pomp, luxury and extravagance. He insisted, however, on etiquette and formality, and was himself a model of good breeding, culture and courtesy.

HADRIAN

THE MODERN MONARCH

Who among men had such wide interests, who was so many-sided and mobile, who thought so quickly, knew so much, surprised even those who stood nearest to him by his knowledge of their most secret thoughts? Who was in everything so supple and yet hard as steel, who so cold in calculation and determined in action? He felt the longing of men and gave it fulfilment in philosophical formulae, ideologies, and illusions, but also in deeds, so that they greeted him with exultation where he appeared.
—Wilhelm Weber, *Cambridge Ancient History,*
Volume XI, Chapter viii, 3.

HADRIAN radiated his own private atmosphere. There was a modernity in his preoccupation with things of moment and his lack of interest in mere emperorship. His education had made him Greek to the core, and under him the Hellenic world experienced a spiritual and material renaissance unequaled at any other stage in the imperial era, either before or since. Indirect as it was, defeated Greece had at last won her victory over Rome.

In the fourth year of his reign, 121 A.D., Hadrian set off on his first journey as emperor. He was perhaps the most traveled monarch in world history, and this wanderlust was one of his most noteworthy characteristics.

Always accompanied by his large secretariat, he traveled from one end of the empire to the other, inspecting the administration of justice wherever he went. Traveling along the roads of Europe, North Africa and Asia by coach, horse, or foot, he and his staff of officials constituted a mobile "directorate" with sweeping political powers.

Gaul, Germany, Greece, Asia Minor and Egypt all saw the arrival of the emperor and his large and silent entourage. Hadrian liked people to be quiet in his presence and made it the principal task of a senior official to see that they were. And in proof that if anything held up these long journeys it would not be symptoms of royal fatigue, Hadrian sometimes marched twenty miles or so in full armor. He habitually wore ordinary clothes and shunned gold, jewelry and weapons.

Everywhere throughout the empire he regrouped his armies almost always with an eye to their defensive, not their offensive potentialities. He recruited bodies of militia in all the frontier provinces of the empire to defend the civilized world against the barbarians. And in his administration of the Roman army he outrivaled all the emperors before him. He forbade officers to accept gifts from their men and prohibited all luxury in the legions. Above all, he was endowed with the remarkable talent for sensing with razor-sharp certainty whether an appointment or a contract for military supplies or building materials was useful and expedient, or whether it had been dreamed up merely to provide some organization with work, or perhaps money. Hadrian ruthlessly swept away everything which was at all unnecessary or unprofitable and kept a tight rein on the money- and time-wasting paper warfare and costly red tape which are the bane of any large empire. Hadrian also built up an ideal type of civil servant.

The emperor's mental flexibility and lack of prejudice were amazing. His very beard was an outward and visible sign of this. It must be borne in mind that ever since the time of Alexander the Great, about five hundred years earlier, the whole of the Graeco-Roman world had gone about clean-shaven, the only exceptions being nonconformists like Christians and philosophers. Socrates wore a beard, as did Plato and Epicurus. And now Hadrian's beard was a token of his archaistic leanings. It was precisely this devotion to an ancient past which put him so far in advance of his time. For all her influence over him, Plotina had nothing to do with this. Hadrian defended his beard. In fact, he decreed that only men with beards or potential beards could become officers, a regulation which weeded out the immature. Quite naturally the wearing of beards became fashionable under Hadrian and his successors.

The soldiers especially adored their emperor who drank with them, ate with them and marched with them, never using a carriage. And so the Roman empire grew even stronger in a era when it had no need to wage war. The Parthian war was speedily brought to an end. Hadrian refused the offer of a triumphal procession, ordering instead that the statue of Trajan, his late predecessor and the real conqueror of Parthia, should be borne into Rome through the Porta Triumphalis.

The Parthians looked upon Hadrian as their friend and redeemer. The Armenians now had their own king and not a Roman governor as in Trajan's time. The Mesopotamians were absolved from paying tribute. Hadrian also made large gifts to the kings of the Albanians and Hiberians in the Caucasus, thereby gaining their friendship for the first time. Even the Bactrian kings of the Hindu Kush sent ambassadors to Hadrian and courted his favor. Rome's international relations had been put on the best possible footing.

But inside the Roman empire, too, nothing escaped the eyes and ears of the emperor. He was everywhere at once, since his agents (*frumentarii*) traveled the world over, reporting whether senior government officials were really doing their job.

Hadrian wanted to be his people's servant, no more—but no less. He always rose to his feet when receiving senators, but insisted that they should wear the regulation toga on duty or in public. He reorganized the whole judiciary and commissioned the celebrated jurist Salvius Iulianus to make a collection of all previous legal decisions, thus paving the way for Emperor Justinian's *corpus juris*. He prohibited denunciations for *lèse-majesté* and ruled that masters no longer had the power of life and death over their slaves. Sentences of death (this applied to slaves too) could only be passed by public courts. Hadrian even issued a decree forbidding the sale of male or female slaves to the brutal gladiatorial schools. Henceforth this could only take place under state supervision and after detailed examination of each individual case.

The penalty for culpable extravagance was strict, but short and sweet: anyone who had squandered property which he was legally obliged to conserve was flogged in the amphitheater and then allowed to go home. Hadrian abolished penal servitude for slaves and freemen alike. It had been the custom, when a Roman had been murdered in his own home, to use torture when interrogating his slaves. The emperor did away with this inhuman practice and laid it down that only slaves who had been close enough to have knowledge of the murder could be interrogated. He also extended the concept of *humanitas* to include slaves because in his eyes they too were human beings.

Then there was bathing. Hadrian decreed that the sexes should be segregated when taking public baths and installed new baths for this purpose. We know, incidentally, that he applied this rule to his own villa, where he had two separate baths.

But Hadrian was not a prudish man. He was modern, both in the world of his day and in retrospect. He was a democrat. Anyone could approach him, and he spoke to everyone, including the poor, and chatted far more often with other ranks than with officers. Once, as he was walking down a street, a woman called to him and asked him something. "I've no time now!" said the emperor. "Then don't be emperor!" she shouted after him. Hadrian turned back and listened to her patiently.

The Romans, being southerners, regarded Germany as a land of hard winters and intense cold. Hence the admiration of the historian Dio Cassius when he wrote that the emperor never covered his head either in heat or cold. "Even in the German snows and the scorching sun of Egypt, Hadrian went about without a hat."

The emperor's Roman biographer, says: "Scarcely ever had an emperor traversed such vast regions at such speed." We even learn that Hadrian climbed Mount Etna in Sicily to watch the sunrise. His contemporaries found this rather bizarre, but there are many references to his penchant for sun worship.

The emperor's second great world tour covered the period 128–134 A.D. Gaul, Spain, Britain and Germany were all inspected. In Britain, Hadrian erected the famous rampart or entrenchment which extended for over sixty miles from the Tyne Estuary to the Firth of Solway and was typical of his defensive thinking. He also strengthened the Germano-Rhaetian *limes*, the frontier rampart between Andernach and the Danube at Regensburg. Something else of note happened during this period: Hadrian dismissed Suetonius Tranquillus, his private secretary and a well-known historian, together with his assistants. Apparently they had taken liberties with his wife Sabina which infringed court etiquette. He was also very displeased with Sabina because she had grown irritable and perpetually ill-tempered. Had he been a private citizen and not emperor, he would undoubtedly have divorced her.

Hadrian was an amazingly accomplished and talented person. He was a good prose writer and an excellent poet, and greatly enjoyed swapping verses with the major poets of his day. He was an authority on Cato, Cicero, Virgil and Sallust, and knew the works of Homer and Plato like the back of his hand. He considered himself such a good astrologer that he set down in writing, every January, what was going to happen to him in the course of the year. Even in the year he died he wrote down, with a fair degree of accuracy, all that fate still held in store for him, down to the actual hour of his death.

The philosophers Epictetus and Heliodorus, orators, musicians, mathematicians, painters, astrologers—Hadrian gave them every possible help and encouragement. But he was also fond of needling them and involving them in caustic debate, poking fun at them much as Frederick of Prussia did at Voltaire. His phenomenal memory enabled him to dictate brilliantly formulated speeches at high speed, retain whole books by heart, and write, listen and chat to his friends all at the same time—"incredible as it may seem," his biographer remarks.

Hadrian also had a very good memory for faces, a characteristic which he shared with other great statesmen in world history. He would even recognize private soldiers again after a lapse of years and address them by name without a moment's hesitation. Indeed, he made it a sort of hobby not only to remember the names of thousands of people but also to be able to spell them. This aptitude aroused the greatest admiration in the Senate and among the inhabitants of the many countries he visited.

He could be witty, too. A gray-headed old man once made a request which Hadrian refused. Soon afterwards the same man appeared again, this time with his hair dyed. Hadrian recognized him immediately. "I have already refused your father once," he quipped.

DIVINE ANTINOÜS

Hadrian was not only the first true philhellene to occupy the throne of the Caesars but also the greatest, in whose footsteps Gallienus followed in the third century and Julian in the fourth. Under Hadrian, Hellenism ... became the formative power in the Imperium Romanum.

—Hermann Bengtson, Greek History.

THE EMPEROR often bathed in the public baths. On one such visit he saw an old man flexing his knees and rubbing his back against the wall "Why are you massaging yourself against the marble?" asked Hadrian. "Because I do not own a slave," the old man answered. The very same day, Hadrian made him a present of several slaves and enough money to maintain them for years. Next time he visited a public bath, the walls were lined with old men bending their knees and rubbing their backs on the marble. Calling them over, the emperor told them to massage each other for a while.

There are many such stories which may be attributed to the great man's whimsical or pungent sense of humor. Another is the fact that with the aid of his architect Decrianus he arranged for the removal of the colossus which Nero had erected in the vestibule of his Golden House. Keeping it in an upright position, he had the statue transported to a spot northwest of what later became known as the Colosseum. The gigantic sculpture must have been some 130 feet high (part of its pedestal still survives), and was so heavy that the emperor's architect had to use a team of twenty-four elephants in order to shift it. Hadrian erased Nero's features and dedicated the figure to the sun.

The emperor was so fond of animals that he built tombs for his pets. His hunter, Borysthenes, even got a pillar complete with inscription.

Hadrian visited Athens three times, in the years 124–125, 128–129, and 131–132. Here he built the so-called City of Hadrian, thus becoming in effect the second founder of Athens. He completed the Olympieum, begun over six centuries before by the tyrant Pisistratus, and built the Temple of Hera, a pantheon, the Stoa and its library, a gymnasium, a temple for Zeus, and an aqueduct. He also got himself initiated into the mystery cult of Eleusis. For Athens, Emperor Hadrian was the symbol and author of a fresh lease of life. Hadrian's Gate, which divides the ancient city from the new, still bears the legend: *Here is Athens, formerly the city of Theseus* on one side, and on the other: *Here is the city of Hadrian, not of Theseus.* Hadrian was so devoted to the Greeks that he founded a "panhellenic confederation" which every Greek city in the Roman empire was to join.

There is no doubt that Hadrian's intentions for Jerusalem were also of the best. Ever since its destruction by Titus the city had lain beneath the Judaean sun like a great open sore. Hadrian began to rebuild it, but on the spot where Jehovah's temple lay in ruins he planned to build a shrine for Jupiter. Enraged by this, the Jews rose in rebellion under their leader and champion Bar Kochba, Son of the Star. Hadrian

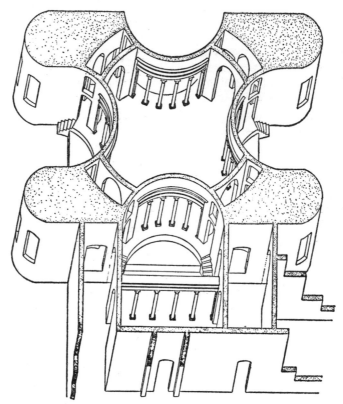

The "Little Palace" of Hadrian at Tivoli. (From *Hadrian und seine Villa bei Tivoli* by H. Köhler)

retorted by instructing his general, Julius Severus, to destroy all their towns. It was a decision which, as a devotee of peace, he found hard to make.

In the year 130 Hadrian visited Egypt with his wife and the usual large entourage. A lady-in-waiting, Julia Balbilla by name, left a few Greek poems engraved on the Colossus of Memnon as a memento of the imperial visit. While he was there, Hadrian suffered a stroke of misfortune which was to cast a shadow over the rest of his life.

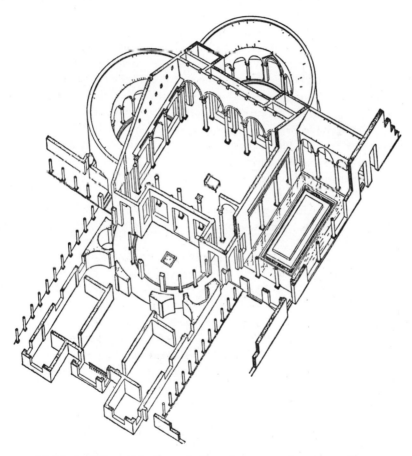

Hadrian's Villa at Tivoli was built to the emperor's own specifications. This is the spacious dining room. (By courtesy of the Verlag Gebr. Mann, Berlin)

On the emperor's staff at the time was a handsome young man named Antinoüs, of whom he was more than fond. (It is written that he lived with him "like a wife.") It appears, though the facts are obscure, that this youth was drowned during a trip up the Nile. That, at any rate, is what Emperor Hadrian is supposed to have said. Dio Cassius, the Bithynian historian, is skeptical and suggests that Antinoüs died for love of Hadrian "because what the emperor had in mind demanded the voluntary sacrifice of another."

This death, accident or not, seems to have overwhelmed the emperor so utterly that he never recovered from his grief. We are told that he mourned for the dead boy "like a wife."

At the place where Antinoüs died, Hadrian founded a town called Antinoöpolis on October 30, 130 A.D. The town stands on the east bank of the Nile, not far from Hermopolis across the river. Whereas the streets of Pompeii were thirty feet across at their widest point, Antinoöpolis had an avenue sixty-five feet wide. Lining this main thoroughfare were baths, temples, a theater, and a building assumed to be Antinoüs' tomb. All the streets ran at right angles like those in New York and were numbered in the same way.

Still unsatisfied, the emperor set up statues and busts of Antinoüs all over the Roman empire. He even came to believe that he had observed a new star in the sky, the star of Antinoüs. He saw Antinoüs as a god, as Osiris, resurrected from the waters of the Nile, and ordained that he should be worshiped in association with Ammon in the temple at Antinoöpolis. In the Greek cities of Asia Minor, Egypt and Europe, the identity of Antinoüs became merged with that of Hermes, Dionysus, Pan, Apollo, and Asclepius. In Italy he was associated with Silvanus.

To Hadrian life had lost all meaning if Antinoüs' beauty and nobility were beyond recall. He built temples and chapels but left them bare of sacred images. For whom were they erected? Was Hadrian in search of a new god? After all, he was an adherent of the gods of Rome, so why the empty temples? One thinks at once of Antinoüs. Perhaps the emperor hoped to meet him, resurrected, in one of them.

Hadrian had built himself a beautiful country villa at Tibur (Tivoli) at the foot of Monte Arcese in the lonely Campagna which was his especial love. Its ruins cover an area of some 160 acres. Each building on the estate was named after one of the famous places Hadrian had visited on his travels. There were libraries, a theater, baths, arcades, while the vigorous and imaginative design of the two palaces, the large and the small, with their wealth of curves, make them unique among the buildings of antiquity. They took more than a decade and a half to complete. No less than sixteen portrayals of Antinoüs have been found there, including statues, busts, and reliefs. What thoughts must have passed through the aging emperor's mind as he strolled through the rooms, cloisters and grounds, alone and unescorted save, probably, for the shade of Antinoüs? His health had now deteriorated, and he began to suffer from nosebleeds of increasing violence.

The emperor built himself a tomb, a gigantic mausoleum which he intended all his successors to use in turn. Although he had seen the pyramids in Egypt, he wanted his own symbol of eternity to be round, round as eternity itself. A site opposite the Campus Martius became a scene of great activity. Antlike, slaves hauled stones and mortar into position, and the grandest tribute to Roman emperorship gradually took shape. The tomb is now the Castle of St. Angelo. Hadrian wanted the urn containing his ashes to repose there in solitary state until the next emperor joined him, and so on into all eternity.

Hadrian had hoped to live for a very long time but he now saw that fate was hovering close at hand, ready to recall him. He had already nominated Lucius Ceionius as his successor in the event of his death, but fate now ruled otherwise.

Hadrian ordered the execution of his ninety-year-old brother-in-law, Servianus, and his grandson Fuscus, aged eighteen. No one had ever seen Hadrian act in anger before. "Bear witness to my innocence, ye gods!" cried Servianus. "I see Hadrian. He wants to die and will not be able to!" It was true. Hadrian's condition grew worse and worse. "It is sad indeed," he wrote, "to want to die and not to be able to."

Then Lucius Ceionius unexpectedly died of a violent hemorrhage and Hadrian, who was now suffering from dropsy, summoned the most distinguished members of the Senate to the palace and addressed them from his sickbed. He presented Antoninus Pius to them and announced that he would be taking over the government. Antoninus, for his part, was required to adopt young Marcus Aurelius as his son and successor.

Meanwhile, Hadrian felt his death grow more imminent with each day that passed. Still as restless as ever, he made a last trip to Baiae on the coast, wanting to look at the sea, the broad and splendid sea which had carried him from country to country, the water which made him feel closer to the soul of his beloved Antinoüs. But he was in agony. So passionately did he yearn to die that he asked first for poison and then for a sword, but to no avail. He promised money and legal immunity to anyone who would kill him but no one volunteered. In the end he sent for Mastor, a former prisoner of war, and with a mixture of threats and promises talked him into killing him. He daubed a cross on his chest to mark the spot where Mastor was to drive his dagger home.

The barbarian took to his heels.

Hadrian wept.

He wept because he could kill others, but not himself. Then the idea suddenly struck him that he might have regained his health and lived longer if only he had received proper treatment. "Many doctors are a prince's death," he is alleged to have said just before he died.

THE GENTLEMANLY EMPEROR

He was a strikingly handsome man of eminent talents and a pleasant disposition. An aristocrat to his finger tips, he was dignified in manner, an accomplished orator, a fine scholar, extremely moderate and abstemious, an industrious landowner, affable, magnanimous, ever respectful of other men's rights. He possessed all these attributes in the right proportion and never made an exaggerated parade of them. That was why he won the esteem of all people of integrity and truly merited comparison with Numa Pompilius.
—Historia Augusta, Antoninus Pius, ii.

HADRIAN, the man of peace, had reigned with such success that the machinery of government was functioning with marvelous regularity and precision.

Hadrian's foresight and wisdom are beyond praise. Evidence of his wisdom was his choice of his successors. Neither Antoninus nor Marcus Aurelius proved a disappointment. Indeed, under these two rulers Rome remained at the highest pinnacle it was ever to achieve. Twenty years of peace: forty years of order and justice.

Yet Marcus Aurelius was the last great figure in this fortunate period, and once he had gone, the ship of state soon drifted into troubled waters and steered a perilous course among the reefs of disputed succession, assassination, and Teutonic invasion.

Antoninus Pius was a handsome, likable man to whom none but the best characteristics were ever attributed. Fifty-two years of age when Hadrian died, he was compared by the Romans with Numa Pompilius, the wise and upright prince of peace who allegedly had been the second king of Rome. They had to go a long way back in history to find a figure comparable to the aristocratic and elegant landowner who was now emperor of Rome. In 147 A.D. the latter-day Numa presided over the celebrations held to mark the nine-hundredth anniversary of Rome's foundation.

Antoninus was born Titus Aurelius Fulvus Boionius Arrius Antoninus at Lanuvium in Latium on September 16, 86 A.D., but his family came from Nemausus, now Nîmes in Provence. Since nobody from the provinces could become a senator without owning land in Italy, the Antonini had bought property in the Campagna. Antoninus lived on his estate, at Lorium, fed his chickens, and devoted himself to the breeding of cattle and horses. It was there that he brought up young Marcus Aurelius. He took a truly paternal interest in his adoptive son, initiating him into the lore of country life and teaching him how to manage an estate properly.

Antoninus occupied the Roman throne for twenty-three years, and throughout that time—in complete contrast to Hadrian—he never left Italy. These were among the empire's happiest years. In fact Edward Gibbon, the famous English historian, went so far as to regard the Antonine period (which includes the reigns of Antoninus and Marcus Aurelius) as mankind's happiest era. The German historian Ernst Kornemann, on the other hand, looks upon the reign of Antoninus as "a succession of grossly wasted opportunities" which caused the Roman empire to retrogress. There is something to be said for both points of view. Rome was still blessed with prosperity and peace, but the Germans were growing stronger in the north and the Parthians in the east. Antoninus should, perhaps, have waged preventive wars in each case, but he lived "with his head in the clouds where external affairs were concerned," as Kornemann puts it. However, it seems grossly unfair to criticize him for that since every monarch or statesman who genuinely believes in the possibility of lasting peace and wishes to spare his people bloodshed does fundamentally live with his head in the clouds. Antoninus was a man of integrity and a good and paternal ruler. Every government decree he issued was painstakingly discussed with his friends and advisers in advance, for the last thing he wanted was to appear autocratic.

For all that, his name makes less impact on the memory than that of such members of the imperial rogues' gallery as Nero and Domitian, or strong-men like Sulla and Antony. It seems to be an unfortunate fact that the world's thrifty, gentle and kindly monarchs are doomed to a shadowy historical existence.

Immediately after Antoninus' accession, the Senate refused to confer on his late predecessor any of the customary marks of respect. They could not forgive him for having executed certain distinguished men. Tearfully Antoninus implored the Senate not to slam the gates of Olympus in Hadrian's face. "If Hadrian was really so wicked and ill-disposed toward you, I am not your emperor. You would have to invalidate everything he did—including my adoption." By such words Antoninus made such an impression on the senators that they eventually awarded Hadrian all the funeral honors due him.

The Senate gave Antoninus the surname Pius, or "dutiful," a title which Roman historians justify on numerous grounds. Perhaps the emperor simply owed the award to his great kindness, friendliness, and prudence. He was also invested with the title Father of the Fatherland, an honor which he at first declined but later accepted, courteously expressing his thanks.

When his wife Annia Galeria Faustina died in the third year of his reign, she was officially deified by the Senate and many coins were minted in her honor bearing the inscription *Diva Faustina* ("the Deified Faustina"). Faustina had a daughter of the same name, and four years after her mother's death Antoninus gave the younger Faustina, an extremely beautiful girl, in marriage to his adoptive son Marcus Aurelius.

Antoninus lived frugally and without ostentation, spending most of his time in the House of Tiberius, his palace on the Palatine, or on his country estate in the Campagna. He avoided making journeys outside the route between his estate and the capital because he considered the expense of traveling with a full escort unjustified.

When in residence at Rome, the emperor was the true focus of world attention. All nations held him in the highest esteem and treated him with great respect. When word came that the Parthian king was planning an attack on Armenia, a letter from Antoninus sufficed to dissuade him. Antoninus made large cash distributions to the people on nine separate occasions. In addition he gave his soldiers a bonus on the day of his daughter's wedding in the year 145, and founded the *Puellae Faustinianae*, an order for destitute and homeless girls, in honor of his dead wife. He also erected many buildings in Rome and completed Hadrian's great tomb which was then regarded as a miracle of building technique.

In the north of Britain Antoninus authorized the construction of a rampart between the Firth of Forth and the Firth of Clyde as a fresh defense against the barbarian tribes. In the year 148 he advanced the famous *limes*, the defensive rampart designed to keep out the Germans, and replaced all its wooden towers by stone ones. The military value of this monumental earthwork was open to question but it was certainly a great feat of organization and a lesson in the use of mass labor. It also demonstrated the emperor's wish to defend his world empire by peaceful means. Peace, order and security were his dominant ideas, so much so that his subjects gratefully declared that Rome needed walls no longer. If Antoninus Pius had not refused the honor, our months September and October would now be known as Antoniny and Faustiny.

This does not mean that Antoninus' reign was free from disasters and evil omens. The soothsayers were ready with their usual predictions. Famine broke out. The great circus collapsed. An earthquake occurred, probably in 140 A.D., and destroyed towns in Rhodes, Cos, and Caria. Fire broke out in Rome, the Tiber burst its banks, a comet was seen in the sky, a two-headed child was born, an Arabian snake tried to devour itself (it got as far as its midriff), and a woman produced quintuplets—beating Madame Dionne in Canada by 1,800 years.

Antoninus became emperor at the age of fifty-two and continued to conduct public affairs until his death, twenty-three years later. One of his greatest preoccupations in his later years was to keep himself fit. He still looked extremely well but he became convinced that his tall figure was becoming a little bent, so he ordered several corsets made of narrow strips of limewood and strapped them to his chest and back to hold himself upright. Anxious not to succumb to the arduousness of his duties, he ate dry black bread every morning before receiving his court officials.

When the emperor knew he was going to die he ordered a golden statue of the goddess Fortuna, to be carried from his bedroom into that of his adoptive son and heir, Marcus Aurelius.

For a while he lay there in a delirium, muttering about government affairs and the kings of distant lands. Then he turned over on his side and fell asleep forever.

THE TIME IS AT HAND

The time is at hand when you will have forgotten everything;
and the time is at hand when all will have forgotten you.
Always reflect that soon you will be no one and nowhere.
—Marcus Aurelius, *Meditations*, vii, 21, and xii, 21.

MARCUS AURELIUS was born on the Caelian Hill in Rome on April 26 of the year 121. So that he was still a youth of seventeen when Hadrian died.

Hadrian had early recognized the boy's capabilities. If he had not, Marcus Aurelius would probably have become a run-of-the-mill civil servant or army officer, and we should have known nothing about him.

At Hadrian's bidding Marcus was given a comprehensive education which he absorbed with notable success. We know the names of his tutors, some of them familiar to us and others quite unfamiliar, some Roman and some Greek. Young Marcus Aurelius was devoted to these distinguished scholars and his admiration for them, coupled with a passion for learning, prevented him from taking more than the bare minimum of sleep. We know that he was instructed in literature, drama, music, geometry, grammar, rhetoric, jurisprudence and, in particular, philosophy. The boy grew up in the true spirit of the Stoic doctrines, living on a diet of bread and figs, sleeping on the hard ground, and devouring one book after another. "I am so weary that I can scarcely breathe," he wrote in a still-extant letter addressed to his old teacher Fronto.

Marcus Aurelius received his *toga virilis*, the garment which a Roman youth wore on coming of age, at fifteen, and Emperor Hadrian at once betrothed him to Fabia, the daughter of Lucius Ceionius Commodus. But the marriage was not destined to last long for when Hadrian died Antoninus Pius took over Marcus' education and dissolved his childhood marriage. Marcus then married Antoninus' twenty-three-year-old daughter, Faustina, a lovely and accomplished girl. Faustina took an active interest in her young husband's studies.

Marcus was now associated with Antoninus in all the more important affairs of state, and the emperor never undertook any course of action without consulting him. The emperor and his adoptive son lived harmoniously together in the Palace of Tiberius on the Palatine, where the prince must have learned a great deal from his conversations with the distinguished old man. But he also continued to attend his tutors' lectures.

As an uncompromising Stoic Marcus Aurelius worked tirelessly to improve himself. All his energies were devoted to the attainment of a state of perfect mental equilibrium which involved self-control and a sense of obligation toward oneself and one's fellow beings. He lived unostentatiously, giving daily audiences to the best men in Rome—not in the great public rooms of the imperial palace or attired in his robes of state, but clad simply in house clothes. His normal outdoor dress was somber in color. He only wore the official toga when accompanying the emperor and was never preceded by torchbearers like other young Roman aristocrats. The thought that he was destined to be master of Rome and the Roman empire was never far from his mind.

Could he be happy, in view of the immense burden he would have to shoulder one day? No, a mind schooled in Stoic rationalism could always see the negative side of everything. He was not happy. He was even a little apprehensive about the future. His inordinate passion for work, the strain of sleepless nights, the ruthless overburdening of his memory and a renunciation of the normal amenities of life all conspired to weaken his constitution. And still he continued to study the great philosophers and perfect his Greek and Latin rhetoric.

Marcus Aurelius was forty years old when Antoninus died but it was in keeping with his shrewdness and deliberation—not to mention his qualms about an emperor's chances—that he summoned Lucius Verus, who had likewise been adopted by Antoninus, and made him coregent, giving him the name Lucius Aurelius Verus Commodus and bestowing on him the titles Caesar and Augustus. By investing his adoptive brother with this last title, Augustus, he placed him on an equal footing with himself. In his ailing condition Marcus Aurelius felt unable to administer the empire on his own and intended Verus to relieve him of some of his military responsibilities. His plan was to divide and share. Thus, for the first time, the empire was governed by two emperors, each with the title Augustus and each with nearly the same measure of authority. But the plan failed and Marcus Aurelius was eventually forced to combat singlehanded the immense difficulties which arose during his reign.

The first thing Marcus and Verus did was to bury their adoptive father in Hadrian's mausoleum. It must have been a great moment when the funeral procession, with its long columns of legionaries, marched up to the doors of the gigantic circular tomb, now fully completed. The top of the magnificent building was crowned by a copse of growing trees and its general appearance was that of an impressive natural feature rather than a man-made edifice.

Marcus Aurelius now called a halt to his studies and laid his books aside, for it seemed that storm clouds were gathering above the huge empire. The new emperor was a philosopher but he could also be a man of action. That was just what philosophy was designed to equip him for.

In the east the Parthians were getting ready to war on Rome under their king, Vologeses III, and had already occupied parts of Armenia and Syria. Marcus Aurelius dispatched his partner and adoptive brother Verus against Vologeses. But unlike Marcus, Verus liked good food, wine and women. Once he had reached the East and tasted the fleshpots of Antioch and Daphne he never wanted to see Rome or another Stoic again, and decided to enjoy life while he could. He at once sent the Parthians an offer of peace which they naturally rejected.

Marcus Aurelius had given his fifteen-year-old daughter Lucilla in marriage to Verus, who was considerably his junior. He was very fond of his adoptive brother-cum-son-in-law and although his hopes that Verus would prove a help to him had been dashed, he remained hopeful and confident. He recalled him from the East, and both emperors were invested with the title Father of the Fatherland.

To protect his eastern flank Marcus now appointed General Avidius Cassius, already governor of Syria, as governor of Asia Minor. It was a necessary step, for while Cassius was driving the Parthians back across the Euphrates and Tigris fresh danger was looming up, this time in the north where the Germans were on the move, as they had been in the days of the Cimbri and Teutons. The Marcomanni and Quadi had broken through the *limes* north of the Danube and were pushing into Pannonia, or lower Austria, under the leadership of Ballomar, king of the Marcomanni. The Romans were hard put to it to hold the Alpine passes, and in the end the Germans even threatened to burst through this last bulwark at Aquileia in northern Italy. Rome was in very real danger in the year 168. It was, in fact, the beginning of a great migratory trend in the Germanic area.

Taking Verus with him, Marcus marched to the relief of Aquileia, forced the Germans to retreat, and then set off in pursuit of the barbarians and crossed the Alps to restore the Danubian frontier. Then Rome suffered a frightful blow. A mysterious epidemic had been introduced into Italy by soldiers from the eastern front, probably from Babylon, known to Romans as Seleucia-on-the-Tigris. Was it the plague? We don't know, just as we don't know what epidemic struck Athens down during the time of Pericles. Thousands died year after year. The dead were trundled out of the capital on carts and barrows. It was the longest and most widespread epidemic in ancient history. The two emperors issued decrees strictly prohibiting the dead to be buried on their own premises, but the epidemic gained ground, ravaged the whole of northern Italy and swooped across the Alps to the Rhine, where it attacked the army, carried off whole legions, and put new heart into the Germans.

The royal brothers agreed that Verus should return to Rome to report to the Senate, but on the way, while still in the company of Marcus, he suffered a stroke and died. The year was 169 A.D. The place, Altinum in Venetia.

After a number of sanguinary battles in gloomy forests or on the banks of remote rivers of which the Romans had never heard, the Marcomanni and Iazyges were defeated. Marcus' defeat of the Quadi was attributed to a miracle. It was a scorchingly hot day when the Romans engaged the Quadi and the legionaries were half dead with thirst. Accordingly the emperor prayed to the gods, who obliged by sending a rainstorm. The Christians explained this marvel by alleging that one of the legions in Marcus' army (the Cappadocian legion XII Fulminata) consisted entirely of Christians. They said that on being informed that the Christians could achieve anything by prayer, Marcus asked them to pray to their god, and their prayers were answered. We are told in moving terms how the Romans caught the precious rain in their shields and helmets, how it mingled with the blood of battle, and how many a man shared the heaven-sent liquid with his dying horse. This fortuitous rain shower is shown in the reliefs on Marcus' column in Rome.

Meanwhile, further barbarian advances were taking place. The Costoboci pushed down as far as Greece and plundered the temple at Eleusis, the Germanic Chatti crossed the Rhine, and the Moors invaded Spain from Africa. The praetorians and other garrison troops were withdrawn from Rome and sent into battle, and on the emperor's orders training establishments were emptied of gladiators, while slaves were armed and assured that if they proved their mettle they would later be granted their freedom. German tribes entered the service of Rome, too, and Emperor Marcus welcomed them with open arms. By dint of an all-out effort a wide strip of territory on the left of the Danube was finally cleared and the last of the Quadi roamed away to the east.

By this time, however, the imperial treasury was exhausted so the emperor decreed public sales, and for two whole months the Forum Traiani was filled with furniture, gold, crystal, ivory and jewels from the royal household. Even the empress's gold-embroidered robes were put up for sale. The emperor did announce, however, that, as soon as the war against the Marcomanni and the other German tribes had been successfully terminated, everyone would be allowed to buy back at their original purchase the articles which he had sold.

Marcus Aurelius had taken over the name Antoninus from his adoptive father. His victories are depicted in 116 reliefs on the Antonine Column in the Campus Martius in Rome. They do not, unfortunately, make as powerful an impact as those on Trajan's Column since the places where the Roman legions had repelled the German invaders were too dismal, strange and unfamiliar to provide the same inspiration. Yet Marcus Aurelius was absent for quite a time in those barbarian regions, remote and awesome lands of the great beech tree, dark spruce and lonely fir. He reached Silesia and the borders of Galicia, defying cold and fatigue to lead repeated cavalry charges in person. It was hardly surprising, therefore, that when he had been unable to send news to Rome for some time, a rumor spread round the Roman world that he had died or been killed in action.

Syria was still under the control of Avidius Cassius, the man whom the emperor regarded as his best governor. Cassius was in fact governing his native land, having been born at Cyrrus. He was a successful man but brutal, violent, and utterly ruthless toward his enemies. He crucified prisoners and discouraged deserters by cutting off their legs.

It was unwise to appoint a man viceroy of his own country, especially when it was so far from the seat of government. Scarcely had the false news of Marcus' death reached Cassius than he instigated a revolt with the object of making himself emperor. It is still uncertain what part Faustina, Marcus' wife, played in this affair. Her husband's weak health and the risks he ran may have convinced her that he would die at any moment, and since Marcus' son Commodus was not only too young but temperamentally quite unsuited to succeed him, Faustina trembled for her position as empress. It is said that she recommended Cassius to take over the throne—and herself—in the event of her husband's death.

Antioch was already swearing allegiance to Cassius when Marcus Aurelius bore down on the renegade general with all sails set. He addressed his troops as follows: "I would willingly abdicate in favor of Cassius, were it for the good of the state. I have endured immense dangers and hardships. For a long time now, I have lived outside Italy. I am an old and ailing man. I can no longer eat without pain or sleep without care. My one dread is that Cassius may kill himself from shame. I fear this because it would rob me of the finest prize which war against Cassius could bring me: to pardon an offender, to remain friends with someone who has abused my friendship, to keep faith with one who has broken faith."

Marcus' fears were realized. They cut off Cassius' head—the head which had, for the few months from about mid-April to towards the end of July, 175, been filled with dreams of imperial sovereignty. A legionary hurried to meet Marcus Aurelius and lay the trophy at his feet but the emperor was so saddened by the gift that he ordered it buried without taking a look at it. Then, while still on his journey eastward, he was greeted by a second piece of bad news. Faustina was dead: Faustina, the wife he had loved so dearly, the woman whom the legionaries had called "Mother of the Camp," the woman of whom Antoninus Pius had said, "Rather in the desert alone with my daughter than in the imperial palace without her."

Had Faustina died a natural death?

Had shame or fear at having conspired with Cassius driven her to take her own life?

The emperor would have nothing to do with such rumors and even ordered some letters which were found in the luggage of a certain Pudens to be burned unexamined. For Marcus had no taste for blood. Even the gladiators at Rome were only allowed to fight in his presence if none of the combatants carried sharp weapons. He refused to allow a lion which had been trained to devour human beings in the circus to enter the arena, in spite of popular demand, and locked up the trainer.

In the year 176 the emperor, accompanied by his fifteen-year-old son, returned to Rome in triumph after his difficult and hazardous journey to the East. He was in a mood of depression. He had lost a good man in Cassius, perhaps because he had placed too much confidence in him, and he was still mourning for his wife. But the great triumph drowned all other thoughts for a period of days and weeks. Marcus Aurelius laid the foundation stone of the Antonine Column, an eternal reminder of the repulse, so important historically, of the second great German invasion. An equestrian statue of Marcus Aurelius still stands on the Roman Capitol today. Once gilded, this famous piece is the prototype of all subsequent equestrian statues, but it owes its survival only to an erroneous belief that it portrayed Constantine, the first Christian emperor.

However, the Germans' offensive strength was far from exhausted, and the emperor's spell of leisure in Rome was of short duration. The enemy had been subdued but danger was still lurking everywhere. Marcus Aurelius therefore decided to clarify the situation by pushing the frontiers of the Roman empire forward to the Erzgebirge, to the Sudetic and Carpathian Mountains. A new legionary camp, Castra Regina (modern Regensburg), was erected on the Danube as a defense against the Marcomanni and two new provinces in Bohemia and Hungary (they were to be called Marcomannia and Sarmatia) had just been formed when the emperor died quite suddenly and unexpectedly in Vienna of a dangerous infection. It is probable that his constitution was already so severely impaired by continuous stomach trouble that it broke down under the effect of a strange and unaccustomed diet. He died on March 17, 180 A.D. The last password he gave was, "Go to the rising sun, my sun is setting."

It was there in Moravia and Bohemia, during the long and lonely nights in camp, that the emperor wrote his world-famous *Meditations*. Composed in Greek, these soliloquies have survived for nearly two thousand years and brought tranquillity and peace of mind to generation after generation, even though the emperor himself never intended them for publication. Since the seventeenth century, over two hundred different translations of the emperor's book have appeared in England alone.

The *Meditations* is a devotional work consisting of dialogues between Marcus Aurelius and himself, and himself and God. Actually he speaks of "the gods," it is true, but that is merely his term for the divine object of his prayers, whether a single god or the universe itself. "Men seek places whither they can retire, abodes on land, on sea, in the mountains. . . . All such desires are childish, when it is possible, at any given moment, to withdraw into oneself. For nowhere does a man find more peace and tranquillity than in his own soul. . . . Consider how many men have been at odds with each other, borne each other envy and hatred, fought to the death, and then lain down for the last time and become ashes. . . . Consider, too, how quickly all is forgotten, remember the chasm of infinity on either side, the futility of approbation, the fickleness and instability of mankind. . . ." Marcus Aurelius had a deep insight into the human soul. "People of a certain disposition will always act in accordance with their nature." Most great philosophers, both before and after Marcus Aurelius, have recognized that character is an immutable factor and that people must be taken as they are.

Marcus also knew that the only way to make an impression on people was by kindness. "Does someone hate me?" he asks. His reply is unhesitating: "That is his own business. For my part, I am kind and well disposed toward everyone and ready to show him his errors, not reproachfully, but . . . sincerely and full of kindness."

The emperor knew his place in history, time, and the world. "Do you grumble at what the course of life brings you? . . . What a tiny part of boundless, infinite time is allotted to each of us. Everyone disappears into eternity. . . . And on what tiny portion of the whole earth's surface do you creep about? Reflect on all this and regard nothing as important save to act as your nature impels and endure what Nature brings you. . . . The whole world is but a dot. What a small speck of it is occupied by the abode of men, and how few of them there are! And what sort of people are they that shall praise you? . . . Do not wait for the perfect State, but esteem it, however small the progress made."

Such were the sentiments of Marcus Aurelius, and it is not too much to call him the greatest royal philosopher that ever lived. "The time is at hand when you will have forgotten everything, and the time is at hand when all will have forgotten you. . . . Reflect that you will soon be no one and nowhere."

Could such a man have persecuted Christians? Have we found a flaw in the great emperor-philosopher?

Well, the reign of Marcus Aurelius saw not only the death of Justin and his six companions but the martyrdom of Metrodorus the Marcionite and Pionius the presbyter, the torture and burning of Carpus and

Papylus at Pergamum, and the voluntary death by fire of Agathonice the Christian. Eusebius gives us the text of a letter written by the churches of Lugdunum (Lyon) and Vienna (Vienne, near Lyon) to the communities of Asia and Phrygia in the year 177. Its frightful tales of mob violence, atrocities and Christians roasted alive, and its descriptions of the torments endured by Blandina the slave girl and the maltreatment of ninety-year-old Bishop Pothinus are like a shrill cry to the heavens. Our comfortable age can scarcely fathom how those early Christians triumphed over agony and death, for we have lost the ability to distinguish when heroism is worthwhile. The Christians, however, were dying for eternal truth.

But none of this took place under the eye of Emperor Marcus Aurelius. He did not personally oppress the Christians, and in his edict to the province of Asia he declined to take any measures against them. Only if they could be proved to have committed political offenses against the Roman state was the state permitted to intervene. But the governors who persecuted Christians in those days operated at a distance where the emperor could not always keep a check on them. Thus Marcus Aurelius was definitely not at the bottom of all this organized suffering. He was the most upright emperor the Roman empire ever had, a Stoic who was the soul of justice and rooted in the ancient Roman sense of duty, a long-suffering philosopher in a hostile world, one of the luminaries of antiquity.

No less a man than John Stuart Mill opined that Marcus Aurelius was a better Christian—in the undogmatic sense—than any of the avowedly Christian monarchs who have ruled since his day. He was probably more humane than any other ruler in history.

The universe and eternity, the great starry heavens and puny little man who carries all happiness and unhappiness about inside him and is really without hope, yet should welcome his destiny without complaint: such were the ideas that coursed through the mind of the lonely emperor as he communed with himself and recorded his meditations during those long nights on the frontiers of the barbarian world, far from Rome. A man of over fifty, he sat there deep in thought, the stillness outside broken only by the muffled calls of sentries changing guard, by the moaning of the wind as it swept across the wild Danubian landscape, or by the distant, infinitely mournful songs of the Marcomanni women as they lulled their wounded sons to sleep. Alone with the huge night sky and man's timid and eternal quest for peace of mind, Marcus Aurelius found an answer: do what your nature demands of you and act as your nature directs. It was a formula which brought him very close to supramundane wisdom and supramundane peace. For, as he himself wrote: "It is quite possible to become a godly man, yet remain unrecognized."

THE MONSTER

He had slain an ostrich, and brought its head across to where
we were sitting. He held the head in his left hand, the bloody
sword raised in his right. True, he spoke not a word, but he
motioned with his head and smirked as if to show that he had
the same thing in mind for us.

—Dio Cassius, lxxii, 21.

MARCUS AURELIUS was the soul of kindness and a wise man who almost succeeded in attaining perfect inner contentment and peace of mind "like the wide sea becalmed." But in the very kindness and optimism of this philanthropic emperor lay his one weakness: he deliberately refused to see his fellow men as they really were. He was boundlessly indulgent toward his wife and made his son emperor in spite of his patent unsuitability.

Nineteen-year-old Commodus haunted his father's deathbed like a shadow. Dio Cassius even insists, allegedly on good authority, that Marcus Aurelius "did not die of the disease which had attacked him" but because of the ministrations of his doctors, "who wished to ingratiate themselves with his son." He even claims that the emperor realized what was afoot but, far from betraying that he knew he was being murdered, told his soldiers to serve his successor faithfully.

Rome had had five good rulers in succession. It seems, in history, as though even intelligence and moderation demand an occasional lapse, as though the course of events cannot be without its darker side, as though only despotism and murder can boost the advent of happier days.

Marcus Aurelius left behind the finest code of rules for living which any pagan Roman could have devised.

What about some rules for his son? Was he not in far greater need of them?

We must bear in mind that Marcus Aurelius was the first emperor for some time to depart from the adoptive system of succession, a system which provided an excellent antidote to the degeneracy so prevalent in the second generation of Roman dynasties. Wise and kind though he was, Marcus Aurelius was obtuse where his own flesh and blood was concerned. For though he engaged the finest scholars of his day in an attempt to instruct and educate Commodus, it was all wasted effort. As a Roman historian ironically pointed out, the success of a palace education is determined by the royal pupil's temperament and his tutors' lack of authority.

At all events, Marcus Aurelius had failed, and history had repeated itself. Seneca was one of the greatest educationalists of all time, yet his pupil was Nero. And now a far greater monster occupied the throne of Rome. Commodus had reigned in partnership with his father for four years and Marcus Aurelius must have noticed a great deal in that time. But he was a Stoic. He knew how to control himself.

Commodus gave clear evidence of his brutality at the tender age of twelve. Finding his bath too cool on one occasion, he ordered the chief bath attendant thrown into the furnace. Fortunately, the slave entrusted with the order did not carry it out but merely threw a sheepskin on the fire. Commodus sniffed the smell of burning and was satisfied.

Now that Marcus Aurelius was dead, Commodus found himself in sole command of a large army and faced with the task of completing the conquest and pacification of the Marcomanni and Quadi and bringing the German wars to a decisive close. Instead he immediately succumbed to every kind of bad influence.

Before long Commodus had surrounded himself with actors and young degenerates who persuaded him that war in these wild regions was far too dangerous and painted horrific pictures of what lay across the Danube. The upshot was that he gave up the war and concluded a peace treaty with the Germans on extremely generous terms, abandoning the new provinces which Marcus Aurelius had so laboriously created. This was not at all the policy envisaged by his father but a retreat undertaken against the advice of the late emperor's friends. It did not, however, prevent Commodus from staging a triumphal return to Rome. The young emperor's boon companion Saoterus sat behind him during the procession, on October 22, 180, and Commodus repeatedly turned round and lavished amorous kisses on him in full view of the spectators.

The misbegotten offspring of one of the greatest Roman emperors then proceeded to squander the resources of his empire as fast as he could. The Senate hated him but cringed and fawned as usual. And the more the emperor felt himself despised, the bloodthirstier he became.

Before long, plans were under way to assassinate him. The conspirators included his sister Lucilla, a man named Quadratus, and Paternus, the commander of the imperial bodyguard, and the actual murder was to be carried out by a certain Claudius Pompeianus. It was an evening in the year 183 A.D. Commodus was just leaving the amphitheater by a dark and narrow gateway, bound for home, when Pompeianus sprang out at him with a drawn sword, crying, "This weapon comes to you from the Senate!" Alas, the foolish man bungled his opportunity. He was arrested and executed, together with Quadratus and numerous others. Lucilla, the emperor's sister, was banished to Capri and there murdered.

Rome seethed with the wildest rumors. The praetorian guard somehow got the idea that the emperor's unpopularity was due to his friendship with Saoterus, whom they promptly murdered. Paternus, the prefect of the guard, had hoped that this would change things, but he too fell prey to the emperor's vengeance and was executed in the company of several other alleged saboteurs.

Commodus was frightened, however, and ceased to appear in public readily and never received letters or messengers unless they had been previously examined by his new favorite, Perennis. Absolutely no one was admitted to the emperor's quarters without Perennis' prior approval. The court took on an almost Oriental atmosphere with the sycophant Perennis administering public affairs and the emperor devoting himself entirely to his own pastimes. Having safely transferred the burdens of government to the shoulders of Perennis, Commodus rushed from one banquet to the next, staggered around his palace roaring drunk, took an endless succession of hot baths, and amused himself with his three hundred concubines, the pick of Rome's prostitutes. He also purchased and kidnapped three hundred young boys specially selected for their physical charms. Once again the Romans had to grin and bear it all, as they had done in the days of Caligula, Nero, Vitellius and Domitian. The emperor personally performed ritual slaughter at the altar, acting as a sacrificial attendant. He fought in the arena, murdered anyone he disliked, robbed people and broke every conceivable law, even killing his wife Crispina. His concubines were forced to participate in the most riotous orgies. He murdered senators, wealthy women, and finally his own son. In the end even his favorite, Perennis, was declared a public enemy and torn to pieces by the soldiery.

The emperor's new man was named Cleander and like Saoterus, he was a former slave from Asia Minor. Cleander was obliged to commit even worse crimes on the emperor's behalf than his predecessor. The guard commanders were changed constantly. Senior appointments could only be obtained by bribery. There was nothing out of which the worthy Cleander could not make money, and before long nobody at court could see through the maze of intrigue with which he surrounded himself. But no courtier's place was secure under an emperor who was constantly in need of new scapegoats. Famine broke out, bread became unobtainable, and rioters surged through the streets of Rome. Cleander was seized by the mob and stoned to death. It goes without saying that the children whom he had fathered on several of Commodus' concubines were also executed, along with their mothers.

Cleander was succeeded in turn by Julianus and Regillus, each of whom was put to death in his turn. Execution followed execution with monotonous regularity. We can still read the long lists of people, consuls, civil servants and courtiers among them, who perished in the emperor's blood bath together with their families.

The Senate introduced a note of hilarity into the situation by giving Commodus the titles Dutiful (Pius) and Fortunate (Felix). The dutiful and fortunate emperor then proceeded to stage an attempt on his own life as an excuse for more murders. Yet another of his names was Britannicus. He cherished a megalomaniac ambition to rechristen Rome "Colonia Commodiana," encouraged in that idea and others of a like caliber by his mistress, Marcia, who later became a Christian. And since it was their only way of ridiculing him, the Senate at once fell in with these suggestions, even according him divine status. He also gave the name Commodianus to: the Senate; the people; the Palace; the legions; the city of Carthage and the African fleet.

We read of the most astonishing goings on at court. Commodus got rid of Motelenus, one of his guard commanders, by presenting him with a gift of poisoned figs. There came a day when one of the palace servants "accidentally" dropped a writing tablet out of a bedroom window. It was unfortunate. The tablet bore the names of innumerable people whom the emperor intended to kill.

Commodus greatly fancied himself in the role of Hercules. Clad in female garb, he would slaughter lions and chained prisoners with his club. Another of his hobbies was to dress cripples up as snakes and shoot them to death with arrows. He also appeared in public as a gladiator and recorded for posterity the number of opponents he had slain. It is almost inconceivable how even a city like Rome could have tolerated all the emperor's whims and fancies.

Sometimes Commodus embraced people fondly, sometimes he showered them with obscene nicknames of his own devising. Once during an inspection he threw Julianus, the guard prefect, into a swimming pool and later made him dance naked before his concubines. He would even enter the sacred precincts of temples, spattered with blood and still lusting for murder. On one occasion he decided to rename every month in the year after his own grandiose titles. Sometimes he felt immensely strong, sometimes weak and ill. His lower body developed swellings which even the finest silken robes failed to disguise. But no sooner had the population hopefully begun to wonder whether they had seen the last of Commodus than he surprised everyone by reappearing in the amphitheater dressed as a woman.

Commodus had become incredibly lazy and had long ceased to discharge any public business. His replies to written requests and petitions bore no relation to their subject matter, and a large proportion of the emperor's letters consisted simply of the word "farewell." For a fee, men could now get their sentences of death transferred to others. On the emperor's authority, the famous *acta urbis* or *acta diurna*, a sort of official gazette, was crammed with scurrilous, sensational and vulgar items of news.

The Romans regarded Commodus as the plaything of his own whims. One day he even ordered the capital to be burned down and was only dissuaded at the last moment, probably by Laetus, the prefect of the praetorian guard. Recognizing that the present emergency had to be brought to an end, Laetus now enlisted Marcia's co-operation in a carefully planned attempt on the emperor's life. When poison failed to act quickly enough, they summoned an athlete who was the emperor's favorite wrestling partner, and the man throttled him to death.

The Roman populace clamored for "the hook." But, curiously enough, instead of being dragged into the Tiber, Commodus' body was laid in Hadrian's mausoleum.

Dangerous buffoon, monster, gladiator and self-styled hero, Commodus had erected statues and effigies of himself all over the city. Now every reminder of him was torn down. Not having built anything himself, he had been in the habit of putting his name on other people's buildings. Wherever he had done so, it was now erased.

It was like the end of some horrible dream. All that remained was a haunting memory of the emperor's drunken, petulant face and the flowing locks which he made his hairdressers dye blonde and sprinkle with gold dust.

AN EMPIRE FOR SALE

Whoever gave the troops the largest bonus was to become
emperor. Julian acquired the hotly contested imperial throne
for about 6000 denarii [roughly $590] per man....
When we received the news, we were seized with fear of Julian
and the soldiers. This applied especially to those who had been
on close terms with Pertinax, among them myself, who had
been honored by him and nominated quaestor, but had fre-
quently brought Julian before the courts in my fight against
injustice.

—Dio Cassius, lxxiii, 11, 12.

"PERTINAX was a man of honor. He reigned for only a short time and was then murdered by his soldiers." These are the opening words of the seventy-third book of the eighty-book history of Rome by Dio Cassius, who was a senator during this period and gives us a graphic description of it. A keen observer of the contemporary scene, he was always there on the spot, watching emperors come and go, sometimes laughing with his fellow senators, sometimes trembling with them, living dangerously in a Rome where death sentences and decapitations were all too frequent.

"The troops have appointed me emperor," declared Pertinax, "but I am not snatching at this honor. I wish to abdicate immediately. My age, my poor health, and my personal affairs do not make the throne an attractive proposition." He went to the Senate and asked Glabrio, the foremost patrician there, to assume the imperial throne in his place. Glabrio politely declined, however, and the other senators were equally reluctant.

"We therefore applauded the great man with all sincerity," Dio Cassius relates, "and confirmed him as emperor. He was a man of the highest character and soundest constitution. Only his feet troubled him."

It was December 31, 192 A.D. Pertinax was sixty-six. Unlike the Senate, the army could not raise much enthusiasm for the mild old man. He appears to have been well-meaning, if scarcely the person to act like an Imperator or retain the throne for very long. But even though he did nothing extremely wrong, he was not popular. The

215

Romans despised his quiet stealthy manner, insipid public speeches and greedy acceptance of gifts, and laughed at his apparent ignorance of his wife's continual infidelity with her musician lover. Yet Pertinax did have his good side.

Commodus had left behind a foul morass of vice, injustice and corruption. His successor did everything within his power to straighten out the mess, stop the praetorians bullying the civil population, reduce the high level of taxes, and generally put the country on an even keel. He tried to model himself on Marcus Aurelius.

Pertinax organized a gigantic sale of all the treasures which Commodus had confiscated and hoarded. Among other articles offered for sale were gorgeous silks embroidered with gold, priceless robes and cloaks in the Dalmatian and Greek style, a gladiatorial toga and the gold and jeweled accouterments that went with it, and vessels of gold, ivory and silver.

Also up for auction were Samnite jars in which Commodus had kept his face lotions, and chariots of the latest design, with carved wheels and movable seats which the occupant could adjust so he never had to sit in the sun. Other chariots were equipped with devices for measuring distances, and still others were cunningly adapted to suit the late emperor's highly individual tastes in vice.

Then it was the turn of Commodus' slaves. His boys and prostitutes were sold, though many of them were soon brought back to the palace to amuse his elderly successor. With an unusual burst of generosity, Pertinax distributed the proceeds of all these sales to his soldiers.

He found it a difficult task to return all the items of property stolen by Commodus (including numbers of confiscated slaves) to their rightful owners, but he did his best. He also cut down on court expenditure and made his son live outside the palace in his original home, sending him to an ordinary school. Even his palace banquets were modest affairs. "He used to invite us to frugal meals," Dio Cassius records.

The new regime with its emphasis on economy not unnaturally aroused widespread displeasure among the praetorian guard, civil servants and courtiers. No longer could the soldiers rob and pillage or the emperor's freedmen behave as they pleased, no longer could the ill-paid bodyguards sleep on duty. Laetus, the commander of the praetorians, soon regretted that he had ever helped Pertinax become emperor, for the old man took to calling him in public stupid blabbermouth and taxed him with giving away secrets. Inevitably there came a day when three hundred soldiers marched on the palace.

The palace guards did not bother to stop them for they had no use for their closefisted master. Pertinax was inspecting the court slaves when he was confronted by the three hundred intruders. Instead of effective action, odd and easygoing man that he was, he treated them to a long lecture. It utterly failed in its object: a spear pierced the emperor's chest. Breathing a prayer to Jupiter, Pertinax covered his head with his toga and died under a rain of dagger blows, a venerable bearded old man who, for a mere two months and twenty-five days, had ruled an empire which had outgrown his kind of innocuous personality. The Senate expressed their deepest regret at the emperor's death, but then nobody cared what the Senate thought, least of all the praetorians who had murdered Pertinax.

Rome now witnessed what was probably the most shameful and ridiculous farce in her history as the capital and the entire empire was offered to the highest bidder, with the late emperor's assassins playing the role of auctioneers, and Sulpicianus and Julian doing the bidding. The officers made no secret of the fact that they would give the throne to whichever of them offered their men the most money and a wild round of bidding began. "Sulpicianus is offering such and such an amount," the brokers shouted. "How much do you raise him by?" Julian immediately increased his offer. "What do you say to that?" the brokers asked Sulpicianus. And so it went on until the imperial throne was finally knocked down to Julian at 6,200 denarii per head. Having paid—or at least promised to pay—each man this not inconsiderable sum (about $700), Julian marched to the Senate with the guards at his back and was proclaimed emperor. His wife Manlia Scantilla and his daughter Didia Clara each received the title Augusta, as is shown by coins of this period, but when Julian summoned them to join him in the palace they did so apprehensively, already scenting the imminence of his downfall.

The Roman populace would have nothing to do with a man who had bought his throne. They pelted Julian so violently with stones as he was entering the palace that his escort of guardsmen had to screen him with their shields. Men and women uttered imprecations while the emperor was performing a sacrifice and begged the gods not to accept his offerings. Then they threw more stones. Julian made a feeble attempt to pacify them by suspending the laws but it did little good. The crowds poured into the circus, sat wherever they pleased, and stayed there all night, hooting, yelling, and calling down curses on Julian's head. In the end they grew tired and hungry and went home without having achieved anything.

Next, the governors of Syria and Upper Pannonia, Gaius Pescennius Niger and Lucius Septimius Severus, rose in arms against the emperor, and Severus marched on Rome with an army. Julian wanted to send the praetorians against him, but their enthusiasm was already on the wane since he could not satisfy their renewed demands for money. Severus seized control of the fleet at Ravenna. Now Julian proposed to send Vestal virgins and priests to meet him, thinking to achieve by entreaty what he could not do by force. The Senate, however, refused him permission, their attitude being that anyone who could not master an opponent by force of arms had no right to rule. Julian had, however, persuaded them to declare Severus a public enemy. Meanwhile, Severus marched on inexorably, preceded by large numbers of spies and soldiers in disguise. Panic-stricken, Julian decided to make peace with Severus and share the throne with him, perhaps intending to murder him later. Severus contemptuously declared that he would rather be the enemy than the colleague of a weakling. That left the desperate emperor with no choice but to build ramparts and ditches, turn Rome into an armed camp, and prepare to give his rival a bloody reception.

Absolute chaos ensued. There was a stream of conflicting orders. Men, horses and elephants bivouacked all over the place. The citizenry quaked in their shoes while the emperor's bodyguards, corrupt and demoralized, did nothing. Maddened by the battle turrets on their backs, Julian's elephants stampeded and threw their riders. And Julian fitted new locks to the palace doors to protect himself from the enemy. "Sometimes we had to laugh at it all," says Dio Cassius, "especially when the emperor barricaded the palace and bolted the doors."

Soon poor Julian was abandoned by everyone. The Senate, taking courage, divested him of his imperial authority. His voice echoed dismally through the deserted palace. He was lying on a couch in his huge bedchamber, pale and trembling, when a legionary flung open the door, rushed in, and plunged his sword into his breast. "What crime have I committed?" gasped Julian. "Whom did I ever put to death?"

After a mere two months and five days, Julian's reign was over.

THE GRIM AFRICAN

Emperor Septimius Severus was strict, unbending, grim. During
the latter years of his life he always had himself borne about
in a litter. When they wanted to depose him on that account,
he said quietly: "A man governs with his head, not his legs."
                                                        —Historia Augusta, Severus xviii, 11.

THE next occupant of the Roman throne, Septimius Severus, was born
at Leptis Minor in Africa on April 6, 146. His family, which could be
traced back for several generations, perhaps had some Punic blood,
even though it had received Roman citizenship much earlier, having
been resident of Rome itself by 90 A.D., by which date it had achieved
equestrian status. And it is recorded that Severus' Latin betrayed his
provincial origin.

His career had been an arduous one: aide to the proconsul in Africa,
tribune of the people, praetor in Spain, student at Athens, where he
also performed "certain sacred rites," governor of the province of
Lugdunensis. His first wife, Marcia, had died, so, being a keen student
of astrology, he proceeded to examine the horoscopes of various marriageable girls. Among them was a beautiful young Syrian whose
horoscope indicated that she was going to marry a ruler of men. Her
name was Julia Domna, and her father, Julius Bassianus, was high-
priest of the sun-god at Emesa in Syria. Severus was extremely pleased
with this gift from the stars—though the stars never told him that
Julia would be unfaithful.

As governor, Septimius Severus was supreme commander of the
Roman troops in the Pannonian districts between the Danube and the
Drave. It was here that his legions proclaimed him emperor on August
13, 193 A.D., at Carnuntum, a town on the Danube twenty-six miles
east of Vienna. He was greeted enthusiastically along the whole route
to Rome, but when the Romans realized that he meant to march into
the city at the head of his troops, there was general panic. Severus was
taking no risks. Ringed by soldiers, he marched to the Capitol and
entered the imperial palace with his bodyguards.

The troops gathered outside, grumbling. They wanted ten thousand
sesterces each, and Severus could not refuse, however little liking he

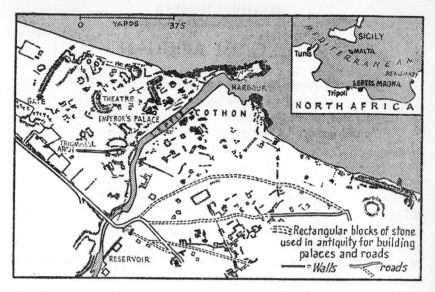

Leptis Magna, founded by the ancient Phoenicians, was the birthplace of Septimius Severus. Here the Romans built a splendid city of marble which now lies in ruins.

had for the idea. But no sooner had he established himself firmly on the throne than he began to govern in his own way. First he disbanded the praetorian guard and formed a new and stronger force from among his own legionaries. Then he saw to it that the dangerously depleted granaries were properly restocked. He dispatched troops to Africa and sent a legion to occupy Greece and Thrace, anxious to forestall any move by his rival, Pescennius Niger, the governor of Syria. Niger had already seized Byzantium but when he saw that the new emperor could show his claws, he offered to share the throne. Severus promptly refused.

Battle was joined near Issus in Cilicia at the close of 193. Niger had the advantage of numbers as well as a vast amount of military equipment, weapons and engines of war, but he was rather a hothead who styled himself "Alexander the Second." On being asked what gave him the right to adopt the name, he pointed to his sword and replied, "This does!" When the battle was over, Niger had lost 20,000 men. He made for Parthia, but got little further than Antioch before Severus had him arrested and beheaded. He then ordered his opponent's head to be impaled on a stake and planted in the ground in front of Byzantium, hoping that the sight would induce the city's inhabitants to surrender. He also punished the citizens of Antioch and Neapolis in Palestine because they had supported Niger.

Then Severus continued to besiege Byzantium which eventually fell.

The Romans promptly massacred all soldiers and officials but spared the ordinary citizens although Severus handed the captured stronghold over to the inhabitants of the neighboring town of Perinthus, who "oppressed it in every way." Dio Cassius says of Byzantium: "I saw the city in ruins, but I also saw it when it was still intact. And I even heard it speak. There used to be seven towers down by the sea. If you shouted to the first it would echo the sound and pass it on to the second; so sharp of hearing were the walls of Byzantium."

While the siege of Byzantium was still in progress, the emperor was already conducting operations against the Osrhoeni, Adiabeni and Arabs, and later he also knocked some sense into the Parthians. Rome of course offered him the inevitable triumph and the Senate conferred on him the titles Arabicus, Adiabenicus and Parthicus.

Then trouble broke out in Gaul under Clodius Albinus. The emperor promptly got his opponent proclaimed a public enemy and marched against him. He encountered Albinus at Tinurtium—probably the modern town of Tournus, which stands by the Saône some nineteen miles north of Mâcon. In the battle that ensued Severus ran into great danger through a fall by his horse.

His vanquished opponent Albinus was hauled before him, more dead than alive, and summarily decapitated on February 19, 197. Then Severus sent the head back to Rome and ordered the trunk left unburied outside the dead man's house for a long time. He then executed countless of Albinus' supporters in the area, noblemen and noblewomen alike. Albinus' official residence, Lugdunum (Lyon), which had been a chief city of Gaul since the time of Augustus, now lost its importance, while Treves began its climb to fame.

Seething with a tyrant's hatred, Severus returned to Rome where he executed forty-one noblemen and senators on the spot.

Severus left a trail of blood behind him wherever he went as anyone who opened his mouth too wide, indulged in witticisms or made equivocal remarks was put to the sword. "Behold the emperor, worthy of his name! He is truly steadfast (*pertinax*), truly strict (*severus*)."

Among others who forfeited their lives was the punster who coined that ambiguous phrase!

An historian of the age considers that Severus went to war more often out of ambition than absolute necessity. And certainly the emperor now opened an offensive war against the Parthians. He took their capital, Ctesiphon, allowed his troops to loot it, instituted a wholesale massacre, and carried off thousands of prisoners. Then he marched through Mesopotamia and turned it into a Roman province once more. The city of Atra refused to surrender, perhaps because of its faith in its first-class, long-range catapults, one of which is said to have been capable of discharging two projectiles at each firing. The inhabitants of Atra also used petroleum, pouring it down on the Romans from their walls and setting it alight. "Thus God helped his city," says Dio Cassius. Severus abandoned the siege.

The emperor then traveled onward to the African provinces where his native city of Leptis was rebuilt on a grand scale. Severus placed such emphasis on his Carthaginian descent that he also erected a great memorial for Hannibal and for Libyssa, the Bithynian town where he died, and effigies of the ancient patron goddess of Carthage, Tanit Caelestis, appeared on Roman coins. There are reminders of Severus all over modern North Africa. The spirit of the Punic Roman emperor still emanates from innumerable ruins, from crumbling temples, triumphal arches, statues, inscriptions, harbor installations, market places, entire towns. A large and quite well preserved temple to the Septimian family still stands at Ciucul in Numidia. Never in the whole of its history, until today, has North Africa experienced such a golden age as it did under Septimius Severus and his successors.

Emperor Severus was a dangerous man but Plautianus, the commander of his bodyguard, was perhaps more dangerous still. He accumulated loot from the four corners of the Roman world, even raiding islands in the Persian Gulf for what were probably zebras, which were sacred to the sun-god.

Plautianus was much more bloodthirsty than the emperor. He castrated one hundred Roman noblemen in his own house, for all of his daughter Plautilla's servants and tutors had to be eunuchs. Before long, Plautianus grew more powerful in some circles than Severus himself and statues of him were erected everywhere.

Severus even betrothed Plautianus' daughter to his own son Antoninus, a young man who was constantly quarreling with his brother

Geta. Indeed both the emperor's sons were bad characters, kept bad company, and had bad manners. "I am so fond of Plautianus," the emperor declared, "that I should like him to outlive me."

Empress Julia had to put up with every sort of hostility from Plautianus as he tried to blacken her in her husband's eyes, conducted investigations into what he termed "the Julia case," and stretched noblewomen on the rack in his search for incriminating evidence. Poor Julia sought consolation in philosophy.

Meanwhile, Plautianus debauched himself with prostitutes and youthful catamites, caroused, crammed his stomach with food, vomited, and generally played the greatest libertine in Rome. Plautianus was firmly in the saddle and no one could dislodge him.

Racius Constans, governor of Sardinia at the time, said, "The heavens will fall before Plautianus has anything to fear." Yet one year later Plautianus forfeited his head, and the heavens did not fall.

A few hairs from the dead traitor's beard were handed to Julia and Plautilla. The two women had only just met. Julia beamed. Plautilla wept. In the words of Dio Cassius: "Thus the most powerful man of my day, who dreamed of climbing ever higher and before whom all quaked and trembled . . . was put to death . . . and his body thrown out of the palace into the street."

Plautilla and Plautius, the dead man's children, were exiled to the island of Lipara where they lived in fear and misery until they were slain by Caracalla. Now that the all-powerful Plautianus was gone for good, Severus' sons, Caracalla and Geta, felt as free as air. They raped women, befriended gladiators and charioteers, and became competitors in crime.

One story of this period is rather amusing. A well-to-do man was suspected of coveting the imperial throne, and a witness declared that he had seen a bald-headed senator eavesdropping. No names were mentioned and all the senators were panic-stricken, not only the actually bald ones but also those who were going thin on top. Dio Cassius, who was a senator himself, wrote: "I cannot here refrain from saying what happened to me, ludicrous as it may seem. I was so perturbed that I involuntarily felt around on my head for some hair. It was the same with a number of others." Then came the further information that the bald-headed man had been wearing a toga trimmed with purple. "Our eyes now turned to Baebius Marcellius, who had hardly a hair left on his head."

On his way to the executioner, Marcellius said to his children, "My only regret is that I have to leave you behind alive."

Realizing that life in peacetime Rome was spoiling his sons and that his armies' discipline was slackening for lack of any large-scale operations, the old emperor set off for Britain, guessing that he would never return from the expedition alive.

It was on this expedition that Severus' wife, Julia Domna, who used to accompany her husband on his campaigns and was known among the troops as "Mother of the Camp," criticized the wife of Argentocoxus the Caledonian for her promiscuous sexual habits. But the woman merely replied, "We conform to nature far better than you Roman ladies. We openly consort with the best, while you live secretly with the worst and commit adultery with them." And "the best" were really tough and intrepid men. Dio Cassius tells us that "they endured hunger, cold and every kind of hardship with ease."

Late in his reign Severus invaded Caledonian territory, probably leading his troops from the sea to the Firth of Forth. Certainly he penetrated quite far into the north of the island, for he noticed "the sun's long sojourn above the horizon." Scotland was to be turned into a Roman province, and inscriptions show us that the country had its own cult dedicated to the Carthaginian goddess Tanit, the emperor's patron deity.

We are told that Severus was borne about in a litter throughout this campaign because he was ill, and afflicted with gout. His sons, too, were a source of worry—especially Caracalla, who seems to have been a complete degenerate, quick-tempered and often scarcely in command of himself. On one occasion he is said to have nearly killed his father with a sword thrust in the neck, only to be deterred by the outcry of the emperor's retinue. Afterward, in his tent, Severus told him, "If you want to kill me, do so. You are in your prime, while I am an old man." But Caracalla made no move.

Seeing old Severus lying there racked with pain, the troops had wanted to proclaim Caracalla emperor in his place. But Severus ordered his bearers to carry him to the court-martial, where he punished them all except his son. "That will teach you," he said, "that a man governs with his head, not his feet."

In the year 211 A.D., the old emperor at last decided to return to Rome. But the Caledonians were still as refractory as ever, and Severus

The still-surviving Pantheon at Rome was a temple sacred to all the gods. It was built by Hadrian between 115 and 125, although the inscription refers to a temple previously built on the site by M. Agrippa. The magnificent circular building symbolizes "perfection," its height and diameter both measuring 141 feet. Light is admitted through the aperture in the roof.

Antoninus Pius, one of the most noteworthy occupants of the Roman throne, was an uncommonly handsome man who combined humanity and warmth with generosity and great courtesy. During his reign (138-161 A.D.) the Roman Empire reached the zenith of its power.

Annia Galeria Faustina, wife of Emperor Antoninus Pius. On her death in 140 A.D. she was proclaimed "Diva Faustina" at her husband's request. The worthy emperor also founded an order for destitute girls, the Puellae Faustinianae, in her honor.

Emperor Marcus Aurelius and his brother Lucius Verus. The two brothers ruled jointly from 161 to 169 A.D. Marcus Aurelius, who survived Verus by eleven years, was the author of the world-famous *Meditations*, written during lonely nights in camp in Moravia and Bohemia.

A bronze equestrian statue of Marcus Aurelius in the Capitoline Square. The Christians, who were persecuted during his reign, would later have melted it down if they had not mistaken it for a statue of pious Emperor Constantine.

This interesting detail from the Column of Marcus Aurelius shows a German woman and her child being led off into captivity.

Over 97 feet high and built of Carrara marble, the Column of Marcus Aurelius was erected by the Roman Senate between 176 and 193 A.D. to commemorate victories over the Marcomanni, Quadi, Sarmatae and Iazyges. The original figure of the emperor, which had disappeared, was replaced in 1589 by a bronze statue of St. Paul.

Publius Helvetius Pertinax, a general who distinguished himself in Rhaetia under Marcus Aurelius and in Britain under Commodus. After the latter's murder he reigned for two months and twenty-five days.

Emperor Commodus reigned from 180 to 192 A.D. He ushered in an epoch of bloodshed, ferocity, and mass murder. This degenerate son of Marcus Aurelius was eventually strangled by the gladiator Narcissus.

Marcus Didius Julianus was a wealthy senator who bought the Roman throne at an auction organized by his predecessor's assassins. He was murdered in 193 A.D., after a reign of only two months.

Emperor Septimius Severus, who reigned from 193 to 211 A.D., was born in Africa and proclaimed emperor at Carnuntum on the Danube. His belief in astrology led him to marry Julia Domna, a girl with a "royal horoscope." He died at Eboracum (York).

The triumphal arch of Septimius Severus in the Roman Forum was erected by the people and Senate in honor of the emperor and his two sons Geta and Caracalla in 203. The inscription refers to the tenth anniversary of his reign, and the figures at the base of the pillars represent Parthian prisoners of war.

Geta, the ill-fated son of Septimius Severus and Julia Domna, who was treacherously murdered by his brother Caracalla in 212 A.D.

Julia Domna, second wife of Septimius Severus, was a beautiful and gifted Syrian woman of intellectual bent. Her son Geta vainly sought refuge in her lap when trying to evade the murderous sword-thrusts of his brother Caracalla.

Plautilla, wife of Emperor Caracalla, was murdered by her bloodthirsty and capricious husband.

Emperor Caracalla, who murdered his brother Geta, occupied the throne of Rome between 212 and 217 A.D. and was the builder of the famous Baths of Caracalla. His real name was Marcus Aurelius Antoninus Bassianus, Caracalla being a nickname derived from the cloak he always wore.

Opellius Macrinus instigated Caracalla's assassination and assumed the throne in his place. This African-born emperor ruled ingloriously from 217 to 218 A.D.

The Baths of Caracalla, begun by Septimius Severus in 206 and inaugurated by Caracalla in 216, could accommodate 1,500 bathers at any one time. The Baths' ornamentations included the Farnese Bull, the Flora, the Farnese Hercules and the Belvedere Torso. Above is a general view of the *thermae*, while the lower picture shows the vaults of the *frigidarium*. Subterranean vaults probably contained heating installations for water- and steam-baths. An earthquake demolished the building in 847.

Emperor Elagabalus reigned between 218 and 222 A.D. During his reign Rome witnessed scenes of debauchery unequaled by anything in her previous history.

Julia Mamaea, mother of Alexianus, the thirteen-year-old boy who, as Emperor, took the name Alexander Severus. Mamaea controlled her son and through him the whole empire.

Julia Paula, beautiful first wife of the priest-king Elagabalus. Here we see her as a young woman of about twenty-six.

Alexander Severus (reigned 222-235 A.D.) had such fine and brilliant eyes that it was said to be hard to meet his gaze. He was a favorite of the Romans and ruled with integrity and moderation. He was too dependent on his mother, however, and was eventually murdered with her.

The nerve center of ancient Rome. The Roman Forum was the focal point of the greatest empire in the ancient world and the hub of Roman life, which reached a peak of activity at about 11 A.M. each day. All traffic was banned here between sunrise and 4 P.M.

Ahura Mazda, the God of Light, is here shown conferring sovereignty on King Ardashir, who transformed the ancient doctrines of Zarathustra into a State religion. (Rock relief at Persepolis, Persia)

This used to be the stronghold of *Ardashir*, King of the Persians. He reigned from 226 to 241 A.D. and founded the mighty Sassanian Empire, which survived until 641.

King Ardashir's palace near Firuzabad must once have looked like this. (Photograph of an accurate reconstruction)

Fire-altars in the lonely highland plateaus of Persia sacred to Ahura Mazda, God of Light, whose prophet was Zarathustra. Mazdaism possessed no temples or religious buildings.

The Saalburg, a complete Roman fort as it must once have looked, reconstructed in the neighborhood of Bad Homburg between 1898 and 1907. The second Rhaetian cohort, comprising 500 men (120 of them mounted), was stationed here in the time of Hadrian.

A *limes* tower complete with rampart, palisade and signal-torch, reconstructed from a relief on Trajan's Column.

The main gate of the Saalburg, the only one of the fort's four gates to have a central dividing wall. At the entrance stands a statue of Emperor Antoninus Pius.

Emperor Maximinus, an uneducated Thracian, was proclaimed emperor in Mainz and ruled from 235 to 238 A.D. He was a first-class army officer.

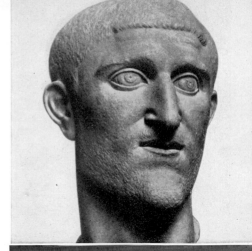

Maximinus' strikingly handsome son shared the throne with his father and was murdered with him on May 10, 238.

Emperor Gordian II reigned in partnership with his aged father for a few weeks in 238 A.D. and was then killed.

This bronze helmet with vizor is a mute reminder of the lavish entertainments of which the emperors and people of Rome never tired.

A Roman shoe, once worn by a legionary in about 200 A.D. Note the excellent workmanship and the up-to-date style designed to keep the foot cool. It was found in an old well shaft, where it had remained in amazingly good condition.

resolved to take the field once more. He died at Eboracum (York) on February 4, while engaged in preparations for this campaign.

Dio Cassius remarks that Severus was always a good friend but a very dangerous enemy. He carried out his plans with dogged resolution. He never lost his African accent, nor did his daughter, who spoke Latin with such a strong intonation that Severus disliked having her in Rome.

Severus was a very early riser, accustomed to rising even before daybreak to listen to reports on every sphere of government activity. He then presided in court until midday, when he went riding, took a bath and sat down to a good lunch with his family. The afternoon was spent in completing the rest of the day's affairs and taking Latin lessons. Late in the afternoon the emperor took another bath and then sat down to his evening meal. It is surprising, in view of his regular habits, that he lived only to the age of sixty-five.

Shortly before his death he sent for his own burial urn. "You will soon contain a man who found the globe too small for him," he said. His last words to his bodyguards were: "*Laboremus.*"—"Let us work!" He wanted to remain active to the last. "Well, hand it over, whatever there is left to do," he whispered, and then died.

"LAUGH, JULIA!"

Geta sustained a fatal wound and, dying,
drenched his mother's breast with blood.
—Herodian, *Imperial History* iii, 4.

"ON THINKING the matter over carefully, I am certain that, in general, no genius has ever bequeathed a really distinguished son to posterity. Most of the great men in history have had either no sons at all or off-spring which mankind could well have done without." So writes a Roman historian who lived after 300 A.D. He quotes, among other examples, Homer, Demosthenes, Virgil, Caesar and Augustus, and considers that the best thing which could have happened to Septimius Severus was never to have begotten Caracalla.

In the Via Giulia at Rome, in the peristyle of the Palazzo Marchese della Rovere-Sacchetti, there is an historical relief known as the "Sacchetti Relief." It depicts Emperor Septimius Severus seated on the *sella curulis* (chair of office) with Geta on the extreme right and Caracalla behind him on the other side. Between the two princes we can make out the jurist Papinian and, standing prominently beside the emperor in the place of honor, Severus' favorite, Plautianus. The figures of Plautianus, Geta and Severus all lack heads. They were purposely mutilated, and we know why.

The relief was commissioned to celebrate the nomination of Caracalla and Geta to the consulship in 205. When Plautianus was beheaded on January 23, his head had to disappear from the sculpture as well. Then Geta's head was obliterated in the year 212, while the emperor's vanished some time later.

Shortly before Septimius Severus died he expressed the wish that his sons get on together and behave as brothers should. Alas, each of them was dominated by an unnatural desire to kill the other. Their father had named them his joint successors in the hope that they would co-operate but even as they stood beside his bier in Eboracum, pro-fessing friendship and mutual admiration, each was secretly planning fratricide. One thing was obvious from the first: only one of them could reign, only one of them could rule, and so only one of them could live. Warily, the two brothers crossed the Channel and traveled through Gaul and Italy, suspiciously watching every sword, drinking with caution and never eating at the same table for fear of poison.

Geta seems to have been more popular with the troops than Caracalla, perhaps because his strong physical resemblance to his father encouraged the soldiers to assume that he was like Severus in character too. Caracalla was probably the more unscrupulous. He first plotted to assassinate Geta during the Saturnalia but unfortunately made his preparations too obvious and failed.

So the two brothers settled down in Rome, dividing the large imperial palace exactly in half and barring every door and passageway leading from one side of the palace into the other with barricades and guards. On the few occasions when the brothers met, it was either in public or in the presence of their mother Julia Domna—and then only if escorted by their bodyguards. All attempts at reconciliation or compromise failed; it was even planned to divide the empire. Caracalla, the elder brother, was to get Europe and western Africa, while Asia and Egypt would go to Geta, whose capital was to be either Alexandria or Antioch.

Julia Domna was most unhappy. At all costs, she wanted to prevent the Roman empire from being dismembered because of her sons' intolerance. As the mother and widow of emperors, she felt that she too would be torn asunder by the proposed partition.

The Senate attempted to reconcile the brothers by offering a solemn sacrifice to the goddess Concordia. The sacrificial beast was already at the altar and the consul on his way to supervise the slaughtering when someone managed to frustrate the ceremony. The consul could not find the attendants, and the attendants could not find the consul. It meant bad days ahead for Rome where nothing was given greater credence than an omen.

Geta was guarded by sentries night and day, and Caracalla saw that he was not going to get at his brother by main force. And so, about February 26 of 212 A.D., he went to his mother Julia Domna and, feigning a sensible desire for reconciliation, asked her to send for Geta. After all, he pointed out, Geta was his brother, and as the elder of the two he wanted to embrace him alone in their mother's house.

Geta trusted his brother for the first and last time. Unescorted, he went to his mother—and his death. Centurions whom Caracalla had concealed outside rushed into the room with drawn swords as Geta, running to Julia and throwing his arms around her neck, cried, "Mother, mother, they are killing me!"

Julia Domna was helpless. She embraced her son in an attempt to protect him with her arms, but the centurions stabbed away at him so enthusiastically that they wounded her in the hand. Geta died on his mother's knee, soaking her robes with blood, and a ghoulish whisper went around Rome: "Did you know? Geta has returned to the lap which bore him!"

Caracalla had triumphed, but from the moment of fratricide he was a haunted and conscience-stricken man incessantly impelled to remove from the world whatever reminded him of his guilt. His twenty-two-year-old brother was dead. Caracalla kept Julia Domna under surveillance day and night, forcing her to laugh as though she were the happiest woman alive and noting down her every word and gesture so that she dared not mourn her loss even in private.

Caracalla went on to become a complete despot, malicious and two-faced, influenced by terror, superstition and witchcraft.

The effects of conscience also seem obvious as Caracalla raced through Rome like a hunted man, constantly claiming that he was in deadly peril. "They want to do away with me. They want to kill me," he whispered to everyone he met. He promised his soldiers huge bonuses. "I am only one of you," he declared. "I want to live for you alone, to be able to reward you handsomely. My treasures all belong to you." The new emperor went so far as to tell his men that he intended to die with them. Then, having recalled all exiles, Caracalla launched a brutal campaign of terror. He dealt out death sentences galore and waded in a veritable sea of blood, using Geta as his eternal pretext. Thousands of men and women were executed, among them Geta's palace servants, soldiers who had supported him, and his friends, male and female. It was enough for someone to have been seen in Geta's half of the palace. The very name Geta became an anathema. On all the monuments and inscriptions in honor of Septimius Severus and his family which have ever been found, whether in Italy, Asia Minor, Africa or elsewhere, Geta's name has been erased.

The celebrated jurist Papinian was another of Caracalla's victims. Emperor Severus had probably confided to him how troubled he was about his two sons and Papinian may have attempted to bring the brothers together. We are told that Caracalla ordered him to justify his murder of Geta to the Senate and the people. Papinian is said to have replied that it was easier to commit fratricide than to defend it, and that to incriminate an innocent victim of murder was tantamount to murdering him a second time. On his way to execution, the famous jurist asserted that any man who took over his post as praetorian prefect without avenging him was a fool. The gods appear to have heeded his words, for the emperor was later murdered by Macrinus, Papinian's successor.

When Papinian was dead the emperor coolly inquired why the executioner had cut off his head with an ax instead of a sword.

But the emperor was far from finished with murder. His next victim was his former tutor, Cilo. Not until the soldiers had seized him and ripped off his senatorial robe and torn off his boots did Caracalla hurry and throw his military cloak around the poor man's shoulders crying, "Do not maltreat my dear old tutor!" Then he ordered the military tribune who had been detailed to kill Cilo executed for failing to cut off his dear old tutor's head.

Rome became a very sad place as all distinguished or respected men went in constant fear of their lives. Several Romans were even executed for having relieved themselves near statues of the emperor.

A CLOAK

The cloak became world-famous. Caracalla *meant a*
cape, and the emperor who wore it was named after it.
He was infatuated with Alexander the Great.
—Dio Cassius, lxxvii, 7.

CARACALLA yearned to be a celebrated general. He was always seeking
new excuses for war, kept large armies permanently mobilized, and
lavished huge sums of money on his soldiers. Having absolutely no
sense of proportion, he gave his men such extravagant rates of pay
that ultimately he had to devalue the coinage, just as Severus had decided to do before him and as Commodus had done before that. Even
so, his father's treasury was soon exhausted. This lack of money was,
however, probably not responsible for the emperor's one act of historical importance: his celebrated granting of citizenship to the entire
free provincial population of the Roman empire in the year 212 A.D.,
thus making the empire a single legal unit for the first time.

Caracalla was hot-tempered, thoughtless, and as overhasty and un-
sound in his decisions as he was prejudiced in favor of his own judgment. He disliked asking advice, especially of people who had put him
under an obligation of some sort. He liked no one and hated everyone,
most of all those who had somehow distinguished themselves. Some
outstanding men he did not murder but he sent off to regions with
unpleasant climates which did not agree with them, thus using "marks
of high esteem" as a way of removing men whom he disliked from
his range of vision. Others had all their property confiscated and were
reduced to penury. In all these measures the emperor was aided by a
certain native cunning, perhaps a legacy from his Syrian mother.

One year after Geta's murder, in 213, the emperor left Rome never
to return. He did not witness the completion of the huge thermae
which were built on his orders and are still among the largest ancient
ruins in Rome today, but spent the remaining four years of his reign
in various provinces of the empire. In August of 213 he crossed the
Rhaetian *limes* and defeated the Germans on the Main, thereafter
adopting the title Germanicus Maximus. In the spring of 214 we read
of him on the Danube.

Caracalla marched on through Thrace until he reached Macedonia where he succumbed completely to his mania to emulate that country's greatest son, Alexander the Great. He spent hours before a mirror with his head on one side, trying to imitate the posture for which Alexander was famous. (The Alexandrines responded by christening him "Alexander's monkey.") He drank from a goblet reputed to have belonged to Alexander, carried weapons which Alexander had reputedly used about 550 years earlier, ordered statues of Alexander erected in every camp, both at Rome and in the provinces, and recruited a phalanx composed solely of Macedonians and Spartans and armed exactly as Alexander's soldiers had once been. The emperor even negotiated unsuccessfully with the king of Parthia, Artabanus V, for his daughter's hand in marriage so that, as heir to the Parthian empire, his suzerainty would extend as far as India, as Alexander's had done long ago.

About this time, the emperor arrived in Antioch with his mother. By now he was suffering from nervous hallucinations, persecuted by the spirits of his murdered victims, haunted by the minatory apparitions of his father and brother. Sometimes he fainted dead away. But Alexandria, the Egyptian city named after the hero he so greatly idolized, temporarily jolted him out of his illness.

The emperor had heard that the Alexandrines despised him for having murdered his brother Geta and it was this which had made him decide to visit their famous city. With his habitual cunning, he invited the city's most distinguished citizens to a banquet and then exterminated them. He occupied every street and rooftop, imposed a curfew and executed many people, friends as well as foes. "The city is very large," Dio Cassius relates, "and, since the wholesale slaughter went on day and night, no one could make any distinctions—even if anyone had wanted to."

Every province had its turn at experiencing the emperor's rapacity, brutality and lack of scruple. Dio Cassius tells us that no one had a good word to say for him. He was given the name Tarantas, the nickname for a gladiator who was small and ugly but belligerent and bloodthirsty. However, he is known to history as Caracalla.

Being unequal to great exertion or extremes of heat and cold, Caracalla ordered himself some special clothes which looked like armor but were not. Clad in these he felt safe from assassination but did not have to endure the weight of real mail. Over his sham armor he wore an unusual red cloak which, unlike the one-piece normal Roman cloak, was tailored from several pieces of cloth and worn heel-length. Its name, *caracallus*, came to be applied to the emperor himself, Caracalla being a variation of the original word. His soldiers were obliged to wear these garments too.

Caracalla's mother, Julia Domna, seems to have managed the affairs of the whole empire with considerable statecraft, both at Rome and at Antioch in Syria where she was on home ground. But since Caracalla paid little attention to her advice, she had to go very cautiously to avoid arousing his violent temper. The fact remains that she maintained written communication with the empire at large, answering official correspondence in Latin and Greek, and gave audiences to senior civil servants, still finding time to devote herself to philosophical meditation.

It was the emperor's fondness for murder and vice, coupled with his habit of leaving the administration of public affairs to others, which finally spelled his undoing. An Egyptian seer had predicted that Macrinus, Caracalla's praetorian prefect, would soon be master of the Roman empire, and declined to withdraw this prophecy even when put in chains and threatened with death.

The emperor, back in Syria again and holding court at Antioch, was notified of this occurrence in writing but being engrossed in a chariot race at the time, he neglected to open his mail—as he often did—and sent the report back to Rome unread. There it was opened by Macrinus, who administered a large proportion of civil affairs on Caracalla's behalf. On reading the fateful document, Macrinus did not waste a moment. Sending for a soldier who was dissatisfied with his lack of promotion, he instructed him to kill the emperor.

By now Caracalla was on a trip from Edessa to Carrhae (modern Haran), the place from which Abraham had once started out for Canaan and where the Romans under Crassus the Triumvir had suffered their first defeat at the hands of the Parthians in the year 53 B.C. There the emperor indulged his pronounced partiality for Oriental magic cults and astrology. He had long ago accepted the Semitic or Syrian sun cult as one of Rome's new religions, and he now decided to pray at the shrine of Luna, the moon-goddess.

Caracalla hurried along the ancient Biblical trails to the moon temple, his mind obsessed with magic. In his craving for deliverance from the pangs of remorse, he failed to notice that his soldiers had become sullen and uncommunicative; that in their hearts they despised him, even though his sole wish was to be one of them. Now only a small squadron of cavalry accompanied the hurrying emperor until, ordering his escort to halt, Caracalla left the main highway and went a short distance into the surrounding scrub "to satisfy the needs of nature." And here the discontented soldier, whose name was Martialis, approached the emperor on some pretext and drove a dagger into his heart. He himself was immediately killed by a Scythian archer in the imperial bodyguard.

Julia Domna could weep at last. She had lost both her sons now, and with them the rank of empress. Grief and loss of status proved too much for her and she soon took her own life.

THE BEAUTIFUL BOY-PRIEST

He wanted not only to abolish the Roman forms of worship, but to snuff out the religions of the entire world, dominated by the thought that the god Elagabalus alone should be worshiped everywhere.
—Historia Augusta, Antoninus Elagabalus, vi.

IT IS extraordinary how totally insignificant people are sometimes raised to the most exalted heights in time of alarm or emergency. They meet with sudden success and attain a prominence of which even they would never have believed themselves capable. Playthings of destiny, they are like kites in the wind which fall in tatters after a short time aloft.

Such a man was Opellius Macrinus. He was not motivated by personal ambition. No, he arranged his emperor's murder out of dire necessity, a necessity forced on him by the precariousness of his position. A common soldier once, Macrinus was Caracalla's praetorian prefect. But then it had been prophesied that he, humble though his origins were, would become emperor of Rome. It was a pleasant prophecy but a dangerous one, so long as another emperor was still alive. And Caracalla was very much alive and might send Macrinus' head rolling at any moment.

Caracalla was murdered on April 6, 217 A.D. Fear had impelled Macrinus to become a murderer, just as fear made him seize the throne.

Macrinus was an undistinguished character. But, with the courage of a man who is gambling for his life, he rose to the demands of an unparalleled situation. Never before had a man who was not even a member of the Senate mounted the Roman throne. Now the time was ripe. Anyone looked better to the Romans than the frightful Caracalla. And as a gesture to the legion's regard for the Antonine name born by his predecessor, Macrinus proposed that the monster whom he had just murdered be declared a god.

It was unheard of for an assassin to honor his victim in such a way. Still more amazing was the fact that the Senate complied with Macrinus' wishes, for his guilt was an open secret. Nevertheless the new emperor's proposal did more to cloak his murderous act than any of his other hypocritical declarations although the legions continued to grumble.

Since there is no better way for a despot to obliterate his past than to cover himself with military glory, in the summer of 217 A.D. Emperor Macrinus marched against the Parthians. All the army's doubts and uncertainties might have vanished and street-corner gossip might have died away after an outstanding victory or two. Great military successes were the Midas touch which would turn an emperor's insecurity into power and glory.

But after a few minor successes and two major defeats by the Parthians, Macrinus put forward peace proposals which Artabanus, the Parthian king, was willing to accept. The emperor then returned to Antioch where he devoted himself to recherché amusements and basked in his exalted rank. He cultivated his beard, strolled majestically about, and conducted audiences in such an affectedly low voice that no one could understand a word he said.

Herodian reports that back in Rome people could at least enjoy a year's freedom from fear, once Caracalla was dead and peace had been signed with the Parthians.

However, the Roman legions soon developed a distaste for their new master. They had no particular stomach for fighting the Parthians, yet the emperor's deplorable peace treaty with the Parthians made them look too obviously a defeated army. Macrinus had even promised to pay Artabanus a large indemnity for war damage, and when he proposed to cap it all by docking the legionaries' future pay the Roman warriors stepped up their plans for the emperor's murder.

Nor were the surviving members of Severus' line content to sit back and let their title, Antoninus, be purloined by a man with no right to it. Julia Domna, late wife of the former emperor, had a sister named Julia Maesa. And Maesa had two daughters, Soaemias and Mamaea, each of whom was the mother of one son: Soaemias of Varius Avitus, and Mamaea of Alexianus. The entire family lived at Emesa, their native city on the Orontes in central Syria, on Macrinus' order. This place, which lay to the north of Damascus, is now known as Homs. At Emesa the family provided high priests for the god Elagabalus (less correctly Heliogabalus) in whose name we rediscover the ancient god Baal of the Old Testament. Elagabalus, a sun-god and the patron deity of Emesa, was worshiped in the shape of a black conical stone "which had fallen from heaven"—a piece of the sun, in fact.

The city of Emesa was famed in ancient times for its sun temple. The city's tutelary deity was the sun god Elagabalus, who was worshiped in the shape of a meteor. Emperor Varius Avitus, later known as Elagabalus, held priestly office in Emesa at the early age of fourteen.

Julia Domna herself had been the daughter of a wealthy priest of Elagabalus and Varius Avitus, Soaemias' son, occupied the same post in Elagabalus' temple at the age of fourteen. Thus the family was closely connected with the cult of Baal.

Fourteen-year-old Varius Avitus was the legitimate son of Soaemias and the Syrian Varius Marcellus. But now his cunning grandmother Maesa announced that he was a natural son of the late Emperor Caracalla. That made him a Severus: and only a Severus—being entitled to the surname Antoninus—could become emperor.

To the grandmother obtaining the throne for her grandson was obviously more important than preserving her daughter's good name. As for the daughter, she did not mind exposing herself to shame, disgrace or scandal as long as her son became emperor. The two women actually succeeded in convincing some of the legions that the priest's son was Caracalla's bastard. And since the Antonines were still honored as gods, it was not long before the new Antoninus was voted honors by cities all over the empire.

Grandmother Maesa was as wily as she was wealthy while daughter Soaemias was ambitious, courageous and hardheaded. Grandson Avitus on the other hand was an effeminate youth who liked spending money. Naturally the handsome young priest was extremely popular with the troops, and his temple was never empty.

Caracalla's alleged offspring was now proclaimed emperor and Macrinus once more found himself in deadly peril. A battle was fought between the legions loyal to young Avitus and those of Macrinus at the village of Immo, 24 miles east of Antioch on June 8, 218. Macrinus, deserted by most of his troops, attempted to make his way in disguise to Italy, but was arrested at Calcedon and soon put to death. And so ended the reign of the first emperor in Roman history never to set foot in Rome throughout his reign.

The handsome boy-priest, known to us simply as Elagabalus after his god, although he did not receive the name until much later, was now undisputed master of the empire. He became the most Machiavellian monster that ever occupied the Roman throne, diabolical in his vicious eccentricities and far outrivaling Nero himself in perverted ingenuity.

When the Senate heard the news of Elagabalus' accession there were the usual scenes of rejoicing as tributes were paid to the new Antoninus and curses were heaped on the late Macrinus and his nine-year-old son.

To prepare the Romans in some degree for his strange appearance, Elagabalus commissioned a life-sized portrait of himself in the vestments of a Syrian priest and sent it on to Rome in advance, where it was set up beside the statue of Victory in the Senate house.

About September 29 of 219 Elagabalus made his ceremonial entry into Rome. Swathed in gorgeous robes, rouged like a girl, his eyes artificially luminous with essences, a pearl necklace about his throat and diadems in his hair, the new emperor entered the city on the Tiber bringing a breath of the Orient with him. At his side sat his mother and grandmother, misty-eyed with rapture and devotion but confronted by the onerous task of controlling the unruly instrument of their ambitions.

The Romans witnessed scenes such as they had never known before. They saw the sacred meteorite pass by in solemn state, borne on a lofty carriage. The Syrian youth had removed his sun-god's image from the temple at Emesa and brought it all the way to Rome. He walked backwards ahead of the carriage so that he should never lose sight of it. Two temples were soon erected for this Baal, one on the Palatine Hill and the other near what is now Porta Maggiore. Emperor Elagabalus wanted to merge the numerous Roman cults and make the god Elagabalus the supreme deity. He even wanted to bring Judaism and Christianity into his temples and enlist them in the service of his god.

Elagabalus very soon divorced his first wife Julia Paula, whom surviving sculptures reveal as a beautiful but rather sullen-faced girl. To publicize the amalgamation of Rome's gods with those of the East and set the seal on his strange religious merger, Elagabalus then married a Vestal priestess, Aquilia Severa, who was sworn to thirty years virginity. He announced that, in his opinion, such a marriage between a high priest and a priestess was most appropriate and expressed his confident belief that any children of such a union would be godlike.

This was among the first shocks which the emperor gave his Roman subjects; it was by no means the last. The emperor of Rome danced round the altars at public festivals to the sound of cymbals, drums and weird anthems sung by Syrian women.

All Rome marveled at the sacred sky-born stone, the new priest-emperor, and the oriental display of exotic colors, incense and music.

But who really was Elagabalus' god—this god to whom he was suspected of sacrificing children from aristocratic families all over

Italy? Actually his god was no more than a combination of self-indulgence, debauchery and vice. But Elagabalus made certain that the people got their handouts although instead of throwing them gold and silver he distributed fattened cattle, camels, donkeys and slaves. And the Roman populace accepted its gifts—and its bizarre ruler.

DROWNED IN BLOSSOMS

*"In a banqueting-room with a reversible ceiling, he once over-
whelmed his parasites with violets and other flowers, so that
some of them were actually smothered to death, being unable
to crawl out to the top."*
—Historia Augusta, Antoninus Elagabalus, xxi, 5.

ELAGABALUS was fourteen when he came to the throne, and only
eighteen when he died.

There were riotous scenes in the imperial palace where he opened
a large bathhouse to the public—not, it may be added, in the service
of Roman hygiene but in order to find victims for his idiotic
amusements.

The emperor was constantly accompanied by a huge athlete from
Smyrna called Aurelius Zoticus. Zoticus, the son of a cook, had been
brought with great ceremony to Rome where Elagabalus welcomed
him into his palace, specially illuminated for the occasion, and appointed him his chamberlain. Zoticus took the most outrageous advantage of his friendship with Elagabalus and amassed a large fortune by
selling promises and concessions to all and sundry. "I told the emperor
this about you," he would whisper to everyone he met, or "The emperor
said that about you." But Elagabalus solemnly went through a form of
marriage with Zoticus and insisted that someone should act as "brides-
maid or bridesmatron."

Elagabalus also nominated a professional dancer as prefect of the
guard, a charioteer as commander of the watch, and a barber named
Claudius as supervisor of the grain supplies. None of these men had
any qualifications for their jobs except debauchery. Aurelius Victor
reports that, generally speaking, Elagabalus "gathered about him the
most obscene people from all over the globe." He gave the three senior
posts in the department of death-duties to a muleteer, a messenger and
a smith. It is no wonder that whenever he visited the Senate or a military camp he took his grandmother with him, for otherwise no one
showed him any respect. It was, incidentally, the first time that a
woman had ever set foot in the senate house.

Mamaea, the sister of Elagabalus' mother Soaemias, had meanwhile
seen to it that her son Alexianus was also promoted to imperial rank

and that Elagabalus adopted him. It was quite obvious that Elagabalus could not go on "reigning" by himself for much longer. His cousin Alexianus was a very able young man who was popular with the army and greatly respected by the Senate. Elagabalus turned morose at the very mention of Alexianus' name, realizing only too well that the people much preferred his cousin to himself. And so, seeing Alexianus' continued existence as a threat to his own position, he hired some soldiers to assassinate him. However, the soldiers occupied the palace to protect Alexianus, not to kill him.

Elagabalus waited anxiously for news of the murder, yet when he heard the tramp of soldiers' feet he was suddenly seized by a nameless fear and hid behind a curtain in his bedroom. He thus managed to escape with his life on this occasion, but still he did not abandon the idea of murdering his cousin. As a preliminary step, knowing that the Senate was on Alexianus' side, he decreed that all its members must leave Rome immediately. Despite this, one courageous senator named Sabinus stayed on in the dangerous city. The emperor angrily ordered a centurion to kill him but, fortunately for Sabinus, the centurion was deaf. Another man who risked his life on this occasion was Ulpian, the great Syrian jurist.

Elagabalus was addicted to banquets, wine, flowers, and perfume. He inaugurated various summer carnivals, each with a different color as its theme. There was a green festival, a pink festival, a violet festival, a blue festival—a special color for each warm summer's day. He blended wine with the most exotic additives, enhancing the bouquet of rose wine, for instance, by mixing it with fragrant fir-cone essence. He showered his banqueting halls with roses, lilies, violets, hyacinths and narcissi, and waded happily through oceans of blossom. Having installed a reversible ceiling in his dining room, he tipped such quantities of violets and other flowers onto his guests that several of them lost their lives when they were unable to struggle out of the suffocating avalanche of blossoms and into the open air.

Elagabalus would only swim in his pool if the water had been perfumed, and the rarest and most precious oils were provided whenever he went bathing with his court. He had swimming pools built a considerable distance from the coast, where it was difficult to fill them with sea water, and then gave them to his friends along with rose-scented water in which he himself had bathed. Once, wanting to see a mountain of snow, he had one transported from far away in huge buckets. His pillows and couches had to be stuffed with hare's fur and the finest turkey feathers, and he always reclined on them surrounded by rare flowers and perfumes. He once had himself and his favorites served a dish of six hundred storks' heads, of which he only ate the brains. On another occasion, he offered his guests twenty-two unusual meat dishes and compelled them to bathe with him in mixed company between each course, swearing all the time how much they were enjoying themselves.

The emperor collected snakes and was fond of letting them loose among the spectators at evening entertainments, roaring with laughter at the people who were hurt in the ensuing panic. Sometimes he harnessed lions to his chariot, sometimes tigers or elephants, always donning the costume of the deity to which these animals were sacred. His pets included small but deadly Egyptian snakes, hippopotami, crocodiles and even a rhinoceros. When he got bored, he drove around nude with lovely young girls, likewise unclad, harnessed in pairs, threes or fours to his chariot. At night he would disguise himself in a wig and visit disreputable taverns where he enjoyed himself riotously. Sometimes he would sit on the threshold of one of his palace chambers, pulling aside the curtain on its golden rings and soliciting any of his courtiers who happened to be passing in a reedy, languishing voice. He was always extremely effeminate in his behavior and used, among other things, to wear a hair net, paint his eyes with white lead and carmine, and pluck his beard. Wherever Elagabalus went and whatever he was doing, whether sacrificing, receiving visitors or addressing the people, he used to dance. He also played charioteer, dressed in a green robe, with his bodyguards, grandmother, mother and numerous concubines acting as umpires. Bowing low, the emperor would beg gold pieces from his officers and the other "umpires" like a common racing driver.

Elagabalus had a good singing voice and could play the flute, horn, organ, and a three-stringed instrument. He is said to have been the first Roman to dress entirely in silk, a material which he prized above all others. He also owned a *tunica* of pure gold, another of purple, and another, from Persia, encrusted with precious stones, which he often complained was too heavy for him. He even wore jewels on his shoes and a bejeweled diadem calculated to enhance his girlish beauty.

At the theater he sometimes laughed so loudly that the audience could not hear the performers. But one of his favorite performances was to assemble all the prostitutes in the capital in a large public building and deliver obscene speeches to them.

When his friends had gotten properly drunk at one of his wild parties Elagabalus used to dowse the lights, lock them in, and let lions, leopards and bears into the room without warning. Actually the animals were docile and harmless, their teeth having been removed, and the emperor only wanted to give his friends a fright, not kill them; but in fact several of them died of shock.

Elagabalus appears to have been the inventor of the air cushion. He used to employ them and then have his slaves let the air out under his friends so that they rolled beneath the table. Again, he lashed several of his boon companions to a water wheel, set it in motion, and enjoyed himself hugely at their expense.

He ordered imitation food to be made out of wax, wood, ivory, clay, marble or stone and served these cunning replicas to his unsuspecting guests while at table with them. He once told his slaves to gather half a ton of spider's web, offering prizes as an encouragement, and when they collected five tons, remarked that it showed how large Rome was. He used to present his friends with jars containing frogs, scorpions, snakes, and even captured flies which he called "tamed bees." On another occasion he bought himself a beautiful concubine for 100,000 sesterces and then kept her untouched, "as a virgin." He sank fully laden ships in harbor on the grounds that such an act demonstrated the greatness of his soul. He executed all the day's business at night and luxuriated in bed for most of the morning. He seldom dismissed his courtiers after an audience without giving them a present—unless they were the thrifty type, of course. The emperor detested thrifty people.

On being told by Syrian priests that he would die an unnatural death, Elagabalus provided himself with red silk cords with which to hang himself, golden swords on which to impale himself, and every conceivable type of poison. He even went to the extent of building himself a tall tower from which to plunge to his death when the critical moment arrived. But his soldiers and bodyguards, especially the latter, did not let it come to suicide.

Once again, Elagabalus was contemplating the murder of his cousin. Once again, all he had succeeded in doing was awakening the murderous inclinations of his bodyguards against his own person. Then, in a last-minute attempt to pacify them and save his life, he visited their camp accompanied by his cousin Alexianus and their respective mothers.

The soldiers never took their eyes off him but watched him like a rat in a trap. Then the atmosphere took on a note of sinister farce when the two mothers started to squabble, heaping the fuel of their hatred onto an already explosive situation. Elagabalus at last tried to escape and hid in a latrine with Soaemias, who sat there trembling with her arms clasped tightly about her beloved son. But mother and son were discovered and slain. Their heads were cut off and their bodies dragged through the gutters to the Tiber, where they were thrown off the Aemilian Bridge with weights attached to prevent their floating to the surface.

The actor, practical joker, charioteer and dancer, the insane voluptuary, the painted woman in masculine attire who had occupied the throne of a world empire was dead at last. He was only eighteen.

THE DARLING OF THE ROMANS

*He intended to build Christ a temple and include him among
the gods—a project which Hadrian is said to have contemplated
earlier.*
—Historia Augusta, Severus Alexander, xliii.

AFTER his half-demented cousin Elagabalus, Alexianus looked to
Roman eyes like a gift from the gods. It was 222 A.D., or 975 years
after the founding of the city—*ab urbe condita*, as the Romans termed
it. It was an age when people believed in miracles and heavenly
manifestations and saw divine portents whenever there was a change of
government. A story at once became current that a great star had
appeared in the sky above the house at Arca Caesarea in Syria as
Alexianus had been born. People had doubtless heard something about
a "king of mankind" and his birth-star, and the idea of an omen of
salvation above the new emperor's place of birth was the logical
outcome.

It was hoped that the fourteen-year old Alexianus would model
himself on Alexander the Great, which was why, as emperor, he bore
the names Marcus Aurelius Alexander Severus in addition to the
habitual load of imperial honors and titles. However, power really lay
in the hands of his astute but money-grubbing mother, Mamaea, who
formed a permanent privy council composed of sixteen wise and respected senators to help her. Its president was the well-known Syrian
jurist Ulpian who, in his additional capacity as commander of the
bodyguard, was invested with supreme imperial jurisdiction.

Mamaea never wanted to be an empress; she merely wanted to hold
the reins of power from behind her son's back, and to restore order.
But she wanted to be the only one to shape her son's ideas and would
not tolerate another woman near him. Alexander married the daughter
of a patrician, chosen for him by Mamaea, but his happiness was short-
lived. His father-in-law, who had received the title Caesar, was executed for high treason when he started taking his new status too seriously and the unhappy bride, whose name may have been Memmia or
Herennia Orbiana, was chased out of the palace by her mother-in-law
and banished to Africa. It so happened that Alexander was deeply in
love with her.

Mamaea molded her young son's character with the utmost care, enlisting the aid of the greatest living teachers. What was more, she was successful, for his nature, not in itself a strong one, was illumined by integrity, orderliness, inner purity and an unquestioning devotion to his mother. Admittedly, this young emperor whom the Romans honored and revered like a god never willingly made a decision of his own. Mild as the gentle wind from Lebanon which blew across his native land, he merely bowed to his responsibilities. But he never shirked a decision—as long as Mamaea was within reach—and he never dared to contradict her.

Alexander had beautiful, brilliant eyes, and people used to say that it was difficult to meet his gaze. He also had a remarkably good memory and was even credited with telepathic powers. And being a distinguished astrologer himself, he permitted the Chaldeans, who had originally been banished from Rome in 139 B.C. and periodically persecuted ever since, to install themselves there once more and pursue their profession freely. It was believed that anyone who could predict the future was a great asset to the state.

The emperor studied geometry, painting, and singing. In contrast to Nero and Elagabalus, however, he only sang in privacy, i.e. in front of his slaves. Roman historians also attributed a large number of other talents to this highly respected emperor, some of which were no doubt invented out of admiration, regard, or a sense of relief that he had survived his villainous cousin and that Elagabalus was dead and gone. Although a Syrian by birth, Alexander was far less Asiatic in manner than his villainous predecessor. And in his anxiety to be a Roman, he always tried to gloss over or disguise his alien origins and was furious when the citizens of Antioch and Alexandria jokingly referred to him as a Syrian priest.

The emperor used to visit the temple at dawn each day where, if we are to believe the *Historia Augusta,* he addressed his prayers not only to the Roman gods and the emperors who had been raised to divine rank, but to the spirits of Orpheus, Christ, Abraham and, when in his private chapel, to Apollonius of Tyana. This remarkable itinerant preacher and worker of miracles from the first century A.D. was represented by legend sometimes as a magician, sometimes as a godlike man. At the instigation of Maesa's sister Julia Domna, who was also a devotee of Apollonius, the Greek author Philostratus wrote a romantic biography of the man. It has survived to the present.

We are told that Alexander Severus intended to build Christ a temple, a project which Hadrian, who erected several temples and left them bare of gods, may have contemplated earlier. It appears, however, that Alexander's adviser successfully opposed this plan, warning against building a temple to the God of the Christians by arguing that everyone would turn Christian and the other temples would be deserted. For all that, the Jews were now granted freedom of worship and it was forbidden to persecute the Christians. That great Father of the Church, Origen of Alexandria, was even invited to levees by Julia Mamaea, the emperor's mother.

The emperor normally spent the early part of the morning hunting, fishing or walking before turning to affairs of state, which never seemed to tire or irritate him. After that he would do some reading. He often dipped into a biography of Alexander the Great, but also studied Plato and read Cicero and Horace. Then came athletics, after which Alexander had himself oiled and swam for an hour. He followed his bath with a snack of milk, bread and eggs which often enabled him to do without a midday meal. In the afternoon he answered official correspondence and worked with his secretaries. After that he was at home to friends and visitors with Ulpian always at his side during the more important interviews.

Alexander was very abstemious and often drank nothing but cold, clear water. In summer he used to mix his wine with a little rose water, his fondness for the bouquet this produced being all he really had in common with his cousin Elagabalus.

Alexander made a clean sweep of the parasites whom Elagabalus had provided with cozy sinecures in the civil service, purging the Senate, palace and army of dancers, catamites and uneducated upstarts. The emperor also discharged all the palace eunuchs and made them the slaves of women commoners or gave them to his friends, declaring that this "third sex" should not be tolerated either by men or by upper-class women. Dwarfs, jesters, male singers with female voices, clowns and buffoons were all proclaimed state property, as were women of easy virtue. There were hard times ahead for corrupt magistrates because the young emperor, so mild in other respects, could be brutal when it came to legal graft.

The emperor made it a principle not to grant appointments to the first to crowd around the trough, preferring to promote modest men of genuine ability who stayed quietly in the background. Doctors, technicians and scholars of all kinds received commissions and well-paid posts, while orphans and children from poor homes got interest-free loans from the state. The whole Senate was given a hearing before any new senator was nominated and was also consulted in the matter of elections to the consulship, as it had been in the old days. When Mamaea advised her son to be rather more strict and severe, Alexander answered that his kind of rule was at least safe and enduring.

The young emperor seems to have been extraordinarily hard-working. We learn that he sat for nights on end poring over the lists of officers and other ranks in his army, checking their strength, ranks and rates of pay, noting the names of men who had earned promotion, and drawing up extensive plans for supply depots and ration dumps which would spare his soldiers the necessity of carrying heavy packs.

On military expeditions through enemy territory, Alexander always provided an ample number of sturdy draft animals. He personally visited the sick and wounded in their leather-tented hospitals and had them transported in carts during long marches. Severely wounded men were left behind in towns in the gentle and efficient care of leading citizens.

Alexander planned all his military enterprises with great forethought. He let his soldiers know the date and time of departure long in advance and informed them how far they had to go. The one thing he obviously never told them was his objective and his plan of operations, fearing that he might alert the enemy and play into their hands. It is little wonder that the legionaries liked their young emperor and felt that he had their interests at heart. They were well clothed, well quartered, and excellently armed. They had swift thoroughbred horses and regulation saddles. Their splendid appearance was living proof of the power and glory of Rome.

However, the fact that it was composed of so many different nationalities made this Roman army a brittle affair. Moreover the men who had served under Alexander's predecessors were spoilt and fundamentally demoralized. On top of this Alexander's well-intentioned plan to settle largish bodies of troops as yeomen farmers in the neighborhood of their frontier garrisons had the unfortunate effect, from a military point of view, of diminishing both their state of readiness and their value as a fighting force.

Alexander attracted businessmen to Rome from all over the world by smoothing over trade difficulties and regulating financial relations.

He imposed reasonable taxes on tailors, linen weavers, glass manufacturers, blacksmiths, silversmiths and goldsmiths, and founded guilds for greengrocers, wine merchants and shoemakers. When the populace asked him to lower prices, he asked them which items of food were too expensive. "Beef and pork," came the reply. Instead of lowering prices, Alexander imposed a ban on slaughtering. When he lifted it two years later there was a glut of meat on the market—and it was dirt-cheap!

The emperor preferred the normal linen toga to robes interwoven with purple or gold; in his opinion, gold thread made any material stiff and unpleasant to wear. He also wore puttees and close-fitting white trousers. On Trajan's Column trousers were the distinguishing mark of a barbarian, yet by the second century A.D. they were already being worn by some of the Roman troops on the Rhine and the Danube, who were encouraged by the colder climate and the example of the betrousered Celts, Germans and Dacians. Now, in the third century, the emperor himself took to wearing trousers.

Alexander entertained the idea of putting all his courtiers into uniforms denoting their rank. They were not to be military uniforms, but merely a means of showing the emperor at a glance with whom he was dealing. He also decreed special clothes for slaves which would make it harder for them to mingle undetected with freemen. However, the legal experts Ulpian and Paulus seem to have put a damper on Alexander's sartorial plans. Apart from anything else, slaves were becoming fewer because many of them had been given their freedom on humanitarian grounds. "According to the law of nature, all human beings are equal," was the enlightened verdict of Ulpian.

The emperor decreed that mixed bathing should be strictly prohibited. And to prevent the public baths (there were eight hundred of them in Rome) from getting into financial difficulties, Alexander gave them the usufruct of the state forests. Baths could be taken in the evening and at night too, since the emperor provided abundant supplies of oil for artificial lighting. In the year 222 A.D. Alexander built what was the last Roman aqueduct on the ancient pattern. Coins dating from the year 226 and bearing pictures of thermae show us how important to the Roman his bath was.

Life in Rome was good, the citizens were contented and the legionaries, at least those of higher principles, were fond of their young emperor. But, because he was just and reasonable and did not load them with money like Elagabalus, as they so often had before, they found his integrity almost more trying than the vices of his imperial fore-runner. Ulpian, who as prefect of the guard was responsible for justice and discipline, they soon came to regard as an enemy. The guards spread a story that he had done away with his predecessors Flavianus and Chrestus, and mutiny broke out. Pursued by the guards, Ulpian sought refuge in the imperial palace. The dramatic scene which fol-lowed clearly shows how dangerous life was for the young emperor and what a tense atmosphere prevailed in the capital. The guardsmen threw themselves on Ulpian and although Alexander tried to protect his friend and adviser with his purple cloak, the soldiers murdered their brilliant and erudite commander before the emperor's very eyes.

Alexander's reaction was sluggish. He could not summon up the courage to take action against the ringleader of the mutiny, a man named Epagathus, so he first appointed him prefect of Egypt and then sent him on to Crete. Only when the guards' memory of Epagathus had faded slightly did the emperor have him tried before a court on the island and executed.

ARDASHIR'S GREAT ACHIEVEMENT

There is no power without an army, no army without money, no money without agriculture, no agriculture without justice.
—Ardashir, King of Persia.

LIKE a fine ray of light out of an overcast sky, a new and quite un-Roman sentiment came to the notice of young Severus Alexander sometime during his reign (222–235 A.D.): "Do unto others that which you would have them do unto you." The non-Christian emperor had this golden rule, which originated in the Proverbs of Solomon in the Old Testament, inscribed on the wall of his palace. It seems certain that he must have heard it from Jews or Christians.

Once when Alexander learned that a soldier had maltreated a poor old woman, the young emperor had him drummed out of the army and made him the old woman's slave. We are told that, being a skilled wheelwright, the soldier was well able to support her, but we are also told that the army grumbled at his punishment. Similar dissatisfaction and internal unrest in time became a threat to the emperor and the empire in general. On one occasion Alexander was forced to disband an entire legion, first giving its members a lengthy lecture in which he addressed them as "citizens," not "soldiers."

Yet Alexander often sat down in his legionaries' dining tent and ate the same food as his men. Though he gave silver shields to the elite of his bodyguard, he took pains to show that he personally could live like a common soldier. Apparently he never felt the fear of his legionaries which had gnawed at so many of his predecessors. "A soldier is harmless," he used to say, "as long as he is well clothed, well armed and well quartered: as long as he has a full belly and some coins in his money belt."

But were the legionaries really so harmless? The great English historian Gibbon asserts, in his famous work on the decline of the Roman empire, that from the reign of Augustus to that of Alexander Severus Rome carried two sorts of enemy within her: tyrants and soldiers. And it was the soldiers who made and unmade the tyrants.

Almost at the same time as Alexander Severus became emperor of Rome, the distant highlands of Iran witnessed one of the most momentous events in their fascinating history. For here the Sassanian empire of Persia was born. Parsa (the original form of the modern name Persia) was once a small province in the huge kingdom of Media. In the year 550 B.C. an intrepid son of this small province overthrew the Median king, captured Ecbatana, the Iranian capital, and made himself "King of Kings." The glory of Cyrus' royal dynasty, the Achaemenids, lasted for about 220 years, until that day in 331 B.C. when Alexander the Great vanquished the Persian empire with his decisive victory at Gaugamela in the plain of the Tigris.

When Alexanders' successors, the Macedonian Seleucids, had been ousted in their turn, yet another non-Persian dynasty mounted the throne of Iran. These were the Parthian Arsacids, members of a race of steppe-dwellers and horsemen who came originally from the region of the Aral Sea in Central Asia and were called the Parni. The Arsacids ruled for five hundred years.

Then in 226 A.D. there was an exact repetition of what had happened in 550 B.C. Once again a youth from Parsa overthrew the Great King. Once again a Persian conquered the empire and founded a new royal line.

Thus Iran was conquered by the little province of Parsa on two separate occasions: by Cyrus in 550 B.C. and by Ardashir in 226 A.D. There in the native land of such conquereors as Cyrus, Darius and Xerxes ancient tradition lived on. Even though they had been dead for more than seven hundred years, people still remembered the great days of the Achaemenids and the way they had tried to conquer Greece and, through Greece, Europe. People still dreamed of world conquest and an empire such as the world had never seen before.

Like so many conquerors, Ardashir came of the humblest origins although later on, as so often happens in history, it was carefully proved that he belonged to a princely house. Our most important source of information about him is the Arab historian Abu Jafar Mahommed

---

In 550 B.C. Cyrus emerged from *Parsa*, the ancient heart of Iran, overthrew the Median King of Kings, captured the Iranian capital, *Ecbatana*, and founded the Achaemenian dynasty. The imposing ruins of the Achaemenids' palaces and tombs stand at *Persepolis*. Their dynasty survived until Alexander's conquest of the Persian Empire in 330 B.C., after which the (non-Persian) Parthian Arsacid dynasty held sway for five hundred years. Then, in 226 A.D., Iran was again conquered by Parsa and Ardashir founded the Sassanian dynasty. The Sassanids' native city was *Istakhr* or *Stakhr* and their new capital was *Ctesiphon*, royal seat of the powerful kings Ardashir and Shapur.

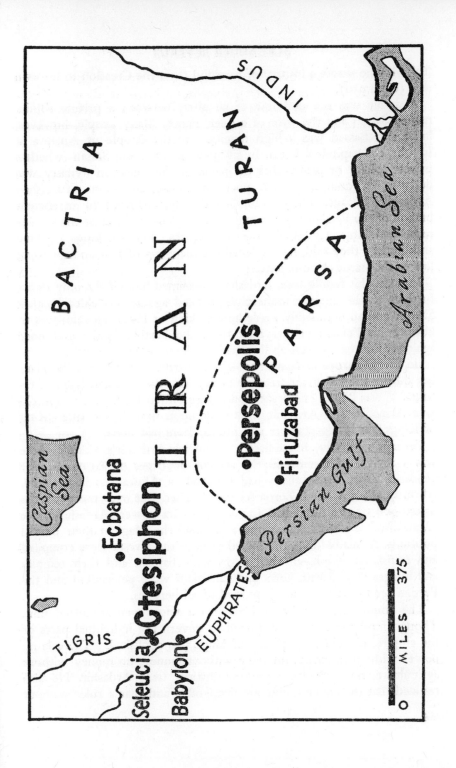

Tabari, who wrote a history of mankind from the Creation to his own day (circa 950).

Ardashir was the outcome of an affair between a private soldier named Sassan and the wife of a dyer, Babec. Many people, however, insist that Sassan was a high dignitary in the temple of Anahita at Istakhr, the capital of Parsa. In any case, it was from Sassan—whether private soldier or priest—that the name of the Sassanian dynasty was derived. Of course, Persian poets and historians soon refurbished Ardashir's lineage. They established that he belonged to an ancient branch of the Persian royal family and was a descendant of the world-renowned kings Cyrus, Darius and Xerxes. The workings of time and destiny, they said, had reduced the members of that ancient royal line to the status of commoners.

Invoking his family tree, Ardashir proclaimed himself the only rightful heir to the ancient monarchy, rebelled against his elder brother Shapur and autocratically made himself king of Parsa. His aim was to liberate his Persian countrymen from the Parthian yoke and once again set the ancient Persian line, which Alexander the Great had swept aside, on the throne of Iran. It took three battles to defeat the Parthians but during the last great struggle in 227 A.D., the Parthian King Artabanus V was killed. His descendants were ousted from every foothold save Armenia, and Ardashir now took upon himself the title "King of Kings," as his forefathers and predecessors had done.

Perhaps naturally, immediately following Ardashir's victory there was a revival of interest in the ancient doctrines of Zoroaster. For centuries now, the Iranians had believed in Ahura-Mazda the god, Ahriman the devil, and Zoroaster the prophet. But over the years the priesthood of the Magi had lost much of its power. Ardashir made "Mazdaism" a state religion and reinstalled the Magi in their official positions. At his bidding, the sacred texts of the Avesta were compiled and translated afresh, all rival faiths were banned and their temples and images demolished. Jews and Christians were persecuted and the Persian ranks were ruthlessly purged of all heretics.

The empire was rigidly welded into a single well-organized unit. Though feudal overlords continued to govern the individual parts of the empire, the old multiplicity of kings was abolished. "There is no power without an army, no army without money, no money without agriculture, no agriculture without justice," said Ardashir. He also realized that throne and altar are inseparable and that a ruler without a religion automatically becomes a tyrant. Acting on this realization he created not only a new empire but a world power.

The emergence of this neo-Persian empire was, historically, of the utmost importance. Now Rome was no longer the only world power; she had a mighty rival in the Sassanian-Persian empire. Spiritually, this new empire soon found itself fighting on two fronts. In the west it tried to repel the onslaughts of victorious Christianity and in the east it resisted the impetus of Buddhism. King Ardashir reigned from 223 to 241 A.D. and his equally distinguished successor Shapur (Sapor) I from 241 to 271. Both these kings strengthened their empire, reached acquisitively eastwards and westwards, and competed with Rome at every opportunity.

The great cultural influence of the Sassanian empire was still making itself felt in the Middle Ages. It was from the Sassanids that we inherited knighthood and nobility, tournaments and mounted duels with the lance, court dress and ceremonial, feudalism and the idea of an established church. The Sassanian era lasted until the victory of Islam in the year 651, when Iran became part of the Caliphate. But let us return to Ardashir. It was obvious that the king's lust for power and prestige would soon encounter Roman opposition. Instead of waiting for trouble, Ardashir went in search of it. Proclaiming himself heir to the old Persian empire, he demanded the return by the Romans of all territory in Asia. Simultaneously he invaded Roman Mesopotamia and Syria. His cavalry pushed on into Asia Minor, showing an audacity and determination which Rome had not encountered for many years.

Alexander Severus sent the Persian king a warning not to invade foreign territory or try to stir up insurrection in Asia. War with Rome, he pointed out, was something quite different from war against barbarian hordes, and he reminded Ardashir of the victories won by Augustus, Trajan and Septimius Severus.

Ardashir retorted by sending a delegation to Antioch in Syria. Here the emperor was one day confronted by four hundred enormous Persians armed with golden weapons and a reply from their master, the "King of Kings": the Romans must surrender Syria and all their Asian possessions, leaving the Persians in control of their ancient empire.

The emperor answered this arrogant request by immediately seizing the four hundred envoys and treating them as prisoners of war.

Still dependent on his mother but with characteristic thoroughness, young Alexander Severus now began planning countermeasures after a last attempt to avert hostilities through diplomatic channels made while wintering in Antioch with Mamaea in 231–232. But an inevitable Roman weakness loomed up once more. The emperor's troops spent an enjoyable winter visiting women's bathhouses, drinking and amusing themselves generally, at the same time making it clear what they thought of the "petticoat regime" which Mamaea directed from behind her son's back. Alexander had the most unruly of his men arrested and put in chains but mutiny threatened to develop. Then, from the tribunal, the young emperor delivered one of the long speeches for which he was renowned, addressing himself both to the accused men and to those soldiers who had not been arrested. "If our discipline fails, we shall lose our good Roman name and our Roman empire. Some Roman soldiers, comrades of yours and men of mine, are leading a depraved life. They drink, they loiter about in baths, they behave like Greeks." The listening soldiers gave a murmur which turned into a shout. "You should shout in battle," cried Alexander, "not in front of your emperor! You should display your strength to the Germans and Persians, not to me. If you despise Roman laws you are not fit to be called Roman citizens!"

But other reports came of mutiny among Roman troops in various other parts of the world. It was not a good omen for the trial of strength in which Rome was soon to be engaged.

In the year 232, three Roman armies took the field against Ardashir. The first marched through Armenia, the second through northern Mesopotamia, while the third, commanded by Alexander himself, moved on the Persians to the south of the Euphrates. The first army met with initial success and advanced as far as Media, looting as it went, but suffered heavy losses on its return journey over ice-bound and inadequate mountain roads. The army which took the route through Mesopotamia had scarcely reached the marshy plains of Babylonia when it was scattered by the numerically superior Persians and their armored cavalry. Roman casualties were severe. Alexander's column, moving too slowly and lacking resolute leadership, suffered from disease and exhaustion.

The outcome of this great clash between Rome and Persia was obvious: Persia had won. For the time being, however, the Persians were unable to capitalize on their victory or even to hold Mesopotamia for they too had suffered losses. Thus Ardashir decided to postpone any further aggression, and the Romans were allowed to reoccupy their abandoned frontier forts. No peace treaty was signed but Alexander went back to Rome pluming himself on having won a great victory, even though his losses had been far too heavy to warrant any such claim.

It was then that the emperor and Rome were faced by a new danger, this time from the north.

THE WALL OF DESTINY

AS MENTIONED earlier, in the year 83 A.D. the Emperor Domitian made a decision which has continued to influence European history to the present day. In order to secure the approaches to the frontier fortress of Moguntiacum (Mainz), call a permanent halt to German encroachments, and protect Roman possessions in Gaul and southwest Germany, Domitian erected a frontier rampart, the *limes*.

The word *limes* originally suggested an impassable boundary such as a cliff, a river, or a mound of stones. Later it came to be applied to the path running between two pieces of land. Thus a *limes* was primarily a narrow balk marking the border between two fields or settlements. In its simple meaning of "boundary path" it was also applied to the strip of unpopulated wasteland on the German frontier. Domitian's contribution was to turn the *limes* from a no man's land into a fortified line. The first move was to cut a path through the forests which could provide the frontier guards with a patrol line.

The idea of a fortified *limes* suited the mood prevailing at the end of the first century A.D. The Roman empire longed for security. Many fields of creative endeavor in the ancient world were showing clear signs of decline and retrogression. Social apathy was setting in. During the second century A.D. the process of spiritual debilitation became even more marked, and in the third century we witness the breakdown of ancient civilization.

Ever since Edward Gibbon's classic work was published, a stream of books have been written about the cause of the Roman empire's decline and fall. It is, as the well-known ancient historian Ernst Kornemann has said, "the problem of problems" and is forever being formulated and solved anew. We probably come closest to the truth by attributing the downfall of the ancient world to a large number of causes. Its deterioration took place in the political, social, economic and, last but by no means least, the spiritual sphere. Among political enemies it was the Germans who, by their struggle with Rome, gave the map of Europe a completely new look.

But there was a time when Rome made an attempt to push farther and farther northwards and draw the whole of German territory into the Roman empire, as Caesar had probably once planned. It must be remembered that in 6 A.D. the region north of the Main between the

Rhine and the Elbe was a Roman province under the administration of Publius Quinctilius Varus, a relative of Augustus.

But Arminius, the chieftain of a small German tribe, in the year 9 A.D. put an early end to the Romans' struggle for possession of the whole of Germany. Varus' three legions were annihilated in the battle of the Teutoburger Wald, and Varus himself was killed.

In 88 or 89 A.D., some eighty years after Arminius had attacked a world empire, Emperor Domitian started to build the *limes*. He was a very autocratic man, like Ch'in Shih-huang-ti, the Chinese emperor who created the long earthwork which later became the Great Wall of China. But he was also a first-class organizer and administrator who saw clearly the manifold dangers along the northern frontier of the Roman Empire. And it was he who defeated the Chatti, Rome's most dangerous enemies at that time, in northern Hesse.

Domitian started the *limes* and Hadrian (117-138 A.D.) strengthened it with a palisade, rampart and ditch. Under Antoninus Pius, Hadrian's successor, the *limes* had been pushed forward and further strengthened until now it ran in a perfectly straight line, regardless of natural features, from the Rhine near Hönningen and Rhein-Brohl down to Regensburg on the Danube, a distance of some 350 miles; a Roman barricade which split Europe in two and was to provide the root causes of so many wars. None of the other frontier fortifications which the Romans erected in trouble spots like Britain, Africa, Syria or Romania ever achieved as much historical importance as the *limes* on the German border.

The great invasion of the empire's northern frontiers began in the year 213 A.D. All along the middle Rhine and upper Danube, i.e. in the forward areas of Upper Germany and Rhaetia, the West Germans and their East German cousins surged forward and the Romans now encountered an enemy called the Alemanni.

Being compounded of *alle* and *Mannen*, Alemanni signified a league of men and indeed they originally were several tribes which had attached themselves to the Semnones, a people that had migrated to this area and now appeared for the first time under this collective name. The Alemanni formed an alliance with the Chatti, the non-nomadic race north of the Main that had given Domitian so much trouble. In the year 213 they all made a concerted crossing of the frontiers of the Roman empire.

The Romans had improved the roads in their northern territories,

COLOGNE
(Colonia Agrippinensis)

Wied

Linz

Weiherhof

Neiderbieber
Alteburg
Höhr

Coblenz

Augst

Seyn

Lahn

Hainhaus   Arnsburg
                Inheide
Hunneburg
                Butzbach   U. Widdersheim
Langeheim   Bingenheim

Moselle

Becheln

Pohl   Holzausen
Kermel   Born
             Feldberg

Langen
Schwalbach

Lorch

Bingen

MAINZ
(Moguntiacum)

Kapersburg
SAALBURG
Homburg   Nidda

Zugmantel
Hofheim
Wiesbaden   Höchst
             FRANKFURT
             Seligenstadt

Heftrich
        Rückingen

Main

Altenstadt

Markoebel

Kinzig

Gr. Krotzenburg
Hainstadt

Stockstadt   Aschaffenburg

Niedernburg

Lützelbach

Worms

Obernburg
Wörth
Trennfurt

Alstadt   Frendenberg
Vielbrunn   Miltenberg
Eulenbach
Würzberg
Hesselbach   Walldüren
Schlossau
Scheidenthal
Eberbach

Wü

Ladenburg
Heidelberg
Altrip
Speyer   Neckar

Neckar-
burken

Osterburke

Gundelsheim   Jagsthau

Wimpfen   Jagst
              Kocher   Ohringe

Heilbronn   Main

STRASBOURG
(Argentoratum)

Mur

Welzheim

Stuttgart   Canstadt
                        Lorch

Elz

260

The Limes, built by the Roman emperors between 83 and 138 A.D. as a powerful bulwark against German attacks. This wall of palisades and stone extended for about 350 miles from the Rhine to the Danube and was supported by towers, forts and military roads. It is a fragment of history which is gradually sinking into oblivion beneath plowed field and woodland.

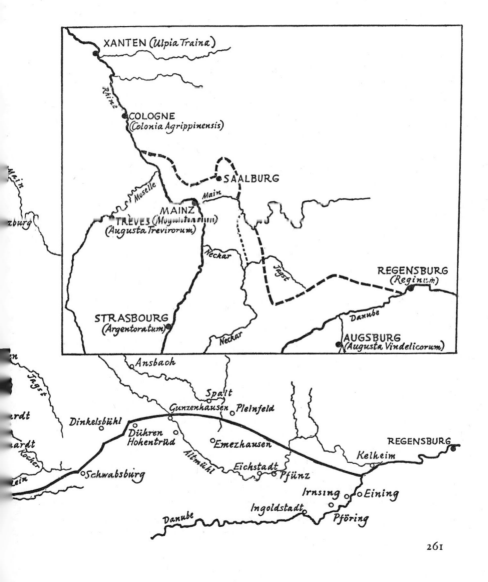

Rhaetia and Noricum, and made extensive preparations. Then, still in 213, Emperor Caracalla defeated the Alemanni in the vicinity of Miltenberg am Rhein. In place of the now-decaying palisade, there arose along the Rhaetian *limes* north of the Danube a stone wall between six and nine feet high and some four feet thick, the so-called *Teufelsmauer* (Devil's Wall), an imposing rampart over one hundred miles long. Elsewhere, the *limes* was an earthwork with a large ditch on the German side and in front of this another smaller ditch into which were driven the stakes which formed the palisade. The stakes were between ten and fourteen feet high and about a foot thick, and the entire network of defenses was never less than sixty-five feet in depth.

We know all this now, and a 130-foot section of this palisade has been reconstructed at Sayn and can be admired from the Pulver-Berg. But for a long time the palisade bothered students of the *limes* a great deal. Tracing the smaller ditch was easy enough, but it was so narrow that it could never have presented any serious obstacle to an attacking enemy and it was difficult to see what the purpose of this outlying hollow could have been, especially since all that was ever found in it was stones, charcoal, iron nails and fragments of slate. Eventually some wooden stakes were discovered in a marsh in the Odenwald where, thanks to the boggy ground (always a splendid preservative), they had remained in excellent condition. The riddle was solved at last. The narrow outlying ditch had served as the foundation of a stockade which ran for mile after mile through forests, over hills and across obstacles. The materials found in the ditch had been used to wedge the stakes securely.

However, the *limes* did not consist merely of a rampart, ditch and stockade. There were also many wooden blockhouses which gave a good view of the surrounding country. Traces of more than a thousand such watchtowers have been found all along its length arranged so the guards could pass information from one tower to the next. During the day smoke signals were used. A shutter in the roof of each tower enabled puffs of smoke to be sent up at varying intervals. At night communication was maintained by fire signals. A flaming torch held motionless indicated the approach of friends; hostile activity was indicated by waving the torch to and fro. So much for "telegraphy" in the first centuries A.D. In cases of emergency trumpet calls could also be exchanged between the towers, thus alerting mile after mile of the defense system.

At regular intervals immediately to the rear of the *limes* stood the quadrangular forts of wood and earth in which the outposts were quartered, while still farther to the rear were large fortresses like Heddesdorf, Bendorf, and Niederberg. The cornerstone of the defense network was represented by the famous legionary camp at Mainz.

The *limes* fortifications also included stone towers. We can get an exact idea of what they looked like from portrayals of them on the columns of Trajan and Marcus Aurelius at Rome, and a reconstruction of one of them has been erected on the Pulver-Berg at Sayn, close to the ruins of a genuine Roman tower.

In the year 232 the Alemanni invaded the Roman empire once again, pouring across the *limes* not only on the Rhine frontier but also in the northern part of the province of Rhaetia. Large numbers of provincials hid their money and valuables in pots and buried them beneath the ground, and since many of them never got a chance to dig their treasures up again it is still not uncommon for people to come across caches of coins today. Rome hastily sent forces from all over the world to the trouble spot. Alexander Severus personally led his legions on a forced march to the *limes*, archers and Parthian deserters were brought from the East to help deal with the mounted hordes of Alemanni, and the Romans hurriedly threw a pontoon bridge across the Rhine near Mainz. The first engagements went well.

Then something appalling happened. Before there had been any decisive engagements mutiny broke out in various parts of the Roman legions. The young emperor disbanded several units. In this crucial moment his mother who, needless to say, was also at headquarters, suddenly hit on the incredible idea of cutting the soldiers' pay. Then, wanting to avoid a pitched battle, on his mother's advice Alexander opened negotiations with the enemy. His soldiers (probably the Pannonian units) were opposed to this: if the emperor was negotiating with the Alemanni it might well mean that he was offering them money which they preferred to have for themselves.

The air was fraught with danger. Had not a druidess called to the emperor, at the very moment of his departure for the war: "Go, but do not hope for victory or rely on your soldiers!"?

As usual, the emperor did not take these threats and omens too seriously. As usual, he ate his evening meal in an unguarded tent. Afterwards, at about the seventh hour, he lay down for a short rest. It was a cool evening in March, 235 A.D. "What is it?" suddenly called the emperor, starting up. "Have you news of the enemy?"

A Roman soldier stood before him, pale and trembling. The man had simply lost his way, and now he found himself standing by Alexander's bed. But then, suddenly struck by the thought that the emperor's continued existence could spell his own undoing, he rushed out, calling to his comrades to come and slay the emperor without more ado. Seizing their swords the men raced into the tent and stabbed their defenseless master to death.

The young emperor had always obeyed his mother and now she had to die with him. She had given birth to a man of integrity, not a hero.

The tragedy of it all was symbolized by what the murderers saw, once the emperor was lying dead in his own blood. The supper dishes had not been cleared away and on them were the remains not of a sumptuous feast, but of ordinary rations like the ones they had just eaten themselves.

THE BAITED BEAR

*He dashed himself against the wall, threw himself on the
ground, shouted loudly and incoherently, and gripped his
sword as though he wanted to kill the whole Senate there and
then. He rent his robes, beat the palace servants, and nearly
tore out his young son's eyes.*
—*Historia Augusta, The Two Maximini,* xvii.

MAXIMINUS was born in a Thracian village at a time when his native
land was still a cultural desert. In him we are confronted by a self-
made man from the outermost edge of the Roman empire who suddenly emerged at the hub of world activity, although he never came
to Rome as emperor. History knows this Caesar as Maximinus Thrax,
that is Maximinus the Thracian.

A big man, violent, uncouth, arrogant but not unhandsome, he is
reputed to have drunk no less than a Capitoline amphora of wine every
day. A Capitoline amphora was a jug whose original was kept on the
Capitoline Hill, rather as the standard meter is in the vaults of the
Bank of Paris today. It held about forty-six pints! In addition, Maximinus reputedly ate forty pounds of meat daily, but no vegetables—
he didn't like them. He could knock a horse's teeth out with a single
blow of his fist. His enormous size and physical strength encouraged
him to believe that he was immortal, but in the theater people used
to laugh at him behind his back. "A man who cannot be killed by one
is killed by many," they quipped.

In the year 232 A.D. Maximinus was commander of the second legion
("Trajan's Own") in Egypt, and during the war with Persia he was
governor of Mesopotamia. Having won a reputation as a gallant and
distinguished officer, he was then given by Alexander Severus command
of all the recruits in the Roman army on the Rhine and became, in
effect, the Roman Director of Military Training. Although a disci-
plinarian, he gave his men the feeling that they were doing a worth-
while job. He refused to allow his legionaries to ply a trade as a side
line, and considered that hunting was the only leisure occupation
worthy of a fighting man.

Maximinus the Thracian was a general after the legionaries' own hearts, and it was not surprising that the mutineers made him Imperator in place of Alexander Severus. When news of his accession reached Rome the Senate resigned itself to the *fait accompli,* although a sizable body of senatorial opinion was opposed to having such an upstart on the throne.

Right at the very outset Maximinus had to cope with an attempt on his life organized by some centurions. He only just managed to foil their plan, which was to lure him across the Rhine into hostile German territory, then cut off his retreat and kill him. The ringleader of this murderous plot is said to have been a man of consular rank named Magnus, who naturally wanted to become emperor himself.

But Maximinus was on the alert and, having exposed the conspiracy, he at once condemned the conspirators to death without the benefit of a trial and their property was confiscated. The Thracian peasant was not a man to be trifled with.

Crossing the Rhine, Maximinus advanced deep into German territory. Along the Main and in what is now Würtemberg he burned villages, drove off cattle, took thousands of prisoners, plundered and devastated everything made by German hands. The emperor's oriental bowmen and African spearmen, Syrians and Mauretanians respectively, seemed in German eyes to be diabolical supermen.

And the Germans? This was how the Roman historian Tacitus had described them a hundred years earlier: "Their shields are black, their bodies painted. They choose dark nights for battle. They spread alarm by the very appearance, gruesome and dismal, of their ghostly ranks. No enemy can withstand the startling, almost hellish sight. For in every battle, the eyes are the first to fall."

The first pitched battle took place in fen country, probably on the borders of northern Würtemberg and Baden, and was fought by the Romans and their foreign mercenaries against the same Alemanni who had broken through the *limes* shortly before. Even as emperor, Maximinus still fought in the front line. It never occurred to him to do otherwise.

The year 235 saw the German threat banished once more, and the remains of new *limes* fortifications erected during this period show that peace had been restored on the Rhine and upper Danube. Henceforth, the emperor called himself Germanicus Maximus, and he now proclaimed his son, a remarkably handsome man, Caesar and joint emperor. Great victory celebrations were held at Sirmium, their winter quarters on the Save near Belgrade. We are told that Maximinus gained successes against the Sarmatians and Dacians during 236 and 237, and in the spring of 238 we see him back in Sirmium, holding court and receiving envoys from Rome and the provinces. Rome itself did not attract him. He felt far more at home in the broad valley of the Save among his soldiers and horses. He was now planning to subjugate all the Germans in the vast area between the Danube and the North Sea.

Maximinus never ceased persecuting those who had supported his predecessor's dynasty, now extinct. He is said to have been extremely brutal in his methods of taking vengeance, crucifying people, crushing their skulls, and throwing them to starving beasts. Perhaps he thought that, as a man of humble origins, his only way of keeping the throne was by instilling fear in his subjects.

His sense of personal inferiority, erroneous as it may well have been, made Maximinus hate the Senate and the whole of the aristocracy. For a while his wife Caecilia Paulina did her best to mitigate this dangerous characteristic, but unfortunately she soon died. Maximinus detested everything that had any connection with his predecessor. So deep was his loathing of Alexander's memory that he decreed a new spate of anti-Christian persecution merely because Alexander had tolerated the Christians. It was not, however, very severe.

Hippolytus and Origen, who had probably been on friendly terms with Mamaea, Alexander Severus' mother, now found themselves in danger. We also read that the Christians Pontianus, the Bishop of Rome, and Hippolytus were exiled to Sardinia in 235 A.D. In Cappadocia and Pontus, too, Christians were persecuted by Governor Serenianus. But in spite of all this Emperor Maximinus is not to be numbered among the classical persecutors of Christianity, for on the other side of the picture he himself ensured the continued existence of the priesthood in Christian communities for reasons of public policy. Nor were the persecutions in Cappadocia and Pontus carried out at his instigation, but because the Christians there had been held responsible for an earthquake.

Maximinus was always in need of money. The empire was large, the enemy active on every frontier, and defense costly. That meant that taxes had to be high and this in turn demanded that harsh methods be employed in collecting them. The emperor cast an especially predatory eye at the temples with their valuable dedicatory offerings of gold and silver. Using any pretext, he melted down sacred images, memorial statues and consecrated objects of every description, and turned them into money. He also confiscated the property of the wealthy. This naturally caused resentment, and it was hardly surprising that some young Roman aristocrats in Africa murdered the imperial procurator at Thysdrus, a coastal town one hundred miles southeast of Carthage, near modern El Djem, when he prepared to expropriate their estates at the emperor's bidding.

The rebels repudiated Maximinus and swore allegiance to a venerable old proconsul named Gordianus. It was the last thing the old man wanted. He screamed, threw himself on the ground, and begged his "benefactors" to leave him alone, but they threatened him with their swords and wrapped him willy-nilly in the purple. The date was 238, and Gordian was eighty years old.

Gordian was extremely rich and took an interest in literature. His joints had stiffened with age and he often fell asleep during meals. Eventually he reconciled himself to the idea of spending the rest of his days on the throne and moved to Carthage with his son, who was proclaimed joint emperor. The Roman Senate ratified the two Gordians' accession and deposed Emperor Maximinus, and the inhabitants of the capital celebrated the "tyrant's downfall" amid scenes of tumultuous rejoicing during which many supporters of the Thracian peasant-emperor were killed.

Among Maximinus' adherents in Africa was the governor of Numidia, a man called Capellianus, who now began to incite his province to rebel against the Gordians. Young Gordian was sent by his father to restore order, only to be killed after a fierce and desperate engagement. Gordian senior thereupon took his own life.

When the news of the Gordians' death reached Rome, with its threat of retribution on the part of Maximinus, the Senate hurriedly elected not one but two emperors from its own ranks: Marcus Clodius Pupienus Maximus and Decimus Caelius Calvinus Balbinus. They were to have exactly equal status and were, with the help of a committee of twenty senators, to organize the defense of Italy against Maximinus. The people and the legions quickly supplied yet a third emperor in the shape of Gordian's grandson, who later became Gordian III. With three emperors, Rome felt itself more than a match for the fourth who was lurking in the north on the German border.

The fourth emperor behaved like a huge, tormented bear. Convulsed with rage, he dashed himself against walls, threw himself on the ground, bellowed, lashed out at his servants, tried to claw his son's eyes out, and finally drank himself into a stupor. Then, sober once more, he mustered his army—which included many German deserters—and marched over the Alps into Italy, taking cavalry and a large baggage train with him. When the German horsemen in his advanced guard reached Emona (modern Laibach), they found it a scene of sinister desolation in which nothing edible was to be found. Five hundred wolves, dread harbingers of famine, had visited the town shortly before. The same sight greeted Maximinus' troops in every town they came to. Rome was opposing them with that most terrible of all foes: silent, gnawing hunger. The first place to offer resistance was Aquileia. Knowing that their town would be razed to the ground if it were captured, the citizens of Aquileia defended themselves with every means at their disposal against Maximinus' attempts to take it. In the end, the emperor's second Parthian legion took a hand—though not by capturing Aquileia. Tired, hungry and desperate, they murdered their own master, Maximinus, and his handsome son.

One month after Maximinus' death the praetorian guard murdered Pupienus and Balbinus, the two senatorial emperors, who had by that time fallen foul of each other. A thirteen-year-old boy now stood as sole ruler of the empire.

Army, Senate and populace all welcomed the choice, for this third Gordian was a grandson of the worthy old man whom fate had treated so badly. Fundamentally, however, young Gordian's accession represented a triumph for the soldiery, who had once more assumed the arbitrary right of choosing an emperor.

But the famous "year of the six emperors," 238 A.D., saw yet another event of great historical significance. It was the year when the Goths crossed the frontiers of the Roman empire at the estuary of the Danube.

THE COMING OF THE GOTHS

He [Gordian III] was a gay youth, handsome, endearing,
universally popular, merry in his life, serious in his letters.
There was nothing which could have made him unfitted to
rule save, perhaps, his youth.
—Historia Augusta, The Three Gordiani, xxxi.

IN 238 A.D. the year when Maximinus the Thracian died, Rome was once more threatened on two fronts: by the German tribes in the north and by the still unconquered new world power in the east, the Sassanian dynasty's Persian empire which since 226 under the first two Sassanid kings, Ardashir and his son Shapur, had revived the ancient Asian threat to Europe. Ardashir died in 239, but his son Shapur proceeded to show the world that, unless it is checked by force, Asia will always creep irresistibly westwards. Ardashir had already captured Nisibis and Carrhae. Shapur now reached out an eager hand for Roman Mesopotamia and Rome's Syrian provinces, even threatening Antioch and the Orontes.

There is something almost pathetic about the way in which Rome sent her boy-emperor to meet the menacing avalanche from the east. Emperor Gordian III may have been only thirteen years old, but he had demonstrated considerable sagacity in the way he extricated himself skillfully from a web of court intrigue, the apron strings of his vacillating and weak-minded mother, and the machinations of the palace eunuchs. In him we see a rare example of a pupil who remained unwaveringly loyal to his teacher. And in the teacher we recognize a man who, like Seneca, stood head and shoulders above his contemporaries. His name was Timesitheus.

While still a prince, young Gordian had married his tutor's daughter, a lovely girl with an even lovelier name: Furia Sabinia Tranquillina. Now, as emperor, he appointed Timesitheus to the highest government posts, while the Senate conferred on him the honorary titles Father of the Prince and Protector of the State. For all his new-found authority, Timesitheus remained staunch in his loyalty to the emperor. The two of them, tutor and pupil, set off on a forced march to the East. Timesitheus showed himself a thoroughly competent commander and Gordian was an intelligent boy. Here is a passage from a letter which he wrote to Timesitheus: "Woe to the ruler to whom no one dares speak the truth. Since such a king cannot mingle with the people, he must accept what he is told or overhear what the majority are saying."

On the way to Asia the Romans picked up more troops from the army on the Danube. Bands of Dacians, prominent among which were the Carpi, at once tried to penetrate the gaps in the frontier defenses. But Timesitheus fought back. He pacified the frontier, hurried on eastwards with the emperor, liberated Syria from the Persians and in a decisive battle at Resaena won back the whole of Mesopotamia for Rome.

Another interesting personality whom we meet with the Roman army at this time was the Egyptian-born philosopher Plotinus, one of the last intellectuals in the ancient world to embody in himself and his philosophy the ancient world's whole range of thought. He was not merely an intellectual, however, but a near saint whose main concern was with the soul and whose life was dedicated to the eternal quest for an invisible god. Plotinus joined the eastern expedition as a scientist in search of information because he wanted to see India and, in particular, wanted to understand the philosophies of Persia, India, and the Far East.

Timesitheus, who had organized the whole expedition so brilliantly, was everywhere at once, paying incognito visits to the sentries at night and asking after their welfare or strolling through the sleeping legionaries' tents. His superb organizing ability made this army, far from home as it was, a fighting force of unparalleled efficiency. "And, because he loved the emperor and the state so greatly, he was respected by all," says the chronicler.

Timesitheus wanted to push on, following in the footsteps of Alexander the Great, to the Indus and perhaps even to China. But it was not to be. He died of a sudden attack of influenza. Such at least was the official cause of death, although the suspicion of poison could not be discounted. It was rumored that he had been given a laxative just before his death by some doctors in the pay of a man who coveted his position: to wit, one Marcus Julius Philippus, the forty-five-year-old son of an Arab or Syrian sheik from the desolate region of Trachonitis in Transjordania. Philip at once began to undermine Gordian's popularity with the troops by sabotaging their supplies and young Gordian proved no match for him. As a man, Philip was uncouth, ill-bred, arrogant and ruthless. And Jacob Burckhardt says, probably with

271

justification: "It is doing Philip too great an honor to regard him as an Arab sheik. He came from the disreputable tribe of southern Syrians east of the Jordan." Gordian attempted at first to oppose Philip, then to co-operate with him, finally to suffer under him. It was all to no avail: he was soon murdered.

We know the very spot where Gordian III died, for on the spot, between Circesium and Doura-Europos, quite near the confluence of the Euphrates and the little Chaboras, a memorial was erected to the young emperor. Philip had the mortal remains of his nineteen-year-old victim taken back to Rome, informing the Senate that he had died of an illness.

As for Plotinus, once the campaign was over he managed to reach Antioch, whence he traveled back to Rome.

An African and a Syrian had occupied the Roman throne; now it was an Arab's turn to rule the Roman empire. Philip the Arab made peace with the Persians in return for concessions and entrusted the further defense of the eastern frontier to his brother Priscus, a step which was an urgent necessity, for Philip himself had to hurry back to the northern frontier. Here he conducted successful operations against the Carpi in the autumn of 246 A.D., and celebrated them by adopting the triumphal title Carpicus Maximus. Dacia had been held once more.

Near what is now Sheba, south of Damascus, Philip founded the city of Philippopolis and conferred on it the rights of a colony. The impressive ruins of its splendid buildings, which were modeled on the palaces, theaters, temples and baths of Rome, still survive. The Thracian city of Philippopolis which had been founded by Philip of Macedon, father of Alexander the Great, was also raised to colonial status.

It was in this year, 247–248 A.D., with decay gnawing at the heart and extremities of the great Roman empire, with Roman sovereignty on the wane, that Philip the Arab held a magnificent festival at Rome. It was the thousandth anniversary of Rome's foundation. Ten centuries had passed since Romulus and his small band of shepherds fortified their humble encampment on the banks of the Tiber.

Actually the date of the great festival should have been April 21, 247 A.D., but Philip had postponed it for a year. Now it was celebrated with great pomp. Foreigners were not allowed to attend and slaves were forbidden to show their faces as choirs composed of twenty-seven boys and twenty-seven girls of the noblest birth invoked the bene-

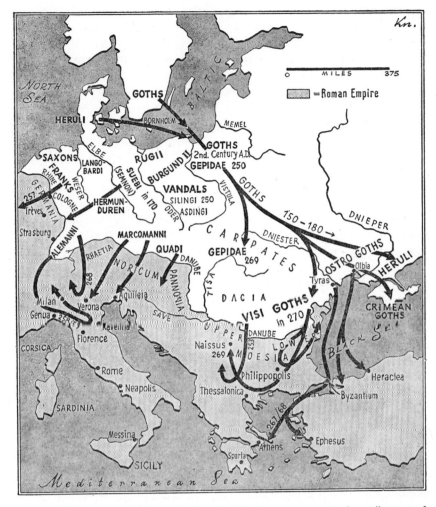

The Goths came partly from the island of Gotland and partly from Öster- and Västergötland in southern Sweden, where their name has survived. Their vast hordes swept like a tidal wave down to the Black Sea, Asia Minor and Greece.

diction of the gods. There were sports in the Circus Maximus, colored lanterns, torches, and dancing and music on the Field of Mars. Sacrifices were offered to the gods on the banks of the Tiber for three nights running. A Roman historian describes all that Rome offered its inhabitants in the way of entertainment during these festivities.

273

Young Gordian had made advance preparations for the triumphal procession which he intended to hold in Rome in celebration of his own and his tutor's victories over the Persians. Now Gordian was dead. But his animals were still there—thousands of them—ready for another emperor to parade before the public or slaughter for their amusement. The list included ten elk, ten tigers, ten hyenas, ten wild lions, ten giraffes, six hippopotami, one rhinoceros, twenty wild asses, thirty tame leopards, sixty tame lions, "a thousand brace of imperial gladiators" (right in the middle of the catalogue!), forty wild horses, and many other "beasts." This bloodshed was intended to herald a new century of glorious history but all it heralded was decline, dissolution and decay. Even at the moment when Philip was making merry in Rome the Frankish vanguard was approaching the Rhine, the Goths, Carpi and Vandals were crossing the Danube, and the Blemmyes were invading Egypt from Ethiopia. In many places provincial landowners were starting to arm their slaves and tenants as an act of self-preservation because the government had ceased to provide them with military protection against the invading barbarians.

The Pannonian legions rebelled, the Goths stormed into Moesia, and the legionaries in the Danube area swore allegiance to a certain Pacatianus. Another Roman, Jotapianus by name, claimed the throne in the East and in Syria a third pretender suddenly appeared in the person of Julius Aurelius Sulpicius Uranius Antoninus. Here Philip lost his nerve and offered to abdicate but the Senate refused to commit itself. Accordingly, he sent his ablest general, Decius, to deal with Pacatianus. But, following a familiar pattern in Roman history, Jotapianus and Pacatianus were both murdered by their own men and Decius was crowned in their place. He was chary of accepting this doubtful honor leading, as it almost inevitably did, to a violent end, but the legionaries threatened him with death if he refused. So reluctantly donning the purple, he marched against Philip and defeated him at Verona in 249. The last Oriental to occupy the throne of imperial Rome had fallen.

During the reign of Emperor Philip the Arab (244–249) the Goths threatened *Dacia* and besieged *Marcianopolis*, the capital of *Moesia*. Emperor Decius (reigned 249–251) suffered a crushing defeat at the hands of the Gothic king Kniva. The Goths then captured *Philippopolis*, and in 251 *Decius* lost his life in battle. All the places indicated on this map were besieged, captured, looted and destroyed by the Goths.

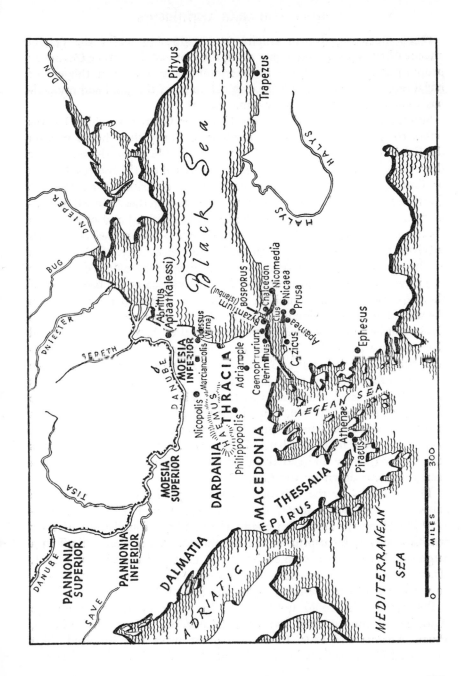

Once more the Roman empire was staggering under the fearful impact of the Goths' onslaughts along the Danube. No other Germanic people played a greater part in determining the history of this era of racial migration. Where was the original home of this bold and mysterious race, and what does their name mean?

Some Romans called the Goths Gothi or Guttones, while Tacitus refers to them as Gothones. According to Pliny, their home was on the Baltic coast and round the Frisches Haff. He expressly states that they were a Germanic people. The Goths called themselves Gutans or Gutos, and in their own country they described themselves as Gutthiuda, *gut* and *thiuda* meaning "people-together." In all probability, some of them came from the island of Gotland and others from Öster- and Västergötland in southern Sweden, where their name has survived to this day. They then settled in the estuary of the Vistula and began to force their way into eastern Europe where their emergence as a powerful nation on the coasts of the Black Sea at the beginning of the third century A.D. coincided with a new threat, the Alemanni, in the west. During the reign of Philip the Arab (244–249) they threatened Dacia and besieged Marcianopolis, the capital of Moesia. Decius forced them to give ground at Nicopolis in the year 250, but they later annihilated a Roman army and sacked the city of Philippopolis in the Haemus range, led by their king, Kniva. They then stormed across Macedonia, pushed southwards as far as Thermopylae, veered to the north and in June, 251 A.D., wiped out the greater part of the Roman army at Abrittus in Moesia (now Aptaat-Kalessi in the Dobrudja).

Right at the start of this battle Decius' son, Herennius Etruscus, was killed by an arrow and shortly after Decius himself was lured into a marsh and cut down by the Goths.

These attacks by the Goths, who loom up so suddenly out of the mists of history, seem almost like irresistible natural phenomena. Fanning out along the Black Sea coasts, they laid the foundations of their maritime power by capturing the Bosphorus. In 253 they set off in a large number of flat-bottomed boats and captured the city of Pityus. Then they took Trebizond and acquired a fleet there, only, in 258, to withdraw to their settlements on the Sea of Azov.

But the Goths could not sit still. In 259 they marched on the Thracian Bosphorus and captured Chalcedon, Nicomedia, Nicaea, Prusa, Apamia and Cius. In a third great wave five hundred ships destroyed Cyzicus. Crossing the Aegean Sea, the Goths landed at the

Piraeus near Athens and from there advanced as far as Epirus. Nothing escaped looting and devastation, from the southern tip of the Peloponnesos to Thessaly in the north. Then, weary at last, the vast hordes made their way back overland to the Danube, although some of them sailed down the coasts of Asia Minor in search of further plunder and destroyed the world-famous Temple of Diana at Ephesus before starting on their homeward journey.

Ancient estimates of Decius that have come down to us are apt to be extremely unfavorable, but this is understandable enough when one considers that it was Decius who first became systematic about the persecution of the Christians. Of course from the time of Nero Christians had been sporadically persecuted and killed, but usually it had been only on a very restricted basis and never in more than a province or a few provinces at a time. Also generally they were not sought out, but only bothered when someone made a formal complaint about specific individuals. But about June of 250 Decius instituted the first systematic persecution to the death of all Christians all over the empire. He was in an extremely grave military situation and decreed that every subject of the empire from little children up must sacrifice to the pagan gods and obtain an official certificate saying he had done so. The penalty for refusing was death. Had this persecution lasted and been carried out with perfect efficiency, there would have been only lapsed Christians and dead ones left in the world. Fortunately some of the magistrates practiced leniency and the persecution died down by about the end of the year due to the Gothic war. It was the first time that all the Christian communities were threatened with their very existence, and Decius' memory in Christian sources suffers accordingly.

THE HOUR OF CRISIS

IT WAS ominous that the head of the Roman state should have lost his life in battle.

Decius was the first Roman emperor to die a hero's death on the battlefield. He fell far from Rome where his men could not even recover his body. But his sacrifice was futile: he could not prevent a Gothic victory. There in the East, on the Danube, a terrible wound had been torn open. Paradoxically, only more Roman blood could staunch the bleeding.

As far as Rome was concerned, anyone who restored the desperate position, closed the breach in the empire's defenses, and once again saved Rome and the empire from extinction would be only too welcome to the throne and all the honors that went with it.

Gaius Vibius Afinius Trebonianus Gallus was governor of Lower Moesia, the region south of the lower Danube. He was well placed, therefore, to redeem Rome's honor and avenge Decius' death. But the Danubian countryside had been devastated and the Goths had carried off many of the surviving inhabitants of Thrace as prisoners, looting, murdering, and taking anything of value with them.

The remnants of the Roman army of the Danube now proclaimed Gallus emperor, and Rome applauded. But Gallus abandoned immense quantites of booty to the Goths. He was obliged to guarantee them freedom of withdrawal and to watch senior Roman officers and dignitaries being led off into barbarian captivity. Worst of all, he promised them a huge annual tribute in gold.

In the course of the centuries the Romans had grown accustomed to *receiving* tributes, and to have to shower their barbarian enemies with such a fortune in gold each year was most unpleasant. They grumbled, and many in the capital mocked Gallus for having made such concessions, though it was not the first time a Roman emperor had been in such straits.

In an attempt to improve his own invidious position Emperor Gallus appointed Hostilianus, the still-surviving second son of his late predecessor Decius, as joint regent. But Hostilianus died. Last of the Decians, he succumbed to the plague which was then raging through eastern Europe and attacked Asia Minor shortly afterward.

Like a forest fire, the rumor at once swept through Rome that Gallus had murdered the son of Decius, the late lamented hero. People began to ask ugly questions. Hadn't Gallus been in reserve while Emperor Decius was doing battle with the Goths? And, if he had been stationed behind Decius' ranks, why hadn't he gone to his commander's aid? Were it not for Gallus, it was whispered in the streets of Rome, Decius might still be alive.

Soon there was a widespread conviction that Gallus had betrayed his emperor.

Gallus had immediately traveled to Rome where he treated the Senate with great deference and then proceeded to snap his fingers at all the sinister rumors. He laughed, drank and made merry in the capital of his menaced empire.

Meanwhile, on the Danube in Lower Moesia, Marcus Aemilius Aemilianus had assumed command. Reassembling the weary Roman legionaries, he attacked the barbarian Goths and drove them back across the Danube. His soldiers naturally hailed him as a friend in need and at once proclaimed him emperor. Aemilianus set out for Italy by forced marches, intending to take Gallus by surprise and dispose of him.

Gallus met his rival, probably on the plain of Spoleto. There the armies of the two imperial adversaries faced one another, well within visual range. Gallus could not prevent his soldiers from making unfavorable comparisons. Their own commander had bought peace on the Danube with Roman gold and had been forced to abandon their best officers to a terrible fate as prisoners of the Goths. Aemilianus, on the other hand, had victoriously stemmed the barbarian invasion. When they learned that they were hopelesly outnumbered and he was willing to reward every deserter that came over to his side, the outcome was assured. The legionaries murdered Gallus and, as was now the invariable custom, his son Valusianus as well.

So ended the civil war. The Senate, which had so recently declared him "public enemy," confirmed Aemilianus as emperor and conferred on him the resounding titles Hercules the Victor and Mars the Avenger, titles in whose glamor the dazzled Aemilianus basked for four short months. They are to be found on coins of the period, of which many are in our museums. People usually buried their money only in time of danger, which is why many of our most comprehensive collections of coinage date from mankind's darkest hours.

Shortly before his death the unfortunate Gallus had hastily dispatched a general named Valerian to Gaul and Germany to fetch the Rhine legions as reinforcements. It is possible that Valerian was that rarity, an obedient and loyal officer at a time when loyalty was at a premium among the Romans and that having arrived too late to save his emperor, he decided to avenge him. It is also possible that he merely took advantage of the situation to have himself proclaimed emperor.

At all events Aemilianus' troops now behaved exactly as those of Gallus had done. They too made comparisons. They too peered out into the world from their camp on the plain of Spoleto. They too recognized the advancing enemy as the better man. They too saw at once that the army sweeping down on them was stronger than their own. They murdered their emperor on a hot, sunny day in August of 253 A.D. He had reigned for only four months. His troops from Raetia proclaimed Consul Publius Licinius Valerianus as emperor. It was unusual for a Roman of this period to become emperor without steeping his hands in blood, but Valerian was such a one. And this time the new Augustus commanded the support not only of the Senate but of the entire Roman world as well.

Valerian, the self-styled "enemy of tyrants," is one of the most tragic figures in Roman history, for he suffered a fate which no other ruler of Rome ever had to undergo. He was sixty years old when he donned the purple. A very erudite man, and a good judge of character, he furthered the careers of efficient officers like Claudius, Aurelian and Probus who were destined to preserve the empire in years to come. Perhaps because of Valerian's age the Senate invested his son with the title Augustus. The name of this joint regent, certainly one of the most original personalities in all Roman history, was Publius Licinius Egnatius Gallienus.

Father and son had been left a sad legacy. The Roman world was threatened on every frontier. In the East, Persia was already a world power like Rome herself. To the north the Germans were trying to settle north of the Black Sea. They were the vanguard of the great interracial migration which was ultimately to sweep across the whole of Italy. Further west Frankish hordes were already looting their way south.

The desperate situation prevailing in the year 254 prompted Valerian to divide the empire. He himself went to the East and installed his court at Antioch in Syria, while his son took over the defense of the West.

It was a crucial decision—crucial because it publicized for the first time the greater importance of the East. The father, as senior emperor, went to the Greek Orient while the son and subordinate emperor remained in the Latin West. It meant that the empire had been divided for the first time. It meant that Rome was gradually ceasing to be the focal point in world history.

It was while Valerian and his son Gallienus were taking their leave of one another, never to meet again, and while the barbarian Goths and Borani were swooping down from the Black Sea to ravage seacoast and countryside that Persia's strong man recognized his moment. Shapur, one of the most important kings to rule Iran since Darius I, now began to make history.

A LIVING DEATH

THE city of Baghdad in Iraq is built partly of stones found on the banks of the Tigris, some twenty-four miles away. The ruins of an imposing palace with a huge curved reception hall had long stood there among the rubble of a vanished settlement, providing a convenient and inexpensive supply of good building material.

This ancient ruined city had an even more illustrious history than modern Bagdad. Ctesiphon, as it was called, was the winter residence of the Parthian rulers after it was built by the powerful king Shapur I, the second great statesman of the Sassanian dynasty. It was Shapur's ambition to realize his father Ardashir's dream of dominating "the whole world."

Like his father, Shapur was a devotee of fire worship. His priests, the Magi, with the powerful backing of state religious sponsorship, were the sole arbiters of ritual orthodoxy, sin and atonement, oracular decrees and the magic arts. A vast, visible empire lay at the feet of Ormazd, the invisible god, and the spirit of his prophet Zarathustra celebrated a great revival in the neo-Persian empire. Yet while Shapur was strict and unyielding, he could also be tolerant. It was during his reign that Mani, one of the most unique figures in the history of religion, propagated his mysterious "doctrine of light and darkness." The first Manichean sermon was delivered on March 20, 242 A.D. On that day, young Mani first proclaimed his religion at Ctesiphon, capital of the empire, under the aegis of King Shapur.

Thirty years later Mani died. But his doctrines spread throughout the world, becoming known to the Romans and even penetrating to the British Isles. They became one of the greatest threats to Christianity, although they were ultimately eclipsed after a long struggle.

In Manicheism, light and darkness appear as two eternal beings. At one time they were distinct from one another, but darkness insinuated itself into light like the Serpent into Paradise and since then evil has existed in the world. Mani's doctrine was really an aberrant off-shoot of Christianity, a strange composite of ancient Persian, Hellenistic, Buddhist and Christian ideas. Indeed, Mani called himself an apostle of Jesus Christ. The Manichean faith recognized certain prophets who had spread "the Light," among them Adam, Noah, Abraham, Buddha, Zarathustra, Mani himself and, most important of all, Jesus, who according to Mani's own words "appeared in Judaea." Christ was "the last prophet before Mani" and Mani regarded himself as "the greatest prophet and apostle of Jesus Christ." Much of this information is to be found in the writings of Saint Augustine, but the close relationship between Manicheism and Christianity has been illustrated by ancient Manichean documents discovered quite recently at Turfan (in the Chinese province of Sinkiang) and in Egypt. It is interesting to note that Mani wrote in Aramaic, Christ's native tongue.

Shapur treated the young religious fanatic with a great deal of understanding and allowed him to propagate his doctrines throughout the empire by missionary activity. Having at first tried to stamp out the Christian faith, which was gaining ground all over the contemporary world, Shapur one day forbade the Magi to persecute the Christians further, deciding to let everyone in the huge Persian dominions seek salvation in his own way. The Magi were allowed to uphold their ancient Iranian god Ahura-Mazda and his prophet Zarathustra, the Manicheans "the Light" and its various prophets, the Jews their Yahweh, the Christians their Christ, the shamans their animistic phenomena and magic spirits, and the Brahmans their huge collection of gods. And all the adherents of every religion were to be permitted to pursue their own ideas and forms of worship in peace and freedom.

At the same time, King Shapur tried to extend and perfect his father Ardashir's religious lifework. Ardashir had commissioned a senior religious official (Tansar) to collect the various texts of the sacred Avesta and had published them as an authorized version. His son Shapur added scientific texts to this canon, including medical, astronomical and metaphysical works from India, Greece, and other parts of the world. The new Persian king was an extremely open-minded man of liberal interests.

It is remarkable what a wealth of religious ideas pervaded the world about 250 A.D. Five great world-conquering ideologies were competing for support among the inhabitants of Europe and Asia: the Jewish-Christian faith in the West, the religion of Ahura-Mazda and Mani's doctrines in Persia, Buddhism in India and, influencing all four, Greek philosophy or Hellenism. But although hard pressed by Christianity and Buddhism, Mazdaism gained new reserves of strength and a fresh lease of life under the Sassanian regime in Persia, probably just because Zarathustra's ancient god was under such heavy fire from every other religion.

Whereas Ardashir had contented himself with being lord of Iran, his son described himself as "Great King of Iran and all other countries." (His Persian title ran: *Shahansha i Eran u Aneran,* or "Great King of Iran and non-Iran.") Shapur was enterprising, cunning and cruel, but he possessed a harem, and there—as with most Persian kings—lay his one weakness and only vulnerable spot.

Anyone who wanted to rule the world would have to deal with the Romans. More precisely, he would have to defeat the Romans and drive them out of Asia. As a good strategist, Shapur knew that before he could do so he would have to secure his right flank. And there on his right flank lay Armenia. In the year 252 A.D., the Persian king occupied the rugged and mountainous country which King Chosroes had defended so successfully for thirty years against every external and internal threat until Shapur at last succeeded in bringing about his assassination. Chosroes' son Tiridates was only a child when the throne passed to him. His kingdom, too, like so many others in history, was destined to be overthrown from within. Opposed by other members of the Armenian royal family, Tiridates had to seek asylum with the Romans, and the opposition party, with one Artavasdes at its head, was only too happy to accept Persian suzerainty.

The collapse of Armenia tore a dangerous breach in Rome's eastern defenses. And Shapur now invaded Mesopotamia, marched through Syria leaving a trail of devastation in his wake, besieged Antioch for a time, and overran Cappadocia. The city of Tyana fell, and Caesarea was hard pressed.

Emperor Valerian was scarcely equal to this situation. He was getting on in years, being past sixty, and the Persia coup came just as the Goths and Borani were renewing their land attacks and piratical raids. The elderly Roman monarch must have won several victories over the Persians, for coins dating from the year 259 bear inscriptions such as *Victoria Parthica* and *Restitutor Orientis* and were evidently struck

---

Valerian left *Antioch,* his royal residence, and marched into *Cappadocia,* but turned back abruptly on receipt of bad news and eventually made his headquarters at *Samosata,* a stronghold on the upper Euphrates. There, supported by the stout fortress of *Edessa,* he intended to stem the Persian advance. However, the Persians effected a breakthrough at *Dura-Europos.* (Excavations have been carried out there since 1928.) At *Naksh-i-Rustam* a scene was hewn into the rock for all time depicting Emperor Valerian kneeling in chains before the Persian king Shapur, who is seated on a horse. The Roman emperor was destined to die in captivity.

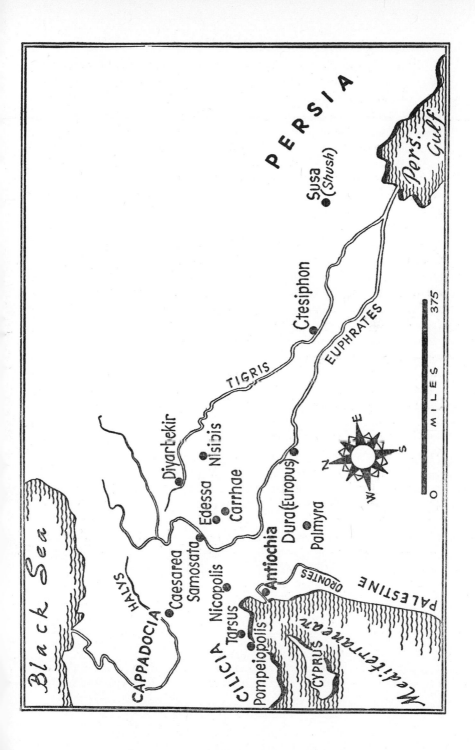

to commemorate victory over the Persians (Parthians) and the pacification of the East. Be that as it may, Valerian was finally reduced to a mood of fear and uncertainty.

This, as has been mentioned, was a period when any Roman general who had gained military successes reached out an eager hand for the imperial purple. Valerian was therefore most reluctant to entrust large expeditionary forces to any one of his generals for it was dangerous to bestow far-reaching powers on a deputy. True, he sent Successianus to deal with the Borani and appointed him praetorian prefect or commander-in-chief. True, he dispatched a certain Felix to Byzantium with orders to prepare the city for a siege. But none of these measures presented any real obstacle to the determined Goths.

Leaving his official residence at Antioch, Valerian at last traveled to Cappadocia, only to turn back abruptly on receipt of bad news and finally make his headquarters at Samosata, a stronghold on the upper Euphrates. Here, supported by the stout fortress of Edessa, he proposed to await the Persian advance.

Shapur now sent his son Hormizd to the Euphrates and the Persians effected a breakthrough at Dura-Europos. This caravan-city on the central Euphrates, one of the largest archaeological sites in the world, has been gradually excavated by the French Academy and Yale University since 1928. At the foot of a steep cliff in the northeast corner of the city flowed the Euphrates, while high above the river stood an acropolis or citadel. Identifiable among the ruins are stone bastions and towers, a rectangular street system, a Roman courthouse, and palaces for officials. Part of the city, probably undermined by the Euphrates, fell into the depths below, but on the remaining walls were found pictures of horsemen in Persian dress. Excavations have proved how stubbornly the Persians besieged the city and how desperately they were resisted. Battles raged beneath the ground as the defenders met tunnel with countertunnel. Archaeologists have found the remains of soldiers with coins in their purses dating from the year 255.

Then, just when things were at their blackest, the Romans were hit by a disaster which increased the hazards of their unfortunate position a thousandfold. Valerian's ranks were ravaged by the plague. The old emperor brooded day and night as to how Rome had offended the heavens while his soldiers, as though struck down by an invisible hand, perished by thousands. The only idea which occurred to the old man in this state of dire emergency was to vent his wrath on the

Christians. Thus since the tragic situation demanded a scapegoat and since Valerian's main concern was to propitiate the heavens and regain the favor of the ancient gods of Italy, he diverted the Romans' gaze from the conflagration in the East to the evils of Christianity.

The Christians prayed for the life and welfare of the emperor, but they prayed to their own God. As Bishop Cyprian said, when subjected to a rigorous cross-examination by the Roman governor of the province of Africa: "I am a Christian. I know no other god than the true God. That is the God whom we Christians serve. We pray to Him night and day for ourselves, for all men, and for the preservation of the emperor." But sincerity did not save the Christians' heads and many of them were executed. The Christian bishop of Rome was slain in the catacomb of the Praetextatus just as he was celebrating Mass. The deacon Laurence was roasted to death, and in Carthage Cyprian was sentenced to die by the sword. In Spain Bishop Fructuosus died a martyr's death. "That is what comes of neglecting to worship the gods and refusing the emperor's countenance a pious salute!" the Roman judge shouted at him. Yes, thought Valerian in despair, if one ceased to worship the gods of Rome they sent plagues, Persians and plagues. But while the vacillating old man managed to wreak havoc among Christians everywhere, he failed to stop the Persians.

In the year 260 Shapur appeared before Edessa. True to its reputation, the city defended itself with great gallantry. Valerian decided to fight it out and sent his army, depleted by the Black Death, demoralized, enervated and half-starved, into the field. It soon became known in the ranks that the emperor himself had abandoned all hope.

Valerian now took a last desperate step. He tried to negotiate with the Persians, offering them a fantastic sum in gold in an attempt to pacify them. The cunning Shapur had a first-class intelligence service, however, and knew exactly how hopeless things were in Valerian's camp.

Shapur at first refused to negotiate, then later allowed himself to be talked into a conference, his only proviso being that Valerian should attend it in person. The unwitting Valerian came, and was taken prisoner. It was a sly and infamous breach of international law, but that did not worry Shapur.

A Roman emperor in barbarian hands, captured, enslaved, and—worst of all—still alive. It was a terrible tragedy, not only for the emperor but for the empire as a whole.

The world had sharp ears in those days. News raced rapidly from country to country despite the lack of telegraph, telephone or airplane. So the report of the emperor's capture smote Rome's armies and provinces like a hammer blow. At Rome, the incessant cries of the bargemen on the Tiber were hushed, the rumble of wagon wheels died away, the carts stopped rattling through the winding lanes, curses froze on the muleteers' lips. Money-changers stared in horrified amazement at coins bearing the old emperor's portrait. Coppersmiths, snake charmers, even beggars held their breath as the shocking rumor ran through fifty miles of Roman streets.

Now the Persians poured westward like a tidal wave. Antioch fell, betrayed to the Persian king's soldiers by Mariades, one of its leading citizens who, having been expelled from the city council for embezzling public funds, decided to turn traitor. It is probable that he arranged the escape of several prominent Antiochians, and the city's mint and treasury were hurriedly removed to a place of safety. But the masses had no inkling that Mariades had betrayed them. They were sitting in the amphitheater applauding when the murderous Shapur's soldiers broke in and at once put everything to the torch, not even sparing the surrounding countryside. Mariades was burned alive on Shapur's orders, probably because he had not been wholehearted enough in his treachery and had allowed the city's store of gold and treasure to disappear in advance.

Numerous small townships and the capitals of Cilicia and Cappadocia, Tarsus and Caesarea all fell prey to the Persians' savage fury, while in Paphlagonia in northern Asia Minor, Persian cavalry reached the shores of the Black Sea. Endless columns of prisoners trudged over the desert tracks of the East, driven to water once a day like cattle. The great Band-i-Kaisar (Mole of the Caesar) at Sostra (Shushtar) in Susiana is said to have been constructed by these prisoners.

We are told that Shapur treated Valerian like a slave until the day he died. From time to time he would parade him in imperial purple and chains, and often when Shapur mounted his horse the Roman emperor had to lie down on his belly so that the Persian king could step on his back. "That is what I call a real triumph," laughed Shapur, "not just painting triumphs on walls, as the Romans do." Valerian was forced to endure such treatment for the rest of his life, and it appears that he survived for many years. And when he at last died Shapur

Balbinus and Pupienus were elected joint emperors by the Senate in 238 A.D., after the deaths of Gordian I and Gordian II. Balbinus took over the civil administration, while Pupienus assumed supreme command of the army. The dual regime functioned for only a brief period, after which the emperors became jealous of each other. Three months later they were both murdered.

The Romans reclined when eating because they thought it either unhealthy or uncomfortable to do so sitting down. Here Emperor Balbinus and his wife are shown lying in effigy on their own sarcophagus.

This philosopher's sarcophagus dating from the 3rd century A.D. probably depicts the Empress Salonina being instructed by Plotinus.

The celebrated philosopher Plotinus of Lycopolis in Egypt, "the last man of the ancient world," accompanied Gordian's expedition against Persia in 242-3. When in Rome, he freely exchanged ideas with Emperor Gallienus and his wife Salonina. Gallienus' thoughts of building him a philosopher's city ("Platonopolis") were abandoned after the emperor's murder. Plotinus believed in a single Creator of all things.

At school on the Moselle in 190 A.D. This fascinating tomb was discovered in the foundations of Constantine's town walls at Neumagen.

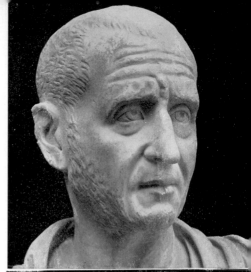

Emperor Decius, the first Roman emperor to be killed in action on barbarian soil. He lost his life while fighting the Goths—very probably because he had been betrayed by General Trebonianus Gallus.

Trebonianus Gallus was proclaimed emperor by the army after the battle of Abrittus. His two years of rule were dogged by misfortune: the Persians overran Mesopotamia, the Goths invaded Moesia, and the Plague raged. Trebonianus and his son were murdered in 253.

Gordian III and his murderer Philip the Arab. Emperor Philip (reigned 244-249) succeeded in inciting the army against young Gordian (below), who was eventually murdered.

Emperor Gallienus was the son of Valerian, who died in Persian captivity. Gallienus wanted to counter Christianity with Plotinus' doctrines and his sincere quest for God. This interesting emperor, who was little understood by his contemporaries, reigned from 253 to 268 A.D.

The walls of Rome were hurriedly built by Emperor Aurelian in 271 A.D. as a protection against barbarian invasion. Since Rome's legionaries were engaged in defending her threatened empire, prisoners of war and Roman artisans were compelled to do forced labor. The walls, which are nearly twelve miles long, ran ruthlessly through residential districts and cemeteries.

Triumphal arch and colonnades at Palmyra. No other city in antiquity could boast a main street like Palmyra's, which was a mile long. It led through this gate and was once a bustling thoroughfare.

The great Temple of Bel (the Baal of our Bible) at Palmyra. Queen Zenobia ruled the city until its destruction by Emperor Aurelian in 273.

Marcus Aurelius Probus would be numbered among the great figures in world history if our information about him were not so scanty. He introduced viticulture into Germany and Hungary and was an extremely successful general. He was killed at Sirmium in 282.

Head of an aristocratic lady from Palmyra. The leading families of this caravan city spoke and wrote Syriac-Aramaic. Like this woman, Zenobia was an Arab.

Emperor Diocletian (reigned 284-305) had an amazing gift for organization. He ruled the world for twenty years and then retired to his palace at Salonae in modern Yugoslavia. Only very few sculptures of this unique historical figure exist.

Emperor Diocletian's residence at Split (Salonae). This palace, which still survives in part, was the largest in the ancient world.

In Rome, the art of dancing was confined to women and children. (One note-worthy exception: Emperor Caligula!) Lovely, graceful dances like the one shown in this relief were introduced into Rome from Greece at the end of the 2nd century.

Illustrating the naturalism of Roman sculpture at the time of Emperor Gallienus (238-268 A.D.). This sarcophagus, symbolizing the unity, even in death, of a Roman married couple (left and right), depicts their mute but fervent affirmation of eternal loyalty. In the center stands the tutelary goddess of marriage.

had him stuffed, painted red, and exhibited in a temple "to the ever-lasting shame of Rome."

It is, of course, possible that the Christians exaggerated the horrors of Valerian's captivity because he had persecuted them so relentlessly. Indeed, a number of historians consider the emperor's hardships to have been very much overdrawn.

One thing seems certain: Shapur was so harassed by the Romans and their allies in the ensuing years that he must have vented some of his spleen on his distinguished prisoner, and it is also well known that Persians of this period were exceedingly brutal. Certainly at Naksh-i-Rustam, near the ruins of Persepolis, a scene depicting the Roman emperor kneeling in chains before the Persian king Shapur, mounted on a horse, was carved into the rock for the benefit of future generations. This well-preserved relief can still be seen there today.

At first nothing could stem the Persian tide and Shapur's armies murdered and looted at will. But at last the retreating Romans re-grouped themselves under a general named Callistus. Callistus, nick-named Ballista, attached himself to Macrianus, the Roman quarter-master general. Collecting some ships in Cilician ports, he set off for beleaguered Soloi (Pompeiopolis), killed several thousand Persians, and gained a great if most unusual victory: he captured the Persian king's harem!

Shapur's attitude changed at once. The unexpected loss of his concubines, not to mention the personal baggage that went with them, apparently cut him to the quick. He set off in the direction of Ctesiphon, his capital, traveling by forced marches. When asked what urgent business he had to attend to at home, he alleged that he "had to celebrate a festival."

Throughout this turmoil the city of Edessa had held fast against time, plague, and Persian attack. King Shapur's line of withdrawal took him through terrain commanded by that fortress. But he knew Edessa too well to risk a fight with his army in its present weakened and depleted condition. Thus the citizens of Edessa lived to see the triumphal day when Shapur, aspirant to world domination, was forced to purchase free passage through their territory with all the money which he had captured from the Romans.

After that the wild, restless and titanic energy of the power-hungry Persian king seems to have waned. Shapur eventually found, in the rulers of the oasis of Palmyra, opponents who were either a match for him or at least curbed his ambition. And toward the end of his reign he was so occupied with internal affairs that he had no time to contemplate a new trial of strength with the Romans. The war-weary king spent the rest of his days carrying out grandiose building projects.

Shapur's coins would indicate, however, that he remained faithful to the ancient Persian deity Ahura-Mazda or Ormazd, god of light. Seventeen hundred years old, these coins portray a remarkably shrewd and alert face and bear the legend: *Worshiper of Ormazd, excellent Shapur, King of the Kings of Iran, heavenly scion of the gods.*

THE GRECOPHILE

GALLIENUS was an exceptionally brilliant man but a prudent one. He stayed in Rome and made no move to liberate Valerian from Persian captivity, not even sending envoys to the Persian king to beg for his father's release. On the contrary, he seemed almost glad to be rid of his parent. In the triumphal march which he staged to commemorate the tenth anniversary of his accession he included some men dressed in Persian costumes to simulate prisoners of war. Several comedians threaded their way through the ranks as though searching for someone. When asked what they were doing, they replied that they were looking for the emperor's father.

Gallienus was a rather unique figure in the history of Rome. He at once abandoned his father's anti-Christian policy and issued an edict of toleration whereby Christian communities had their confiscated property, churches and cemeteries restored to them. In fact the emperor became almost a patron of Christianity, which is why adherents of the ancient Roman faith credited his memory with so few good traits and the Christians made the most of his merits, which were probably considerable.

During his reign the Roman world experienced a brief Hellenistic renaissance. Like Hadrian, Gallienus was an admirer of Athens and an enthusiastic champion of Greek culture. He too traveled to Greece and had himself initiated into the mystery cult of Eleusis. Eleusis in Attica was the chief center of worship of the goddess Demeter. All who participated in the mysterious rites were sworn to secrecy and no author in antiquity ever broke silence on the subject; hence our almost complete ignorance of the rituals involved. We do know, however, that they included certain dramatic performances designed to stimulate religious emotion. Gallienus struck coins depicting himself as Demeter and adopted the name Galliena in his capacity as a female deity. Ludicrous though this may seem to us, we must remember that people of the time were much closer to the goddess's secret.

Gallienus' wife was a remarkably sensitive and cultured Greek woman named Cornelia Salonina who came from Bithynia and has unfortunately been paid too little attention by students of history. When she died a coin was minted in her honor bearing the words *Augusta in pace*. Is it possible that Salonina was a Christian?

The emperor and his consort were both devotees of the greatest contemporary Greek philosopher, Plotinus of Nicopolis (in Egypt), the creator of neo-Platonism. Neo-Platonism was a rebirth of the old Platonic ideas, at a time when Greek philosophy revived once more, once more proclaimed its great mission and, in an era of chaos, disclosed its deep yearning for God. Plotinus described man's goal as "to become godlike." There is little doubt that he was acquainted with Christianity. Neo-Platonism was born at a period when those who believed in the ancient gods of Rome and the mysteries and cults of the East were in many respects not far removed from the Christians and their novel beliefs, for the ancient faith and the new were both Europeanized by Hellenistic philosophy. Gallienus did not end the persecution of the Christians because he regarded them as harmless. He merely decided that the only way to refute them was with the spirit, not the sword.

The emperor wanted to counter Christianity with Plotinus' ideas and his sincere, moving quest for God. In this Gallienus may well have been influenced by his wife Salonina, who accompanied him wherever he went and was actually in camp with him when he was assassinated. All over the Roman world men of intellect—Christians among them—were enjoined by the emperor to promote the most valuable concepts of ancient classical culture. Europe is indebted to Gallienus for passing on a large measure of the Greek genius and way of life.

Ironically enough, during his reign the sorely tried Roman empire was subjected to a series of disasters. In 262 A.D. numerous towns in Asia Minor were destroyed by earthquakes and year after year outbreaks of plague took their frightful toll.

Gallienus patterned himself on Augustus. He tried to deal with every threat, every infringement of the Roman frontiers, immediately and with a vigor and vigilance worthy of his illustrious model. Yet at other times, so Eutropius tells us, he could be strangely immobile and apathetic.

Gallienus repelled German attacks on the Rhine for seven long years and succeeded in halting the wild hordes of Alemanni, Heruli and Goths. He fortified threatened cities. (One can still clearly distinguish, at Verona for example, the speed and urgency with which walls were built on his orders.) At the same time, he was constantly harassed by would-be usurpers. So many ambitious men cast covetous eyes at the throne during this period that Roman history lumps them together under the heading of "the Thirty Tyrants."

A man named Postumus set himself up as an independent emperor at Treves (Augustus Treverorum). He erected magnificent buildings there, ruled Gaul, Britain and Spain, and issued coinage which gave the impression that the entire world belonged to him. Despite the numerous successes which he won over Postumus, Gallienus eventually had to concede that the traitor was master of the Gallic provinces. When, anxious to spare the lives of many thousands of soldiers, Gallienus nobly challenged him to a duel, Postumus replied that he was not a gladiator. The pretender was finally murdered by his own men at Mainz. The *limes,* Hadrian's great system of defense, had been meant as a guarantee of lasting peace. Now a constant state of war prevailed and the frontier fortifications had completely given way.

Gallienus instituted a considerable number of reforms in the army. He created a mobile reserve ready for instant use, recruiting his cavalry, now the most important arm, from among the Dalmatians, Moors and Germans. This "flying squad," designed for speedy dispatch to threatened frontier areas, was stationed at Milan and was as mobile as the new conditions of war demanded. The Persian campaign had shown that Roman infantrymen were not maneuverable enough to cope with the swift Iranian cavalry. For all that, the infantry remained what it was two thousand years earlier and still is, nearly as long afterwards: the hard core and essential backbone of any powerful army.

Gallienus is the only emperor in this violent and sanguinary epoch who was able to celebrate the tenth anniversary of his accession. This he did in the autumn of 263. Five years later the emperor could be seen hurrying back to Italy from the Danube, fresh from victories over the Goths and Heruli, whose plundering raids had brought them as far as Athens and Corinth. Gallienus now besieged the insurgent cavalry general Aureolus in Milan.

The emperor was a vigorous, alert man who always acted quickly. It was this very alertness and capacity for lightninglike decision which spelled his doom. He was told that Aureolus, beleaguered in Milan, had made a sortie. It was a ruse and conspirators were lurking outside the emperor's tent. He rushed out without helmet or armor and fell mortally wounded.

Gallienus was an utter individualist with a mind of his own who was little understood by his contemporaries. Even death did not win him immunity from the misfortune which had dogged him throughout his life, for his family was massacred with him. But he helped pass on to us the spirit of Greece and was one of the great figures in Roman history, despite our comparative lack of information about him.

The most amazing thing of all is that, in a period when the empire was dogged by attack, defeat and betrayal, the ruler of Rome found time to forge plans for a unique project. He almost agreed to install the great Plotinus in a settlement in Campania modeled on Plato's political doctrines, where all devotees of the spirit of Plato could forgather and engage in exalted creative activity. Even though Platonopolis, as the ideal city was to be called, never became a reality, the project remains a silent memorial to the singular mind that gave it consideration.

SHE RODE LIKE A SOLDIER

IN THE Syrian desert stand the lonely ruins of Palmyra. No one who wanders among the silent colonnades, through the shattered temples and palaces, and over the debris of a myriad tumbled stones can fail to recognize that hundreds of years went into the building of the place, and that a great past lies buried there.

Midway between the Mediterranean and the Euphrates, Palmyra once stood astride the main route between the civilization of the Persian Gulf and the metropolitan cities of the Mediterranean. It was a rendezvous for caravans from the whole of the Roman empire and the Far East. Wares from Emesa on the Orontes and valuable merchandise from Doura-Europos and the Euphrates area arrived on camel back and were unloaded here, and dealers in precious stones and rare pearls plied their trade. The city's market place was piled high with goods from China, India, Persia and southern Arabia: balls of silk, incense candles, ivory—the treasures of a world.

The oasis was famed for its abundant water supply, which was stored in huge subterranean reservoirs. Beside the broad, mile-long main avenue, bounded at one end by a triumphal arch, stood the great sun temple. Seven hundred and fifty rose-white pillars (of which 150 are still standing) gleamed in the sun and massive buildings soared into the deep blue Syrian sky. It was a true feast of Greek, Roman and Oriental architecture. A number of archaeologists have worked on the oasis during the last twenty years and new ruins are constantly being unearthed. A careful examination of the temple of Baal-Shamin the sun-god has led to the discovery of an altar and a ritual banqueting hall, while Palmyra's splendid theater has only recently been excavated.

Palmyra made world history. More than that, Palmyra once aspired to world domination, and the hands which reached for that prize were the slender hands of a woman.

The inhabitants of Palmyra were Arabs who spoke and wrote Aramaic, the language of Christ. Greek was used as a secondary language, but the aristocracy of Palmyra undoubtedly belonged to the Arab race. Merchant clans with hundreds of years of tradition behind them, traders who preceded Marco Polo by centuries in their expeditions to China and back, and some of the best archers and armored cavalry in the contemporary world: these were the pillars of Palmyra's strength.

With Valerian captured by the Persians and the empire, under his son Gallienus, menaced on every side, it was left to an Arab to save the Roman world. The name of this man, a prince of Palmyra, was Septimius Odenathus. Far away in the desert, in the eastern world, he and his city kept faith with Rome, even disposing of a pretender to the Roman throne and driving the Persians out of Mesopotamia and Armenia. Gallienus gratefully entrusted him with the defense of the East, and before long he had become governor general of the entire Orient.

Odenathus and his splendid city thus attained a unique status: to all intents and purposes, the lord of the oasis was an emperor. Odenathus was murdered in the year 267 at the height of his career. Perhaps he had become too powerful for the emperor's liking. The sheik was succeeded by his son, falsely so-called Prince Vaballathus Athenodorus, but since the boy was much too young to rule, the administration of Palmyra's affairs was taken over by his mother, Queen Zenobia.

Zenobia was a Greek name, the queen's oriental name being Bat-Zabbai, or "daughter of Zabbai." Queen Zenobia traced her ancestry back to the rulers of Egypt, to the dynasty which had produced the great Cleopatra who was of Macedonian stock. However, she is said to have been more beautiful than Cleopatra and considerably more chaste—exaggeratedly so, in fact. History relates that she only permitted her royal husband Odenathus to embrace her once a month—and then only for the purpose of procreation.

Zenobia had worked hard to school her almost masculine intellect under the famous philosopher and rhetorician Cassius Longinus, who instructed his beautiful pupil in Greek language and literature. He had a cosmopolitan background, having taught in Athens and being himself the pupil of a very well-known Egyptian. In his own and his pupil's eyes, Egypt was the absolute and universal criterion of greatness. Longinus was one day to become Zenobia's most trusted adviser.

A woman of wide interests and unusual intelligence, Zenobia spoke fluent Syrian, Aramaic, Greek and Latin. The amazing military successes of her husband Odenathus were in no small part due to his consort's advice, courage, determination and presence of mind. Imagine what it must have meant when the Arab prince attacked the mighty Persian empire and knocked at the very gates of Ctesiphon, the Persian capital! The contemporary Oriental world admired and respected the gallant couple, and the Romans at first looked upon Odenathus and Zenobia as the avengers of their captured emperor, Valerian.

Whenever King Odenathus was not occupied with affairs of state at Palmyra or actually engaged in a military campaign, his favorite pastime was hunting. We learn that he killed lion and panther. There must have been large forests in Syria at this time, for bears are also mentioned. Zenobia often accompanied Odenathus on these hunting expeditions and showed no less dash and bravery than her husband. Having successfully inured herself to heat and cold, she never traveled in a closed carriage but rode like a cavalryman and often marched for many miles at the head of her troops. By the time Odenathus died Palmyra was a flourishing caravan-city which controlled the whole of Syria and a large part of the East. Neighboring countries such as Arabia, Armenia and Persia feared Zenobia's enmity and sought her favor.

But Zenobia was still dissatisfied. Wasn't Longinus always rhapsodizing about Egypt? Wasn't Egypt the crowning glory of civilization, the five-thousand-year-old pearl of the contemporary world? Wasn't Egypt the granary of the Roman empire? And hadn't Zabdas, Zenobia's chief of staff, spent many nights expounding to her the best plan of attack? Zenobia wanted to rule Egypt, the land of the Pharaohs and, so she claimed, of her own forefathers. She would not rest until she had plucked this tempting fruit for herself and her young son. Accordingly she sent a large army under the command of Zabdas to the Nile and simultaneously launched an attack on Arabia. It was an ideal moment. Probus, the Roman prefect, was absent from Egypt. He hurried back as fast as possible, but it was too late. The Palmyrenes had conquered Egypt, and Probus committed suicide.

At Rome Gallienus had been succeeded by Claudius II, an extremely efficient army officer from Illyria (modern Yugoslavia). He fought Rome's battles with great success for one and a half years, defeating the Alemanni at Lake Garda and decisively worsting the Goths at Nish. His victories laid the foundations of the empire's reconstruction, but he died of the plague in the year 270.

Claudius II was followed by Aurelian, a man who combined great physical strength with a coolly calculating mind and well-disciplined military ability. He was outstandingly courageous and carried each of his military operations through with copybook precision and great tenacity. Once he had decided on a plan he would never freely deviate from it. By far the most distinguished of all the Roman officers in Illyria, Aurelian had made his mark in the war against the Goths and was the obvious successor to the throne.

The new emperor lacked three things: charm, tact, and a subtle appreciation of the intellectual. For all that, his reign was a time of unparalleled achievement. First he signed a treaty with Zenobia to protect his rear, intending to rule the West himself and leave the eastern half of the empire under the control of Zenobia and her son. Then he began to tidy up. The Roman empire was being eaten away on every side. Aurelian repelled a Vandal invasion of Pannonia. The Juthungi and Alemanni heavily defeated him at Piacenza and Rome itself was threatened, but he saved the situation and was finally victorious at the battle of the Ticino. It was his invariable policy to recruit defeated enemies into the Roman army. He fortified Rome with walls twenty feet high, thirteen feet thick, and twelve miles long, creating a mighty bastion of defense which was interspersed with towers and eighteen gates. It was built by noncombatants and prisoners of war, Rome's legionaries having better things to do in the outside world, and is still one of the sights of the city. The emperor abandoned the province of Dacia and left it to the Goths. Now at long last he had his hands free for the great game in the East.

The world waited expectantly for the clash between the tough and brilliant soldier and the worldly-wise, ambitious queen. Flushed with success, the Palmyrenes had remained in Egypt and minted coins at Alexandria with the head of their own King Vaballathus on one side and that of the Emperor Aurelian on the reverse. But before long (from March 11, 271, onward) they were striking coins on which only the Palmyrene king's head appeared. In the summer of 271, Zenobia raised her own status to that of Augusta, or empress, and entitled her son Augustus. Palmyra had seceded from the Roman empire and thrown down the gauntlet.

Aurelian was not a man to tolerate this sort of behavior. Breaking off relations with Palmyra, he assembled a large army and wrested Egypt from Zenobia's control. At the close of 271 the emperor's massive columns rolled eastward. The city of Tyana on the borders of Cappadocia offered resistance but was taken. The emperor treated the citizens with great leniency and the news of his behavior encouraged a large number of other cities to open their gates to him. Zenobia now relied on getting some support from the king of Persia, but King

Shapur was very old and unwilling to forget that he and Zenobia had been bitter enemies.

At Antioch battle was joined anew. Zenobia was present in person but her run of military success was at an end. Although outnumbered, Aurelian defeated the Palmyrene cavalry and Antioch fell into his hands. Once more, the emperor shrewdly spared the lives of the civil population.

Zenobia's defeated soldiers trudged back along the endless caravan trails, their morale at a low ebb. Aurelian then offered the queen peace terms, calling on her to surrender and pointing to the large number of men who had lost their lives in the battles on the Orontes. "Yes, but they were only Romans," retorted Zenobia, and engaged the emperor yet again at Emesa. After a bloody battle the Roman legionaries again won the day.

"The sun-god of Emesa has deserted his home and given victory to Rome," declared Aurelian and adopted this god of light, an oriental deity which had been subjected to the refining influence of Greek culture, as the Romans' national god. The sun temple was dedicated on the Field of Mars at Rome on December 25, 274. It was an attempt at heathen monotheism, for only a universal and omnipresent god like the sun-god could hope to make a fight of it with the new God of Christendom.

But Rome's soldiers were exhausted. They advanced on Palmyra by forced marches, broiled by the pitiless sun. The city had ample supplies and a siege presented almost insuperable difficulties, especially since the Romans were perpetually short of water. Aurelian was wounded by an arrow, but the greatest officer on the throne since Trajan refused to abandon his cause. In the end Zenobia fled on a dromedary to seek help from the Persians once more. But Roman cavalry had set off in pursuit and Zenobia had only reached the Euphrates and was just stepping into the boat which was to take her to the other bank and freedom when she and her son were seized by the Romans. Palmyra, unnerved by Zenobia's flight, abandoned further resistance. When the Syrian queen was led before Aurelian he asked her how she had dared to rebel against the masters of Rome. Zenobia answered with great dexterity that she had never been able to regard his predecessors or, indeed, any of the men who had forcibly taken possession of the throne as Roman emperors, and added: "You alone are my conqueror and lord."

But the captured queen soon lost her initial *sang-froid*. She trembled

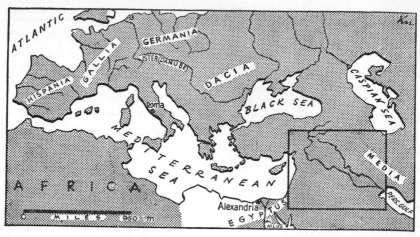

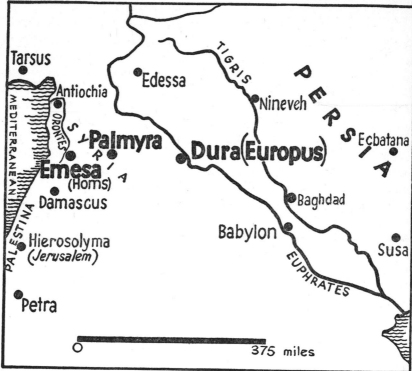

Palmyra used to be the commercial rendezvous between the metropolitan cities of the Mediterranean and the cultural area of the Persian Gulf. This caravan city reached its zenith under the Arab queen Zenobia. Her army was defeated by Emperor Aurelian at *Emesa*, and she was finally captured at *Dura-Europos* just as she was about to escape across the Euphrates.

when she learned that the legionaries were clamoring for her execution and, forgetting that Cleopatra, her model, had taught the world that a queen should die rather than live in dishonorable captivity, she betrayed all her friends, teachers and confidants, claiming that her resistance to Rome had been engendered by bad advisers who had taken advantage of her feminine weakness.

Aurelian thereupon promptly beheaded Zenobia's leading counselors. Among those who fell prey to the cowardice of this woman who had so recently seemed one of the most courageous personalities in world history was Longinus. He died as a philosopher ought to die. Utterly serene, never complaining, comforting his fellow victims, and reserving all his sympathy for his unfortunate mistress, he went to his death with absolute composure.

Countless treasures fell into the Roman emperor's hands as the treasure chambers and storerooms in the temples and public buildings of the world's most prosperous oasis yielded up their contents to the victorious Romans. Apparently Aurelian spared private property, and once again he exercised his now proverbial leniency toward the inhabitants of the city.

But hardly had he crossed the Bosphorus on his way home than he heard that the Palmyrenes had risen against him once more. This time, with truly Asiatic brutality, he vented his rage on men, women and children alike. Not even the peasants who lived in the neighborhood of the city were exempted. The emperor ordered everything to be destroyed. Nevertheless, when he saw Palmyra lying in ruins he regretted his decision and gave the few surviving inhabitants permission to rebuild the city. His act of clemency came to nothing. Palmyra was never to rise again above the station of a little desert village, and its ruins have lain untouched for seventeen hundred years.

The emperor had almost reconquered the Roman world when a new and singularly interesting figure appeared on the scene. Firmus was a shipowner and papermaker of Greek origin who had left Seleucia in Syria and settled down in Alexandria, where he amassed a vast fortune by manufacturing papyrus. He also did a thriving trade in Chinese silk, using the town of Coptos as his base. During the years circa 270 "Firmus silk" was being transported by ship and camel train from one end of the world to the other and Firmus' ships were regularly traversing the Indian Ocean. Clothes-conscious ladies in Rome and Palmyra dressed themselves in his silks. No sooner had Firmus heard that Aurelian had left for home after his first conquest of Palmyra than he joined forces with some Nubian desert tribes, instigated a revolt, and decided, at the beginning of 273, to promote himself from paper king to Roman emperor. However, Aurelian's legions restored order here too, and we learn with some regret that the enterprising paper and silk magnate took his own life.

The emperor's triumphal procession through Rome bade fair to surpass anything which the Eternal City had seen before. Twenty elephants, four tigers, two hundred tamed animals from Libya and Palestine and sixteen hundred gladiators all paraded by. There were banners captured from many defeated nations, treasures from Asia, ambassadors from Ethiopia, Arabia, Persia, India and even China, and endless columns of prisoners, among them Goths, Vandals, Sarmatae, Alemanni, Franks, Gauls, Syrians and Egyptians. Then came the gorgeous wardrobe of the captive Zenobia and, finally, the queen of the East herself, choicest prize of all. A slave led her along on the end of a golden chain welded about her neck. The lovely woman looked ready to collapse under the weight of her own jewelry as she was forced to walk along ahead of her magnificent battle chariot—the very same chariot in which she had hoped to enter Rome in triumph.

Aurelian's triumphal chariot was drawn by a team of four stags captured from the Goths. Hour after hour the amazing procession wound through the streets of Rome. At first the crowds were lost in silent admiration, then they cheered. Then they fell silent again and stared with bated breath. For in the parade of prisoners was Tetricus, senator and would-be emperor who had arbitrarily seized control of Gaul. Never before had a Roman senator marched through Rome as a prisoner in a triumphal procession. The emperor was lenient with him, however, and gave him a government post in southern Italy, namely supervisor of morals in Lucania.

We are told that Aurelian treated Zenobia with the utmost consideration and gave her a villa at Tibur (modern Tivoli). The Syrian queen, once so proud and courageous, proceeded to lead a blameless existence as the wife of a Roman senator. Her daughters married into leading Roman families, and her descendants are said to have been living in Rome as late as the fifth century.

THE ADMINISTRATIVE GENIUS

Diocletian was a shrewd character, gifted with sharp-sightedness and a penetrating intelligence. He tried to divert on to others the bitterness caused by his severe measures. He spent his old age as a private citizen on his country estate at Salonae. His rare magnanimity was demonstrated by the way in which he voluntarily relinquished his lofty status for the rank and condition of a private citizen—the only man to do so since the foundation of the imperial regime.
—Eutropius, *History of Rome*, ix.

AS A GREAT soldier-emperor, Aurelian had fought successfully against the Goths and Vandals. He had brought the Alemanni to a standstill and made Rome the strongest fortress in the world. He had reunited Gaul with Rome. He had destroyed Palmyra and captured Queen Zenobia, first exhibiting her to the Romans as an item of booty in his triumphal parade and then settling her in a villa at Tibur and marrying her to a senator.

Zenobia's conqueror was now master of the world and God's deputy on earth. His lonely supremacy brought him gradually closer to the Christian emperors who were later to rule "by the grace of God." However, Aurelian's god was not the God of Christianity, but rather the sun-god which had given him victory over Zenobia and with it mastery of the world. Jupiter Capitolinus, hitherto the senior member of the Roman pantheon, was now superseded by the oriental sun-god, the invincible national deity who was greater than all other gods. By promoting a single god, Aurelian's sun cult illustrated the astonishing development of the ancient mind and, being virtually monotheistic, foreshadowed the possibility of future state recognition for the God of Christianity.

Aurelian governed in the Oriental manner, godlike and by divine right. His grasp extended to every quarter of the world, to north, east, south and west, to the skies and the sun. But, incomparable soldier-emperor that he was, he died through a stupid mischance, either through blind fate or human folly.

At the end of 274 he had set off for the East once more, intending to wrest Mesopotamia from the Persians and reconquer it for Rome. The final act unfolded at Caenophrurium, between Perinthus and Byzantium, in the autumn of 275. The man who had set a nearly impotent empire on its feet again, owed his death to the machinations of an insignificant private secretary.

This secretary, Eros by name, had for some trivial reason aroused the emperor's disfavor. Overapprehensive of Aurelian's anger, Eros forged a letter purporting to show that the emperor meant to execute all his bravest warriors. He then showed it to the men involved and they, imagining that they were in mortal danger, resolved to murder their inflexible master. They only discovered their mistake after the great monarch was dead. Eros was executed but the damage was done.

The army was so dismayed that for once it did not select a new emperor from its own ranks but left the choice to the Senate. The long-departed era of senatorial supremacy seemed to have returned in September of 275 when Senator Tacitus was elected emperor. Such an honor was tantamount to a death sentence, considering how few emperors died from natural causes. Tacitus was seventy-five years old. He conscientiously marched against the Goths in Asia Minor, only to die of disease at Tyana about April, 276. He was succeeded by an Emperor Florian who "ruled" for all of three months before being deposed.

The army of the East now chose another Illyrian, Marcus Aurelius Probus, the ablest officer in the Roman service. Had history been kinder to him, this emperor would be ranked among the greatest for he succeeded, by a series of bold and brilliant strokes, in restoring Roman possessions to full strength. He liberated Gaul from the Germans in a single year, repelled hostile attacks on every frontier of the empire, on the Rhine, the Danube, and in Upper Egypt, dealt with insurgent mountain tribes and usurpers in the provinces, settled large numbers of German prisoners in the Roman empire, did a great deal for his native Pannonia, launched soil improvement schemes, and introduced viticulture into Germany and Hungary. He was killed at Sirmium in 282, just as he was preparing for a Persian campaign. He reigned one year longer than Aurelian, achieved as much or even more than he did, and was known, like Aurelian, as "God and Lord." Yet historical records give him such poor coverage that we know relatively little about him.

Probus' successor, Carus, and his sons Carinus and Numerianus, rulers of West and East respectively, made only fleeting appearances on the imperial stage. All three died violent deaths, as was only to be expected.

Constantius Chlorus, born in Illyria, was nominated by Diocletian as Caesar of the West. His Helena, who built numerous Christian churches and was later canonized, bore him a son who was to become Constantine the Great. Constantius was a victorious general of great ability and a magnanimous ruler. He died in Britain, at York.

The Porta Nigra at Trèves was the most massive gatehouse ever built by the Romans and formed part of the imposing city fortifications constructed in the 4th century A.D. It is possible that the gate was built by Constantine.

The tomb of Caecilia Metella on the Via Appia. Caecilia lived in about 50 B.C. and belonged to a very blue-blooded family which produced six consuls.

►

The Aqua Claudia, one of the eleven aqueducts serving Rome in the imperial era, was constructed by Claudius in 52 A.D. Running across bridges and through tunnels, this "stone canal" brought over 40 million gallons of water into Rome daily from the vicinity of Arsoli, 45 miles away.

The Bridge of Cestius. The man who gave his name to this bridge lived in about 10 B.C. As a tomb, he built himself a pyramid 120 feet high which is still to be seen in Rome today.

►

Restoration of the Roman aqueduct at Spoleto, Toscana.

Roman soldiers advancing on a town. 4th-century mosaic in the Sta. Maria Maggiore.

Sarcophagus attributed to Helena, mother of Constantine. The relief shows the emperor's triumphal procession.

Constantine the Great, the world's first Christian emperor. By linking Christianity and throne together for the first time in history he became the pioneer of a new era. Recent research has greatly enhanced our understanding of this emperor.

Constantine's triumphal arch in white marble was voted him by the Senate in 312 A.D., to commemorate the emperor's victory over Maxentius at the Pons Mulvius. This imposing monument was completed in 315 A.D., the tenth anniversary of his reign. The inscriptions refer to Constantine as "Founder of Peace."

Constantine's Basilica was a massive brick building which dominated the Roman Forum. Although its designer is unknown, it has decisively influenced European architecture.

The Praetorians formed the bodyguard of the Roman emperors. They served for sixteen years, received triple pay, were permitted to wear sumptuous armor, golden accouterments and tall plumes, and frequently influenced accession to the throne by selling their allegiance to the highest bidder. Their normal strength was ten cohorts each of five hundred men (or, from the time of Septimius Severus onward, about a thousand). Constantine disbanded the Praetorian Guard in the year 312.

This mosaic in a Roman tomb represents Christ as *Hēlios* or *Sol Invictus* ("invincible sun"). With the introduction of the oriental sun-cult by Emperor Aurelian, himself the son of a sun-priestess, Sol Invictus became the foremost Roman god and remained so until superseded by Christianity. This interesting mosaic illustrates how the sun was adopted into Christian symbolism and transformed. Our own "Sunday" is a relic of the Syrian sun-cult.

Numerian took part in a successful Persian expedition commanded by his father and led a victorious army back from Ctesiphon after Carus' sudden death. In autumn, 284, the Roman forces reached Nicomedia, where a gruesome discovery was made. For some time an unbearable stench had been issuing from the emperor's litter which was now found to contain a putrefying body. Numerian was dead, and his litter-bearers had been toting a corpse around Asia. The murderer was his father-in-law, Arrius Aper. Naturally it was not long before he paid for his deed.

Men are complex creatures. No one can be summed up in a few catch phrases, which is why good historical writing is such an art, cramming as it must a lot of truth into a little space. Gaius Aurelius Valerius Diocletianus was one of the most complex figures in world history, a character with a multitude of lights and shadows, neither an ordinary man nor a universal genius, no brilliant soldier but one of the greatest administrators of all time, a human being with human failings, a ruler who made several big and serious mistakes. The last great pagan emperor, Diocletian marked the end of an epoch, not the beginning.

Before his accession he was known as Diocles, and we know he came of very humble origins. His native land was Dalmatia and his home town is assumed to have been Salonae, since he later built a large palace there. The precise year of his birth is unknown but coin portraits dating from 305, the year of his abdication, show him as a man of about seventy.

The troops proclaimed him Augustus, or emperor, at Nicomedia in Bithynia on November 17, 284. Addressing the army, he gazed up at the sun with drawn sword and swore a sacred oath that he was innocent of Numerian's death. Then, quick as lightning, he drove his blade through the man standing next to him. It was the praetorian prefect Arrius Aper, his predecessor's father-in-law.

The story has a point. It had once been prophesied to Diocles that he would become emperor if he killed a wild boar, in Latin *aper*. Now the boar lay dead at his feet. The prophecy had been fulfilled; no trivial matter in those days of dark superstitions, magic incantations and mysterious formulae. The soldiers were dumbfounded. They liked that sort of thing. The new emperor was obviously a quick thinker, and the gods were on his side.

But Diocletian did not possess the conventional daring and magnanimity of the heroic figure who seeks danger and glory, abhors intrigue, and challenges bold men of his own stamp. Edward Gibbon, who drew a very subtle portrait of him, thought that his already strong character gained further schooling from experience and a study of human nature, that he was a blend of generosity and meanness, lenience and severity, stubbornness and flexibility, and that he often cloaked extreme hypocrisy under a bluff soldierly exterior. But above all, Gibbon said, Diocletian had acquired the ability to subordinate his own and other people's emotions to the dictates of his ambition. He could always find the most elaborate and cogent reasons for any action he undertook. H. Mattingly describes the effect of such a man on his contemporaries. Apparently "he was an object of intense admiration—tinged with a certain uneasiness and distrust."

Diocletian surrounded himself with imperial pomp and soon made it clear that he regarded himself as God's agent on earth. There was a religious aura about Diocletian's monarchy which stemmed from an emphasis on his divine right to rule, the supernaturally sacred character of the imperial office, Oriental-style court ceremonial, and emperor worship as a means of paying direct homage to the highest earthly ruler, God's deputy in the world. This restatement of the emperor's central authority probably suited the mood of the time, for people were tired of the frightening national crises of the third century. "If any means of saving the Roman empire still existed—and this was the nation's general belief—it had to come from above," writes Rostovzeff.

While he sometimes held court at Nicomedia (modern Ismid, not far from Istanbul), arrayed in his state robes of silk and gold, with pearls and precious stones on his shoes, Diocletian spent most of his time traveling through Asia and Europe, defending the Empire and receiving the homage due a god. The emperor of Rome had become unapproachable. The supernatural radiance which people ascribed to the emperor now began to appear as a nimbus in portraits of him. The master of the world sat in his Sacrum Palatium in solemn isolation, and anyone who wanted to see him was passed on from one steward and eunuch to the next until he reached the Holy of Holies, where he had to fall before the monarch and address him as a god. This custom of *proscynesis*, which entailed falling on one's knees and kissing the hem of the imperial purple, hailed from the court of ancient Persia and even the emperor's own family were required to comply with it. The emperor's title and normal mode of address was now Lord (*dominus*), not First Citizen (*princeps*), as Augustus had once styled himself. The Principate had become the Dominate.

Diocletian had one daughter, Valeria, but no son. He realized that the empire was too large for one man to govern alone and so, in midsummer 285, he promoted his comrade-in-arms Maximian to the rank of Caesar and sent him to Gaul. Shortly afterward, in recognition of his achievements there, he proclaimed him Augustus, or joint emperor.

There were now two emperors, Maximian in the West and Diocletian in the East. The Augusti were looked on as brothers, an honorary relationship which put Diocletian's co-emperor on a par with himself. Diocletian still retained the premier position in the empire, however. He had chosen to rule the East simply because it presented the knottiest diplomatic and military problems. It was there that the frontiers had to be held against the Persian Sassanids and there that the greatest economic strength lay. The scales of power had tipped irrevocably in favor of the East.

Diocletian had mounted the throne at Nicomedia, the city which would one day see him take his leave of the purple. He made it his royal residence and ornamented it with such splendid buildings that a generation later the orator Libanius called the city "the most beautiful metropolis in the world." The eastern half of the empire had stepped into the spotlight, while Rome, profligate, spoilt, sadistic city of arenas, magnificent thermae and amphitheaters, was forced to retire to the wings.

Even Maximian spent very little of his time in Rome. In order to be nearer the threatened northern frontiers he lived in Milan, which at this period began in some aspects to eclipse Rome in importance. Diocletian and Maximian's dual sovereignty functioned excellently and lasted for seven years. Diocletian was wise and careful enough to invoke the gods in sanctifying and perpetuating his new system of government. From now on, he reigned under the aegis of Jupiter Optimus Maximus, the supreme god, and adopted the religious title Jovius, while his partner Maximian received the title Herculius. And since Hercules was also a hero and acted as Jupiter's right-hand man in heaven, the titles symbolized the two holy emperors' collaboration on earth.

Between them, Diocletian and Maximian defeated a whole host of enemies—Burgundians, Alemanni, Franks, Sarmatae, Goths, Arabs—none of whom had been giving the Romans a moment's peace since the victories of Claudius, Aurelian and Probus.

The two rulers met once in Milan, for despite the vast distances and the difficulties of communication they kept in the closest touch. The inhabitants of Milan gave them an enthusiastic reception after their journey across the snow-covered Alpine roads. The worthy citizens' only worry was how to deal with two emperors: their ceremonial was only adapted to one.

When in 293 Diocletian realized that even two emperors were no match for the unremitting threats from outside the empire and the vast administrative problems within, he founded his famous tetrarchy, or "rule of four." Each of the emperors, the eastern and the western, took on an assistant. The title of the premier emperors remained Augustus, while the assistant emperors assumed the title of Caesar. Both the new Caesars had previously commanded their respective emperors' body-guards and were reliable men whom Diocletian had selected with characteristic skill.

Maximian's assistant, Constantius, was to govern Gaul from Treves, which made Treves an imperial residence and led to its becoming one of the loveliest and most important cities in the West. Galerius became Diocletian's Caesar, and administered the whole region south of the Danube from the Inn to the Black Sea. His residence was at Sirmium (Mitrovitza) on the lower Save. In order to draw the bonds between the four emperors even tighter, the Caesars were adopted by their Augusti and it was planned that they were to succeed their seniors after twenty years, thus giving the latter a chance to abdicate and leave the throne alive, rather than be assassinated. But it did not stop there. The Caesars had to divorce and marry the daughters of their exalted patrons. The imperial quartet is immortalized in the Piazza San Marco at Venice by a harmonious group of four porphyry statues which can still be seen today.

Diocletian still occupied the dominant position. At his own bidding he was honored as "the founder of everlasting peace" and accorded the title Invictus, or "invincible."

Only rarely in human history has so artificial a device been such a practical success. Usually working hand in hand, the four emperors governed, guarded, and gained victories in their respective corners of the world.

The history of Roman achievements between the years 295 and 305 includes a great victory over the Alemanni, victories on the Danube, successful operations in Africa, the quelling of an Egyptian revolt, the expansion of Roman sovereignty in the East across the Tigris, the building of more *limes* fortifications, and the eventual reconquest of Britain whose governor, Carausius, had revolted in 287 and defeated Maximian's fleet in a naval battle in 289.

This period also saw the erection of a contemporary wonder of the world, the magnificent Baths of Diocletian at Rome. This building surpassed in size and splendor all the other eight hundred baths in the capital, including the Baths of Caracalla. Out of the vast central hall of these baths with their high cross-shaped vaults and pillared façades Michelangelo made his Church of Santa Maria degli Angeli. The rest of the site is now occupied by Italy's national museum.

Planning, co-ordination, organization and construction were all second nature to Diocletian. He built arsenals at Antioch, Edessa and Damascus, and probably at Irenopolis (Cilicia) and Caesarea (Cappadocia) as well. Dye works and wool and linen mills sprang up, new roads were constructed throughout the empire, frontier defenses erected. Imposing buildings and palaces took shape in four royal residences at Nicomedia, Sirmium, Milan and Treves. The gloomy, craglike Roman ruins at Treves are still there to remind us of this period. Carthage, Antioch and countless other cities all showed visible signs of the inaccessible emperor's urge to build. At Daphne in Syria there arose two palaces, five baths, a stadium, and a shrine dedicated to Hecate. The temple of Apollo at Miletus was extended and a new bathing establishment at Alexandria brought welcome relief from the heat.

But that was not all. Emperor Diocletian's passion for organization prompted him to create one of the strongest regimes in the ancient world. An increasing number of civil servants were appointed and the city councils and individual government officials lost some of their autonomous powers as everyone was made responsible to a superior. The official hierarchy grew with startling rapidity until it reached almost unheard-of dimensions and efficiency. Every aspect of administration in the huge political system had to be dealt with by an all-powerful bureaucracy. The system was brilliant in its simplicity. Even the central government officials were no more than servants of the people, of law and order, of the state. And in line with this new concept of government, the empire was organized into twelve administrative regions or *diœceses*.

What was the reason for all these measures? Well, something radical had to be done after the disasters of the third century. Reforms were urgently necessary and the Roman empire had to be safeguarded, once and for all, against internal and external dangers. The ancient Roman virtues had long since vanished, and where the old-fashioned disposition was lacking only a system could take its place. In this case it was Diocletian's government machine. Nothing else could have saved the empire.

National moods come in waves. A warlike mood, soon exhausted, is followed by a peaceable mood of longer duration. That is why when normally volatile nations develop a much-vaunted love of peace, it is usually no more than a symptom of fatigue and not a sign of "reformed national character." After Caesar's victory over Pompey and a century of bloody civil war, the Romans were affected by a sort of fatigue, a peaceable inertia which never really deserted them again.

Once the battle of Actium had been won in 31 B.C. and Egypt had been conquered in 30 B.C., Augustus demobilized, cutting the army almost to half strength and leaving only twenty-eight legions in service. These were stationed on the frontiers, and no reserve army was provided in the interior. The danger of such disarmament was demonstrated in 9 A.D. at the battle of the Teutoburger Wald in which Varus lost three legions. Augustus, the great statesman and founder of the Principate, was really the heathen author of the ideal of universal peace, as is testified by the famous Ara Pacis Augustae (Altar of Augustan Peace) at Rome. And this romantic mood permeating the Augustan age, this exalted yearning for eternal peace, this light which preceded the Christian Gospel passed from one emperor to the next. Even though Trajan, Rome's last great soldier-emperor, took the offensive against the Dacians and Parthians, a plan which Caesar entertained and was only prevented from carrying out by the fatal coup on the Ides of March, 44 B.C., Rome's new world policy remained essentially defensive.

After Augustus there was a second retreat from militarism. This was the policy of Hadrian, who on his accession in 117 renounced the aggressive policy of his predecessor Trajan. Overflowing with the idea of *Pax Augusta*, he wanted to be the "illustrious servant" of state and people, an emperor of peace ruling with the wisdom of Hellenism.

Thus the empire was weakened by demilitarization yet again, at a time when Rome was hemmed in by nations whose standard of civilization was rudimentary, and who were only waiting for a chance to fall on the wealth of the Roman empire. What made the third century A.D. so exceedingly dangerous for Rome was that cultural dissolution had set in. People had developed a penchant for mystery religions, and the romantic concept of Augustan peace had been transformed into pacifism proper. Quite uninfluenced by such peaceable ideals, the Germans in the north were surging to the attack with primitive momentum, while the East, dormant since Alexander's day, had awakened to new vigor since the year 226, under the Persian empire resurrected by the Sassanids.

The Roman legions stationed on the frontiers were now quite un-Roman in appearance, having long been recruited not only from Italy but also—even mostly—from the frontier territories. And as the blessings of Roman civilization had penetrated to the outskirts of the empire, so camp life had become softer. The sands were fast running out when Diocletian reinforced these frontier troops by creating a highly mobile reserve or army of the interior.

It was only to be expected that the sweeping efforts to revitalize national defense, the expansion of the army, the powerful and omnipresent bureaucratic system, the enlarged and much more costly royal household and the extensive building program all combined to increase the need for fiscal reform. The emperor fixed the level of taxation at the beginning of each year and no one knew in advance what he would have to pay in the coming twelve months. Rates of payment were assessed by *iugum* and *caput*, *iugum* being a yoke of land (about 0.6 of an acre but variable depending on the quality and fertility of the land), and *caput* being the "head" (cf. "poll" tax) of the man who worked the *iugum*. Female labor was rated at half a head.

Iugatio, or taxation, took into account not only the number of yokes and heads but also the number of cattle. Everything had to be declared and the peasant-farmer, being responsible for his land and his "heads," was duty-bound to pay the taxes imposed. To make the whole business easier for the state, his freedom of movement was restricted and he was tied to his plot of land for better or worse. The towns also had to levy the money and manufactured articles needed by the government, and a group of rich town councilors (*curiales*) were held responsible for the prompt payment of their fellow citizens' dues and had to underwrite them with their own resources. Understandably, the councilors would often have preferred to evade this duty, but a ban was imposed on their movements too, and their responsibilities devolved on their children when they died. Manual laborers and shopkeepers had to join obligatory guilds or corporations and were taxed accordingly. An army of civil servants worked night and day to prevent tax collectors from bilking the exchequer and the taxpayers to any serious degree.

In this way, farmers, laborers and tradesmen were kept in line, the economy was paralyzed, and much of everyday life was fettered to the government machine. But the officials, while growing ever more powerful, had their own fears and worries. Dishonesty was rife. By his sweeping controls and the thorough system of taxation which produced the constant flow of money needed to finance his immense building programs, the administration and the armed forces, Diocletian had perhaps increased the general apathy. The three maxims of existence were: keep mum, obey, and pay. Only the city of Rome was granted exemption from taxes, the ancient capital's last remaining privilege.

The influence of early Christian writing has evoked much harsh and negative criticism of the last non-Christian emperor and his measures. But there was no accurate market research or advanced theory of economics in those days, and the science of sociology had not yet been invented. Recent history had shown that the empire's decay could not be halted unless its economic and financial resources were properly organized, and that military security could not be achieved without great public sacrifices. Diocletian's solution of the problem was a war economy, as we would term it today. His prime object, because it was a dire necessity, was the maintenance of an army. It is a situation not without some startling parallels today!

We know now that Diocletian's planned economy had many failings. What is remarkable is that our own century, despite its exact knowledge of history, has experimented with these methods all over again, only to stand aghast when they break down. Even price ceilings were tried out at this period. In the year 301 the emperor froze all prices, wages and salaries at a uniform level throughout the empire, supposedly to prevent the imperial court and the imperial army from being overcharged. Anyone who exceeded the maximum prices was executed. The system met with no lasting success, even though it was preceded by an attempt at currency stabilization on the basis of a gold standard. The goods disappeared from the shops, a flourishing black market sprang up, and blood flowed. "People were now too frightened to bring anything salable to market, and the cost of living increased to a much worse degree," wrote the Christian author Lactantius in his *De Mortibus Persecutorum* (*How the Persecutors Died*).

Diocletian's tariff of maximum prices appeared as an edict in 301 and was published throughout the empire on stone tablets, several of which have survived. Their lists of goods for which maximum prices were fixed give us a glimpse of everyday existence in a long-vanished age and bring the Roman empire to life once more.

The upper class Romans of this period kept a good table, and the profusion of items bought and sold make amazing reading. In the poultry line, geese, partridge, wild and domestic pigeon, grouse, duck and peacock were all normal fare for the well-to-do. Sparrow, thrush, goldfinch, dormouse and quail were regarded as delicacies. In addition, "individually fed" or fattened turtledoves could be purchased.

For vegetables there were carrots, artichokes, asparagus, and most of the other species of vegetable known to us today. A lot of fruit was eaten too, of course. We read of rose apples, figs from Syria, dates, peaches, cherries, apricots and sweet melons. There were also almonds, walnuts, "rockfish," and Egyptian wine.

The maximum price tablets, fragments of which are continually being unearthed in former Roman provinces, their text engraved sometimes in Latin, sometimes in Greek, and sometimes in both languages together, provide us with a complete guide to contemporary modes of travel. There were sleeping cars, freight cars, and parlor cars. Axles, wheel hubs, carriage seats and horseshoes (though not of the modern nail-on type) were manufactured. We read of dust covers for litters, hooded cloaks, garments with simple fasteners, short capes, and close-fitting underclothes of hare's fur. There was a thriving trade in sheepskin for hats and caps, linen cloths, bedclothes, mattress covers and pillowcases, reed pens, ink, and parchment processed with saffron.

One or two of the handicrafts and professions mentioned are also very interesting. There were craftsmen who specialized in marble overlays for floors and walls, mosaic artists, polishers, veterinary surgeons, sheepshearers, barbers, seamsters, tailors, bath attendants, schoolmasters and solicitors. As far as the study of economic history is concerned, Diocletian's maximum price law is the most important and comprehensive piece of evidence to have survived from antiquity.

We do not know how long this law remained in force, but it had lapsed by 305 at the latest, the year of Diocletian's abdication. The stone tablets give us a thousand indications about the life of the time. But they reveal it as a life regimented down to the last detail. Co-ordination was the watchword of the period, and co-ordination involved a general simplification of life within the confines of the state, in spite of the distinction still drawn between a slave (*servus*) on the one hand, and a bondsman peasant (*colonus*) or member of a compulsory trade union on the other.

Emperor Diocletian was a staunch believer in the ancient Roman god Jupiter. However, he also recognized the Iranian god Mithras, long modified to suit Graeco-Roman taste, not merely because Mithras hailed from the East but because the legionaries were fonder of worshiping him than any other god.

In the year 303, when Diocletian saw that the old Roman world was disintegrating under the impact of Christianity, he launched an oppressive campaign against the Christians, probably at the instigation of Galerius. Diocletian's persecution of the Christians had a prologue. One of the emperor's sacrifices miscarried and Galerius, who was present, managed to attribute its unfavorable outcome to the clandestine activities of the Christians. All the servingmen and women in the palace were at once ordered to sacrifice to the gods of Rome, and anyone who refused was flogged.

Since it had come to light that the palace itself was cankered by the doctrines of Christianity, the emperor decided on a "purification" of the army and extended the purge to the civil service as well. Compulsory sacrifice throughout the armed forces and the government resulted in the dismissal of countless nonconformists.

Lactantius, who was born in the Roman province of Africa in 250 A.D. and became a Christian in 301, described the horrors of persecution and God's judgment on the persecutors in his above-mentioned work, *De Mortibus Persecutorum*.

Diocletian was much too clever to decree a Christian pogrom in the grand manner. But in religious conflicts one evil leads to another, and the early morning of February 23, 303, saw the ominous beginning of a brutal campaign against the Christians.

Within sight of the imperial palace at Nicomedia stood a Christian basilica. From the palace the Christians could be seen going to daily service, a peaceful community, but one which was growing at an astonishing rate.

All at once the doors of the church were flung wide. There was a feverish search for "the effigy of God," sacred texts were burned, and the emperor's troops, officers and men alike, milled about in disorder, looting and robbing. Before many hours were past the tall church had been razed to the ground. The edict of purgation was now extended to the whole empire. Such Christians as had clung to their civil or military appointments in defiance of the first purge were threatened with imprisonment, but there was no bloodshed as yet.

One courageous Christian in Nicomedia pulled down the proclamation and tore it to pieces with the scornful words: "Only victories over Goths and Sarmatae are posted here!" Diocletian and Maximian sentenced him to be burned at the stake for *lèse-majesté*. There is a report on this in the Roman martyrology. The emperors apparently gave orders that "no form of torture should be left untried, but the man endured them all with such serenity of mind and expression that no one could detect in him the slightest sign of anguish." He was, Lactantius tells us, "duly roasted, exhibiting marvelous endurance throughout, and finally burnt to ashes."

Shortly afterward, Diocletian's palace at Nicomedia was set on fire and the emperor was nearly burned to death. Diocletian ordered his entire domestic staff put to the rack.

After another fortnight had elapsed the palace went up in flames once more. Galerius immediately cast suspicion on the Christians, although we read in Lactantius, "He had again ordered the fire to be kindled himself." Lactantius' description is detailed, dramatic, and full of a fierce vitality, but we have no reason to distrust him, by and large, for he was an eyewitness of these events. Moreover, the Christian historian Eusebius confirms that Galerius was the real instigator of the persecutions.

Diocletian was in a difficult position. Even his wife Prisca and his daughter Valeria had been convinced by the new Christian ideas, and both were secret converts to Christianity. Now they too were compelled to sacrifice to the old gods. Members of the palace staff who refused to follow their example were tortured to death. Bishop Anthimus of Nicomedia died a martyr's death, and any Christian in that city who fell into the hands of the emperor's executioners was treated as a convicted incendiary. No time was wasted on legal proceedings: the slaughter went on without trial or verdict. Diocletian's chamberlain, Petrus, died from the effects of the rack. Donatus, who refused to betray his faith, lay in a dark dungeon for six years, was stretched on the rack no less than nine times, and emerged alive. Dorotheus and Gorgonius, two senior court officials who opposed the persecution of the Christians, were put to death most cruelly. They were followed by thousands of martyrs of whom the most famous were Saint Sebastian and Saint Agnes who died at Rome, Saint Lucia at Syracuse, Saint

Catherine at Alexandria, and Saint Barbara at Nicomedia. More Christians were martyred in Egypt and at Tyre, Saragossa and Treves. And if other Christians buried those who had died for their faith, the bodies were dug up again and flung into the sea lest the homage paid to the dead should attract new converts.

Yet in many parts of the empire the Christians encountered overt or secret indulgence from officials who were unwilling to participate in the bloodshed. In Gaul and Britain, which were governed by Constantius, churches were pulled down but Christians suffered no bodily harm. There were farcical scenes in several provinces when the governors dragged Christians before pagan altars and, having once got them there, released them on the grounds that they had done sacrifice. The Christians repudiated this by loudly reaffirming their faith. On the other hand, there were sadistic governors who invented ingenious new methods of torture and execution. When a small town in Phrygia—it may have been Eumenia—resolutely declared for Christianity, it was cordoned off by legionaries and its inhabitants burned alive. Then there were governors who did their utmost never to put Christians to death, not out of leniency but of sadism. They bragged that they had never killed a Christian: their ambition was to break the believers' morale. Lactantius reports that when a Christian prisoner "cracked" after two solid years of resistance, the governor of Bithynia was as proud as if he had defeated an entire tribe of barbarians. Among the most humane governors were those who executed the Christians as quickly and painlessly as possible. But elsewhere, particularly under Galerius' jurisdiction in the East, the witch-hunt raged on a scale hitherto unknown in the empire. No atrocity was too horrible for the ancient gods of Rome and heathendom as, in their death throes, they decided to sell their sovereignty as dearly as they could. It was an eye for an eye and a tooth for a tooth. Christianity's triumph was won with pain and anguish, not to the jubilant sound of Sunday hymns.

There was another side to it, of course. We must not forget the Christians' readiness, their willingness to sacrifice themselves; even, in some cases, the way they jostled one another in their eagerness to die a martyr's death. Some believers, especially women, actually clamored to be executed because they were Christians. Others threw themselves in front of wild beasts in the arenas, and still others were so outspoken that they simply compelled governors to take notice of them and their beliefs.

The Christians never made any concerted attempts to thwart their persecutors by rebellion. Instead they yielded to the heathen authorities and rendered to Caesar what was the Caesar's. Nevertheless, they showed great courage and endurance as, in sublime emulation of Christ, they triumphed by fortitude, not force. Their sheer ability to endure pain was beyond all belief and cannot adequately be described here. These intermediaries between Christ and ourselves who, by giving their lives for a Christian victory and refusing to let the Gospel be silenced, were directly responsible for passing on to us all the concepts of Christianity—which embraces the bulk of our ideas and of western culture in general—belonged to a different age from the cynical, skeptical and often fainthearted age in which we live today. They clung tenaciously to their point of view and died for it because they firmly believed that eternal bliss awaited them when they had drawn their last breath. But this belief in a reward hereafter cannot diminish the merits of their self-sacrifice. The very existence of such a faith is marvelous enough. It demonstrates Christ's enormous influence, the stupendous power of His initial impact on the world, His amazing spiritual strength. It explains how Christianity was able to set out on its everlasting journey through time and eternity.

Diocletian at first restrained the outbursts of hatred against the Christians in Nicomedia because he wanted to keep the situation under control. His second edict did no more than order the arrest of Christian clergy. One repeatedly gets the impression that Diocletian himself was in favor of moderation, and it must be admitted in all fairness that to call him "heathen" is something of a prejudgment. Far from being superstitious, he was a man who had an implicit faith in the gods who had made Rome great, the elder deities invoked by Romans and those who wanted to be Romans. The African author Arnobius gave an intelligent, forceful and courageous exposé of their failings in a seven-volume work written at the height of the persecutions in 305: "Your cause, too, was new when it began. But the value of a religion must be judged by its god, not by its duration, and it matters not on what day one begins to worship, but whom one worships. Is anyone older than He? To whom does eternity owe that which makes it eternity? Is it not His uninterrupted existence which insures that the everlasting ages continue to unfold? But your gods were men. For where there are weddings, marriages, births, wet nurses, handicrafts and infirmities, where conditions of liberty and slavery prevail, where wounds, blows, blood, amours, desires and sensuality are, where all emotions are born of changeability, there nothing divine can exist."

Diocletian thought otherwise. The tall, lean man with the pale face and the powerful nose was firmly rooted in the ancient beliefs. He respected the ancient religion, watched anxiously for divine omens, and gazed with half-tremulous curiosity at the entrails of slaughtered animals for manifestations of the will of Heaven. His real hatred was reserved for the Manicheans, members of the Persian sect which followed the religious founder Manes. Diocletian burned these men alive with their scriptures, executed them or sentenced them to penal servitude in the mines, seeing in them not only religious fanatics but political enemies who were supporters and agents of the Persian king. To his way of thinking there was inherent in any propagation of the Manichean religion a danger that the gods of Persia and his Persian enemy would gain ground. Jupiter, and only Jupiter, was Diocletian's god and the tutelary god of the empire. Firmly believing that Jupiter had made him great, he was determined to safeguard the ancient forms of worship.

Diocletian was not prone to religious ecstasy, not a fanatic, anything but a visionary. As a hardheaded organizer, he was quite unimpressed by Christianity. The idea of adopting new gods, let alone *one* incomprehensible foreign god, seemed far too chancy. It might mean courting the vengeance of the ancient Roman pantheon. Diocletian's faith in the perpetuity of Roman civilization, the Latin tongue and Rome's world mission was unshakable, and he is the only emperor in late antiquity who was still anxious to carry out a Roman political concept. The Graeco-Byzantine state in the East was a counterblow to the ideals of this last genuine prophet of Romanism.

In the year of the Christian persecutions, Diocletian met Maximian at Rome to celebrate the twentieth anniversary of his reign. But by now his mental condition was disturbed and growing worse all the time. A year later, while traveling to Nicomedia, he suffered a nervous breakdown and nearly died.

It is uncertain what actually happened, but the emperor may have had a seizure or perhaps a stroke. In any case on December 13, 304, prayers were said for him in the expectation that his end was near. But it was as if the emperor's mental powers had rallied in sympathy: though a shadow of his former self and greatly weakened, he appeared in public again on March 1, 305. Two months later, on May 1, he and his co-emperor abdicated with due ceremony. Maximian resigned at Milan.

Diocletian's formal abdication took place at the foot of a hill not far from Nicomedia, before the army which he had led to so many victories. With tears in his eyes he declared that he was old, ailing and in need of rest.

The two Caesars, Constantius and Galerius, now stepped into the shoes of their seniors and a second tetrarchy, or rule of four, was born.

For twenty years Diocletian had ruled the world. For twenty years he had defended the empire and built up his vast and formidable administrative machine. Now, after twenty years, the great planner was retiring to Salonae in his native Dalmatia, just as he had perhaps envisaged long ago when he formed the tetrarchy.

All the old man wanted was complete peace and quiet. He was determined to enjoy his retirement too, which was why he had taken the precaution of building the vast palace at Salonae, designed, in keeping with his thorough and orderly nature, on the austere lines of a Roman camp. Diocletian's palace was in fact castle, country house and town all rolled into one. The soldier-emperor wanted to live in a fortress because he was concerned for his personal safety. There were many secret Christians at court, and Diocletian still did not trust Christians.

The east and west sides of the palace were over seven hundred feet long, and the whole structure formed a trapezoid, or irregular-sided quadrangle. The massive walls enclosing it on the north, east and west were nearly seven feet thick. The south face of the palace, which looked out over the sea, was eighty feet high and just under six hundred feet long.

Thirty feet above the ground and built into the side facing the sea was a pillared gallery with twenty-four arches. There the old emperor strolled up and down, day after day, a prey to depressing thoughts and disquieting memories, gazing out to sea and listening to the muffled roar of the waves pounding away at the foundations of his castle.

Advancing age had made the emperor increasingly cautious and mistrustful. An underground passage leading to the sea provided him with instant means of escape in case of emergency.

The fortified palace of Salonae was so enormous that during the Middle Ages a whole town grew up around and inside it. This was the town of Spalato, or what is now Split in Yugoslavia. As late as 1926 the old palace still contained 278 houses and 3,200 inhabitants. No modern visitor to Diocletian's massive seaside retreat can fail to be amazed by the emperor's will to build.

Diocletian's living quarters in the south face contained all that an emeritus ruler of the world could want: a *triclinium* (dining room), *cubicula* (bed chambers), *nymphaea* (halls with pools, fountains and statues), *bibliothecae* (libraries), *balnea* (baths)—every possible comfort and amenity known to Roman and Hellenistic architecture.

Along the inside of the walls at ground level ran storerooms, granaries, slaves' quarters, stables and bakehouses, while the upper story provided accommodation for officers and courtiers (The emperor had brought his court with him.)

Three large gates led into the palace. The main gate, which faced Salonae, was the famed Porta Aurea, some fifteen feet high and thirteen feet wide. Excavations undertaken between 1904 and 1910 have established that this gate went down for another nine feet below the surface.

Diocletian installed a temple to Jupiter in the palace so that he could always be close to the ancient Roman god he worshiped.

An aqueduct five miles long, running partly beneath the ground and partly high above it, brought fresh water to the palace from the river Jadar. For 730 yards of its journey this conduit was supported on arches whose pillars soared in places to a height of fifty-five feet. What is more, when the aqueduct was restored in 1878–1879, one-third of its original length needed virtually no repairs before use. Water was important to the old emperor because the ruling passion and greatest solace of his later years was his vegetable garden.

Freemen and slaves, Greek master craftsmen and Greek artisans, local masons and stone porters, all worked on Diocletian's palace. The masonry for the walls was obtained from neighboring quarries, but the material for all the pillars—rose granite, porphyry, gray, red and white marble—came from marble quarries in Egypt. Colossal statues were also ferried from Egypt to beautify the place.

Inside the palace at Salonae Diocletian built himself an octagonal mausoleum enclosed by twenty-four pillars. The emperor meant to lie there in everlasting peace, but even in death Christianity wreaked its revenge on him. The emperor who had wanted to save the Roman world and the gods of Rome from extinction and had yearned to sleep under the protection of those gods lost the final battle. His last resting place was transformed into a Christian church, the Cathedral of Spalato.

THE WORLD'S FIRST CHRISTIAN EMPEROR

About the hour of noon, when the day was already declining, the emperor had seen with his own eyes, so he said, the victorious emblem of the Cross formed out of light, up in the sky above the sun, and near it the words: "Through this you will conquer."

—Eusebius, *Life of Constantine*, I, xxviii.

DIOCLETIAN's colleague Maximian had followed his example and laid aside the purple, just as the two supreme masters of the empire had agreed long ago. But at the time of the double abdication Maximian was still interested in government. His health was probably stronger than Diocletian's, and he had not lost his taste for forging plans and playing the great game of imperial chess in which the pawns were countries, armies and enemies. Inactivity, leisure and honorable retirement were abhorrent to him, and we shall soon see how long such a man could tolerate voluntary exile.

Once more there were four rulers, two Augusti or emperors, and two Caesars or assistant emperors. It was another tetrarchy on the Diocletian pattern, though the two Augusti, Constantius in the West and Galerius in the East, were quite dissimilar in character.

Constantius, the elder, was bighearted and loved good wine, good living, and pretty girls. He had distinguished himself as a young general in Illyricum, where he had occupied a senior appointment. It is uncertain whether the general brought his young mistress, Flavia Helena, with him when he moved to Naissus (modern Nish), or whether he first met her there in the Roman fortress on the banks of the Nissava. At all events, she was the daughter of an innkeeper, and her Illyrian lover, being of humble origins himself, was very happy with her though he never married her. Constantius and Helena were pagans, but the child that lay in its cradle at Naissus was destined to become the first Christian emperor in the world.

Helena later found Christianity through her son, built numerous churches (among them the Church of the Nativity at Bethlehem), rediscovered Christ's cross, and was eventually canonized. But when Constantius was admitted into the tetrarchy by Diocletian he had to repudiate his beloved Helena and marry Theodora, the daughter of his senior emperor, Maximian. His legal wife bore him two sons and three daughters while Constantine, Constantius' first child, who had been born outside the sacred bounds of Diocletian's political system, was separated from his parents and his stepbrothers and sisters and brought up in Diocletian's court. The boy could not, therefore, have been exposed to any early pro-Christian influence on his father's part. However, his father had an instinctive feeling for the religious climate of his day. He had shown the relatively few Christians in his part of the empire that pagans too could be tolerant. Like other Romans in authority, he had been obliged to pull down many churches in the course of Diocletian's anti-Christian campaign but he had never sentenced any believers to death. As a worshiper of the sun-god he was a pagan with monotheistic leanings, like Seneca, Epictetus, Marcus Aurelius, Apollonius of Tyana, and Plotinus before him. His son later liked to paint him as the first Christian emperor. "My father alone practiced works of gentleness and invoked the Saviour with admirable piety in all his actions." It is worth noting that Constantius called one of his daughters Anastasia, a name which was only favored by Jews and Christians at that time as it means "resurrection." He is also said to have summoned Christian priests to his court.

In very recent times, a new bust of the emperor has been discovered in England. Constantius Chlorus (his surname meant "pale") once again reconquered Britain for Rome. He sailed up the Thames and stood on the site of London. What is more, he died in England, at Eboracum (York), the same town where Septimius Severus had breathed his last.

Galerius was quite another character. He was hard and merciless. Lack of forethought frequently led him to commit blunders, but he was incredibly ambitious and, as we have heard, persecuted the Christians ruthlessly in the years 303–304, and it was he who as Caesar convinced Diocletian of the need for a reign of terror. The self-assurance with which he had persecuted the Christians was matched by his cocksure attitude toward his new mission as Augustus and one of the senior members of the tetrarchy.

The two Augusti, pale Constantius in Gaul and robust Galerius on the Danube, watched one another suspiciously. A factor which heightened the tension was that the new assistant emperors, or Caesars, Severus and Daia, were cat's-paws of Galerius and blindly devoted to him. As a consequence Galerius was virtually sole master of a world ruled by four emperors. Constantius on the other hand could not do anything which did not suit Galerius, and every move he made was carefully noted by Galerius' henchman.

Constantius was also under a different sort of threat. His son Constantine was at Galerius' court, in the power of his undeclared enemy. The boy had grown up in the East away from his father and his mother Helena, having received his military training under Diocletian. There at Nicomedia, in the palace of the great man who was shaping and reorganizing the world, he saw world policy in the making and felt the hot, exciting breath of history on his cheek. At first, as an outsider and the son of a woman unrecognized by the tetrarchy, he was kept under strict and unremitting supervision. But there came a day when he was promoted to *tribunus primi ordinis*, and there is little doubt that Diocletian's keen eye sometimes lighted on the tall, handsome, fairhaired youth as a potential successor. But it could not be. The tetrarchy was not a hereditary system and senior emperors could not select a Caesar from their family circle, so the young man saw himself passed over. He was present when Diocletian abdicated and appointed Daia Caesar instead of him. From then on he was obliged to stay in Galerius' court like a hostage, for his presence there guaranteed the suspicious emperor immunity from any hostile move on the part of Constantius. True, the brave and ambitious young man was given a senior post and distinguished himself in battle against the Sarmatae on the Danube frontier, but he was never allowed to evade the watchful attentions of the emperor or his spies.

Meanwhile Constantius was preparing for an expedition against the Picts and Scots in Britain. We now come to a most interesting moment in world history. Constantius sent messengers to Galerius requesting his imperial colleague point-blank to send his son to assist him in his campaign. Now it was Galerius who was in an awkward position. He could not refuse to release Constantine; that would have been construed as open hostility. But to grant Constantius' request was to give father and son freedom of action. Always an ugly customer in a tight spot, Galerius chose a third course. To reach his father Constantine would have to pass through territory under the control of the Caesar Severus. Galerius therefore sent him off on his long journey but apparently expected Severus to have him intercepted and arrested on the way. Only this would explain why Constantine hurried furtively from one post station to the next like a criminal on the run, killing his exhausted horses so that his pursuers could not use them.

The long-awaited meeting between father and son took place on the coast at Boulogne, just before the crossing was made. Constantine fought the British tribes at his father's side and became very popular with the troops. When after a long illness Constantius finally died at Eboracum, the Romans' barbarian army at once proclaimed Constantine emperor. It was July 25, 306. Once more a delegation set off on the long journey to Galerius with orders to inform him of what had happened and request his confirmation.

Galerius reacted with great cunning. He appointed his faithful henchman Severus an Augustus and recognized Constantine as a Caesar. Constantine declared himself satisfied with his subordinate status for he possessed, as his best modern biographer, Josef Vogt, emphasizes, "the happy knack of being able to wait." Meanwhile his father's death had put new heart into the Alemanni and the Franks. Constantine attacked without delay. Capturing their kings, Ascarius and Ragaisus, he threw them into dark dungeons of the amphitheater at Treves and had them torn to pieces by wild animals in the arena there. Then he reorganized the Rhine fleet and built a bridge across the river near Cologne.

While all this was going on ex-Emperor Maximian, who had withdrawn from public affairs at the same time as Diocletian, was restive on his country estate in Lucania in southern Italy. He too had a son, Maxentius. Perhaps he found it hard to understand why Constantius' illegitimate offspring should have been proclaimed emperor and had his Caesarship confirmed by Galerius when his own son had been denied such an honor. Perhaps Maxentius was pleading his own case to him. At all events Maxentius bided his time in the vicinity of Rome while his father forged plans and brooded in southern Italy.

Severus, who governed Italy, was exceedingly unpopular at Rome. Rome's importance as a world center had already been short-circuited by Maximian's choice of Milan as his official residence. Furthermore Diocletian had always ruled far from Rome, and the city and its inhabitants had made a poor impression on him when he paid them a visit. Now Severus proposed to disband the Roman guards and subject Italy to a penal level of taxation. The Romans' wrath knew no bounds. Rome was an imperial city, the city which had made the empire great. And Rome was due to celebrate another century of existence in the coming year and her inhabitants wanted to be able to hold their heads proudly erect as citizens of an imperial city once more. The guardsmen refused to accept the order to disband and Maxentius, who was conveniently at hand, was proclaimed emperor. Rome had regained her imperial status for the last time.

This time Galerius was uncooperative. He had reluctantly sanctioned Constantine's promotion but now he decided to show his claws. Although Maxentius was his son-in-law, being the husband of his daughter by his first marriage, he had an irresolute, unsoldierly nature —well compensated by arrogance—which Galerius particularly detested. He ordered Severus to march against him. Maxentius and his father made an efficient combination, however. They managed to capture Severus by a ruse, and he was put to death just as Galerius himself was taking the field against them.

Odd things happened in those days, and no holds were barred in an imperial wrestling match. Ex-Emperor Maximian won Constantine over to his own and his son's side by giving him his daughter's hand in marriage. Fausta, as she was called, was not yet of marriageable age but Constantine was obviously very much in love with her. Maximian, old age and impatience getting the better of him, then proclaimed Constantine Augustus on condition that his new son-in-law accorded him the same status. The bond between the two men was duly sealed by public professions of mutual esteem. But old Maximian's cup of contentment could never be full while his son was still lording it at Rome. Arriving there after a hurried journey, he tore the imperial purple from Maxentius' shoulders in the presence of his assembled troops. However, Rome's legionaries were on the son's side. Maxentius was their own emperor, whereas Maximian had always ruled from Milan. The old man had miscalculated and, being in the weaker position, was forced to flee. Naturally he sought refuge with his son-in-law Constantine.

The tetrarchy was in ruins. Diocletian's grand design had collapsed. It had never been anticipated that an ex-emperor would re-emerge from oblivion with an unabated thirst for power. Only a *deus ex machina* could save the day and Galerius decided to produce one. He invoked the aid of Jupiter himself, or rather "Jovius," the old pensioner of Salonae. Almost a forgotten man after his three years of retirement, Emperor Diocletian was invited to attend a conference at Carnuntum, the most important Roman fortress on the Danube front in the year 308. Diocletian left his majestic palace by the sea and traveled to the Danube as a private citizen to preside over the celebrated conference, at which

325

Maximian and Galerius were present. It was the last time anyone managed to coax him away from his vegetable gardens and into the world of imperial administration.

To stroll through the ruins of Carnuntum, to see the foundation stones of the fine palaces and houses there, to trace the outlines of the army camp, to stand in the silent arenas of the once pulsing civil or military amphitheaters and absorb their atmosphere, to read the intensely human messages of filial and parental affection on the numerous tombstones or visit the Museum Carnuntinum, Austria's newest museum devoted to Roman history, and stand before the altar to Mithras is to be brought strangely close to the vanished age of Rome. There on the altar stone, consecrated in the year 308, are engraved the names of Diocletian, Maximian, Galerius and Licinius. It was there that old Diocletian himself once stood. It was there in Carnuntum that he said, when the discussions were at their height, "If only you would grow cabbages far away in Salonae, as I do, you would be the better for it." Mommsen once said of Carnuntum: "The Viennese have a Pompeii on their doorstep, but they do not know how to make the most of it." Well, today they do. A whole world lies there, unearthed before our eyes: religious sculptures and consecrated altars, statues and statuettes, dancing maenads and stark torsos, coins, bowls, jugs, urns, glass beakers, glass bottles, spoons, tweezers, surgical instruments. The visitor to Carnuntum will carry away with him a vivid impression of the decisive influence exerted on the world by Roman emperors far from home, of the efforts they made to defend the Danube frontier, and of the immeasurable strength with which the long arm of Roman civilization and creative energy thrust its way into what was once barbarian territory. He will also realize that, even for an old and weary emperor like Diocletian, distances simply did not exist.

The results of the conference were threefold: Maximian had to promise to retire from politics for good, Licinius (one of Galerius' comrades-in-arms) was promoted to Augustus in place of the murdered Severus, and Maxentius, the Roman rebel, was declared a public enemy.

The old fox had once more brought his matchless genius for administration to bear on a disintegrating world. He had restored order. But several men were missing from the conference couches at Carnuntum, ambitious rulers who still wanted to transform the world.

Soon jealousy raised its head once more. Naturally enough Constantine and Daia did not take kindly to Licinius' sudden promotion to

Salonae (modern Split in Yugoslavia) is the site of an impressive palace which Emperor Diocletian built circa 300 A.D. and to which he retired after his abdication in the year 305. *Carnuntum*, the most important Roman fortress on the Danube front, witnessed the famous Conference of the Three Emperors in 308 A.D. Those present included Diocletian, Maximian and Galerius. Constantine the Great was born at *Naissus* (modern Nish).

Augustus. Both wanted full imperial rank for themselves. As for Maximian, the turbulent old man found retirement as distasteful as ever. Before long he was trying to turn his daughter Fausta against her husband and stirring up insurrection among his son-in-law's troops. But his luck had run out, and he was captured and ultimately died by his own hand.

Constantine now broke away from the whole chaotic system. First he announced that he was descended from Emperor Claudius II, whose victories over the Goths had won him the surname Gothicus. Then as the tutelary god of his new Flavian dynasty Constantine adopted Emperor Aurelian's Sol Invictus, or invincible sun-god. Having calmly established himself as the scion and descendant of a famous imperial family with an illustrious name, Constantine made no bones about his hostility toward Maxentius. He declared him a tyrant and set to work to win the support of the Christians in Rome and throughout Italy.

For his part, Maxentius looked around for an excuse to make war on Constantine. He suddenly discovered a deep affection for his late father, and announced that Constantine had murdered the old man without just cause. Then he began to pull down statues of Constantine in Rome. It was a declaration of war.

Mustering troops from Germany, Gaul and Britain, Constantine led them across the Alps. Maxentius, with a far larger army, waited for him in Rome. He had erected some magnificent buildings there, among them a circus at San Sebastiano outside the city, the *urbis fanum* or Temple of Rome, and his celebrated Basilica Nova which was the most massive covered building in the ancient world. This basilica was modeled on the great bathrooms in the thermae and consisted of a vaulted hall. It not only served as a social or commercial meeting place but also housed the *tribunal,* or law court. It later influenced the design of many Christian basilicas, or early churches, and was Michelangelo's model for St. Peter's.

As we have already heard, Rome was preparing to celebrate a centenary in the year 313. She was anxious to regain her status as queen and focal point of the world, but to do so she needed a victorious emperor with an illustrious name. Her citizens therefore at first thought that Maxentius was the answer to their prayers but they soon found out that their idol was nothing but a ruthless, vicious and self-seeking despot.

Constantine ultimately arrived outside Rome with 90,000 infantry and 8,000 cavalry. Maxentius, whose forces numbered 170,000 and 18,000 respectively, decided to shut himself up in the city and accordingly demolished the bridge across the Tiber. His plan was to repel all Constantine's attacks from within the impregnable confines of the metropolis. There he stayed, sacrificing to the gods and poring over the Sibylline Books. Sibylla is a very ancient name which originated among the Eastern Greeks in Asia Minor, and the Sibyls were prophetesses and priestesses, often of Apollo whose inspired predictions are described by Virgil in the *Aeneid*. Maxentius read in their pagan prophecies that he was bound to repel Rome's attackers. He had built a pontoon bridge across the Tiber, chained together in two sections so that it could be cut apart in case of necessity. Now he led his army across it and engaged the enemy on the other side of the Tiber by the Milvian Bridge.

Constantine's first move was to launch a cavalry attack, then fling his infantry into battle behind it.

His outnumbered legionaries now more than made up for their inferiority in numbers by displaying an overwhelming superiority in courage and morale. Maxentius' troops fought badly, their ranks wavered, then broke, and the whole army began to stream back across the bridge into the city. Unfortunately the bridge parted at a crucial moment and Maxentius plunged to a watery death in the Tiber. Nobody dared to evince any joy when the news of his death filtered into the streets of Rome; the citizens were obviously terrified of Maxentius and doubted the truth of the report. Writing in about 450, the Greek historian Zosimus painted a graphic picture of the atmosphere in the city. Not until Maxentius' head was exhibited on the end of a spear did the paeans of rejoicing burst forth.

Constantine executed a number of his late adversary's supporters and had the compliant Senate rededicate Maxentius' buildings to him and proclaim him supreme Augustus. On October 29, 312, the emperor made a triumphal entry into Rome where he was hailed as a liberator and harbinger of peace as he led his army along the Via Flaminia and into the city through the Porta Triumphalis. "Constantine's Arch" was, in fact, begun by Maxentius on his own behalf. It was not completed until 315, three years after the triumph itself.

A Roman triumph was invariably accompanied by a visit to the Capitol where the victorious emperor sacrificed to Jupiter. The whole of the heathen world expected Constantine to do so as a matter of course, especially since this was his first visit to Rome and the Senate in particular, deep-rooted in the Roman faith, viewed any recognition of the ancient gods with satisfaction. But Constantine avoided the Capitoline temple and did not offer sacrifice. Something extraordinary must have taken place within him before the battle of the Milvian Bridge. So it appeared, at least, and so legend would have us believe. Scholars have written numerous works on the subject of this inner transformation and modern authorities believe that we are very near the heart of the mystery. It is easy to understand why so many theologians and historians have been preoccupied with Constantine's religious experience. We are products of an age which is lacking in faith, barren of great religious experience, hungry for revelation, lacking in inner perception. Vision is something almost totally denied to our age of speed, logic and skepticism. But, apart from Christ's influence and the conversion of Saint Paul, Constantine's spiritual transformation was the most momentous religio-psychological event in world history. In the year 312, before the battle of the Milvian Bridge, the Roman emperor from Illyricum became the first ruler in the world to recognize the omnipotence of the Christian God. Eusebius, the ablest and most prolific author in the Christianized Roman empire and a contemporary and favorite of Constantine's, describes the emperor's experience as a vision. Lactantius, who was also alive at this time, describes a similar dream, probably a separate incident.

Apparently Constantine saw a phenomenon of light—a sign made up of sun and cross united in the sky—and was told in his sleep to put the heavenly symbol on his soldiers' shields. Constantine complied with this suggestion and ordered his men to carve the Greek letter χ on their shields, representing the *ch* in Christ's name. At the top of the rising stroke he added a hook to express the letter *r* in "Christ," thus transforming the emblem into a sort of monogram: ☧.

Further evidence of Constantine's vision is supplied by his military helmet, which also bore a replica of the two initial letters in Christ's name, the Greek letters *chi* and *rho*. Portrayals of the emperor's monogrammed helmet can still be seen on coins minted only a few years after the battle at the Milvian Bridge which was fought in 312. Three years later, in 315, the silver medallion of Ticinum was struck. It displayed, at the tip of the crest on the emperor's helmet, the monogram ☓. In this case the *rho* was vertically superimposed on the *chi*, but they still represented the first two letters in Christ's name.

Is Constantine's vision authentic or apocryphal? Did he really see it? Was it fact or fiction?

Our most important source, Eusebius' *Vita Constantini*, is still an object of controversy today. Eusebius, one of the great scholars of his day, pursued his biblical studies in Palestine, at the theological school at Caesarea. The school had been founded by a man named Pamphilus (hence Eusebius' surname Pamphili) and possessed one of the most famous libraries in the contemporary world, the library of Origen, the

Father of the Church who had been tortured during the Christian persecutions under Decius and died in 254 as a result of his maltreatment.

Eusebius (circa 260–340) wrote a number of important works. His
Life of Constantine is a true hymn to the triumph of Christianity—with
the emphasis on "true," for modern scholars are becoming increasingly
convinced that all Eusebius' main assertions are correct.

However, a number of authorities seek to prove that Eusebius did not
write the *Vita Constantini* at all. Had such a work existed in the fourth
century, they say, it would have been mentioned or quoted by authors
of that period. Because fourth-century authors make no reference to a
biography of Constantine by Eusebius, their silence is taken to imply
that the work was a Christian forgery of later date. The Belgian scholar
Henri Grégoire makes an erudite and ingenious case for this point of
view.

But Eusebius was a pious man and to him love of truth and Christianity went hand in hand. He was writing about an age in which he himself
lived and a man whom he knew extremely well. Constantine told him
all about his vision of the cross in the sky with his own lips. According
to Eusebius, before his battle against Maxentius at the Milvian Bridge
the emperor called upon God to reveal to him who He was, and while
Constantine was praying a divine symbol appeared to him. High in
the sky above the sun he saw, formed by light, the victorious emblem
of the cross, and near it the words "Through this sign you will conquer" or, in Latin, "*hoc signo vinces.*"

Constantine certainly told people about his vision. On that point
there is general agreement. Whether the vision was genuine, on the
other hand, is a matter of interpretation. No vision can be anything but
subjectively genuine, i.e. genuine only so far as the recipient is concerned, and every vision presupposes a *readiness* to receive it. What will
always remain a mystery, of course, is the connection between visual
image and subjective idea, the way in which one arises from the other,
and the part played by the extrasensory factor which we call divine
power. The important question is whether Constantine was expecting
such a vision, whether he was ready for it, whether he wanted to see
the sign of the only true God, whether he believed in it. Remarkably
enough, modern authorities are coming to the conclusion that the vision
was genuine and not fabricated, simply because the former assumption
is more probable. Heinz Kraft argues very convincingly that the invention of visions does not fit in with Constantine's personality. "The

vision is splendidly attested, and Constantine's Christianity after 312 cannot seriously be disputed." Kornemann, the well-known classical historian, says: "It is a vital and no longer deniable fact that the God of Christianity was made manifest to the soul of the greatest and most powerful man of his time, and became a personal experience."

On the other hand Jakob Burckhardt, Swiss historian, art expert and philosopher, unfortunately saw in Constantine a man who made the most of Christianity purely for political ends. And Henri Grégoire's verdict on the vision of the cross is that it was a piece of apocryphal, tendentious and utterly worthless legend.

The fact that the vision has acquired a legendary flavor over the years and that the emperor's conversion strikes one as abrupt and almost miraculous is due to the lack of attention bestowed upon Constantine's spiritual development. His gravitation toward Christianity was not an abrupt step but the logical outcome of his sense of mission; his "growing Christianization and belief in his own calling" (Heinz Kraft) not a feat of spiritual gymnastics but a slow and gradual process. Finally, Constantine was deeply aware of his vocation and must have had an abundant source of inner strength. That alone could explain his decision to do battle with Maxentius in the year 312 when his prospects looked so bleak. Rome was thought to be impregnable, the opposing forces were numerically superior, and experience gained in numerous German campaigns could not be put to advantage in besieging the most modern fortress in the world. And, apart from anything else, the heathen prophets or *haruspices* had advised the emperor not to open hostilities.

So it was his sense of mission alone which spurred him on. That was why he embarked upon the most vital struggle in his life under the emblem of the invisible God, and why he turned increasingly toward Christ, God's mediator, whose doctrines and adherents no emperor before him had ever managed to eradicate.

Constantine knew all that. He had seen the futility of Christian persecution while at the courts of Diocletian and Galerius. As a young man who probably, even at that stage, sympathized with the Christians, he had detested both men. And who knows what he saw and never gave away! An extremely interesting discovery was made in Diocletian's palace at Split. On one of the bricks was scratched the outline of a fish rather like a dolphin. Everything indicated that the sign had been left there in great haste, and whoever was responsible had turned the brick around so that the fish faced inwards and was hidden from sight.

The fish, usually represented as a dolphin, was the emblem of Christ because the Greek word for fish—*ichthus*—contained the initial letters of the expression *Iesus Christus Theou Uios Soter*, "Jesus Christ, God's son, Redeemer." We shall never know who felt impelled to bear witness to his secret love for Christ while the palace was being built, but Constantine probably saw many such evidences of hidden faith during his young days at court there and they must have given him food for thought. Two additional factors were the influence of his tolerant father and the tragic death of Galerius, the anti-Christian emperor. For Galerius died in frightful agony, a victim of cancer, and in his terror he imagined that the dread disease had been sent by the God of the Christians. And so, on April 30, 311, shortly before his death, the brutal persecutor of the Christians had issued an edict granting religious freedom to all believers.

All this must have left its mark on Constantine, quite apart from the fact that the world had reached a critical point in its spiritual development. Constantine had himself passed some well-defined landmarks in his intellectual career. He had groped his way forward slowly and cautiously. He had believed in Jupiter, Hercules and Apollo. Then he had reached something much nearer Christianity, a monotheistic belief in the invisible, invincible sun-god. He ended by identifying the invisible sun-god with the God of Christianity. That was why his sacred emblem may also have been a cross without a tip: ⳨ —a *T* surmounted by the sun. As yet Constantine made no explicit mention of Christ's name. That would have been forcing the pace. The Senate was still unconverted, as were most of the empire's inhabitants. Hence the inscription on Constantine's triumphal arch: *By inspiration of the deity*. The sculptural ornamentation on it was still appropriate to the sun-god. But the expression "deity" in the dedicatory text distinctly shows that the point of transition between sun worship and Christianity had been reached.

Constantine probably believed with all sincerity that he owed his victory to the Christian god, for he handed over the Lateran, Empress Fausta's palace, to the Pope as an episcopal residence. According to Roman Catholic tradition there has been a papacy ever since the time of Saint Peter, over whose grave stands the great church which was named after him and begun by Constantine in 324. Constantine also authorized the building of the Lateran Basilica, "mother and chief of all Christian churches." Finally, he returned all property confiscated from the Christian communities in Africa and exempted ecclesiastical dignitaries from taxation.

The man who linked Christianity and the crown for the first time in history became the pioneer of a new era in world history.

SUBLIME HAPPINESS

*He alone among Roman emperors worshiped God the supreme
lord with extraordinary piety, he alone proclaimed with candor
the teaching of Christ, he alone glorified his Church like none
other within the memory of man, he alone eradicated every
error of polytheism and all kinds of idolatry.*
—Eusebius, *Vita Constantini*, lv, 75.

CONSTANTINE'S vision marked the moment when the sign of the
Cross was handed over to Western civilization. If the transformation
of gods and symbols was a gradual and carefully controlled process, it
was only due to Constantine's remarkably keen instinct for what the
Roman empire would tolerate and what it was ready to accept. We
now accept the Cross as a matter of course. But we can scarcely assess
what it meant for the emperor of a pagan world first to find his way
inwardly to this symbol of an alien religion and then to give his
spiritual discovery practical expression.

Modern textual research, after a period of doubt, has again veered
toward Eusebius and acknowledged Emperor Constantine as a Christian monarch. Constantine's conversion to Christianity is regarded as
sincere and authentic by most of today's authorities, among them Alföldi, de Cavalieri, Baynes, Palanque and Vogt. But, modern authorities apart, the sincerity of the emperor's Christian faith is vouched for
by a man whose statement cannot be disputed, Constantine's own
nephew, Julian "the Apostate." This highly individual personality who
occupied the imperial throne from 361 to 363 was brought up on a
strict brand of ascetic Christianity but later renounced the Christian
faith and tried to further the empire's reconquest by heathendom.
Julian can hardly be described, like Eusebius, as one of the emperor's
panegyrists, since he deeply detested him, but his hostile tirades against
Constantine contain repeated allusions to his uncle's abandonment of
the sun-god and conversion to Christianity.

Emperor Constantine was greatly affected by his miraculous vision.
Summoning Christian priests, he questioned them about their God and
the meaning of the sign which he had seen. They told him that Christ
was the only-begotten son of God and that the sign was a symbol of
immortality and of the victory which He had won over death during

335

His sojourn upon earth. They also described the nature of His influence on mankind.

How old was the monarch who posed such fundamental questions and received the momentous answers which were to decide the course of European civilization? The date of Constantine's birth is hotly disputed. Joseph Vogt puts it at 285. If this is correct, Constantine would have been only twenty-seven when he saw the sign and became a young man with a great spiritual mission, a mission in which he believed with ever-increasing certainty until the hour of his death.

After his victory over Maxentius, Eusebius tells us, Constantine publicly conveyed tidings of the Son of God to the Romans. And all nations "who dwelt as far as the western ocean joyfully celebrated their sense of redemption at festive gatherings. They never tired of singing hymns of praise to the victorious hero, pious servant of God, and benefactor." By the grace of God, salvation had come to the Roman world in the person of Constantine.

There were still three emperors in the Roman empire: Constantine, Licinius, and Maximin Daia. Constantine now set about to strengthen the ties between himself and Licinius. In February of the year 313 an impressive wedding took place at Milan. Constantine gave Licinius his stepsister Constantia in marriage. Important man though Licinius was, ruling as he did the Balkan and Danubian territories, Constantia cannot have regarded her forthcoming marriage with any great joy. Being past the age when he could reasonably expect to have children, Licinius forced her to adopt a son he had had by a slave. It was a political marriage. Constantine had wanted it so and Constantia, as a dutiful Roman, complied with her stepbrother's command.

At Milan the two emperors agreed to grant universal freedom of worship. (Christianity also came within the scope of this decree.) But they publicly professed their allegiance only to the *summa divinitas* (the "supreme deity"). It was still a little too early to make any explicit reference to the God of Christianity. The Milan agreement also restored Christian property and places of assembly and granted recognition to individual Christian communities. In future every man was to be allowed to live according to the religion of his choice, a right which naturally benefited the Christians most of all. In order to win Licinius' support for this ideal, render Christianity even more attractive to him, and enable the new religious policy to be carried out on the widest possible scale, Constantine promised his colleague additional territory at the expense of Valerius Maximinus Daia, then ruling in the East.

Daia must have seen the threat inherent in the Milan agreement, for he decided to anticipate Licinius at a moment when Constantine was engaged in operations against the Rhenish Franks and could not come to his partner's aid.

This Daia was not a congenial character. He was a brutal and superstitious Illyrian of very lowly origins whose rise to power had brought on megalomania, a sensualist with a predilection for wine and women, and an utter political and military failure. The severity with which he persecuted the Christians, on the other hand, far exceeded that of Diocletian, even though the latter's brilliant organizing ability had lent his punitive and exterminatory measures a special horror. Maximinus Daia prided himself on being the most autocratic of all autocrats, appropriated whatever he took a fancy to, and declined to recognize the rights of private individuals. Now, in the winter of 312–313, he decided to try to alienate the troops in Thrace and Illyria from Licinius, their thrifty, almost miserly master, by indulging in reckless bribery. Daia did not know the meaning of caution. He whipped his pack animals savagely across the snow-covered mountains of Asia Minor, sustaining heavy losses from exhaustion and exposure on the way. But he captured Byzantium after a siege lasting only eleven days, took Perinthus, and marched on Adrianople. Battle was joined on May 1, 313.

As at the Milvian Bridge, each side invoked different gods. It is worth noting that Licinius' soldiers prayed to the "invincible sun-god" before the battle, not to the God of the Christians although some historians have theorized that the litany sung by Licinius' troops to the *summus deus* (the "highest god") was also Christian. Christian tradition, however, records the appearance of an angel.

Maximinus Daia's soldiers had to rely on the ancient Roman gods, on soothsayers and heathen oracles. Although outnumbered, Licinius won the day. It was yet another triumph for the invisible God, if not explicitly for the God of Christianity.

Maximinus naturally executed the soothsayers who had forecast that he would be victorious. Eusebius describes how harshly he was punished by fate. He evidently became a victim of leprosy. "His innermost entrails were ceaselessly gnawed away.... For the whole of his body had been transformed as a result of his gluttony into a vast mass of fat,

337

which was now decomposing." In his pain and distress Maximinus acknowledged his guilt before God, suspended persecution of the Christians, ordered their churches to be rebuilt by imperial decree, and begged them to pray for him. Eusebius tells us that Maximinus richly deserved his punishment; that he not only burned, beheaded and crucified Christians, threw them to wild beasts or hurled them into the sea, but also maimed large numbers of men, women and children in one eye and one foot and sent them to the mines where they wasted away pitiably and died. He ended by becoming blind himself, but he lived long enough to escape to Asia Minor where he died at Tarsus in the autumn of 313. "Personal experience has taught me to acknowledge the God of the Christians as the only god," he said. Licinius meanwhile ordered Maximinus' wife thrown into the Orontes and executed his son and daughter, aged eight and seven respectively. Or so at least are the details which have come down to us from Christian, and thus admittedly biased, sources.

That left only two rulers, Constantine in the West and Licinius in the East. Diocletian's four-emperor system had collapsed for good and all. The imperial brothers-in-law were now free, if they wanted, to construct a new Roman empire based on peace and religious toleration.

Still under the influence of his Milan meeting with Constantine, Licinius began by ordering the governors of the eastern provinces to sanction freedom of worship. Gradually, however, his tolerance toward the Christians gave way to hatred and he began to persecute them.

Constantine recognized the danger. In order to create a buffer state between his own world and that of Licinius, he married his stepsister Anastasia to a certain Bassianus, whom he appointed Caesar and put in charge of Italy and Illyricum.

Licinius, innately pugnacious and quarrelsome, arranged for Bassianus' brother Senecio to incite the new Caesar to murder Constantine. Fortunately Constantine unmasked the plot, executed Bassianus, and demanded that Licinius hand over Senecio. Licinius refused and in 314 war broke out between the two emperors for the first time. On October 8 of that year Constantine won a battle at Cibalae on the river Save. After a second but indecisive battle in Thrace an uneasy peace was concluded by which each ruler was to confine himself to his own half of the empire. This left Constantine with by far the larger share and marked the first so complete division of the Roman world. Henceforth two large and distinct states confronted one another with mutual distrust, their rulers forbidden to set foot in each other's domains.

In the summer of 315 Constantine visited Rome to celebrate the tenth anniversary of his accession, and once again he omitted to sacrifice to the heathen gods. On the other hand, a meeting took place between him and Pope Silvester at which it must be assumed that the building of churches in Rome was discussed. Christians were now entrusted with high offices, the image of Sol Invictus vanished from Roman coinage, and Sunday became a national holiday.

This latter measure symbolizes the whole period of flux and development in which the momentous transition from sun worship to Christianity took place. *Sun*day, or *dies solis*, formed a bridge between the two religions. It had always been the first day in the heathens' planetary week, while to the Christians it was a day of reunion for all believers. Now *dies solis* became the official day of rest, which suited both Christians and worshipers of the sun-god. Until the introduction of this arrangement the first day of the week had never been a holiday. It was about this time, too, that the Christians began to celebrate the birth of Christ on December 25, the birthday of Sol Invictus. That was how Constantine, as a servant of the great religious enlightenment of his day, built a Christian world out of heathendom and its feast days.

His rival went in the other direction. In the year 321 Licinius opened an all-out campaign against the Christians. Churches were torn down, ecclesiastical dignitaries condemned to death, believers thrown into prison. Eusebius tells us: "Licinius was convinced that we were doing everything and seeking to attain God's grace only for Constantine's sake." Many Christians "even had to undergo an entirely novel form of death. Their bodies were cut up into many pieces with the sword and, after this cruel and atrocious punishment, thrown into the depths of the sea as food for the fishes." When the Goths crossed the Danube and invaded Roman territory in 324, Licinius should have driven them back but he refused to budge. In order to defend the Roman world Constantine was forced to violate the frontiers of the eastern empire and march through Licinius' territory on his way to meet the Goths.

There followed a last bitter struggle for undivided sway over the Roman world. Licinius once more resorted to the gods of heathendom. Surrounding himself with soothsayers, Egyptian prophets, poisoners, sorcerers, priests and augurs, he sacrificed to the heathen gods and questioned them as to the outcome of the war. With long-winded dictum and sonorous verse, hymn and oracular pronouncement, the motley crew of visionaries declared that he, Licinius, would win. The augurs, too, saw victory for Licinius in the flight of birds and the priests read the same thing in the quivering entrails of slaughtered animals.

"This moment will show which of us is mistaken in his beliefs," said Licinius. "If our gods are victorious we shall take the field against all the ungodly"—in other words, the Christians.

Constantine once again fought beneath the "redeeming emblem of victory" and on July 3, 324, he won a great battle against Licinius at Adrianople. He was now master of Europe but Byzantium was still occupied by his rival's forces, so he gave orders for a siege. Meanwhile Licinius fled to Asia where he was finally caught and defeated by Constantine at Chrysopolis. Byzantium and Chalcedon surrendered shortly afterward.

Constantia, Licinius' wife, implored her stepbrother Constantine to pardon him. The emperor acceded to her request and allowed Licinius to settle down peacefully in Thessalonica.

But life without power and intrigue was not for Licinius, and he treacherously opened negotiations with the barbarians on the Danube. This breach of good faith resulted in his being condemned to death by the Roman Senate and executed at Constantine's instigation.

Sole ruler of the Roman world, Constantine now proclaimed the triumphal power of his miraculous emblem. He felt that he was the elect of God. Sweeping aside all remaining obstacles to Christian faith and religious observance, he professed himself the executor of divine will.

Christians now occupied senior government posts and in Rome a Christian became *praefectus urbi*. The Christian communities also received imperial grants for the building or restoration of their churches. Senior Christian bishops formed a sort of privy council about the emperor, who began to regulate and direct ecclesiastical affairs.

The Christian communities were far from being a united and harmonious whole, however. There were too many theological schools, too many dogmas, too many conflicting views. The Christian doctrines were veiled and obscured by problems, doubts, contradictory opinions, sectarianism and heresy—that ominous hallmark of the period. A Greek word, *hairesis*, originally meant "choice" and was used to express doctrinal unorthodoxy. It was a time when the Christians, "at odds with the ancient philosophy, were fashioning their belief into a doctrinal system" (Vogt).

Constantine longed above all else for the unity of the Christian Church, a unity which was for him summed up by the word "catholic," *katholikos* being the Greek for "universal." But the outlook was unpromising, especially in the East where the most diverse views were being passionately upheld. At Alexandria in the year 318 a priest named Arius proclaimed a new Christian dogma. He held that Christ and God the Father were two distinct entities, similar but not consubstantial. Arius was excommunicated by his own bishop, Alexander, but received support and encouragement from other bishops in the East and began to propagate his views, thus reducing eastern Christians to a state of turmoil and agitation.

In an effort to settle the dispute Constantine summoned bishops from all over the empire to a conference in the imperial palace at Nicaea in Bithynia between May and July, 325. He decreed the inauguration of a public "mail service" to enable all the bishops to attend and ordered the necessary draft animals to be put at their disposal.

So the servants of God assembled at Nicaea, no less than 320 of them, predominantly bishops from the eastern part of the empire. There were men noted for their wisdom and deliberation, others who had distinguished themselves by their austere way of life, and still others who had won fame by their very humility. There were venerable old graybeards and young Christian firebrands only recently recruited into the service of God. The emperor spoke in Latin, and it is indicative of the polyglot nature of the assembly that his words had to be translated. He was more widely understood when he used Greek. Persuading some and shaming others, he finally succeeded in achieving unanimous agreement on all the points at issue. It was resolved, at the emperor's request, to celebrate Easter on the same day throughout Christendom, "for our Saviour bequeathed to us but one day of redemption, the day of His most holy Passion; and His Catholic Church was to be one Church, in accordance with His will."

The synod's most important single act was to settle the controversy which Arius had aroused. The orthodox Christian faith was laid down for all time in the so-called Nicene Creed.

At a second Nicene council held in the year 327 Constantine attempted to convert Arius to this creed, only to encounter the opposition of Bishop Athanasius. After a dispute lasting many years, Athanasius was removed from office and banished to Treves.

Between the two councils, in the year 326, Emperor Constantine did something which was to lie heavy on his conscience as a Christian. His wife Fausta fell in love with his eldest son Crispus, born of a liaison with a concubine named Mamertina.

Desperately disappointed when she found herself rebuffed by her stepson, who was only twenty years old, and realizing that her blandishments were falling on deaf ears, Fausta reached a frightful decision. She slandered Crispus to Constantine by pretending that the young man had tried to rape her. The details of the affair are obscure but that seems to be the main outline. One cannot help thinking of Philip II of Spain and Don Carlos, or Peter the Great and the execution of his son Alexis. Burckhardt refers also to Soliman the Magnificent and his worthy son Mustapha, who met his doom through the machinations of Roxolane.

Constantine was on the point of celebrating the twentieth anniversary of his reign. Had Crispus reminded his father of the proximity of this jubilee which would, under Diocletian's system, have marked the time when he ought to relinquish the throne? Was Fausta playing Phaedra to her stepson's Hippolytus? She had three sons of her own by Constantine, and it could well be that she was maligning her stepson in order to guarantee their right of succession. Whatever the reason, the emperor, normally so circumspect, lost his head on this occasion. He had his son executed at Pola in Dalmatia without giving him a chance to explain the true facts of the case. Young Crispus, who had himself been married at the age of fourteen, was entirely innocent and the hoax was ultimately exposed by Helena, the emperor's pious mother. Now it was Fausta's turn to die. They induced her to take a steam bath in the palace thermae and then boosted the temperature until she was asphyxiated. After these tragic events Constantine published an edict prohibiting cohabitation with concubines throughout the Roman empire. He clearly regretted his own part in the affair and felt that it was his own infidelity which had driven his wife to attempt adultery.

Another event falls into this period: the epoch-making foundation of Constantinople as the capital of the world. Constantine had considered other cities as potential world capitals, among them Serdica (Sofia), Salonica, Sirmium, even Troy. But he finally settled on Byzantium, which stood not far from the administrative metropolis of his predecessor Diocletian. Constantinople was to become a Christian Rome, a Rome of the East, and the new city was, in fact, laid out very much on the Roman pattern. Building began on November 26, 326. On May

11, 330, Constantinople was officially inaugurated as New Rome. It was to last eleven centuries, until the Turks took it on May 29, 1453 A.D.

Constantine solved the problem of succession by allotting one portion of the empire to each of his three sons and a fourth to his brother's son. During Easter Week, 337, the ruler of the world fell ill. He hurriedly set off for the medicinal springs at Drepanum, which he had renamed Helenopolis in his mother's honor. But his health failed to improve and so, filled with forbodings of death, he had himself taken to Ancyrena, a suburb of Nicomedia in Bithynia.

He was not baptized by Bishop Eusebius of Nicomedia until he was on the point of death. The moment was deliberately chosen. Having committed all his life's sins as a non-Christian, he could now enter the world to come entirely free from sin.

Constantine had really wanted to be baptized in the Jordan, "in the waters of which our Redeemer Himself received baptism as an example to us," as he put it. "This is the moment for which I have hoped so long, craving for it and yearning to find salvation in God." On the last day of Whitsuntide, 337, the Roman emperor who had seen God's sign and passed it on to the West as a sacred legacy closed his eyes forever.

The great man's body was brought to Constantinople in a golden coffin and set on a lofty bier in the largest and most splendid room in the imperial palace. Candles sparkled around him in golden candlesticks as he lay in his baptismal gown, his only adornment a diadem, for he had refused to touch the imperial purple once he had been baptized. Sentinels stood guard over him night and day, and senior officials, dignitaries and military commanders tiptoed in silently at the normal hour of audience, fell on their knees and paid homage to the monarch. Court ceremonial continued to be observed with unwavering, clock-work regularity "for him who, alone among mortals, was still an emperor after his death."

Not until Constantius, the only one of the emperor's sons to put in an appearance, had arrived in the grief-stricken city was the coffin transferred to the Church of the Apostles. This was the church which Constantine himself had erected "to an incredible height," as we are informed, near the walls on the outskirts of his new metropolis. Eusebius tells us its roof gleamed so brightly in the sun's rays that it could be seen from a great distance. Constantine had built his mausoleum in conjunction with this church. It contained twelve memorial stelae, one for each of the Apostles, and the emperor's sarcophagus was hauled into the center so that it was guarded by six Apostles on either side. The master of the world had aspired to become the thirteenth herald of the true faith. He had hoped, with joyous and invincible confidence, that after his death he would be regarded as an apostle.

His body did not lie there forlorn or neglected. He had decreed that services should be held in the mausoleum so that he could hear the prayers spoken in honor of the Apostles who stood close by his coffin.

Constantine died a sublimely happy man. Not only had he won his way through to the only true faith, but he was to lead countless millions of other men to the same religion after his death. He was sublimely happy because he knew that immortal life awaited him, life everlasting and divine light.

LIST OF ROMAN RULERS FROM
MARIUS TO CONSTANTINE

THE REPUBLIC
(*Circa* 510 B.C.–30 B.C.)

THE PRINCIPATE
(30 B.C.–A.D. 284)

The Julian-Claudian Dynasty (30 B.C.–A.D. 68)

The Flavian Dynasty (69–96)

The adoptive emperors (96–138)

The Antonine Dynasty (138–192)

The Severan Dynasty (193–235)

The soldier-emperors (235–284)

THE DOMINATE
(284–337)

BIBLIOGRAPHY

I. Classical Sources

AMMIANUS c. 332–400 A.D. Ammianus Marcellinus with English trans. by J. C. Rolfe, 3 vols. 1935 and 1937 in Loeb Classical Library. — APPIAN c. 160 A.D. Appiani Historia Romana, Ed. L. Mendelssohn and P. Viereck, Leipzig 1905 and 1939. — ARNOBIUS c. 305 A.D. Adversus nationes, Ed. by C. Marchesi, 2nd Ed. Turin 1953. — ARRIAN c. 95–175 A.D. Arrian von Nikomedeia, Ed. by A. G. Roos, 2 vols. 1907 and 1928. — AUGUSTUS 63 B.C.–14 A.D. Imperatoris Caesaris Augusti operum fragmenta, Ed. by Henrica Malcovati, 3rd Ed. Turin 1948. — MARCUS AURELIUS 121–180 A.D. Marcus Aurelius with English trans. by C. R. Haines in Loeb Classical Library, London 1924. German trans. by W. Capelle, Stuttgart 1953. — AURELIUS VICTOR c. 360 A.D. Sexti Aurelii Victoris Historia Romana cum notis integris Dominici Machanei, Eliae Vineti, Andreae Schotti, Jani Gruteri, Amsterdam 1733; or: Ed. of F. Pichlmayr, 1911. — CAESAR 100–44 B.C. C. Juli Caesaris Commentarii, De bello Gallico and De bello civili, Ed. by A. Klotz, Leipzig 1950 and 1952. Alexandrian, African and Spanish Wars, with English trans. by A. S. Wag, London 1955 in Loeb Classical Library. Guerre d'Afrique, Texte établi et traduit par A. Bouvet, Paris 1949; also A. Klotz, Gnomon 23, 1951, 40 ff. — CICERO 106–43 B.C. M. Tulli Ciceronis scripta quae manserunt omnia, Leipzig 1923 ff. The Correspondence of M. Tullius Cicero, arranged according to its chronological order, with a revision of the text, comment., and introduct. essays by R. Y. Tyrrell and I. C. Purser, Dublin and London, Vol. I 1904, Vol. II 1906, Vol. III 1914, Vol. IV 1918, Vol. V 1915, Vol. VI 1899, Vol. VII 1901. — INSCRIPTIONS. Inscriptiones Gracae, Vols. I–XIV, Berlin 1890 ff., and Corpus Inscriptionum Latinarum, Vols. I–XVI, Berlin 1893 ff., published by the Preussischen Akademie der Wissenschaften. Cagnat, R.: Inscriptiones Graecae ad res Romanas pertinentes, 4 Vols. Paris 1901–1927. — CASSIODORUS c. 487–583 A.D. Flavius Magnus Aurelius Cassiodorus: Orationes, Fragments edited by L. Traube; Variae, edited by Th. Mommsen in Monumenta Germaniae Historica, Auct. Antiquiss. XII, Berlin 1904; Chronica, edited by Th. Mommsen, MGH A.A. XI, Berlin 1904; Historia ecclesiastica, edited by W. Jacob-R. Hanslik, Vienna 1952. — DIO CASSIUS c. 155–235 A.D. Cassius Dio Cocceianus, Ed. by Ph. U. Boissevain, 4 Vols., 2nd Ed. Berlin 1955. — EUSEBIUS c. 260–340 A.D. Eusebius von Caesarea, Ausg. der Historia ecclesiastica von E. Schwartz, 5th Ed. Berlin 1955. — EUTROPIUS 364–378 A.D. Breviarium ab urbe condita, Ed. by F. Rühl, Leipzig 1909. — HERODIAN 3rd century A.D. Herodianus, Ed. by K. Stavenhagen, Leipzig 1922. — HISTORIA AUGUSTA probably written c. 400 A.D. Scriptores Historiae Augustae, Ed. by E. Hohl, 2 Vols., Leipzig 1927. — JOSEPHUS c. 37–100 A.D. Flavius Josephus, complete works, Ed. by B. Niese, 7 Vols., 2nd Ed. Berlin 1955. — JULIAN 332–363 A.D. The Works of the Emperor Julian, with English trans. by Wilmer Cave Wright, 3 Vols., in Loeb Classical Library, London–New York 1953.—LACTANTIUS c. 250–c. 318 A.D. Ed. by S. Brandt in Corp. Script. Ecclesiast. Latin. XXVII, 2, Vienna 1897. Also Ed. by I. Pesenti, Turin 1921. De mortibus persecutorum, Ed. by I. Moreau, Paris 1954—MALALAS 6th century A.D. Chronographia, edited by L. Dindorf, Corp. Script. Byzant., Vol. XV, Bonn 1831. A. Schenk Graf von Stauffenberg, Die röm. Kaisergeschichte bei Malalas, Stuttgart 1931 (partial edition of Malalas with commentary). – NEPOS c. 99–c. 24 B.C. Cornelius Nepos, De viris illustribus, Ed. Halm, Leipzig 1871. Also: Ed. with notes by K. Nipperdey-K. Witte, 11th Ed., Berlin 1913. Text and German trans. by W. Gerlach, 2nd Ed. Munich 1952. – OROSIUS, 5th century A.D. Paulus Orosius, Historiae adversus paganos, Ed. by C. Zangemeister, Leipzig 1889. – PETRONIUS 1st century A.D. Cena Trimalchonis, Ed. by H. Schmeck, 4th Ed. Heidelberg 1954. Also edited by W. B. Sedgwick, 2nd Ed. Oxford 1950. – PLUTARCH c. 45–c. 125 A.D. Plutarchi vitae parallelae, Ed. C. Lindskog and K. Ziegler, Leipzig 1914–39. – PLINY THE ELDER 23–79 A.D. Gaius Plinius Secundus, Naturalis historia, Ed. L. Jan, Leipzig 1854–65. 3rd Ed., C. Mayhoff 1892–1909. – PLINY THE YOUNGER 62–c. 113 A.D. Gaius Plinius Caecilius Secundus, Epistulae and Panegyricus, Ed. M. Schuster, Leipzig 1933. – PLOTINUS c. 204–270 A.D. Schriften, übers. von R. Harder, Leipzig–Hamburg, 1930–56. – PROCOPIUS fl. 565 A.D. Prokop von Caesarea, Ed. by Haury, 3 Vols., Leipzig 1905–1913. – RES GESTAE DIVI AUGUSTI, Monumentum Ancyranum Ed. Th. Mommsen, 2nd Ed. Berlin 1883. – SALLUST 86–c. 35 B.C. Sallusti Catilina, Iugurtha, Fragmenta ampliora, Ed. by A. W. Ahlberg-A. Kurfeys, 2nd Ed. Leipzig 1955. Appendix Sallustiana (epistulae, investivae), edited by A. Kurfeys, 2 Vols., Leipzig 1950–55. – SENECA c. 4–65 A.D. Divi Claudii Apokolokyntosis, Ed. by C. F. Russo, 2nd Ed. Florence 1955. – SUETONIUS c. 69–140 A.D. Gaius Suetonius Tranquillus, De vita caesarum, Ed. by M. Ihm, Leipzig 1922. Also Ed. by J. C. Rolfe in Loeb Class. Libr. 1914. German trans. by A. Lambert, Zürich 1955. Suetonius, Ed. by I. Lana, Turin 1952. – TACITUS 55–120 A.D. Cornelii Taciti Annales, Ed. by C. D. Fisher. Historiarum libri, Ed. C. D. Fisher. Opera minora edited by H. Furneaux in Scriptorum classicorum bibliotheca Oxoniensis, London 1952. Or: Historien und Annalen, edited by C. Halm-G. Andresen-E. Koestermann, Leipzig 1950–1952. Germania, Agricola, Dialogus, same editors, Leipzig 1949. De origine et situ Germanorum, Turin, 1949 (Corp. Script. Lat. Paravianum). Die historischen Versuche, übers. von K. Büchner, Stuttgart 1955. – TERTULLIAN c. 160–230 A.D. Tertullian, Apology, De Spectaculis, Minucius Felix, Octavius, with English trans. by T. R. Glover in Loeb Class. Libr., London 1953. Or: Quintus Septimus Florens Tertullianus, Ges. Ausg. in Wiener Corpus Scriptorum Ecclesiasticorum Latinorum, Vol. 20, 1890. Apologeticum, herausg. u. übers. von C. Becker, Munich 1952. – XIPHILINOS 11th century. Text in the above-cited edition of Dio Cassius. Also in: Histoire Romaine écrite par Xiphilin, Zonare, Zosime, trans. from the Greek by Cousin, Paris 1778. – ZONARAS 12th century. Text ed. by L. Dindorf, Leipzig 1868–75, and Th. Büttner-Wobst, in Corp. Hist. Byzant. Vol. III, Bonn 1897. – ZOSIMOS c. 500 A.D. Text ed. by L. Mendelssohn, Leipzig 1887.

II. General Bibliography

ALBERTINI, E.: L'empire romain, 3rd Ed., Paris 1938. – ALTHEIM, F.: Niedergang der Alten Welt, Vol. I and II, Frankfurt a.M. 1952. – id. Literatur und Gesellschaft im ausgehenden Altertum, Halle 1948–50; also E. A. Thompson in Journ. Rom. Stud. XLI, 1951, 204 f. – id. Gesicht vom Abend und Morgen (Fischer Bücherei), Frankf. a.M.-Hamburg 1955. – id. Die Soldatenkaiser, Frankfurt a.M. 1939. – id. Rom und der Hellenismus, Amsterdam-Leipzig. – BENGSTON, H.: Einführung in die alte Geschichte, 2nd Ed. Munich 1953. – id. Griechische Geschichte von

BIBLIOGRAPHY

den Anfängen bis in die römische Kaiserzeit, Munich 1950. — BERNHART, M.: Handbuch zur Münzkunde der römischen Kaiserzeit, 2 Vols., Halle 1926. — BICKEL, E.: Geschichte der römischen Literatur, Heidelberg 1937. — THE CAMBRIDGE ANCIENT HISTORY, Ed. by S. A. Cook, F. E. Adcock, M. P. Charlesworth. Vol. IV (The Persian Empire and the West), Cambridge 1939; Vol. IX (133–44 B.C.), Cambridge 1951; Vol. X (44 B.C.–70 A.D.), Cambridge 1952; Vol. XI 70 A.D.–192 A.D.), Cambridge 1936; Vol. XII (193 A.D.–324 A.D.), Cambridge 1939. — CARCOPINO, J.: Das Alltagsleben im alten Rom zur Blütezeit des Kaisertums, aus dem Franz. übers. von L. Schaukel, Innsbruck-Vienna 1949. — CUMONT, F.: Lux Perpetua, Paris 1949. — DAREMBERG, C., and SAGLIO, E.: Dictionnaire des antiquités grecques et romaines, 10 Vols., Paris 1877–1918. — DELBRÜCK, H.: Weltgeschichte, Part I, Altertum, Berlin 1924. — DESSAU, H.: Geschichte der römischen Kaiserzeit, 2 Vols. in 3 Parts, Berlin 1924–30. — v. DOMASZEWSKI, A.: Geschichte der römischen Kaiser, 2 Vols., 3rd Ed. Leipzig 1922. — DUNBAR, F. L.: Rom. Sechshundert Bauwerke der Ewigen Stadt. Berlin 1943. — FRANK, T.: Economic History of Rome, 2nd Ed., Baltimore 1927. — id. An Economic Survey of Ancient Rome. I. Rome and Italy of the Republic. II. Egypt. III. Western Provinces. IV. Eastern Provinces. V. Rome and Italy of the Empire. Baltimore 1933–1940. FRIEDLÄNDER, L.: Darstellungen aus der Sittengeschichte Roms, Ed. by G. Wissowa, 4 Vols. 9th and 10th Ed., Leipzig 1920–22. — GELZER, M.: Das Römertum als Kulturmacht, Histor. Zeitschr. 126, 1922. — GIBBON, E.: Decline and Fall of the Roman Empire, in Everyman's Library, 434, 6 Vols., London 1954. — GLOTZ, G.: Histoire générale, Histoire romaine II–IV, Paris 1933–47. — GROEIG, E.-STEIN, A.: Prosopographia Imperii Romani, 4 Vols., Berlin 1933–52. — v. HARNACK, A.: Mission und Ausbreitung des Christentums in den ersten drei Jahrhunderten, 2 Vols., Leipzig 1924. – HOMO, L.: Les institutions politiques romaines, L'évolution de l'humanité, Vol. 18, Paris 1933 — id. L'empire Romain, Paris 1925. — id. La civilisation romaine, Paris 1930. — id. Les empereurs romains et le christianisme, Paris 1931. — id. Le haut empire (Collection histoire générale, Glotz), Paris 1933. — id. Nouvelle histoire romaine, Paris 1941. — id. Le siècle d'or de l'empire romain, Paris 1947. — JEFFERSON LOANE, H.: Industry and Commerce of the City of Rome (50 B.C. to A.D. 200), Baltimore 1938. — KAHRSTEDT, U.: Geschichte des griechischrömischen Altertums (Weltgeschichte in Einzeldarstellungen, Vol. II), Munich 1952. — id. Kulturgeschichte der römischen Kaiserzeit, Munich 1944. — KORNEMANN, E.: Römische Geschichte, 2 Vols. 3rd Ed. edited by H. Bengston, Stuttgart 1954. — id. Weltgeschichte des Mittelmeer-Raumes, edited by H. Bengston, 2 Vols., Munich 1949. — MATTINGLY, H.-SYDENHAM, E. A.: The Roman Imperial Coinage, 5 Vols., London 1923–33. — MOMMSEN, TH.: Römische Geschichte, I–III, Leipzig 1854–56; V, 1885. — NIEBUHR, B. G.: Römische Geschichte I und II, Berlin 1811 and 1812; III, Berlin 1832. — NIESE, B., and HOHL, E.: Grundriss der römischen Geschichte nebst Quellenkunde, 5th Ed., in "Handbuch der Altertumswissenschaft," ed. by W. Otto, Munich 1923. — NORDEN, E.: Die römische Literatur, Leipzig 1954. — THE OXFORD CLASSICAL DICTIONARY, ed. by M. Cary, J. D. Denniston, J. Wight Duff, A. D. Nock, W. D. Ross, H. H. Scullard, Oxford 1953. — PARIBENI, R.: L'Italia imperiale, Storia d' Italia illustrata, 1938. — PARKER, H. M. D.: The Roman Legions, Oxford 1928. — PAULY, A.-WISSOWA, G.: Real-Encyclopädie der classischen Altertumswissenschaft, new revision, Stuttgart 1894 ff.

BIBLIOGRAPHY

– Piganiol, A.: Histoire de Rome, 3rd Ed. Paris 1949. – Reallexikon für Antike und Christentum, ed. by T. Klausner, Vol. I, 1950; Vol. II, 1954, also Numbers 17-19, 1955-56, Stuttgart. – Rodenwaldt, G.: Die Kunst der Antike, Hellas und Rom (Propyläen-Verlag), Berlin 1927. – Rostovtzeff, M.: Social and Economic History of the Roman Empire, Oxford 1926. German Translation, 2 Vols., Leipzig 1929. Italian Translation (new version), Florence 1946. *id.* A History of the Ancient World, 2 Vols., Oxford 1926 and 1927. German: Geschichte der Alten Welt, 2 Vols., Leipzig 1941-42 (Reprinted Wiesbaden). – De Ruggiero, E.-Cardinali, G.: Dizionario epigrafico di antichità romane, Rome 1886 ff. – Salmon, E. T.: A History of the Roman World from 30 B.C. to A.D. 138, London 1944. – Schanz, M.-Hosius, C.: Geschichte der römischen Literatur, I–IV, Munich 1914-35. – Seeck, O.: Geschichte des Untergangs der antiken Welt, 6 Vols., Berlin 1920–21. – Stein, A.: Der römische Ritterstand, Munich 1927. – Taeger, F.: Das Altertum, 5th Ed. Stuttgart 1953. – De Tillemont, M. L.: Histoire des Empereurs, 3 Vols., Paris 1911 (1st Ed. 6 Vols. Paris 1690–1738). – Vogt, J.: Römische Geschichte, I, Die Römische Republik (as Vol. VI of the "Geschichte der führenden Völker"), Freiburg i. Br. 1932, 2nd Ed. 1951. – Wagenvoort, H.: Roman Dynamism, Studies in Ancient Roman Thought, Language and Custom, Oxford 1947.

III. Special Publications

The historical treatises which are contained in the encyclopedias, compendiums, and general histories (under II) are not mentioned separately here.

MARIUS AND SULLA

Berve, H.: Sulla, Neue Jahrib. f.Wiss. u. Jugenbild, VII, 1931, 673 ff. – Carcopino, J.: Sylla ou la monarchie manquée, Paris 1931. – v. Domaszewski: Bellum Marsicum, Sitzungsber. d. Wiener Akad. 201, 1, 1924. – Hill, H.: Sulla's Military Oligarchy, Proceedings of the Classical Association, XXVIII, 1931. – Lanzani, C.: Mario e Silla, Catania 1915. – *id.* L. Cornelio Sulla dittatore, Milan 1936. – Levi, M. A.: Silla, Milan 1924. – Passerini, A.: Caio Mario come uomo politico, Athenaeum 1934. – Reinach, Th.: Mithradates Eupator, König von Pontos, Leipzig 1895. Robinson, F. W.: Marius, Saturninus and Glaucia, Bonn 1912. – Schur, W.: Das Zeitalter des Marius und Sulla (Klio-Beiheft 46), Leipzig 1942.

CICERO

Boissier, G.: Cicéron et ses Amis, Paris 1865. – *id.* La Conjuration de Catilina, Paris 1905. – Carcopino, J.: Les secrets de la correspondance de Cicéron, 2 Vols., Paris 1947; also J. P. V. D. Balsdon, Journ. of Rom. Stud. XL, 1950, 134 f. – Cary, M.: Pompey's Compromise. Classical Review XXXIII, 1919, 109. – Ciaceri, E.: Cicerone e i suoi tempi, 2 Vols., Milan, Rome, Naples 1926, 1930, Vol. 1 in 2nd Ed. 1939. – Cowell, F. R.: Cicero and the Roman Republic, London 1948. – Frisch, H.: Cicero's Fight for the Republic, Copenhagen 1946. – Hardy, E. G.: The Catilinarian Conspiracy, Oxford 1924. – Klinger, F.: Ciceros Rede für den Schauspieler Roscius, Munich 1953. Also Schmid, W., Gnomon, 26, 1954, 317. –

BIBLIOGRAPHY

KROLL, W.: Die Kultur der Cic. Zeit, 2 Vols., Leipzig 1933. – VOGT, J.: Ciceros Glaube an Rom, Stuttgart 1935. – SEEL, O.: Cicero, Stuttgart 1953. Also John H. Collins, Gnomon 27, 1955, 279 ff. – ZIELINSKI, TH.: Cicero im Wandel der Jahrhunderte, Leipzig 1929.

POMPEY

BOAK, A. E. R.: The Extraordinary Commands from 80 to 48 B.C., Amer. Hist. Rev. XXIV, 1918–19, 14 ff. – GELZER, M.: Gn. Pompeius Strabo und der Aufstieg seines Sohnes Magnus, Abh. Preuss. Akad., phil.-hist. Kl. 1941, Nr. 14. – id. Das erste Konsulat des Pompeius und die Übertragung der grossen Imperien, Abh. Preuss. Akad., phil.-hist. Kl. 1943, Nr. 1. – id. Pompeius, Munich 1949. Also F. E. Adcock, Journ. of Rom. Stud., XL, 1950, 135 ff. – GROEBE, P.: Zum Seeräuberkrieg des Pompeius Magnus, Klio X, 1910, 374 ff. – GUSE, F.: Die Feldzüge des dritten Mithridatischen Krieges in Pontus und Armenien, XX, Klio 1926, 332 ff. – MEYER, E.: Caesars Monarchie und das Principat des Pompeius, Stuttgart and Berlin 1922. – VAN OOTEGHEM, S. J.: Pompée le Grand, bâtisseur d'empire, Brussels 1954. – SCHULTEN, A.: Sertorius, Leipzig 1926.

CAESAR

COLLINS, J. H.: Caesar and the Corruption of Power, Historia IV, 1955, 445 ff. – COLOMB, G.: La bataille d'Alesia, Lons-le-Saunier 1950; also F. Miltner, Gnomon 23, 1951, 210. – GELZER, M.: Caesar der Politiker und Staatsmann, 1943. – GUNDOLF, F.: Caesar, Geschichte seines Ruhmes, Berlin 1925. – HOLMES, T. R.: Caesar's Conquest of Gaul, Oxford 1911. – KLOTZ, A.: Caesarstudien, Leipzig 1910. – MOMMSEN, TH.: Die Rechtsfrage zwischen Cäsar und dem Senat, Ges. Schr. IV, Berlin 1906. – RAMBAUD, M.: L'art de la déformation historique dans le Commentaires de César, Paris 1953 (Annales de l'Université de Lyon); also Collins, J. H., Gnomon 26, 1954, 527 ff. – STRASBURGER, H.: Caesars Eintritt in die Geschichte, Munich 1938. – SYME, R.: The Roman Revolution, Oxford 1951. – TAYLOR, L. R.: Party Politics in the Age of Caesar, Berkeley 1949. – WALSER, G.: Caesar und die Germanen, Historia, Einzelschriften, Heft 1, Wiesbaden 1956.

MARK ANTONY, CLEOPATRA, AUGUSTUS

ANDERSON, H. A.: Cassius Dio und die Begründung des Principates, Berlin 1938. – BÉRANGER, J.: Recherches sur l'aspect idéologique du principat, Basel 1953; also Wickert, L., Gnomon 26, 1954, 534 ff. – CARCOPINO, J.: Le mariage d'Octave et de Livie et la naissance de Drusus, Revue Historique CLXI, 1929, 225 ff. – McCARTHY, J. H.: Octavianus puer. Classical Philology XXVI, 1931, 362 ff. – GARDTHAUSEN, V.: Augustus und seine Zeit, 2 Parts in 6 Volumes, Leipzig 1891 to 1904 with Supplement 1916. – GRANT, M.: From Imperium to Auctoritas, 1946. – HAMMOND, M.: Hellenistic Influences in the Structure of the Augustan Principate, Mem. Americ. Acad. Rome XVII, 1940. – HEINZE, R.: Die augusteische Kultur, Leipzig-Berlin 1933. – HOLMES, T. R.: The Architect of the Roman Empire, Oxford, I, 1928; II, 1931. – HÖNN, K.: Augustus und seine Zeit, Vienna

BIBLIOGRAPHY

1953. — Homo, L.: Auguste, Paris 1935. — Klinger, F.: Tacitus über Augustus und Tiberius, Munich 1954; also Béranger, J., Gnomon 27, 1955, 436 ff. — Krencker, D., and Schede, M.: Der Tempel in Ankara (Archäol. Institut d. Deutschen Reiches), Berlin and Leipzig 1936. — Levi, M. A.: Ottaviano Capoparte, 2 Vols., Florence 1933. — Magdelain, A.: Auctoritas principis, Paris 1947. — Otto, W., and Bengtson, H.: Zur Geschichte des Niederganges des Ptolemäerreiches, Munich 1938. — v. Premerstein, A.: Vom Werden und Wesen des Prinzipats, Munich 1937. — Reinhold, M.: Marcus Agrippa, New York 1933. — Rodenwaldt, G.: Kunst um Augustus, Berlin 1942. — Schmitthenner, W.: Oktavian und das Testament Caesars, Munich 1952. — Schönbauer, E.: Die Res gestae Divi Augusti in rechtsgeschichtlicher Beleuchtung, Vienna 1946 (Sitz.-Ber. Akad. Wien, Phil.-hist. Kl. 224, 2). — Seeck, O.: Kaiser Augustus, Bielefeld-Leipzig 1902. — Studi in occasione del bimillenario Augusteo, Rome 1938. — Volkmann, H.: Kleopatra, Munich 1953. — Weber, W.: Princeps I, Stuttgart 1936. — Weigall, A.: Cléopâtre, sa vie et son temps, Paris. — id. Marc-Antoine, sa vie et son temps.

TIBERIUS

Baker, G. P.: Tiberius Caesar, London 1929. — Ciaceri, E.: L'imperatore Tiberio e i processi di lesa majestà. Processi politici e relazioni internazionali, Rome 1918, 249 ff. — id. Tiberio successore di Augusto, Milan 1934. — Drexler, H.: Die Germania des Tacitus, Gymnasium 59, 1952, 52 ff. — Dürr, F.: Die Majestäts-prozesse unter dem Kaiser Tiberius, Heilbronn 1880. — Ehrenberg, V., and Jones, A. H. M.: Documents Illustrating the Reigns of Augustus and Tiberius, Oxford 1949. — Koestermann, E.: Die Majestätsprozesse unter Tiberius, Historia, IV, 1955, 72 ff. — Marañón, G.: Tiberius (trans. from the Spanish), Munich 1952; also M. Gelzer, Gnomon 26, 1954, 345. — Marsh, F. B.: The Reign of Tiberius, Oxford 1931. — Mommsen, Th.: Römisches Strafrecht, Das Staatsverbrechen, S. 537–594, Leipzig 1899. — Rogers, R. S.: Criminal Trials and Criminal Legislation under Tiberius, Middletown 1955. — Schott, W.: Die Kriminaljustiz unter dem Kaiser Tiberius, Erlangen 1893. — id. Studien zur Geschichte des Kaisers Tiberius, 2 Vols., Bamberg 1904–1905. — Scott, K.: Tiberius' Refusal of the Title of Augustus, Classical Philology, XXVII, 1932, 43 ff. — Vittinghoff, F.: Der Staatsfeind in der römischen Kaiserzeit (Neue Deutsche Forschungen, Vol. 84), Berlin 1936. — Walker, B.: The Annals of Tacitus, Manchester 1953, 82–110.

CALIGULA

Balsdon, J. P. V. D.: The Emperor Gaius (Caligula), Oxford 1934. — Maurer, J. A.: A Commentary on C. Suetonii Tranquilli vita C. Caligulae Caesaris, Chapters 1–21, Philadelphia 1949. — Ucelli, G.: Le navi di Nemi, Rome 1952.

CLAUDIUS

Bell, H. J.: Jews and Christians in Egypt, London 1924. — The Acts of the Pagan Martyrs. Acta Alexandrinorum, ed. by H. A. Musurillo, London 1954; also W. Schubart, Gnomon 27, 1955, 212 f. — Momigliano, A.: L'opera dell'imperatore

BIBLIOGRAPHY

Claudio, Florence 1932. — Scramuzza, V. M.: The Emperor Claudius, Cambridge, Mass. 1940. — Stähelin, F.: Kaiser Claudius, Basel 1933. — Suhr, E. G.: A Portrait of Claudius, American Journ. of Archaeology 59, 1955, 319 ff.

NERO

Charlesworth, M. P.: Nero, Some Aspects, in Journ. of Rom. Stud. XL, 1950, 69 ff. — Henderson, B. W.: The Life and Principate of the Emperor Nero, London 1903. — Levi, M. A.: Nerone e i suoi tempi, Milan 1949; also Ernst Hohl in Gnomon 23, 1951, 108 ff. — Lietzmann, H.: Petrus und Paulus in Rom, Berlin 1927. — Schur, W.: Die Orientpolitik des Kaisers Nero, Klio-Beiheft 15, Leipzig 1923. — Weege, F.: Das goldene Haus des Nero, Jahrb. d. Archäol. Inst. XXVII, 1913, 127 ff.

PETRONIUS

Bagnani, G.: Arbiter of Elegance, Toronto 1954. — Heraeus, W.: Zum 75. Geburtstag, ausgew. und herausg. von J. B. Hofmann, Die Sprache des Petronius und die Glossen, Heidelberg 1937.

SENECA

Benoît, P.: Sénèque et St-Paul, Rev. Bibl. 53, 1946, 7–35. — Deissner, K.: Paulus und Seneca, 1917. — Giancotti, F.: Saggio sulle tragedie di Seneca, Rome-Naples 1953; also Handel, P., Gnomon 27, 1955, 183 ff. — Paul, A.: Untersuchungen zur Eigenart von Senecas Phoenissen, Bonn 1953. — Waltz, R.: La vie politique de Sénèque, Paris 1909.

GALBA, OTHO, VITELLIUS

Henderson, B. W.: Civil War and Rebellion in the Roman Empire, 1908. — Hohl, E.: Der Prätorianeraufstand unter Otho, Klio XXXII, 1939, 307 ff. — Klinger, F.: Die Geschichte des Kaisers Otho bei Tacitus, Leipzig 1940. — Zancan, P.: La crisi del principato nell'anno 69 d.C., 1939. — Passerini, A.: Le due battaglie presso Betriacum, Studi di antichità classica offerti a E. Ciaceri, 1940, 178 ff.

VESPASIAN

Bersanetti, G. M.: Vespasiano, Rome 1941. — Graf, H.: Kaiser Vespasian, Untersuchungen zu Suetons Vita Divi Vespasiani, Stuttgart 1937. — Henderson, B. W.: Five Roman Emperors (Vespasian–Trajan), Cambridge 1927. — Homo, L.: Vespasien, l'empereur du bon sens, Paris 1949; also E. Hohl in Historia, II, 1954, 474 f. — Weber, W.: Josephus und Vespasian, Stuttgart 1921.

TITUS

Companion to the study of Pompeii and Herculaneum, Rome 1938. — Conte Corti, E. C.: Untergang und Auferstehung von Pompeji und Herculaneum, 7th Ed.,

BIBLIOGRAPHY

Munich 1951. — MAJURI, A.: Pompeji, Novara 1953. — FURCHHEIM, F.: Bibliografia di Pompei, Ercolano e Stabia, Naples 1891. — SCHEFOLD, K.: Pompejanische Malerei, Basel 1952.

DOMITIAN

CASE, S. J.: Josephus' Anticipation of a Domitianic Persecution, Journ. Bibl. Lit. XLIV, 1925, 10. — GSELL, S.: Essai sur le règne de l'empereur Domitien, Paris 1894. — HERZOG, R.: Urkunden zur Hochschulpolitik der röm. Kaiser, Vespasian und Domitian, Sitz.-Ber. Preuss. Akad., 1935, Nr. 32, 967 ff. — KÖSTLIN, E.: Die Donaukriege Domitians, Tübingen 1910. — PATSCH, C.: Der Kampf um den Donauraum unter Domitian und Trajan, Sitz.-Ber. Wiener Ak. 217, 1937, 1. Abh. — PICHLMAYR, F.: T. Flavius Domitianus, ein Beitrag zur röm. Kaisergeschichte, Amberg 1889. — SYME, R.: The Imperial Finances under Domitian, Nerva and Trajan, Journ. of Rom. Stud., XX, 1930, 55 ff., also Sutherland, C. H. V., id. XXV, 1935, 150 ff.

TRAJAN

ALFÖLDI, A.: Zu den Schicksalen Siebenbürgens im Altertum, Budapest 1944 (Ostmitteleurop. Bibl., ed. by E. Lukanich, 54). — CICHORIUS, C.: Die Reliefs der Trajanssäule, 2 Vols., Berlin 1896–1900. — v. DOMASZEWSKI, A.: Die Dakerkriege Traians auf den Reliefs der Säule. Philologus, LXV, 1906, 321 ff. — GARZETTI, A.: Nerva, Rome 1950; also H. Volkmann in Gnomon 24, 1952, 115 f. — LEPPER, F. A.: Trajan's Parthian War, Oxford 1948. — PARIBENI, R.: Optimus Princeps, 2 Vols., Messina 1926–27. — PARVAN, V.: Dacia, Cambridge 1928. — PETERSON, E.: Trajans dakische Kriege, 2 Vols., Leipzig 1899–1903. — WEBER, W.: Traian und Hadrian in "Meister der Politik," I, 2, Stuttgart 1923. — id. Rom, Herrschertum und Reich im 2. Jahrh. n. Chr., Stuttgart 1937.

HADRIAN

VON BUREN, A. W.: Recent Finds at Hadrian's Tiburtine Villa, Am. Journ. Arch. 59, 1955, 215 ff.—DÜRR, J.: Die Reisen des Kaisers Hadrian, Vienna 1881. — FRASER, P. M.: Hadrian and Cyrene, Journ. of Rom. Stud. 1950. — GRAINDOR, P.: Athènes sous Hadrien, Cairo 1934. — HENDERSON, B. W.: The Life and Principate of the Emperor Hadrian, London 1923. — KÄHLER, H.: Hadrian und seine Villa bei Tivoli, Berlin 1950; also R. Naumann in Gnomon 23, 1951, 216 f. — OLIVER, J. H.: Documents Concerning the Emperor Hadrian, Hesperia X, 1941, 361 ff. — D'ORGEVAL, B.: L'empereur Hadrien, Paris 1950. — PERRET, L.: La titulature impériale d'Hadrien, Paris 1929. — PRINGSHEIM, F.: The Legal Policy and Reforms of Hadrian, Journ. Rom. Stud. XXIV, 1934, 141. — STRACK, P. L.: Untersuchungen zur röm. Reichsprägung des 2. Jahrh., 3 Vols., Stuttgart 1931–37. — WEBER, W.: Untersuch. z. Gesch. des Kaisers Hadrian, Leipzig 1907. — id. Römisches Herrschertum und Reich im 2. Jahrh. n. Chr., Stuttgart 1937.

BIBLIOGRAPHY

ANTONINUS PIUS

BRYANT, E. C.: The Reign of Antoninus Pius, Cambridge 1895. – DODD, C. H.: The Cognomen of the Emperor Antoninus Pius, Numismatic Chronicle XI, 1911, 6 ff. – HÜTTL, W.: Antoninus Pius, I. Prague 1936; II. 1933. – LACOUR-GAYET, G.: Antonin le Pieux et son temps, Paris 1888. – SCHELL, F.: Untersuchungen zur Geschichte des Kaisers Pius, Hermes LXV, 1930, 177 ff. – TOYNBEE, J.: Some "Programme" Coin-types of Antoninus Pius, Classical Review XXXIX, 1925, 170 ff.

MARCUS AURELIUS

CARRATA THOMES, F.: Il regno di Marco Aurelio, Turin 1953. – DODD, C. H.: Chronology of the Eastern Campaigns of the Emperor Lucius Verus, Numismatic Chronicle, XI, 1911, 209 ff. – FARQUHARSON, A. S. L.: The Meditations of the Emperor Marcus, 2 Vols., 1945. – LAMBRECHTS, P.: L'Empereur Lucius Verus. Essai de réhabilitation. L'Antiquité classique, III, 1934, 173 ff. – MARTINAZZOLI, F.: La "Successio" di Marco Aurelio, Bari 1951; also D. A. Rees in Gnomon 24, 1952, 274 ff. – MOMMSEN, TH.: Der Markomannenkrieg unter Kaiser Marcus, Ges. Schriften IV, 487 ff. – NEUENSCHWANDER, H. R.: Marc Aurels Beziehungen zu Seneca und Poseidonios, Bern and Stuttgart 1951; also Leeman, A. D., in Gnomon 24, 1952, 277 ff. – VON PREMERSTEIN, A.: Untersuchungen zur Geschichte des Kaisers Marcus, Klio XI, 1911, 355; XII, 1912, 167; XIII, 1913, 70. – SEDGWICK, H. D.: Marcus Aurelius, a Biography, Yale Univ. Press 1921. – v. WILAMOWITZ-MOELLENDORFF, U.: Kaiser Marcus, Berlin 1931.

COMMODUS

CUMONT, F.: Jupiter summus exuperantissimus, Arch. f. Relig.-Wiss. IX, 1906, 323 ff. – HOHL, ERNEST: Kaiser Commodus und Herodian, Berlin 1954. – MOMMSEN, TH.: Perennis, Ges. Schriften IV, 514 ff. – VON PREMERSTEIN, A.: Protest des Gymnasiarchen Applanos gegen seine Verurteilung durch Commodus, Philologus, Suppl. XVI, 1923, 2, 28. – ROSTOVTZEFF, M.: Commodus-Hercules in Britain, Journ. Rom. Stud. XIII, 1923, 91 ff. – WEBER, W.: Probleme der Spätantike, Stuttgart 1930, 67 ff. and 87.

PERTINAX AND JULIAN

WERNER, R.: Der historische Wert der Pertinaxvita in den Scriptores Historiae Augustae, Klio, XXVI, 1933, 283 ff. See also Barbieri, G., in Stud. ital. fil. class. XIII, 1936, 183.

SEPTIMIUS SEVERUS

HASEBROEK, J.: Untersuchungen zur Geschichte des Kaisers Septimius Severus, Heidelberg 1921. – NEUGEBAUER, K. A.: Die Familie des Septimius Severus,

BIBLIOGRAPHY

Antike 12, 1936, 155 ff. — PLATNAUER, M.: The Life and Reign of the Emperor Lucius Septimius Severus, Oxford 1918.—RÉVILLE, J.: La Religion à Rome sous les Sévères, Paris 1886. — SCHULZ, O. TH.: Vom Prinzipat zum Dominat, Paderborn 1919.

GETA, JULIA DOMNA, CARACALLA

BICKERMANN, E.: Das Edikt des Kaisers Caracalla in P. Giessen 40, Berlin 1926. — KORNEMANN, E.: Grosse Frauen des Altertums (Julia Domna), 252 ff., Wiesbaden 1952. — REUSCH, W.: Der historische Wert der Caracallavita in den Scriptores Historiae Augustae, Klio, Beiheft XXIV, 1931. — SCHULZ, O. TH.: Der römische Kaiser Caracalla: Genie, Wahnsinn oder Verbrechen, Leipzig 1909. — WILLIAMS, M. G.: Studies in the Lives of Roman Empresses: 1. Julia Domna, Amer. Journ. Archaeol., VI, 1902, 259 ff.

ELAGABALUS

BASSET, H. J.: Macrinus and Diadumenianus, Diss., Michigan 1920. — BESNIER, M.: in Glotz, Histoire Romaine, IV, 76–80. — BUTLER, O. F.: Studies in the Life of Elagabalus, Univ. of Michigan Studies, New York 1908. — HAY, J. S.: The Amazing Emperor Heliogabalus, London 1911. — HÖNN, K.: Quellenuntersuchungen zu den Viten des Heliogabalus und des Severus Alexander in Corpus der S.H.A., Berlin 1911. — KORNEMANN, E.: Grosse Frauen des Altertums (Julia Maesa und Julia Mamaea, 273 ff. and 280 ff.), Wiesbaden, 1952. — ROOS, A. G.: Herodian's Method of Composition, Journ. Rom. Stud. V, 1915, 191 ff. — SMITS, J. S. P.: De fontibus e quibus res a Heliogabalo et Alexandro Severo gestae colliguntur, Diss. Amsterdam, 1908.

ALEXANDER SEVERUS

GORLICH, E.: Alexander Severus und der Ausgang des Principates, Aevum XI, 1937, 197 ff. — HOPKINS, R. V. N.: The Life of Alexander Severus, Cambridge Historical Essays, XIV, 1907. — JARDÉ, A.: Etudes critiques sur la vie et le règne de Sévère Alexandre, Paris 1925. See also Göttinger Gelehrte Anzeigen, 1929, 504. — MACCHIORO, V.: L'Impero romano nell'età dei Severi, Riv. stor. ant. X, 1905–6, 201; XI, 1906–7, 285 and 341. — VON SICKLE, C. E.: The Terminal Dates of the Reign of Alexander Severus, Class. Philol. XXII, 1927, 315 ff. — THIELE, W.: De Severo Alexandro Imperatore, Berlin 1909. — WILLIAMS, M. G.: Studies in the Lives of Roman Empresses, Julia Mamaea, University of Michigan Studies, Human. Ser. I, 1904, 67.

THE SASSANIDS

CHRISTENSEN, A.: Les gestes des rois dans les traditions de l'Iran antique, Paris 1936. — id. L'Iran sous les Sassanides, Copenhagen–Paris, 2nd Ed. 1944. — ENSSLIN, W.: Die weltgeschichtliche Bedeutung der Kämpfe zwischen Rom und Persien, Neue Jahrb. f. Wissensch. und Jugendbild. IV, 1928, 399.—HERZFELD, E.: Archae-

BIBLIOGRAPHY

ological History of Iran, London 1935. – Nöldeke, Th.: Tabari. Geschichte der Perser und Araber zur Zeit der Sassaniden. Aus der arabischen Chronik des Tabari übersetzt, Leyden 1879. – Pagliaro, A.: Notes on the History of the Sacred Fires of Zaroastrianism. Orient. Studies in Honour of C. E. Pavry, London 1933, 373 ff. – Rostovtzeff, M.: Res gestae divi Saporis and Dura, Berytus VIII, 1943, 17 ff. – Sarre, Fr., and Herzfeld, E.: Iranische Felsreliefs, Berlin 1920. – Schaeder, H. H.: Iranica, Abh. Gött. Gel. Ges. 1934, 10.

VARUS AND THE LIMES

Dragendorff, H.: Westdeutschland zur Römerzeit, 2nd Ed. Leipzig 1919. – Fabricius, E.: Die Entstehung der römischen Limesanlagen, Trier 1902. – Haller, I.: Der Eintritt der Germanen in die Geschichte, Berlin 1944. – Hettner, F., v. Sarwey, O., Fabricius, E.: Der obergermanisch-rätische Limes des Römerreiches, 14 Vols., 1894–1938. – Jacobi, H.: Das Kastell Saalburg, Berlin 1937 (Limeswerk, 56. Lieferung). – John, W.: Die Örtlichkeit der Varusschlacht bei Tacitus, Göttingen 1950; also E. Hohl in Gnomon 23, 1951, 211. – Judeich, W.: Die Überlieferung der Varusschlacht, Rhein. Mus. 80, 1931, 301 ff. – Koepp, F.: Die Römer in Deutschland, 3rd Ed. Leipzig 1926. – id. Lichter und Irrlichter auf dem Wege zum Schlachtfeld des Varus, "Westfalen" 13, 1937. – id. Varusschlacht und Aliso, Münster 1940. – Kolbe, W.: Forschungen über die Varusschlacht, Klio XXV, 1932, 141 ff. – Kornemann, E.: Die neuesten Limesforschungen im Lichte der römischen Grenzpolitik, Klio VII, 1907, 73 ff. – id. Die Varusschlacht, in "Gestalten und Reiche," Wiesbaden 1943. – Mommsen, Th.: Der Begriff des Limes, Ges. Schr. V (1885), 456 ff. – Norden, E.: Altgermanien. Leipzig-Berlin 1934.

MAXIMINUS THE THRACIAN

Bersanetti, G. M.: Massimino il Trace e la rete stradale dell'impero romano. Atti III congr. nazionale di studi romani I, 1934, 590 ff. – id. Studi su Massimino il Trace, Rivista Indo-Greco-Italica XVIII, 1934, 215 ff. – id. Studi sull'imperatore Massimino, Epigraphica III, 1941, 5 ff. – Hohl, E.: Maximini duo Juli Capitolini. Aus dem Corpus der sog. Historia Augusta herausgegeben und erläutert, Berlin 1949; also R. Nierhaus, Gnomon 23, 1951, 464 f. – Homo, L.: La grande crise de 238 après J.-C. et le problème de l'Histoire Auguste, Rev. Hist. CXXXI 1919, 201 ff., and CXXXII, 1919, 1 ff. – van Sickle, C. E.: A Hypothetical Chronology for the Year of the Gordians, Class. Philol. XXII, 1927, 416 ff., and XXIV, 1929, 285 ff. – Uhlhorn, G.: Maximinus Thrax, in Realencyklop. für protest. Theol. XII, 456.

PHILIP THE ARAB AND DECIUS

Foucart, P.: Les certificats de sacrifice pendant la persécution de Decius (250), Journ. des Savants, 1908, 169. – Jensen, P. J.: Plotin, Copenhagen 1948. – Knipfing, J. R.: The Libelli of the Decian Persecution, Harv. Theol. Rev. XVI, 1923, 345 (Greek text with English trans.). – Manley, I. J.: Effects of the

BIBLIOGRAPHY

Germanic Invasions on Gaul 234–284 A.D., Univ. of Calif. Publ. in History, XVII, no. 2, 1934, 25. — LIESERING, E.: Untersuchungen zur Christenverfolgung des Kaisers Decius, Würzburg 1933. — RAPPOPORT, B.: Die Einfälle der Goten in das römische Reich, Leipzig 1899. — SALISBURY, F. S.: The Reign of Trajan Decius, Journ. Rom. Stud. XIV, 1924, 1 ff. — SCHMIDT, L.: Geschichte der deutschen Stämme bis zum Ausg. der Völkerw. I. Die Ostgermanen, 2nd Ed. Munich 1934; II. Die Westgermanen, 2nd Ed. Munich 1938. — UHLHORN, G., and GÖRRES, F.: Philippus Arabs, in Realencyclop. für protest. Theologie, XV, 331.

GALLUS AND AEMILIANUS

ALFÖLDI, A.: Die Hauptereignisse im römischen Osten zwischen 253 und 260 im Spiegel der Münzprägungen, Berytus IV, 1937 (1938). — MATTINGLY, H.: The Reign of Aemilian, in Journ. of Rom. Stud. XXV, 1935, P. 55. — MOMMSEN, TH.: "Weltreich der Caesaren" (Title of the Phaidon-Verlages!), Amsterdam 1955, 216–219 (on Gallus and Aemilianus).—PROSOPOGRAPHIA Imperii Romani, Art. on Aemilianus, Vol. I, no. 430.

VALERIAN

ALFÖLDI, A.: The Reckoning of the Regnal Years and Victories of Valerian and Gallienus, Journ. Rom. Stud. XXX, 1940 — ROSTOVTZEFF, M. I., BELLINGER, A. R., BROWN, F. E., WELLES, C. B.: The Excavations at Dura-Europos Conducted by Yale Univ. and the French Acad. of Inscr. and Letters, Prelim. Report, 1935–36, Part III, New Haven 1952.

GALLIENUS

ALFÖLDI, A.: Der Usurpator Aureolus und die Kavallerie-Reform des Kaisers Gallienus, Zitschr. f. Numismatik XXXVII, 1927, 198, and XXXVIII, 1928, 200. — id. Die Vorherrschaft der Pannonier im Römerreich und die Reaktion des Hellenentums unter Gallienus, in 25 Jahren röm.-germ. Kommission, Frankfurt 1930. — HOMO, L.: L'empereur Gallien et la crise de l'empire romain au 3e siècle, Revue Hist. CXIII, 1913, 1 ff., 225 ff.—MANNI, E.: L'impero di Gallieno, Rome 1949; also Hohl, E., in Gnomon 24, 1952, 116 f. — SCHLEIERMACHER, W.: Römische Archäologie am Rhein 1940–50, Historia, II, 1953, 94 ff.

ZENOBIA AND AURELIAN

CLERMONT-GANNEAU, CH.: Odeinat et Vaballat, Rev. Biblique XVII, 1920, 382 ff. — CREES, J. H. E.: The Papyri and the Chronology of the Reign of the Emperor Probus, Aegyptus I, 1920, 297 ff. — DAMERAU, P.: Kaiser Claudius II. Gothicus (Klio-Beiheft XX, 1934). — DANNHÄUSER, E.: Untersuchungen zur Geschichte des Kaisers Probus, Jena 1909. — FÉVRIER, J. G.: Essai sur l'histoire politique et économique de Palmyre, Paris 1931. — FISHER, W. H.: The Augustan "Vita Aureliani," Journ. Rom. Stud. XIX, 1929, 125 ff. — HOMO, L.: Essai sur le règne de l'empereur Aurélien (270–275), Paris 1904. — id. De Claudio Gothico Roman-

BIBLIOGRAPHY

orum imperatore, Paris 1903. — JORGA, N.: Le problème de l'abandon de la Dacie. Rev. Hist. du Sud-Est Européen, I, 1924, 37. — KORNEMANN, E.: Grosse Frauen des Altertums, Zenobia, 288 ff., Wiesbaden 1952. — SCHLUMBERGER, D.: La Palmyrène du Nord-Ouest, Paris 1951; also Kahrstedt, U., Gnomon 24, 1952, 446 ff. — SEYRIG, H.: Palmyra and the East, Journ. Rom. Stud., 1950, Parts I and II. — STARCKY, J.: Palmyre, Paris 1952; also Kahrstedt, U., Gnomon 24, 1952, 446 ff. — RICHMOND, I. A.: The City-Wall of Imperial Rome, Oxford 1930.

DIOCLETIAN

BULIC, F.: Kaiser Diokletians Palast in Split, Zagreb 1929. — BOTT, H.: Die Grundzüge der diokletianischen Steuerverfassung, Frankfurt 1928. — DÖRNER, K.: Ein neuer Porträtkopf des Kaisers Diokletian, Die Antike, Vol. 17, Berlin 1941. — ENSSLIN, W.: Zur Ostpolitik des Kaisers Diokletian, Sitz.-Ber. Bayer. Akad. d. Wiss., Phil.-Hist. Kl., Munich 1942. — HERAEUS, W., zum 75. Geburtstag, ausgew. u. herausg. von J. B. Hofmann, Zum Editcum Diocletiani und Neue Studien zum Maximaltarif Diocletians, Heidelberg 1937. — HUNZINGER, A. W.: Die diocletianische Staatsreform, Rostock 1899. — MELONI, P.: Il regno di Caro, Numeriano e Carino, Cagliari 1948. — MOMMSEN, TH., and BLÜMNER, H.: Der Maximaltarif des Diocletian, Berlin 1893. — NIEMANN, G.: Der Palast Diokletians in Spalato, Vienna 1910. — SESTON, W.: Dioclétien et la tétrarchie, I, Paris 1946. — STADE, K.: Der Politiker Diokletian und die letzte grosse Christenverfolgung, Frankfurt 1926. — TAUBENSCHLAG, R.: Das römische Recht zur Zeit Diokletians, Cracow 1925. — WEILBACH, F.: Zur Rekonstruktion des Diocletians-Palastes in Bulićev Zbornik, Naučni prilozi posvećeni Franu Buliću, Zagreb-Split, 1924.

CONSTANTINE

ALFÖLDI, A.: The Conversion of Constantine and Pagan Rome, Oxford 1948; also Straub, J., Gnomon 24, 1952, 117 ff. — id. On the Foundation of Constantinople, Journ. Rom. Stud. XXXVII, 1947, 10 ff. — CARNUNTUM-Jahrbuch 1955 (Römische Forschungen in Nieder-Österreich, edited by E. Swoboda), Vienna 1956. — DE' CAVALIERI, P. F.; Constantiniana, Vatican City 1953; also Vogt, J., Gnomon 27, 1955, 44 ff. — BURCKHARDT, J.: Die Zeit Constantins des Grossen, Leipzig 1880, 5th Ed. Stuttgart 1929. — DELARUELLE, E.: La conversion de Constantin, Etat de la question, Bull. Lit. Ecclés, 54, 1953, 80 ff. — DÖRRIES, H.: Das Selbstzeugnis Kaiser Konstantins, Abh. der Gött. Akad. d. Wiss. 3. F. Nr. 34, 1954. — EICHHOLZ, D. E.: Constantius Chlorus' Invasion of Britain, Journ. Rom. Stud. XLIII, 1953, 41 ff. — FESTGABE zum Konstantins-Jubiläum 1913 für Antonio De Waal, Freiburg i. Br. 1913. Included there: Dölger, F. J., Die Taufe Konstantins und ihre Probleme. Von Landmann, K., Konstantin der Grosse als Feldherr. Leufkens, J., der Triumphbogen des Konstantin. Müller, A., Lactantius' De mortibus persecutorum. Pfättisch, J. M.: Die Rede Konstantins an die Versammlung der Heiligen. Wittig, J., Das Toleranzreskript von Mailand 313. — FREND, W. H. C.: The Donatist Church, a Movement of Protest in Roman North Africa, Oxford 1952; also v. Campenhausen, H., Gnomon 25, 1953, 194 f. — GRÉGOIRE, H.: Les

BIBLIOGRAPHY

persécutions dans l'empire romain, Brussels 1951; also v. Campenhausen, H., Gnomon 25, 1953, 464 ff. — JANIN, R.: Constantinople-Byzantine, Paris 1950. — KÄHLER, H.: Konstantin 313, Jahrb. d. Deutsch. Arch. Inst., 67, Berlin 1953. — KRAFT, H.: Kaiser Konstantins religiöse Entwicklung, Tübingen 1955. — L'ORANGE, H. P.: Studien zur Geschichte des spätantiken Porträts (Instituttet for sammenlignende Kulturforskning), Oslo 1933. — MONCEAUX, P.: Histoire littéraire de l'Afrique chrétienne 5, 1920, 147 f. — MOREAU, J.: Zum Problem der Vita Constantini, Historia IV, 1955, 234 ff. — NESSELHAUF, H.: Das Toleranzgesetz des Licinius, Hist. Jahrb., edited by J. Spörl, 74, Munich-Freiburg 1955. — PIGANIOL, A.: Histoire Romaine IV, 2e partie: L'empire chrétien, Paris 1947. — v. SCHOENEBECK, H.: Beiträge zur Religionspolitik des Maxentius und Constantin (Klio-Beiheft 43), Leipzig 1939. — SCHWARTZ, E.: Kaiser Constantin und die christliche Kirche, 2nd Ed. Leipzig-Berlin 1936. — STEIN, E.: Geschichte des spätrömischen Reiches I, Vienna 1928. — STRAUB, J.: Konstantins Verzicht auf den Gang zum Kapitol, Historia IV, 1955, 297 ff. — SWOBODA, E.: Carnuntum (Röm. Forschungen in Niederösterr.), 2nd Ed. Vienna 1953. — VOGT, J.: Die Bedeutung des Jahres 312 für die Religionspolitik Konstantins des Grossen, Zeitschr. f. Kirchengesch. 61, 1942, 187 ff. — id. Constantin der Grosse und sein Jahrhundert, Munich 1949; also Ensslin, W., Gnomon 21, 1949, 328 ff., and N. H. Baynes, Journ. Rom. Stud. XLI, 1951, 155 ff.–id. Streitfragen um Konstantin den Grossen, Mitteil. d. Deutsch. Arch. Inst., Röm. Abt., 58, 1943 Munich. — id. Die Vita Constantini des Eusebius über den Konflikt zwischen Constantin und Licinius, Historia II, 1954, 463 ff. — VITTINGHOFF, F.: Eusebius als Verfasser der Vita Constantini, Rhein. Museum 96, 1953, 330 ff.

nades at Palmyra — the great Temple of Bel at Palmyra — Probus — Head of an aristocratic lady from Palmyra — Diocletian — Diocletian's residence at Split (Salonae) — Relief of women dancing — Detail of a sarcophagus symbolizing marital unity

following page 304

Constantine Chlorus — The Porta Nigra at Trèves — Tomb of Caecilia Metella — Restoration of the Roman Aqueduct at Spoleto, Toscana — The Aqua Claudia — The Bridge of Cestius — 4th-century mosaic (Sta. Maria Maggiore) — Sarcophagus attributed to Helena, mother of Constantine — Constantine the Great — Constantine's triumphal arch and Basilica — *The Prae-*

torians (relief) — Mosaic representing Christ as *Helios* or *Sol Invictus* (Roman tomb)

Maps

Drawings

INDEX

Bat-Zabbai, 296
Baynes, 335
Beards, wearing of, 185
Belgium, 51
Belgrade, 267
Bendorf, 263
Bengston, Herman, 189
Berenice, Queen, 162
Bethlehem, 133, 321
Betriacum, 148, 152
Birt, Theodor, 102
Bishop Athanasius, 341
Bishop of Rome, 170
Bithynia, 17, 48, 178, 305, 316, 341, 343
Black Death, 287
Black market, 312
Black Sea, 26, 28, 56, 60, 273, 276, 280, 288, 308
Blandina, 207
Blemmyes, 274
Boadicia, Queen, 128
Bohemia (Marcomanni), 205
Bona Dea, 50
Borani, 281, 286
Borysthenes, 189
Bosphorus, 276, 301
Boulogne, 30, 97, 324
Brahmans, 283
"Bread and circuses," 81
Britain, 52, 150, 157, 170, 181, 187, 197, 224, 259, 293, 308, 316, 322, 323, 328
 conquest of, 97, 103, 106
 insurrection in, 127, 128
British Isles, penetration of Manicheism to, 282
Britons, 52
Britannicus, 106, 107, 109, 110, 112, 113, 161
Britannicus (one of Commodus' names), 212
Brundisium, 44
Brutus, Marcus, 61, 62, 78
Buddha, 282
Buddhism, 255, 283
Burckhardt, Jacob, 271, 332
Burgundians, 307
Burrus, 114, 121, 134
Byzantium, 220, 221, 286, 304, 337, 340, 342

Caecilia Paulina, 267
Caecilius, Quintus, 50

Caelian Hill, 199
Caenis, 156, 157
Caenophrurium, 304
Caesar, Julius, 13, 15, 18, 20, 24, 34, 35, 40, 43, 46, 48–53, 54–59, 62, 63, 64, 79, 85, 95, 140, 226, 258, 310
Caesar as a title, 156, 200
Caesarea (Cappadocia), 157, 162, 284, 288, 309, 330
Caesarion, 56, 69
Caesars, the, 17
Caesonia, 95, 98
Calcedon, 237
Caledonian territory, 224
Caledonians, 224
Caligula, Gaius Caesar, 18, 30, 87, 91, 92–98, 100, 106, 123, 124, 134, 141, 146, 150, 151, 157, 170, 211
Caliphate, the, 255
Callistus, 289
Calpurnia, 51, 61, 107
Cambridge Ancient History, William Weber, 184
Campagna, the, 102, 192, 196, 197
Campania, 100, 162, 183, 294
Campania, Gulf of, 93
Campus Martius, 193, 203
Cannae, 23
Capellianus, 268
Cape Matapan, 70
Capitoline hill, 178, 265
Capitoline temple, 329
Cappadocia (Caesarea), 170, 267, 284, 285, 286, 288, 298, 309
Cappadocian legion XII Fulminata, 202
Capri, 13, 80, 83, 89, 90, 92, 211
Caracalla, 223, 224, 226–233, 234, 235, 237, 262
Carausius, 309
Carcer Mamertinus, 52
Caria, 198
Carinus, 304
Carnuntum, 219, 325, 326, 327
Carpathian Mountains, 205
Carpi, the, 271, 272, 274
Carpicus Maximus, 272
Carpus, 206
Carrhae (Haran), 232, 270
Carthage, 33, 212, 222, 268, 287, 309
Carus, 304
Casca, 62
Cassius, 61, 62, 63, 65, 78

INDEX

INDEX

Milan, 293, 307, 309, 318, 324, 325, 336, 338
Miletus, 309
Militia, 23
Mill, John Stuart, 207
Miltenberg am Rhein, 262
Milvian Bridge, 329, 330, 331, 337
Minerva, 153
Minos, 140
Minturnae, 27
Misenum, 93, 163
Mithradates, 26, 27, 29, 34, 45, 56
Mithras, 314, 326
Mitrovitza (Sirmium), 308
Moesia, 274, 276, 279
Moguntiacum (Mainz), 258
Mole of the Caesar (Band-i-Kaiser), 288
Moltke, Count Helmuth von, 178
Mommsen, Theodor, 31, 40, 44, 48, 56, 57, 87, 326
Monastir (Ruspina), 57, 58
Moneylenders, 35
Monte Arcese, 192
Monumentum Ancyranum, 82
Moors, 202, 293
Moravia, 205
Mount Etna, 187
Mount Tabor, 158
Mummia Achaica, 140
Munda, 59
Musa, Antonius, 81
Museum Carnuntinum, 326
Mutiny of Roman troops, 256

Naissus (Nish), 297, 321, 327
Naksh-i-Rustam, 284, 289
Naples, 40, 117
Naples, Bay of, 163
Narcissus, 102, 107, 108
Nemausus (Nîmes), 195
Neo-Platonism, 292
Nepos, Metellus, 41
Neptune, Temple of, 81
Nero, 13, 15, 16, 18, 110, 111–128, 129, 133, 138, 140, 142, 143, 145, 146, 147, 148, 152, 156, 157, 164, 168, 170, 189, 196, 211, 246, 277
Nero Claudius Caesar (Ahenobarbus), 109
Neronia, 118, 119
Nero's court, 132
Nero, statue of, 158, 159

Nero, Tiberius Claudius, 84
Nerva, 16, 173, 176
Nicaea, 276, 341
Nicene Creed, 341
Nicomedes, 48
Nicomedia (Ismid), 276, 305, 306, 309, 314, 315, 316, 317, 318, 319, 323, 343
Nicopolis, 44, 276, 292
Niederberg, 263
Niger, Gaius Pescennius, 218, 220
Nile, the, 56, 181, 192, 297
Nile canals, 80
Nîmes (Nemausus), 195
Nish (Naissus), 297, 321, 327
Nisibis, 270
Nissava, 321
Noah, 282
Nola, 82
Noreia, 23
Noricum, 262
North Sea, 267
North Sea coast, 22
Nubian desert, 302
Numantia, 20
Numerianus, 304, 305
Numidia, 20, 59, 222, 268
Nursia, 156

Octavia, 68, 69, 70, 109, 113, 121, 122, 128
Octavian Augustus, 62, 63, 64, 69, 70, 71, 78, 81, 84
Octavius, Gaius, 27, 63
Odenathus, Septimus, 296, 297
Odenwald, 262
Oedipus, Seneca, 134
Östergötland, 273, 276
Olthaces, 45
Olympia, 119
Olympieum, 189
Olympic Games, 119
Olympus, 196
"On the Brevity of Life," by Seneca, 135, 137
"On Peace of Mind," by Seneca, 137
Orange (Arausio), 23
Orestilla, Aurelia, 36
Orient, the, 296
Oriental architecture, 295
Origen of Alexandria, 247, 267, 330
Ormazd, 282, 290
Orontes, 235, 270, 295, 299, 338
Orpheus, 246

INDEX